For Mario and Elena, on a
German literary genre that owes
its decisive impulse, in the
Romantic period, to Italian,
French, and Spanish literature
            with my warmest regards

            Don Enrique.
            Henry H.H.Remak

Structural Elements
of the German Novella
from Goethe
to Thomas Mann

North American Studies
in Nineteenth-Century German Literature

Jeffrey L. Sammons
General Editor

Vol. 14

PETER LANG
New York • Washington, D.C./Baltimore
Bern • Frankfurt am Main • Berlin • Vienna • Paris

Henry H.H. Remak

Structural Elements of the German Novella from Goethe to Thomas Mann

PETER LANG
New York • Washington, D.C./Baltimore
Bern • Frankfurt am Main • Berlin • Vienna • Paris

Library of Congress Cataloging-in-Publication Data

Remak, Henry H. H. (Henry Heymann Herman).
Structural elements of the German novella from Goethe to Thomas Mann/
Henry H.H. Remak.
p. cm. — (North American studies in nineteenth-
century German literature; vol. 14)
German and English.
Includes bibliographical references and index.
1. Short stories, German—History and criticism. 2. German fiction—19th
century—History and criticism. 3. German fiction—20th century—History
and criticism. 4. Short story—Technique. I. Title. II. Series.
PT747.S6R46   833'.0109—dc20   96-8309
ISBN 0-8204-3451-5
ISSN 0891-4095

Die Deutsche Bibliothek-CIP-Einheitsaufnahme

Remak, Henry H. H.:
Structural elements of the German novella from Goethe to Thomas Mann/
Henry H.H. Remak. –New York; Washington, D.C./Baltimore; Bern; Frankfurt
am Main; Berlin; Vienna; Paris: Lang.
(North American studies in nineteenth century German literature; Vol. 14)
ISBN 0-8204-3451-5
NE: GT

Cover design by George Lallas.

The paper in this book meets the guidelines for permanence and durability
of the Committee on Production Guidelines for Book Longevity
of the Council of Library Resources.

© 1996 Peter Lang Publishing, Inc., New York

Printed in the United States of America.

Dedication

To the American *Germanist* par excellence,

Renaissance man,

connoisseur of the *Novelle*,

and inspiring friend:

Frank G. Ryder.

Contents

Preface

The republication of critical essays dating from 1957 to 1987 entails problems. Scholarship evolves and textual interpretations should reflect, in some manner, whether positively or negatively, the evolution of academic thinking. Bringing the essays up-to-date represented, therefore, one, perhaps compelling option. I did not take it. Why? First and foremost, frankly, because rewriting one's own erstwhile publications is much more agonizing than writing them in the first place. Secondly, the mix of older and newer casts seldom works out: the cracks are only too noticeable. Third, whatever one may think of my premises, they have remained steady (though not monolithic) since I started tackling the novella as an art form thirty-five years ago (teaching it preceded, by several years, publishing on it: a sequence which, I think, is healthy). I hope they have proved somewhat enduring not because I am afraid of change but because the strategy of approach has worked well with particular texts – which is or should be the ultimate verification of all theory. Fourth, since deconstruction there has not been much interest, to put it mildly, in traditional genre scholarship, and the novella is certainly a traditional genre going back six hundred and fifty years or more. And fifth, in literary scholarship, despite the ubiquitous, hyperbolic claims made for new methods, time has shown that all approaches to literature, unlike most scientific methods, are, in essence rather than execution, accumulative, not substitutive, from the philological and biographical nineteenth century positivism via *Geistesgeschichte* (History of Ideas, History of Mentality) to the New Criticism, Structuralism, Deconstruction, Marxism, Neo-Marxism, communication theory, speech action, performance and agency theory, reception studies and reader analysis, feminism, Foucault, Lacan, Bakhtin, and the New Historicism. Each of them retains its potential: it all depends on the relevance of the approach to the particular texts and on the execution of that approach.

So it has seemed preferable, all in all, not to tamper with my original text except for minor formal adjustments, all the more so since a scholarly text should, like the literary text to which it refers, be taken as a whole, not just as a string of observations that can be rearranged at any time in any manner.

I have also preserved the oral character of some of the presentations which have resulted in the chapters of the book. Our academic lingo has become so thick that some oral lightening, perhaps even brightening, should not be unwelcome. Besides, it fits the oral origins of the novella.

This book carries an English title despite the fact that the majority of its contents are in German. This emphasizes my desire to have this basic analysis of major structural components of what has been, for generations, the most effective narrative genre introducing German literature to American undergraduates recognized as an American contribution to German scholarship regardless of the language of a particular chapter, for every part of the book was written in America and many of its ideas have been tested in the American classroom. The point of view taken: a close and repeated textual scrutiny leading to empirical conclusions rather than deductive abstractions is much closer to the Anglo/American tradition than to the German one. I am very partial to the necessity, if American *Germanistik* is going to have any profile based on its own cultural experience such as British or French *Germanistik* possess, of *also*, not *only* writing as an American and for an American audience. But I also recognize that we just do not have the *Hinterland* here to satisfy our desire to be an integral part of *Germanistik* in general and that the centers of *Germanistik* remain in German-speaking countries. There is also an organic advantage, perhaps even for American students and scholars, of treating so literary, refined, and profiled a genre as the *Novelle* in the language of its primary composition. And I have tried to present my German in a way that will be accessible and, I dare hope, at times perhaps even enjoyable to English-speaking readers. Furthermore, all chapters (but not the two pieces in the appendix) are preceded by a summary or synopsis in English, more elaborate if the chapter is in German, and sometimes in telegram style if it is extra long. Finally, I have, in the Preface and in the Introduction, attempted to give a general picture, in English, of the *Novellenproblematik* and an introduction to the ideas set forth in the book.

What is the rationale for the organization of this book? It is largely based on the historical evolution of the *Novelle* in the XIXth and early XXth century. I start out with a general vista of Goethe's relationship to the novella genre, followed by two particular applications of the novellesque in Goethe's work. Both are literary versions of autobiographical experiences: 1) young Goethe's infatuation with the "Frankfurter Gretchen" as described in his *Dichtung und Wahrheit*, 2) mature Goethe's love for the 'beautiful Milanese woman' from the *Italienische Reise* (1788) and its affinities with the story of the "Frankfurter Gretchen" as well as with his father's (authentic? imagined? both?) account of a love affair from a 'close distance' with another Milanese woman almost half a century before, as related by Johann Caspar Goethe in his own 'Italian journey'. Then comes a survey of selected structural components of the novella in German classicism and romanticism, followed by the same approach to three of Keller's novellesque stories: *Kleider machen Leute, Die drei gerechten Kammacher,* and *Romeo und Julia auf dem Dorfe.* The next two chapters examine four phenomena often associated with the novellesque in relevant stories from Keller to Bergengruen: "Wendepunkt" (Turning point), "Pointe" (Punch line), Allegory, and Symbol. The penultimate chapter covers the role of the "Rahmen" (frame story) in the modern history of the novellesque in German literature, and, having started with Goethe, we appropriately end up with the novellesque elements in four of Thomas Mann's stories: *Der kleine Herr Friedemann, Tobias Mindernickel, Tristan,* and *Mario und der Zauberer.*

I have not striven to give this book a mechanical uniformity in the external presentation of the various chapters. While they are all directed toward different aspects of novellesque structure, they are shaped by the particular approach chosen for the particular topic at a particular time. Organically related content must take precedence over formal smoothness.

There is, of course, no claim made to have addressed *all* novellesque features in *all* relevant German stories from Goethe to Mann. In practice this would be an impossibility. And even in theory to expect adherence to an entire set of generic characteristics in every work associated with a certain genre is an absurdity, a straw man set up for the purpose of torpedoing any normative interpretation.

The inclusion, in the Appendix, of a review is very likely a novum that will result in some raised eyebrows. It requires two explanations. The first one is that there is a thoughtlessly inherited and almost unquestioned tradition in the assessment of literary scholarship of academics that relegates a review to an automatically inferior and quasi irrelevant factor in evaluating the work of a scholar. Reviews are, however, an irreplaceable service to scholarship without which we could hardly work. There are mediocre reviews as there are articles and books, but the better and best ones require more than just summarizing the contents of the book: they must locate and present articulately the thrust of the book's argument. This is no easy task. First, because a good many books are sloppily written and it is hard to make out their overall argument. A lot of reviews are better written, clearer than the book they discuss. (The contrary, of course, may also be the case). The art of book reviewing (and it *is* an art) has become even more difficult because so many scholarly books today do not *intend* to have a profiled thesis, they just present highly differentiated observations and have even elevated resistance to conclusions to a deconstructionist ideology or at least desideratum. A *good* review should also assess the book *critically* though fairly, especially since many, probably most scholars read more scholarly reviews than scholarly books (time problem!). A both descriptive and evaluative review demands a not only quantitative but qualitative grasp of a field. A lot of original insights normally associated with articles and books are also found, if more crisply, in good, better, and best reviews. So reviews should be, like all scholarship, read and critically evaluated, just like articles and books, not dismissed *eo ipso* as an 'inferior' or secondary genre.

In this particular case, my review of Paine also contains beyond a specific presentation an assessment of the then current state of novella criticism, not duplicated by any other chapter in the book. So it made double good sense to include it.

The encyclopedia entry about the *Novelle* preceding the Paine review is included for similar reasons. Again, "Encyclopedia" contributions tend to be tagged, automatically, as inferior to articles and books because they are considered summaries of existing scholarship serving dissemination rather than projecting original ideas. But that depends on the nature and quality of the particular contribution which needs to be read and appraised rather than ignored or 'demerited' as such. In this particular case, I also make connections between novellas not duplicated in other parts of my book, so the entry is included in the Appendix since it may be helpful to some readers.

Both entries, in a modest way, serve *communication* among scholars which is in dire straights because we put a premium on 'critical creation' with its idiosyncratic terms rather than on replicable dissemination in a common language.

In this book we have footnotes, numbered within each chapter, that complement specific statements in the text, as well as occasional endnotes that refer to the chapter topic as a whole.

Information about the original publication of the essays that form this book is given after the Appendix.

All titles of scholarship *utilized in this book* are collected and listed, alphabetically (by authors), at its end. It is a working bibliography and does not claim to be complete or up to date.

Two indices (topics, names) complete this *ouvrage*. The extent and the limitations of the topical index are explained in its foreword.

The non-occurrence of a particular title throughout the book does not necessarily mean that it has not influenced my thinking on the novella: all it means is that I have not made conscious use of it in a particular context.

Why did I not update the bibliography? Had I done so, the relevant scholarship discussion in my essays would have to be significantly revised in the light of the new material, and those secondary insights might well, in turn, have led to modification of my primary reading. I will not gild the lily: updating would have been desirable. Various commitments made it impossible to do so. It was either getting out what I have systematically worked toward in the last forty years, an overall view of novellesque structure in German literature in the light of close textual reading from, approximately, the 1780's to mid XXth century, or forgetting about it for good. So I present it for whatever it is worth without claiming it represents the latest account of relevant scholarship.

I have assuaged, to an extent, this deficit by including in the Introduction and Appendix II assessment samples of significant scholarship on the Novelle subsequent to the one considered in the different chapters. In the main body of the book, however, I have to be satisfied with having worked up a good deal of secondary *Novelleliteratur* published prior to the writing of the particular essay. To some readers, these criticisms will illustrate evolutionary stages of scholarship on the German novella and thus may have historical value. But much of this criticism also reflects different approaches to the Novelle irrespective of the date. Most of it is by no means irrelevant to viable current avenues of access toward the total meaning of novellas. As a matter of fact, one of the startling myopias of *Novelle* scholarship in the last three or four decades is precisely its reluctance to recognize how much there is that is productive in past novella criticism all the way back to Goethe and Wieland. I suspect that at least one of the principal reasons for this neglect is the inherent pressure – external and internal – on scholars to come up, at any price, with highly original interpretations rather than saving what is worth saving in the scholarship of others. Negative, iconoclastic positions are more likely to lead to individual academic laurels than sifting, combining, utilizing, and finally synthesizing the research of others. Current scholarly entrepreneurship does not look kindly at positive (though far from uncritical) evaluation of the research of our predecessors. It tends to denounce as futile or reactionary any normatively oriented research. Deconstruction in literary research of the 1950's and 1960's, at least in North America, tended to be anti-formalistic; of the 1970's, 1980's and early 1990's anti-normative and/or ideological (predominantly from the "left"). Despite its intriguing originality and frequent flashes of intellectual brilliance, this is all the more regrettable because the highly sophisticated and yet, in many ways, organic genre of the novella has tended, over centuries, to attract criticism of commensurate *finesse*. Furthermore, my own interpretations and 'theorizing' are based on frequent re-reading and re-teaching of particular texts more than on a complete utilization of all relevant scholarship. I am even tempted to make a virtue out of what other scholars may consider a sin: it is better, if time is short, to re-read and re-teach primary texts than to re-read and add to secondary scholarship on them. This is particularly so because my approach in this book is, unfashionably, structural and intrinsic, not at all because I reject context as a relevant factor in the interpretation of literature including the novella, but because it happens to fit the historic *Gestalt* of the genre. In doing so I exercise an organic option but make no exclusive claims for the method.

The not only long but rich history of research on the German novella, not to speak of the non-German one which has had a strong impact on German scholarship, has too often been dismissed, without reasonably impartial and constructive examination, as hopelessly contradictory and at a definitive impasse. No free scholarship has *ever* reached – nor is it desirable that it do so – 'definitive' agreement or general 'consensus' status on any significant, specific literary topic, but the use of these illusory epithets ("definitive", "general consensus") remains common in rejecting old or justifying new scholarship.

I have tried to write in an intelligible manner open, I dare hope, even to the generalist not that interested in the technical but rather in the structural secrets of the novellesque. It has been my conviction since I started writing for publication fifty-six years ago that the Humanities, as their name implies, are and should be intelligible to any sentient human being of some ability and curiosity, and that includes writing – even and perhaps especially scholarly writing – whose raison d'être is precisely to make literature, as a central part of the Humanities, more accessible, more interesting, more meaningful to humans who read (and there are some left). Here I gratefully acknowledge the influence of French (prior to Barthes) and of British writing which has managed to stay relatively clear of the ravages of abstruse theory and ideology. Recondite writing in the Humanities is a form of Humanities suicide. And it will not do any good for the defenders of convoluted lingo in the Humanities to point to the arcane nature of publications in the Sciences and in Medicine. The Sciences and Medicine have so much going for them in our culture, their eventual benefits to each individual are so deeply trusted that they *can* and, by their nature, *must* use very specialized language even though the Sciences do a much better job than the Humanities in communicating with the public through such journals as *Science, Nature, Scientific American,* and *The* xvi

American Scientist. The Humanities are a much vaguer ingredient of the American conscience, in part dimly positive, in part suspected of trying to substitute their secularized selves for the much sturdier reliance of Americans on religion. The ultimate aim of this study is to enable its readers to apply selected structural yardsticks to novellas and novellesque stories *not* included in this book, to become interpreters on their own.

While I hope I have something to offer, in this book, to seasoned scholars, I am particularly hopeful to give students a solid basis from which they can make up their own minds on novellesque structure or non-structure. In this sense I practice (but with common sense, I hope) the analytic side of the presently much maligned New Criticism. Some students, including graduate students, are exposed too early – before they have enough textual and theoretical experience – to ideological and theoretical angles that 'marginalize' 'traditional' scholarship and cultivate an "in" lingo that runs counter to the professed or implied democratic motivations of much of current scholarship. If I err, as some will say, on the 'constructive' side, that side is badly in need of equal time.

It was not possible to include in this volume my book-length study[1] of the novellesque metamorphoses of the story of "la belle lingère" told, sequentially, by the Marshal de Bassompierre (1579-1646) in his *Journal de ma Vie* (1665), Goethe in his *Unterhaltungen deutscher Ausgewanderten* (1794/1795), and Hugo von Hofmannsthal in the "Erlebnis des Marschalls von Bassompierre" (1899/1900). In it I examine the three versions of this "sich ereignete unerhörte Begebenheit" from the following angles of novellesque structure: "Hochpotenziert, Ironie und Paradox, Spannung (Dilemma) > Krise > Katastrophe > Pointe > Entspannung > Stiller Reiz, weiter nachzudenken, Auslösender und Auflösender Wendepunkt,

---

[1]*Novellistische Struktur: Der Marschall von Bassompierre und die schöne Krämerin* (Bassompierre, Goethe, Hofmannsthal). Berne and Frankfurt am Main, Peter Lang, 1983, 124 p.(No. 46 in *Germanic Studies in America*, ed. Katharina Mommsen).

Metaphysische Dimensionen, Schicksal gegen Persönlichkeit, Sachlichkeit, Sprachlicher Takt, Epische Bewältigung des Dramatischen, Gleichgewicht zwischen direkter und indirekter Rede, Erzählsilhouette-Profil, & Bildliche Verstärkung".

In the course of reading the book, the reader will undoubtedly discover a good many reiterative statements about the structural constituents of the novellesque genre in Germany. Removing these duplications (I prefer to call them reinforcements) would also mean, however, the eliminations of constant references to the fundamental structure of the novellesque in the various chapters of the book. I am, unabashedly, presenting a *systematic argument*, even at the risk that for some reader these 'repetitions' might create the impression of a certain relentlessness. So be it: there is so much centrifugality in our current scholarship that a dosis of centripetality cannot hurt. Furthermore, let us face it, not very many scholars read entire scholarly books these days. Most of us, alas, pick from books what we need. If this is so, I would not want to limit observations on the fundamental structural characteristics of German novellesque stories to *one* chapter.

I cannot claim to have analyzed, let alone synthesized all major elements composing the novellesque as I see it in German novella-like stories. Essentially I dwell on the "eine", "sich ereignete" (authentic), the "unerhörte" (including dilemma > crisis > (near) catastrophe), the "Begebenheit" (actual occurrence), the "Auftakt", the "Wendepunkte" (*aus*lösender, au*f*lösender), the "Pointe", (including the "metaphysische Pointe"), "Falke", "Silhouette", allegory and symbolism ("Dingsymbol" > "Leitmotiv" > "Signal"), and the frame ("Rahmen"). Secondarily I have something to say about the oral origin of the novellesque; the epic control of the dramatic content (heightening the tension), distance and 'objectivity' in telling the story, which intensifies (rather than detracts from) the impact of the irrational; extreme (often criminal) events; stylization; the transparency of language vs. the non-transparency of events; the complex relationship of the "sich ereignete" to the "selbsterlebte"; the autobiographical; irony and paradox as a consequence of the clash between the rational and the irrational; the surprising links between "Novelle" and "Märchen".

xviii

This book concentrates on the German novella. It does not essentially reflect my comparative interests in the non-German novella of the time. Nevertheless, in several portions of the book I do graze the subject: in the Goethe chapters, the survey of the novella during German Classicism and Romanticism, and the two Appendix pieces. The comparative approach to the modern novella offers vast and untilled opportunities, and I hope that others will dig into them.

I have repeatedly criticized current works of scholarship because of the absence of a general conclusion. Yet I am guilty of the same sin, it would seem. In my defense, I can only say that by tracing some of the principal structural components of the German novella from Goethe to Thomas Mann (and occasionally beyond) I have at least arrived at the synthesis of each constituent component treated and that a synthesis of the syntheses will have to await a subsequent occasion.

Finally, my thanks. To the best of my recollection, I never took a course on the *Novelle*. My interest in it came after inheriting a graduate course from a retired colleague in the 1950's. I want to thank the various chairs of the Department of German at Indiana University (Hubert J. Meessen, Frank G. Ryder, Sidney M. Johnson, Albrecht Holschuh, and Stephen Wailes) for giving me the opportunity to teach it at fairly regular intervals, on the undergraduate and graduate levels, from then on to the mid-1980's, and to Frank Trommler and Horst Daemmrich for letting me teach it as a visitor at the University of Pennsylvania in the fall semester of 1984. Two year-long novella research fellowships by the John Simon Guggenheim Foundation (1967-1968) and the National Endowment for the Humanities (1977-1978) as well as a NEH Summer Seminar on "The Structure of the German and European Novella" (1977) helped immensely, and it is impossible for me to gauge what I have learned from my students in the novella courses and seminars throughout the years, not to speak of the published scholarship on the *Novelle*. Indiana University has provided me, for this particular study, with very generous research support, and I am grateful to Vice-Presidents Kenneth R.R. Gros Louis and George E. Walker, in particular, for direct support. The heroines and heroes of the story are, however, my highly computerized but very humane typists/word processers who had to deal with a difficult bi-lingual manuscript: Barbara Goetze, Ruth Mudrow, and Jeff Kennedy in the Department of Germanic Studies, Linda Prince in the Department of Spanish and Portuguese, and especially my cheerful and undaunted typist of most of the book and of the camera-ready copy, Beth Watt in the Office of International Programs, all at Indiana University, Bloomington. Greg Ketcham's help with the Bibliography, Indices, and general proofreading has been invaluable. Kathy Iwasaki and Lisa Dillon of the Peter Lang staff, New York, Production Managers of this book, have lent their expertise to this undertaking. The Editor of the XIXth Century German Literature Series at Peter Lang, Professor Jeffrey Sammons of Yale University, a long-time friend, has been unobtrusively but effectively encouraging and patient.

My genuine thanks must also go to my friends, Dr. Jean Creek and Dr. Mark Wisen, for keeping me in good shape during the ups and downs of this enterprise, and to their brides, Donna and Linda, for keeping *them* in good shape. My wife, my children and their spouses, not to speak of our grandchildren, are frankly puzzled by the strange fascination the *Novelle* has exerted on me but have kept up my (sometimes flagging) spirits in innumerable ways during the many years of gestation of this book.

Bloomington, Indiana
May 1995

Introduction

I will *not*, in this introduction, offer an elaborate justification of each element of novellesque structure as I see it. That is the job of the book, each chapter of which addresses itself deliberately, systematically but far from exhaustively to one or more structural components of the genre. In several of them I summarize my structural hypothesis beyond the particular angle of the chapter topic.

My novella interpretations are based, *cum grano salis*, on inductive reasoning. Certain structural elements are tentatively identified, by their recurrence, from the reading and re-reading of novellesque stories (not necessarily novellas) and then tested against other stories of the general type. That a deductive hypothesis – structural elements suggested by others – is involved in the perspective is unavoidable: with a genre of such long historic continuity (650 years by now or more) it is impossible to start out with a *tabula rasa*. The important thing is the systematic testing and retesting of these hypothetical elements against the actual texts within, to be sure, the ineluctable limitations of time and energy to which we are all subject.

It is, I know, dangerous in these anti-normative days to provide the reader with a chart-like list of typological structural components which immediately conjures up echoes of dated positivism if not – worse – of canonical oppression. But I am doing so anyway, because my hypothesis has far-reaching historical[1] plus strong, direct, inductive textual roots and has been reinforced or modified over many years through constant re-reading and re-teaching seminal novellesque texts. I believe it is in a good position to compete with theories with more eclectic theoretical/ideological slants than

---

[1] For the historical evolution of the structural characteristics of the German novella, see, at long last, a refreshingly straightforward, judicious, narrated reference source in English: Siegfried Weing, *The German Novella: Two Centuries of Criticism*, Columbia, South Carolina (USA), Camden House, 1994.

2

perspectives of the complete text. Furthermore, I do not only want to be read (what author does not?) but I want to be read by non-experts (including students) who need a reasonably solid (not inviolate) structural pattern which they can (and should) test against their novellesque readings, with a good chance that there will be modifications of perspective based on precisely that experience.

Structural Characteristics of the Novella[2] (Working hypothesis)

> *Eine sich ereignete unerhörte Begebenheit* (an actual, authentic, unheard-of, extraordinary occurrence. One central event.)
>
> *Neu, Neuigkeit, Neuartig* (new, newsworthy, novelty. Oral origin. Related to journalism.)
>
> *Profil, Falke, Silhouette, Dingsymbol* (marked profile; silhouette; concrete, object symbols)
>
> *Bericht, nicht Rechtfertigung* (report, not justification)
>
> *Sachlichkeit* (matter-of-factness, distance, objectivity, economy, discipline, preciseness in presentation)
>
> *Spannung* (tension)
>
> *Dilemma* –> *Krise* (Crisis) –> *[beinahe?] Katastrophe* ([near] catastrophe) –> *Pointe:* ultimate, frequently ironic twist, often in the last or penultimate sentence of the final paragraph, suggesting, via an internal postscript, an unexpected, strikingly and tersely formulated new angle, or implied or explicit commentary by the author/narrator, a thoughtful teaser that offers –> *stillen Reiz, weiter nachzudenken:* stimulation for retroactive hypotheses, for the continuation of the story by the listener/reader.
>
> *Wendepunkte* (reversals, crucial turning points)
>
> 1) *Auslösender Wendepunkt* (release of central novellesque conflict) –>

---

[2]To avoid monotony I will, selectively, use 'novella' for *Novelle*, knowing that the German variety is both part of the overall genre but also has its own historical features.

2) *Auflösender Wendepunkt* (resolution of central novellesque conflict)

(The major novellesque turning points are not identical with illusory, epic, or psychological turning points of the story as a whole.)

Drama, episch bewältigt (drama in epic prose: direct vs indirect discourse.) Tension between dramatic/sensational events and calm presentation.

Rahmen (frame)

Voller Akkord [3] (full chord beginning)

Ironie, Paradox

Geschick/Schicksal, Zufall, Notwendigkeit gegen *Willen und Persönlichkeit* (destiny, chance, necessity vs will and personality)

Hochpotenziert (highpoweredness)

Intelligence, sophistication; aristocratic, upper bourgeois elements in novellesque structure, audience, readership.

Durchsichtige Sprache, undurchsichtige Begebenheiten, L e e r - stellen (Transparency of reporting language in tension with opaqueness [gaps, causes, indeterminacy] of events). The novella is the perfect genre for gaps of indeterminacy. Like a good newspaper reporter the novella author 'reports' as facts only what he 'knows', what has been 'verified', and that very soberly, precisely. Let the reader fill in the gaps and thus become the co-creator of the novella. The combination of firmness and openness is one of the strongest contributing factors to the efficacy of the genre.

Even though my typological approach to the *Novelle* is pragmatic, text-driven, and tries consistently to strike a balance between type and individual characteristics, any normative slant in American literary scholarship today runs strongly against the current. There is — and has been since the

---

[3]Term coined by Nino Erné, *Die Kunst der Novelle,* Wiesbaden, Limes, 1956.

4

beginning of my interest in the genre four decades ago – a further distinguishing countercurrent to my approach to the novella. I want to rehabilitate *criticism* as a truly *critical* evaluative function. Academic "literary criticism" has largely become descriptive, not axiological – in fact, decidedly and consciously anti-axiological. It has become endlessly analytic – and shuns not just synthesis but, in many cases, even limited conclusions. There are causes for this in the deep structure of our culture: the oppositional role of the core of academia, personal ideologies, the reward system, the daunting mountains of evidence blocking judgement. We have left the *real criticism* – a critical stance – to the newspaper and periodical critics. This has been a big mistake that has mightily contributed to our marginalization in society.[4] In part it has been a false conclusion from our laudable desire to be objective, to emulate the sciences. On the contrary: it is precisely our constant *striving* for objectivity (not ever attainable – not even desirable – in its illusory, pure form), it is our being monitored by other critics as well as by ourselves (which is the essence of the scholarly enterprise), it is our *systematic* and *historical* training as academics that should put us in a position of being more reliable evaluators than non-academics. This assumes, I realize, that we have a critical literary knack in the first place, and I readily admit that some 'amateurs' may possess more of this than some of us.

Norms as a working hypothesis may strike the contemporaries of various shades of deconstruction and relativism as a scholarly fairy-tale of

---

[4]For a discussion of Comparative Criticism in greater depth see my "Comparative Criticism: Cultural and Historical Roots in the Theoretical Forest", *Neohelicon* (Budapest), XVII, No.1, 1990, 161-199, "The Uses of Comparative Literature in Value Judgements" (in *Komparatistik*. Festschrift für Zoran Konstantinovic, Heidelberg, Winter, 1981, 127-140), and "Between Scylla and Charybdis: Quality Judgement in Comparative Literature", in *Aesthetics and the Literature of Ideas*, Essays in honor of A. Owen Aldridge, ed. François Jost and Melvin Friedman, Newark, Delaware, University of Delaware Press, 1990, 21-33.

olden days. But what has brought about change is itself subject to change, just like the New Criticism, so firmly in the saddle, has ceded the track to Structuralism, Deconstruction, Intertextuality, Neomarxism, Reception Aesthetics, Reader Response, Communication theory, Speech Action, and the New Historicism. The academic consumer appetite for new theories is as voracious, because promoted by the inherent interests of the trade, as lay consumer appetite for edible, potable, and other creature comfort goods, or rather – all too often – just for new packaging. History does not repeat itself: it is reincarnated. Continuity will always be the counterbalance to change. As Thomas Mann said, when you row in a boat and it leans too far to the right you shift your weight to the left, and vice versa. Despite the current infatuation with "change" – whatever that means –, neither life nor literature are imaginable without continuity. It is just a matter of degree, and beyond a certain balance both are unhealthy. My book is neither a glorification of continuity nor blindness toward change: it is a study of their interaction, of historic and existential continuity and historic as well as individual change.

The hoped – for suitability of this book to students as well as mature scholars is anchored in its *Textbezogenheit*, its inductive reasoning, controllable, correctable, and improvable by students as well as their teachers because they, too, have access to the same, widely taught canonical texts as the author of this book. "Canonical" is certainly not an "in", positive word to many scholars today. It has been charged with being the intention or the result of a kind of conservative, if not reactionary conspiracy by the literary/scholarly/academic establishment, by an oligarchy, to block change, to stifle nefarious dissent. In spite of this, canonical texts continue, if only for practical reasons, to be widely read in colleges and universities, and since this book hopes to benefit students, too, it makes sense to write about texts they are more likely to read than others.

But there is more to be said for the canon, too. "Canonical" texts have proved their mettle through generations of readers, critics, and scholars of different origins and inclinations, living in different times and cultures, under different circumstances. The test of the times is not infallible, especially not in what they neglect or forget and leave for later generations to discover or rediscover. But the test of the times is, on the whole, a more reliable scrutiny by way of "longue durée" than the often ideologically motivated inclinations or resentments of some members of *one* – the present – generation. The test of a great work of literature is precisely that it reveals new meanings to different generations in different cultures, that its corroboration comes from different sources, times and places.

What may seem, in my definition of novellesque structure, determined and determinative, perhaps apodictic and prescriptive, is an overdue reaction to the fetish of disintegration that has engulfed contemporary literary scholarship in America. It will, I hope, at least to some extent, compensate for the new conformism of incoherence, of ideological suspicion, of text dissipation, by calling attention to the basic "longue durée" but, at the same time, also to the range of variations which are the prerequisites of great literary texts. It is my intention to show what proportions, or misproportions, of both are responsible for the quality, or lack of such, of a given literary, novellesque work. Our times have witnessed an academic aversion to the recognition of quality as not only *a* but *the* major factor in literary criticism.[5] Quality somehow is supposed to smack of elitism, and elitism is politically suspect.

---

[5] I have discussed the loss and the restitution of the "value" factor in contemporary literary evaluations (criticism) in "The Uses of Comparative Literature in Value Judgements", (see Footnote 4); "Comparative Interpretation and the Question of Value Judgement: Edgar Allan Poe's *The Fall of the House of Usher* and Meïr Goldschmidt's *Bjergtagen I"* *(Spellbound I)*, in *Literary Theory and Criticism*: Festschrift in Honor of René Wellek, ed. Joseph P. Strelka (Bern, Peter Lang, 1984), II, 1189-1214; "Between Scylla and Charybdis: Quality Judgement in Comparative Literature", (see Footnote 4); "Comparative Value Judgements: Integration and Isolation in Camus' *La Peste* (1947) and Grass' *Die Blechtrommel* (1959)", *Mélanges* offerts à Albert Gérard, in *Semper Aliquid Novi*: Littérature Comparée et Littératures d'Afrique. Janos Riesz, Alain Ricard, & Véronique Porra, eds., Tübingen, Narr, 1990, 167-174.

Quality, so it is held, is in the eyes not only of "the beholder" but of *all* beholders, regardless of their preparation and insight (and, sometimes it seems, regardless of the text). At times it would seem that the opaqueness of the language of deconstructionist and other "postmodern" scholarship, although 'undemocratic' to the extent it remains mysterious to many outside the anointed disciples, is in no danger of being 'oppressive' since it is, except to the members of the "cénacle", hermetic. The legendary precision of the language of the novella has spurred me on to write as clearly and distinctly as I can. If I have succeeded only to some extent, I will at least have the moral satisfaction of giving my critics direct access to my erroneous ideas.

In contrast to the contemporary, widespread and tenacious current of open-ended relativism in American literary study, I have taken, in this comprehensive analysis, what I hope will be seen as a sensible, workable, replicable (by students as well as seasoned scholars), productive approach that does not posit absolute and inviolate characteristics of a uniform type of *Novelle* but identifies and describes components of the *novellesque*[6] which, in diverse combinations with each other and also with non-novellesque elements, and with different success, allow us to trace the particular density, profile, and effectiveness of the novellesque in stories tending in that direction.

Depending on the findings in each textual case, we may reach the conclusion that indeed a particular story is sufficiently novellesque to be designated as a *Novelle*, or not. Whatever the conclusion in each case, whatever the particular generic-structural mix of elements, the analysis is not, like so many today, elusively open-ended but leads to a reasonable conclusion, to a possible building stone toward an inductive theory or generalization about the overall genre of the novella. The history of this genre is too long and too continuous to be dismissed as a succession of heterogeneous terms, concepts, and just 'stories'. Novellesque structure is, in the strikingly balanced

---

[6]I prefer "novellesque" to "novellistic" since the latter may, too easily, be taken for "nove*l*istic".

8

characterization of Goethe, "Geprägte Form, die lebend sich entwickelt."[7]

While the novella as a distinguished art form for half a millennium is certain to endure notwithstanding the ups and downs of literary genres, it is clear that it has declined in the last three decades, not only as a creative practice but also as a scholarly target. In the introduction to my 'Theory and Practice of the Novella: Gottfried Keller' essay in this volume, written in 1962, I already record, to be sure, that it is being eclipsed though not replaced by the short story. I also noted at that time that for generations preceding the 1960's the novel had somehow not been respectable enough to be at the center of academic scholarship[8] which, especially in the period of the New Criticism, was more attuned to the lyric, the intrinsically most 'literary', most poetic, most disciplined of the literary genres (including the poetic novel), and previously to the drama, hallowed by its exemplary first climax in classical antiquity and subsequently by its second golden age in modern times (Calderón, Lope de Vega, Tirso de Molina, Shakespeare, Corneille, Racine, Goethe, Schiller). The epic in verse had always occupied a front rank in literary esteem (at least in official regard if not in actual reading popularity), even way into the nineteenth century.

Well, the situation has changed dramatically since 1962. 'Tight', controlled, structured art forms like the drama, the novella, the lyric have clearly descended on the scale of scholarly as well as readers' 'esteem in action'. The novel, on the contrary, now rules the roost (academia, publishers, readers, reviews). The most and increasingly protean art form (the "well-made" XIXth century novel is, not in its popularity with readers but in the ranking by the younger generations of scholars, quasi "passé"), it is clearly the present favorite object of literary analysis, corresponding to the increasing inclination of young writers to aim for the 'ultimate' (the novel), the 'big hit',

---

[7]"Urworte, Orphisch".

[8]It has been recorded that in many American drugstores and bookstores there used to be – perhaps still are – two different sections, marked "Literature" and "Fiction".

immediately rather than gradually climbing toward it by way of the 'smaller', more restrictive genres. Its 'heteroglossia' (Bakhtin) suits the relativism which has become the yardstick of most of the influential contemporary scholarship, especially in the western world.

Intrinsic studies of the German novella have, as noted elsewhere, sharply declined since the 1970's, after a peak in the 1950's and 1960's. This is in line with the cult of fluidity and indeterminacy or multi-determinacy of contemporary research: the limitless expansion of 'text' and its submersion in context; the emphasis on theory, on the one hand, and on intertextuality, on the other; Foucaultian and feminist extra-literary determinism; demotion of the aesthetic; and the substitution of essentially unverifiable reader expectation and response for plausible value judgements.

There is no danger that we will return, in the foreseeable future, to what is sometimes referred to, derogatorily, as generic "straightjackets". Far greater is the clear and present peril that 'anything goes', democracy in literary research going haywire. Genres and other traditional literary forms, whatever excessive claims may have been made for them in the (now distant) past, are part of the existential need to balance substance and form, freedom and restraint. Every generation discovers new combinations, with which we will have to get more familiar before we judge them. But that does not necessarily mean that the older ones have lost *validity*; they may just have lost academic *popularity*: two terms that, our American proclivities notwithstanding, are not synonymous. We are presently in a cult period for "change" and "innovation" without reflecting whether these are inherently good. Communism, Fascism, and Nazism were certainly drastic changes in our century, but were they for the good? Is technology always for the good? We must be very cautious in scholarship not to be intimidated by what are essentially advertising slogans.

Structures of genres or sub-genres that have stood the test of time with all its ups and downs, as the novella and the novellesque have, are likely to have something to contribute to the literary evaluation of a particular story. Generic structures were not mandated by religious prophets. They have developed over time, sloughed off dead skin and absorbed new texture. They have endured because they make sense in terms of storytelling which, whether now or a thousand or two thousand or more years ago, is and has been a basic need and pleasure of mankind. Novellesque structure cannot be ignored as *one* of the evaluative elements of particular novellesque texts. Disregarding the generic tradition to some extent may work in some cases but not in others. It is one of the principal aims of this book to decide when and to what extent it works and when it does not, to restore *value* to e*valu*ation, *critic*ism to analysis and, finally, to help arriving at *synthesis,* however tentative.

Literature as a practiced art is not necessarily "in" with academic scholars, particularly of the younger generation, and the novella *is* an aristocratic, refined, sophisticated, "élitist", historically proud art form to boot, although highly effective with readers of sundry origins because of its integrative balance, its concentrated, disciplined control of an explosive content. In its best specimens, it is a supreme example of the fusion of substance and form. But current American researches are looking in other directions, toward ideology and/or theory, and tend to view with suspicion any claims of high esthetic quality, of successful and even admirable total integration of a *Gesamtkunstwerk.* We are living in a jaundiced age of academic criticism. Even in the heyday of novella scholarship, it was rare to look at the structure of a novella in terms of the total text as presented by the author, at the concatenation of the structural components rather than one or two of them. 'Totalism' has been my aim and, I hope, at least to some extent, my practice. It is all the more needed today because the "work", the tangible/visible text has been declared a ploy and submerged into an 'implied' context, a sea devoid of aesthetic profile. This may work for some types of writing and can add dimensions to the understanding of the novella, but it is not compatible with the structural approach which retains its validity for a self-conscious art form like the novella. The present world of scholarship is rich in thesis and antithesis but sorely deficient in synthesis. Ultimately, this may be fatal to us: however preliminary or hypothetical any syntheses are bound to be in this forbiddingly complex universe of ours, it is our duty to draw conclusions rather than drowning in unproductive analyses.

A normatively oriented, structural analysis of certain novellas does not necessarily presuppose that the author had a systematic, conscious – let alone scholarly – command of the theory of the novella and of its history. On the other hand, there is surprisingly rich evidence, from Goethe and Friedrich Schlegel via Heyse, Storm, Conrad Ferdinand Meyer, and Gerhart Hauptmann to Hofmannsthal, Thomas Mann and Werner Bergengruen of *Novella* authors' awareness of the history of the genre, its distinct profile, and of their partly inductive, partly instinctive knowledge of the "rules" of the genre.[9]

It is, of course, not my intention to rate the novellas treated in this volume mechanically according to the storytellers' observation (or the contrary) of the traditional structural elements of the genre. (The 'quantitative' accusation commonly lodged against 'traditional' scholarship on the novella by nominalists/relativists is grossly inflated anyway). It is not the number of novellesque elements in a particular story that is decisive: it is the efficacy of their function, their interaction or lack of such, it is their effect on the overall profile and the quality of the novellesque story that matter.

Polheim maintains his intransigently negative stance toward the term "novella" in the preface ("Vorwort") and the introductory essay on genre problematics: "Gattungsproblematik" (pp. 9-16) of the major *Handbuch der*

---

[9]It speaks for the integrity of scholarship that Karl Konrad Polheim, several years after his admirably comprehensive account of "Novellentheorie und Novellenforschung (1945-1963)" (*Deutsche Vierteljahrsschrift für Literaturwissenschaft und Geistesgeschichte*, Sonderheft, XXXVIII, October 1964, 208-316), in which he rejects the very term "Novelle" in favor of "Erzählung", nevertheless edited the most useful *Theorie und Kritik der Deutschen Novelle von Wieland bis Musil* (Max Niemeyer, Tübingen, 1970, XVI + 197 pp.) which includes the view of the novella as a living genre by such creative writers as Wieland, Friedrich Schlegel, Herder, Jean Paul, Willibald Alexis, Goethe/Eckermann, Wilhelm Hauff, Theodor Mundt, Tieck, Karl Immermann, Heinrich Laube, Karl Gutzkow, Grillparzer, Hebbel, Eichendorff, Storm, Wilhelm Heinrich Riehl, Heyse, Keller, Spielhagen, Fontane, Conrad Ferdinand Meyer, Louise von François, Ferdinand Kürnberger, Paul Ernst, Heinrich Hart, and Robert Musil.

12

Deutschen Erzählung (Düsseldorf, Bagel, 1981) edited by him which enlists the collaboration of thirty-four Germanists representing a "Who's Who" of the guild in several countries, but he is commendably tolerant in allowing his collaborators to make use of various derivatives of "Novelle" where they wish even though he favors the general and indistinct term "Erzählung".

Although I have, for the reasons given, not updated my bibliographies beyond the references used for the original publication, there is little indication of significant change in the direction of *Novelle* research since these essays first saw the light of day. The successor of Benno von Wiese's widely distributed handbook on the *Novelle* (Sammlung Metzler. Realien zur Literatur, Volume 27, 1963; eighth corrected edition, 1982, VI + 95 p.), Hugo Aust's rich and conscientious *Novelle* (ibid, Volume 256, 1990, X + 185 p.) steers an uneasy, inconclusive, sometimes confusing course between stability and instability, between realism and nominalism of the genre. On the one hand, it gives due attention to the theoretical premises, to the natural, situational origin of the genre (conversation, intended effect, narration, quality) and to structural components (coyly disguised as "vocabulary") such as length, the event ("Begebenheit") with Goethe's famous modifiers ("Eine", "sich ereignete", "unerhörte"), concentration (turning points, symbolism), the frame, intertextuality ("Erzählung nach Mustern"), and its proclivity for appearing in collections of similar stories. But in its valuable discussion of more recent *Novelle* research it waxes quasi dithyrambic about the brilliant but, in its conclusion, nihilistic dictum of Karl Konrad Polheim that the existence of the *Novelle* is an illusion and that all we can and should say is that it is a story of medium length (Aust, 42-48). That is the much ballyhooed mouse that came out of the mountain of the legendary Emil Staiger seminar via Bernhard von Arx. And yet Polheim and Aust write book-length studies about the "Novelle"! The very style of Aust, highly concentrated but also tortuous and overwritten, reflects his existential quandary. A healthy, straightforward antidote to the studied verbal complexity engaged in not just by Aust but by current (not only German) scholarship – quite in contrast to the nuanced but luminous and elegant prose of von Wiese – is Siegfried Weing's survey of *Novella* research (*The German Novelle: Two Centuries of Criticism*, Camden

House, Columbia, South Carolina, 1994) which, while not uncritical, generally takes a constructive view of past *Novella* research and ends with a sensible accommodation of the various points of view documented.

In an exceptionally refreshing and dryly ironic essay on the fate of the novellesque in German twentieth century literature,[10] James M. Ritchie has qualified and modified the general opinion[11] that the psychological binge of this century's literature, aided and abetted by Freud, Schnitzler, and Thomas Mann on the one hand, and the vogue of the time-saving short story in line with modern tempo, on the other, have impaired, nay 'smashed' (von Grolman) the strict paradigm of the novellesque which was no longer in tune with the preoccupations of the twentieth century. While not, in my judgement, invalidating the claim of the phenomenal rise of psychological literature since Dostoevski nor the inroads made by the short story, both, whether directly or indirectly, at the expense of the conscious and highly disciplined art form of the *Novelle*, Ritchie adduces telling evidence for the continuity of the genre not only in what might loosely be called the conservative camp (Paul Ernst, Emil Strauss, Erwin Guido Kolbenheyer, Rudolf Binding, Werner Bergengruen, Ernst Wiechert), not to speak of clearly "völkische Blut und Boden" novellas (e.g. Hans Grimm)[12] but also on the "liberal", even psychologizing side

---

[10]"Die strenge Novellenform im Zwanzigsten Jahrhundert", in Friedrich Kienecker & Peter Wolfersdorf, eds., *Dichtung Wissenschaft Unterricht. Rüdiger Frommholz zum 60. Geburtstag.* Paderborn, Ferdinand Schöningh, 1986, 252-264.

[11]Ritchie cites particularly E.K. Bennett's *A History of the German Novell*e, Cambridge University Press, London, 1934 (first edition) and Adolf von Grolman's "Die strenge Novellenform und die Problematik ihrer Zertrümmerung", *Zeitschrift für Deutschkunde* 43, 1929, 609-627.

[12]Ritchie shows convincingly the politically dictated gray areas between official, non-official, and anti-official (but never threatening) "inner emigration" novella writers during the Nazi era, particularly in the case of

14

(including exile literature): Arthur Schnitzler, Carl Spitteler, Bruno Frank, Stefan Zweig, Leonhard Frank, Gottfried Benn, Günter Grass, and Martin Walser. I hope, myself, to have demonstrated in this book the survival of novellesque structure in several twentieth century stories by Thomas Mann. The continuity of the novella as an art form in the literature of the DDR (Louis Fürnberg, Stephan Hermlin, Anna Seghers, and Christa Wolf) noted by Ritchie is less surprising in view of the essentially very conservative, stylized, literary prescriptions of communist regimes, themselves distortions of the likewise conservative but decidedly quality-oriented literary tastes of Marx.

British scholars are noticeably prominent in the rate and quality of attention they give to the German novella. One wonders about the deeper structure of this attraction. Perhaps it is – as the British may perceive it – the relative lack of concern of scholarship in Germany with form and structure, with close textual reading (*explication de texte*), German propensity toward philosophy and abstraction compared to British common sense, realism, textual pragmatism, and aversion to theoretical models. Whatever the cause, E.K. Bennett, H. M. Waidson, John M. Ellis, Martin Swales, Brian Rowley, Roger Paulin, and James M. Ritchie are among the principal British contributors to important (and very readable) *Novella* research.[13] Ellis' categorically nominalistic, negativistic verdict on any normative endeavor or

---

Stefan Andres (258-259).

[13]E.K. Bennett, *A History of the German Novelle*. Cambridge (U.K.), Cambridge University Press, 1934. 2d revised edition (by H.M. Waidson): ibid., 1961. John M. Ellis, *Narration in the German Novelle*. Cambridge (U.K.), Cambridge University Press, 1974. Martin Swales, *The German Novelle*, Princeton, Princeton University Press, New Jersey, 1977. Brian Rowley, "*The Novelle*", in Siegbert Prawer, ed., *The Romantic Period in Germany*, London, 1970, 121-146. Roger Paulin, *The Brief Compass. The Nineteenth Century German Novelle*, Oxford (U.K.), the Clarendon Press, 1985. James M. Ritchie, "Die strenge Novellenform im zwanzigsten Jahhundert", see Footnote 10 in this Introduction.

generalization places him at the extreme margin of British scholarship. In general, however, British scholarship on the *Novella* since Bennett (1934) tries to steer a middle course between the normative, (inductively rather than deductively arrived at), the textual, and the contextual/historical foundations of the period. The results are level-headed and eminently productive in teaching as well as in research aimed at publication, but also uneasily veering between commitment and laissez-faire. Swales, Paulin, and Ritchie all illustrate this tug-of-war. Swales hits the nail on the head when he sees the XIXth century chasm between the axiom of social and individual order, on the one hand, and the reality of social and individual disorder, on the other, as the deep root of novellesque themes and structure: of the 'central event', 'chance and fate', realism, the tension between the poetic and the prosaic, the subjective and the objective, symbolism, and the *Rahmen* or Narrative Frame. But he minimizes the impact of the novella, a successful art form over six centuries, on subsequent novellesque stories, as well as the *organic* relationship of a particular thrust of storytelling to narrative structure, and embraces the alleged "nebulousness" (a very questionable judgement or at least choice of terms) of the novella as a decided asset. (p. 16). He comes close to the relativism of deconstruction by asserting that a definition of the novella "is nonsensical" and that "we must concern ourselves with the debate itself". (p. 17)[14]. And he loads the dice a bit by choosing as his exhibits XIXth century stories short on the dramatic and therefore much less likely to demonstrate "strenge Form".

Roger Paulin's book – like Swales', on the XIXth century German *Novelle* – tends also, like other British scholarship on the subject, sometimes humorously, to be on an engaging but also frustrating casual side: see e.g. his chapter headings: "'*or avenne che...*': The Novelle from the Renaissance to 1790" (nine pages!); "'*unterhaltend*' and '*befriedigend*': Goethe's renewal in 1795"; "'*etwas muss geschehen*': The Romantics"; "'*moralische Erzählungen*': Heinrich von Kleist and the Novelle tradition"; "'*schildert*

---

[14]See e.g. the very influential work of the philosopher Richard Rorty and of the later (converted) Gerald Graff.

Alles': The Biedermeier Novelle"; "'Freude an der Welt' : The Realist Novelle"; "'die *Schwester des Dramas'*: Shakespearean themes in the Novelle"; "'*unerhörte Begebenheit'*, '*Wendepunkt'*, '*Falke'*: Definitions in their context"; "'*von ziemlich gleichem Werthe'*: The case of Theodor Storm". Like many contemporary *Novelle* scholars he first demolishes a straw man by dismissing research that posits, he claims, the myth of the 'pure' uniform novella. He makes many fine observations on the rating of the German *Novelle* in European and American literature; "the [German] novel is the product of the city, the Novelle of the province" (p. 5); on the pro's and con's of German fragmentation, but on the whole the approach is eclectic, there is a kind of British fear of the systematic, and there is no real conclusion – a fault endemic, alas, to much, perhaps most of current scholarship (but considered no fault by its authors since their approach is axiomatically open-ended).

My curiosity of long standing about the novella is connected with my interest of even longer origin (since my high school days, as a pupil of the Collège Français in Berlin) in the facets of Franco-German literary and cultural relations. The inception of the novella is Romanic. It flourished, in that chronological order, first in Italy, then in France, then in Spain. Through German classicism and romanticism, both equally attracted to Mediterranean literatures though for very different reasons, it experienced an astonishing Golden Age in XIXth and early XXth century Germany.[15] This is the period

---

[15]This is not to claim any exclusivity for the German novella of the nineteenth and early twentieth century. It is, for certain purposes and in the 'right' literary and cultural ambiance, a natural art form practiced in many places (i.e., Scandinavia, Central and Eastern Europe, the British Commonwealth). For a spirited argument on behalf of American novellesque tales, see Werner Hoffmeister, "Die deutsche Novelle und die amerikanische "Tale": Ansätze zu einem gattungspsychologischen Vergleich", *The German Quarterly*, 63, No. 1, 1990, 32-49.

into which all of my chapters fall. The uneven striving of German *Novellisten* to join the Romanic sense of form and effect to the German preoccupation with content, contemplation, ethics, and inner development is woven throughout the texts examined in this book.

The lack of an inner priority of form, of style, of structure in the value system of German "Literaturwissenschaft", which has had an almost devastating effect on Novella research in the last two decades, would much less readily occur in the Romanic cultural sphere where the novella has originated. The novella was grafted, with remarkable success, on the German literary tree, but from time to time the original nature of the tree asserts itself and rejects the graft. Yet the novella is better suited than any other literary form to be a bridge between content and form, idea and art, history and interpretation. The formal core of the novella has been verified over centuries. It stands in constant polar mutuality with content. It does not at all exclude an evaluation of ideas but sets artistic limits to it. Beyond those limits the tale is no longer a novella.[16]

Even its original habitat, the Romance world (Italy, France, Spain), the birthplace and nurturing agent of the novella for centuries afterwards, and for all its greater adherence to traditional form than is generally found in the Germanic orbit, seems to have been affected in its most recent scholarship on the subject by the influence of the minimalist (non-) definition of the novella by Walter Pabst[17] – echoing that of Emil Staiger as reported by Bernhard von Arx for the German novella – as a 'story of medium length'. Even though the recent survey of the history of the novella in these three countries since the

---

[16]See my "Theorie und Praxis der Novelle: Gottfried Keller", p. 147.

[17]Novellentheorie und Novellendichtung: Zur Geschichte ihrer Antinomie in den romanischen Literaturen. Heidelberg, Winter, 1953. 2d, enlarged and improved edition: ibid., 1967. (In Spanish: *La novela corta en la teoriá y en la creación literaria. Notas para la historia de su antinomía en las literaturas románicas.* Madrid, 1972).

18

middle ages is entitled *La Nouvelle Romane*[18] and at least half of the sections carry this term in their titles, the editors, in their preface as well as their introduction, insistently shy away from the term and make it an elusive, mysterious, "genre bref énigmatique" or "insaisissable", impossible to categorize, a problem "éternellement insoluble", respecting no norms, no border, "eternally beyond definition"[19]. This cult of the impossibility of arriving at anything halfway coherent and tangible about a historically profiled and continuous literary form plays it safe, for if you say you can't define anything, how can one attack a non-definition? Yet, this convenient counsel of despair is the high fashion of today's scholarship and is responsible for its (often brilliant) sterility.

Literary value judgement, my conviction that, at some point, there is a connection no matter how qualified and differentiated between genre structure and literary quality, is likely to be the most controversial part of the matrix of this book. What is my argument in favor of this minority view?

Most people would agree, even today, that a dramatic play, to be good theatre, needs to observe 'laws' or rules of the stage: tension, economy, dialogue, sufficient objectivity and differentiation between and within characters to give each side credibility, profile, surprise. For the lyric, too, there will be widespread agreement that a good lyric poem must have a density and a freshness of language and thought combined with a personal message that goes directly to the individual reader/listener.

For prose forms, however, there has always been much more latitude, which seems almost limitless today. But the novella has a long European history as a disciplined drama in prose, as a unique blending of features resulting in a type whose perennial appeal resides precisely in the stylized cooling of cataclysmic events. It is a formal tour de force melding direct and

---

[18](*Italia, France, España*) .Ed.José Luis Alonso Hernandez, Martin Gosman, & Rinaldo Rinaldi. Amsterdam/Atlanta, Rodopi, 1993.

[19]Ibid., VII, IX - XII.

indirect discourse. Therefore it is realistic to assume that there *is* a connection between novellesque substance and form, on the one hand, and literary quality, on the other, always with the proviso that this cannot be a mechanical checklist but has to be decided, on a case to case basis, by the application of general genre criteria but leaving open the many possibilities of combination and compensation. There *was* a time when the rules tended to be too strict, too pedestrian and therefore needed to be challenged, even defied. There *is* a time now where ignoring the rules has led to a sweeping fad, a guideless chaos where some restructuring is as imperative as destructuring was in earlier periods. And if literary criticism in academia wants to keep any pretense of having an impact outside of our "solemn troops and sweet societies" (John Livingston Lowes), then we better heed the public outcry for value judgements. If we don't do it, I shudder to think what less competent and reasoned sides will – and already-do, all too readily.

Chapter I
Goethe and the Novella

Summary

After passing in review the cardinal components of novellesque structure including Goethe's observations on the subject within his creative works as well as outside them, I test, one by one, the three constituents of Goethe's deservedly famous definition of the novella, "eine Begebenheit / sich ereignete / unerhörte" against the first four inside stories of his Unterhaltungen deutscher Ausgewanderten *(1794-95) as well as "Die wunderlichen Nachbarskinder" in* Die Wahlverwandtschaften *(1808), the* Novelle *(1828), and "Die pilgernde Törin", "Der Mann von funfzig Jahren" and "Nicht zu weit" in* Wilhelm Meisters Wanderjahre *(1829). The congeniality or non-congeniality of classicism, in general, and of Goethe, in particular, with certain inherent and continuous features of the novellesque tradition of Romanic cultures (Italy, France, Spain) are delineated. On the basis of harmony or the lack of such between novellesque structure and the* Gestalt *of specific stories, value judgments are arrived at: of the novellesque stories transposed by Goethe from foreign models, the second ("Klopfgeschichte"), third, and fourth ("Bassompierregeschichten") of the* Unterhaltungen, *and "Die pilgernde Törin" in* Wilhelm Meisters Wanderjahre *are the best. The outstanding novellesque story written by Goethe without close adherence to foreign or domestic prototypes is not a novella as such but a protracted and occasionally interrupted episode in* Dichtung und Wahrheit *(1811), Part I, Book VI: the story of the "Frankfurter Gretchen." Embryonically but distinctly and exquisitely novellesque is, further, the story of the "schöne Mailänderin," also interrupted from time to time, in the* Italienische Reise *(second Roman sojourn, published 1829). The essay concludes with a succinct historical and critical assessment of Goethe's role in the evolution of the novella, or rather the novellesque, its continuity and change.*

———————

Goethe's adaptation – Germanization, if you wish – of a genre that had originated and flourished in Romanic territory for almost four hundred and fifty years constitutes a notable example of cross-cultural input into the evolution of European literature.[1] I hope to make a little contribution to several facets of this process: Romanic-Germanic literary interaction; the definition of the novellesque; the symbiosis of content and form, type and text; and the analysis as well as the assessment of some of Goethe's novellesque works in the light of that definition.

There is an almost novellesque paradox about scholarship on the German novella. While the novella thrived throughout the nineteenth century and the early twentieth, research on the subject, while not negligible, was relatively modest in quantity. Ever since World War II writers have greatly slowed down in writing novellas, but novella scholarship has mushroomed. It is even more ironical that in the last fifteen to thirty years highly nominalistic views on the German novella have increasingly asserted themselves without in the least inhibiting research on a genre that is not supposed to exist. Finding the novella to be a nonphenomenon after well over six hundred years of apparently fooling smart people, including academics, is certain to send not only historical scholars into a state of deep melancholia but might, heaven forbid, even raise questions in the minds of the disinterested populace about the usefulness of literary scholarship as such. Fortunately, things may not be as bad as the dialectic of scholars eager to make their mark as iconoclasts may suggest. Ironically – once again – most of the nominalists themselves, after having launched their theoretical lightnings against the myth of the novella,

---

[1]Now and then this essay parallels portions of Chapter IV, "Die Novelle in der Klassik und Romantik" which I originally contributed to Volume XIV, "Europäische Romantik I," of the *Neues Handbuch der Literaturwissenschaft*, Wiesbaden: Athenaion, 1982, 291-318. In an attempt to interest a wider circle of scholars and students I have given only the barebones of references. The critical evaluation of the secondary literature has to be left for another occasion.

22

merrily go on working with it in practice. There has also been, in the most recent past, an effort to rescue the term in some way or another. And most nonspecialists continue, of course, to operate with it, unaware of how controversial it has become.

Much of the nominalistic argument, I submit, is flawed by a wrong premise. Stripped to its essence, the assumption seems to be that there is an absolute theoretical prototype, *the* novella, and if that exclusive model is not overwhelmingly realized in every specific novella then there is no such thing as the novella. We come much closer to reality, I suggest, by saying that there are existential options — Staiger called them the dramatic, the epical, the lyrical — which occur in literature as in life in all kinds of mixtures, but their prevalence or intensity in any particular work may justify calling it a drama, an epic, a lyric. The novellesque (and I propose this coinage because "novellistic" may too easily be taken as a reference to the novel, not the novella) is basically a synthesis of the dramatic and the epic in prose form. If that combination, moving within approximate confines and with some kind of balance, predominates in a story we can call it a novella — not *the* novella. (I admit that it is linguistically and stylistically awkward to use "novellesque" exclusively. Therefore I sometimes backslide into "novella." In such cases, unless I refer to a particular story, I mean the novellesque). This merger of the dramatic and epical in prose form has evolved certain specific characteristics, partly through logical consequence, partly through success, that give the novellesque a certain profile. For this profile to be verified it is normally necessary that a goodly number of these features be present, but there are probably few novellas — certainly few good ones — that contain *all* these traits. Furthermore, the absence of even major characteristics may be compensated for by the extraordinary intensity and effectiveness of others present. Most novellas, then, will have nonnovellesque components also: the didactic or the psychological or the lyrical, the moral tale or the ghost story or the fairy tale. But they are secondary. The novellesque represents the norm, a novella the relative particularization of the norm.

How about the objection: so what whether it is called a novella or a tale or a short story or a novel? What difference does it make? Three reasons why it does. 1) Any literary work of art will, through comparison with a norm, yield dimensions and fine points it is less likely to reveal when contemplated in isolation. Norm <–> text comparison enriches textual analysis. 2) It also benefits norms. Norms must be constantly tested against texts and, if necessary, revised accordingly. One of the cardinal weaknesses of much contemporary German and French theory is precisely that it compares theory to theory, not theory to text, or that text is sporadically used to corroborate theory rather than shape it. 3) Genres, subgenres, or types are no longer, if they ever were, forms of artistic and scholarly repression. They are essentially natural, whatever their misapplications in practice. If a story tending in a novellesque direction mingles jarring elements in its composition, the mismatch may well affect its plausibility, effectiveness, its overall quality. But the novellesque may be found in other, especially related media. Certain portions or aspects of novels, autobiographical fiction, travel stories, ballads, anecdotes, even fairy tales may contain concentrations of the novellesque that may be "purer" than those encountered in some supposed "novellas."

Scholarship has let itself in for much grief by not adopting an analytical, critical stance toward novella nomenclature. Some German authors are knowledgeable about novellesque history and criteria: Goethe, Tieck, E.T.A. Hoffmann, Hebbel, Storm, Hofmannsthal, Musil, Bergengruen. What they say about their and others' stories must be taken seriously. But even in their cases what they say and what they do is often very different. Furthermore, the designation "novella" for prose of medium length has proved to be enormously prestigious and even remunerative ever since Boccaccio. The fact that an author or an editor calls a story a "novella" may mean something or next to nothing. It depends. Contrariwise, the greatest novellas of German literature, Kleist's, were not published as novellas but as tales — "Erzählungen." The decisive factor is not under what label a story has been launched but what it *is*.

It is therefore necessary, before discussing some of Goethe's novellesque works, to tell you what are, in my judgment, the constituents of the novellesque. I apologize for the apodictic impression that my list may make on you, but time is short.

The best definition of the core of the novellesque is still, after a century and a half, Goethe's "eine sich ereignete unerhörte Begebenheit" (the "one authentic unheard-of event"). The news item is reported because it happened; it requires no other justification except that it must be *interesting*. The happening is largely supposed to speak for itself. Didactic, moralizing interventions by the narrator are as out of place in the novellesque as they would be in a well-reported newspaper story. Such intrusions would only undermine the authenticity of the occurrence. Just as in a newspaper a novella does not require an omniscient narrator. Some of the very best novellas (Kleist!) report events certain facets of which do not seem to be known or clear to the narrator. They surprise him as much as they astonish the reader (take, for example, the first four stories in Goethe's *Unterhaltungen*). Thus novellesque occurrences seem more determined by chance or destiny than by personal will.

The authenticity of the novellesque report is safeguarded by the matter-of-factness and objectivity of the narration and the distance kept by the narrator. In some novellas the frame enhances this distance. The frame also fits the socio-conversational origin of the novellesque situation: stories *told* (not *read*) to an audience, a feature of the *Decamerone* integrally maintained in the *Unterhaltungen*, still observed in the "Wunderlichen Nachbarskinder" (hereafter cited as *WN*) of the *Wahlverwandtschaften*, becoming increasingly pro forma or unspecified in the stories inserted in *Wilhelm Meisters Wanderjahre* (hereafter cited as *WMW*), and abandoned in the *Novelle*. The audience, originally entirely aristocratic (*Decamerone*), still is predominantly so in the *Unterhaltungen* and in *WN*, grows more and more bourgeois (*WMW*, E.T.A. Hoffmann's *Serapionsbrüder*) but retains its sophistication.

A novella must mediate an interesting action interestingly since it also has a social mission. Therefore tension is indispensable to the novellesque. The evolution of this tension in a novella may go through some or all of these stages: dilemma > crisis > catastrophe or near-catastrophe > final effect (the nearest equivalent other than 'punch line' I can find to "Pointe") > release from tension > quiet stimulus for reflection. Dramatic peripeteias ("Wendepunkte") appear in the novella as turning points, especially the releasing ("auslösende") and the resolving ("auflösende") ones.

The literary novellesque, unlike the newspaper report, implies that the event reported be not only shocking but significant. While the nucleus of a novella often corresponds to an actual event and a number of excellent novellas keep some of the exact wording of the original document recording the event, the literary narrator furnishes most of the language for his report, he must select, omit, and complete. This is what might be called "the literary difference." The closer the narrator can integrate invention with the record, the more authentic his novella is likely to be. His manner of narrating will be economical, concentrated, taut. Objective length is far less important a factor in determining whether a story is a novella than the subjective brevity to the reader. One of the most difficult novellesque requirements for German scholarship to grasp is that a good novella does not say everything—on the contrary: the less it explains, the more it conveys. German lyrics are often exemplary by their sparing use of words, their suggestive power, but German prose, primary or secondary, tends to be prolix. Since a novella is condensed and disciplined, the linguistic and stylistic configuration of every sentence counts. Artistic expectations are all the higher just because the author must respect the autonomy of the events. The reluctance of German scholarship in the last sixty years or so to take the actual event seriously is, in part, due to its fear of being tagged as positivistic and, in part, to the romantic belief that the more the author invents, the greater the literary merit of his work. On the contrary, the best novellas are artistically preeminent through *how* they report or simulate to report, by what they do *not* explain, by what they leave to the reader to complete, to explain, to interpret. Nothing is more novellesque than the polarity between the lucidity, the soberness of its language and the impenetrability of the events. This makes a productive cocreator of the intelligent reader. The more charged the events, the more disciplined their representation (Goethe at his best, Kleist). This polarity is one of the principal causes of novellesque tension. Sophisticated formal restraint applied to explosive happenings, a device also related to the presence of women among the listeners and, later on, readers, makes of the novella, with few exceptions, a genre for gourmets. The gradual transition from an aristocratic to a

26

bourgeois genre while keeping aristocratic expectations intact (a marked feature, by the way, of French literature) occurred during Goethe's lifetime, in and through his works.

The combustible material that nourishes the tension of the novellesque is fed by disharmony between human intelligence and human passion, between rationality and irrationality, sense and senselessness. The notion of fateful senselessness, or at least lack of explicability, getting the better of intelligence, courage, and justice foments irony and paradox in the novella.

The novellesque – again like a good newspaper report – prefers the visual, the concrete. Given the German penchant for abstractions, this will pose difficulties for German novellas. The picture, the image must speak for itself. It should not be dragged in allegorically but must be an organic part of the event. It gives the novellesque its object orientation, its profile. The well-known novellesque notions of silhouette, falcon, and object-symbol ("Dingsymbol") are different sides of the same coin. The acoustic-musical equivalent to the central object in a novella is the auditory leitmotif (see, for example, the first two stories in Goethe's *Unterhaltungen*).

At best the coherence of a novella bestows representativeness upon each of its parts. Like the overture to an opera the very beginning of a novella is said to be the microcosm (Nino Erné's "Voller Akkord") reflecting the macrocosm of the total work.

This is the context in which I will examine Goethe's novellas or presumed novellas. Much of the grief of contemporary *Novellenforschung*, whether of Goethe or not, occurs because novellesque tales are looked at as just stories whose every ingredient is considered without a systematic probing of their genre-oriented structure.

Where did Goethe discover the novellesque? In Italy and France, principally; in Spain, secondarily: in Boccaccio's *Decamerone* (1348-1353), in the *Cent Nouvelles Nouvelles* (author uncertain, 1462-1486), in Bandello's *Novelle* (1554-1573), in Marguerite de Navarre's *Heptameron* (1559), in Cervantes' *Novelas ejemplares* (1613), to name only a few. These works do not only carry novellesque material but anecdotes, jests, fairy tales, legends, moral tales, adventure stories, character portraits, *etc.*. The impurity of this mix will be inherited by Goethe. But it is the novellesque element among them that has had the greatest impact on the shaping of quality prose literature in Western and Central Europe.

Goethe found these congenial sources in the foreign civilizations to which he felt most attracted. The novellesque owes its origin to the enviable ability of Mediterranean cultures to join the release and entertainment functions of interesting occurrences deviating from official social and moral norms with the redeeming value of artistic discipline. The novellesque displays an irresistible combination of Italian and French *joie de vivre* tinged by determinism, unabashed realism about the facts of life balanced by economy and refinement of language. It takes an objective, somewhat detached view of actions judged by their interest rather than their morality. It displays sophistication of approach, and, when necessary, a thin veneer of morality not taken too seriously by either the author or the intelligent reader. Its realism in content and stylization in form, its urbanity, its visual orientation, its elegant vitality were bound to appeal to Goethe's keen sense of what German culture, tending toward the abstract, the ponderous, and the mediated required for equilibrium. With his profound empathy for the Italians and the French, Goethe must have found their distinctive combination of intelligence and passion particularly fetching, because they made up for the German tradition of dialectically separating rationality from irrationality. In the Romanic literary orbit, passion, particularly an illicit one like adultery, is rewarded, provided it is genuine and generous, or punished, if it is mean and unsavory, depending on which side can muster more intelligence and skill. In Cervantes' *La Fuerza del sangre*, as in Kleist's related *Die Marquise von O...*, the raped and dishonored heroine finally manages – and deserves – to get the better of the transgressor and salt him away in matrimonial bliss not only because of the genuineness of their reciprocal attraction distorted by their first encounter and on the strength of the woman's unblemished and steadfast character but because of the intelligence, even the craftiness of her and her family's strategy in righting a wrong. True love is not enough: it must be guided by brains and adroitness. The indirect manner which saves face and honor is, in true Romanic tradition, a better way of solving amorous problems than open confrontations.

In the "Prokuratorgeschichte" of Goethe's *Unterhaltungen*, taken from *Cent Nouvelles Nouvelles*, you have a beautiful example for the workings of this devious process. Had the procurator rejected the advances of the young wife it would have been an insult to her and probably to her husband; had he taken advantage of the older husband's prolonged absence it would have been cheap; it is only via the round-about but delicate, psychologically superb strategy of the procurator that the desired aim, morally, psychologically, and narratively satisfying, is achieved. The covert passion of Honorio for the princess in Goethe's *Novelle* (1828) is not denounced or eradicated, but neither is it – can it be – satisfied. It is deftly acknowledged, she knows it, he knows it, but no word has been spoken, no deed has been done that would cause lasting embarrassment to the princess. In contrast, the lack of intelligence of the flirtatious wife in Goethe's "Nicht zu weit" in *WMW* (1829) has as much to do with the impending shipwreck of her marriage as the moral and social questionableness of her behavior.

The impact of the Romanic novellesque is not exhausted by simply pointing to plots lifted from Romanic texts. As a cultural phenomenon, it had a penetrating impact on Goethe's thinking and may imbue stories in which direct links with Romanic models do not exist. German culture has shown, long before and ever since Goethe, a remarkable curiosity about foreign civilizations, but this exceptional passive receptivity has much more rarely resulted in significant departures in active German literary endeavors, in primary texts. Goethe's writing was productively stimulated by Romanic classicism, including the novella, and through his works the influence continued in the nineteenth century German novella.

We cannot deal on this occasion with the considerable variations and the historical evolution of the Romanic novella, but need to mention at least that Goethe was receptive to the serious moral and ethical turn in Cervantes' novellas. This leads to the question: what did German classicism, principally Goethe, see in the Romanic novellesque that was particularly kindred to it? The need, I think, to circumscribe passion, a process indispensable to any dramatic genre or blend, to classicism, and to the existential accommodation deemed so vital to the continuity of Mediterranean culture. This balance is enforced not only by the counterweight of rationality and expediency but by linguistic discipline and tradition, by stylization. Human dignity against devastating odds is maintained by linguistic, by artistic dignity. Form compels distance, objectivity. Compactness, economy control southern expansiveness.

But German classicism is, on the other hand, less congenial to other features of the Romanic novellesque such as the higher social and individual worth attached to what is entertaining, interesting, amusing, to practical compromise, to hedonism, to vitality as an ultimate value. Goethe's novellesque writings reflect, on the one hand, this vitality most impressively (as, for example, in the two Bassompierre stories of the *Unterhaltungen* or in the "Pilgernde Törin" of *WMW*), but, on the other, do not escape the classicistic perils of blunting the profile of the novellesque through excessive stylization and didactic dilution of what are supposed to be uniquely silhouetted, "unheard-of," extraordinary events. The dramatic, unpredictable, lifelike occurrences and turning points of the novella are, not infrequently, screened, smoothed, slowed up, "epicized" and didacticized in Goethe's novellalike tales.

With these social, historical, cultural, structural, and artistic implications in mind, we will now analyze some aspects of Goethe's novellas. The texts examined include the frame and the "Binnenerzählungen" (except for the "Märchen") of Goethe's *Unterhaltungen deutscher Ausgewanderten* (1794-1795), "Die wunderlichen Nachbarskinder" in the *Wahlverwandtschaften* (1808), the *Novelle* (1828), and "Die pilgernde Törin," "Der Mann von funfzig Jahren," and "Nicht zu weit" in *Wilhelm Meisters Wanderjahren* (1821, 1829).

First, what does Goethe himself have to say about the novellesque either in his stories or in commenting about his work?

Neither in the frame nor in the six inside stories of the *Unterhaltungen* is there a single mention of the term "novella." But the presence of the phenomenon counts for more than the nomenclature, and the configuration of the novellesque has a rather distinctive place in the frame which, like Boccaccio's, assembles an aristocratic crowd fleeing from a catastrophe and trying to entertain itself, but is far more elaborate, differentiated, and interesting than Boccaccio's. There, Goethe dwells again and again on some key terms of the novellesque. There is reference to the therapeutic value of relating "überraschende Vorfälle" and "neue Verhältnisse." There is the clergyman's unconventional, realistic stress on the newness of a story: "Was gibt einer Begebenheit den Reiz? Nicht ihre Wichtigkeit, nicht der Einfluß, den sie hat, sondern die Neuheit." There is, twice, emphasis on the authenticity of a novellesque story as its prime and overriding asset: "Der Alte behauptete, (die Geschichte) müsse wahr sein, wenn sie interessant sein solle; denn für eine erfundene Geschichte habe sie wenig Verdienst," and, from Karl, "Jedes Phänomen, sowie jedes Faktum, an sich (ist) eigentlich das Interessante. Wer es erklärt oder mit anderen Begebenheiten zusammenhängt, macht sich gewöhnlich eigentlich nur einen Spaß und hat uns zum Besten, wie zum Beispiel der Naturforscher und Historienschreiber. Aber eine einzelne Handlung oder Begebenheit ist interessant, nicht weil sie erklärbar oder wahrscheinlich, sondern weil sie wahr ist."

Freedom of subject, including risqué ones, must, says the Baroness, be compensated for by socially acceptable form. The best combination is a story that is entertaining while we listen to it, but "sie hinterlasse uns einen stillen Reiz, weiter nachzudenken."

Goethe was, then, aware of the novellesque. How systematically is another question. And other theoretical statements in the frame fit other types of stories (moral tale, ghost story, "Familiengemälde"), and they, too, are represented in the *Unterhaltungen*.

Even if we did not know from Goethe's diaries and other documents that this awareness of the novellesque was subsequently fortified by his explicit use of the term "Novelle," his creative work would furnish the evidence. *WN* in the *Wahlverwandtschaften* were not only subtitled "Novelle" by him when the novel was published but the novella is cited specifically by Goethe, two decades later, in his famous conversation with Eckermann of January 29, 1827; "In jenem ursprünglichen Sinne einer unerhörten

Begebenheit kommt auch die Novelle in den *Wahlverwandtschaften* vor." To boot, in the novella itself and immediately after its conclusion the narrator describes what the novellesque is all about. The first formulation is almost an anticipation of the quasi unbearable novellesque tensions of the "Unerhörte" in Kleist's novellas:

> Sich vom Wasser zur Erde, vom Tode zum Leben, aus dem Familienkreise in eine Wildnis, aus der Verzweiflung zum Entzücken, aus der Gleichgültigkeit zur Neigung, zur Leidenschaft gefunden zu haben, alles in einem Augenblick – der Kopf wäre nicht hinreichend, das zu fassen; er würde zerspringen oder sich verwirren.

And just three paragraphs thereafter the narrator gives one of the most sensitive analyses of the nuclear role of the "sich ereignete Begebenheit" known to me. As soon as the story of the *WN* has been related by the companion of the lord to the group assembled, Charlotte leaves the room "höchst bewegt,"

> denn die Geschichte war ihr bekannt. Diese Begebenheit hatte sich mit dem Hauptmann und einer Nachbarin wirklich zugetragen, zwar nicht ganz wie sie der Engländer erzählte, doch war sie in den Hauptzügen nicht entstellt, nur im einzelnen mehr ausgebildet und ausgeschmückt, wie es dergleichen Geschichten zu gehen pflegt, wenn sie erst durch den Mund der Menge und sodann durch die Phantasie eines geist–und geschmackreichen Erzählers durchgehen. Es bleibt zuletzt meist alles und nichts, wie es war.

As to *WMW*, Goethe worked on the three inserts with the most marked novellesque features, "Die pilgernde Törin," "Der Mann von funfzig Jahren," and "Nicht zu weit," off and on, from 1807 to 1829, but I have not found more than occasional curt notations on their novellesque characteristics such as, e.g.,

32

his conversation with Sulpiz Boisserée of September 20, 1815: "Meisters Wanderungen. Novellen. Bestimmte Zahl der verschiedenen möglichen Liebesverwicklungen. Pilgernde Schöne..."

And, finally, there is the famous definition of the novellesque in the conversation with Eckermann already cited, "eine sich ereignete unerhörte Begebenheit," repeated, without the "sich ereignete," for emphasis, and the significant decision by Goethe to call a just completed, major story by its generic name, *Novelle*, perhaps with Wieland's *Novelle ohne Titel* (1804) in mind. His justification is very revealing about his concept of the novella not only then but previously, and about the evolution of the genre in Germany in the thirty-odd years that had elapsed since the *Unterhaltungen*:

> "Wissen Sie was, sagte Goethe, wir wollen es die *Novelle* nennen; denn was ist eine Novelle anders als eine sich ereignete unerhörte Begebenheit. Dies ist der eigentliche Begriff, und so Vieles, was in Deutschland unter dem Titel Novelle geht, ist gar keine Novelle, sondern bloß Erzählung oder was Sie sonst wollen."

It is amazing and ironic that Goethe anticipated and refuted the current nominalists who wish to depersonalize the novella and make it an unprofiled ingredient of the vast and amorphous type called "Erzählungen." It is also ironic, however, that Goethe's practice contributed itself to the expansion and diffusiveness of the "ursprüngliche Sinn" of the novellesque to which he refers in the next sentence, cited earlier. His practice is sometimes consistent with his theory, sometimes not, and it is more often than not inconsistent even within the same story.

In the final portion of my essay I will try an approach not so far attempted in Goethe or novella scholarship, and that is to take the salient components of novella structure, of my empiric hypothesis, and test each of them, one by one, against Goethe stories tending in a novellesque direction. I will limit myself, for the time being, to the "eine Begebenheit," the "sich ereignete," and the "unerhörte."

The "one event," the "eine Begebenheit" needs, for a change, to be taken more literally: a real, compact, self-contained occurrence which should have what Heyse called a silhouette. If there are a series of events there must be a tight sequential unity to them, and *one* must be the culminating or decisive one. In the first Bassompierre story of the *Unterhaltungen* it is the meteoric, ephemeral but unforgettable affair of a subsequent Marshal of France with an enigmatic beautiful shopkeeper's wife; in the second one ("the veil") the regular adultery of another Bassompierre with a likewise mysterious beautiful woman. In the "Pilgernde Törin" it is the tramp-like arrival of another mysterious woman of high refinement in the von Revanne household; father and son fall in love with her; she disappears. An amusement-oriented wife and mother in "Nicht zu weit" leaves her family stranded and is then herself literally as well as figuratively ditched – for the coach in which she and her beau are riding ends up in a ditch, and he then ditches her in favor of another woman in the coach. When she finally gets home, her husband is no longer there. He has met an old flame of his. Here the story ends.

As Goethe himself has singled out the *WN* in the *Wahlverwandtschaften* as an exemplary novella by his standards, let us take a closer look at its silhouette. Two children of neighbors, a boy and a girl, of about the same age, destined by their parents for each other, fight in such a way that their parents are compelled to give up their matchmaking plans. The girl becomes engaged to another, worthy but less strongly profiled young man. The first young man, now a soldier, returns, the bride is seized by a strong passion for him of which he is not aware. Shortly before his planned departure he invites the bridal pair to a cruise, she jumps overboard, he saves her, swims with her to shore, not far from which they are sheltered by a young couple. They fall into each other's arms, swear eternal mutual faithfulness, receive wedding clothes from their just married hosts, put them on and thusly arrayed appear before the respective parents of bridegroom (one does not quite know which of the two bridegrooms!) and bride. The in-laws, it is intimated, will give their blessings to this fast switch.

The story, only six to eight printed pages long, turns, in a wider sense, on *one* event: the practical consequences of the love-hatred of girl and boy from childhood on. It culminates, more specifically, in the decisive water and land happenings. Clarity of the lines, tension, pace, absence of digressions, dilemma, turning point releasing the novellesque action (the girl jumps into the water to commit suicide – or to be saved by the man she wants desperately to capture? Who knows?? At any rate, a very novellesque ambiguity)[2], crises, threatening catastrophe (aquatic and social), resolving turning point (the inofficial couple requests and will probably receive parental blessings): all these are novellesque. But, as one looks more closely, the silhouette, especially towards the end, turns out to be conventional. It carries the marks of abstract invention, of melodrama. The youth who saves a recalcitrant but basically equiattuned belle from great danger and thus wins her for himself is a very traditional theme. That he and the young woman are being sheltered, of all people, by a just-married couple whose wedding attire is still hanging around, that the clothes happen to fit the second couple to a *T*, that it then appears in these bridal garments before the parents, implores their blessings and most likely receives them all in a jiffy (what the lawful bridegroom has to say about it the narrator does not tell us) – all this would be judged, were it not written by Goethe, to be pure melodrama, not plausible as a "sich ereignete

---

[2]The actual source of this "unerhörte Begebenheit" is to be found in the story from an English newspaper which Goethe utilizes, in October of 1787, to teach English to another of his novellesque heroines, the "schöne Mailänderin" with whom he is falling in love during his second sojourn in Rome: "Ich blickte schnell hinein und fand einen Artikel, daß ein Frauenzimmer ins Wasser gefallen, glücklich aber gerettet und den Ihrigen wiedergegeben worden. Es fanden sich Umstände bei dem Falle, die ihn verwickelt und interessant machten, es blieb zweifelhaft, ob sie sich ins Wasser gestürzt, um den Tod zu suchen, sowie auch, welcher von ihren Verehrern, der Begünstigte oder Verschmähte, sich zu ihrer Rettung gewagt" (*Italienische Reise, Zweiter Römischer Aufenthalt, Goethes Werke,* ed. Erich Trunz, Hamburg: Christian Wegner, 1959, XI, 424).

Begebenheit," non-authentic, a literary concoction. We further note that the time frame is very vague and that this novella manages not to mention a single solitary name of a person or a location: an extreme example of classicistic stylization and generalization that does not attain the minimum of selectively precise reporting demanded by the novellesque.

In the two paragraphs immediately preceding the *WN* the story is introduced as being told by the companion of the lord after he has, as the author puts it, stretched the attention of his audience to the highest degree by stories both strange and terrifying, whereas now, in the *WN*, he will relate a story strange, to be sure, but gentler than its predecessors ("eine zwar sonderbare aber sanftere Begebenheit"). That means, I think, an event with a happy ending. Even though the novellesque and a positive conclusion are not mutually incompatible, it strikes us that the happy resolution of this novella is far less compelling than the conflict preceding it. Goethe's novellesque stories, particularly those inserted into novels, tend to have taut, incisive novellesque beginnings followed by increasing diffuseness and a conventional resolution, or sometimes no resolution at all. Goethe may have recognized the problem himself in his conversation with Eckermann of January 29, 1827 when, referring to the story he finally entitled *Novelle*, he says:

> Es kam sodann zur Sprache, welchen Titel man der Novelle
> geben solle; wir taten manche Vorschläge, einige waren gut
> für den Anfang, andere gut für das Ende, doch fand sich
> keiner, der für das Ganze passend und also der rechte
> gewesen wäre.

Goethe's trouble is that he wants to report an extraordinary event as such but also wants to write a moral-psychological-classicistic 'exemplary' novella in the sense of Cervantes. He is cognizant of the principal structural conditions for such a novella but the artistic execution of the idea falters in the second, novellesque part of the story whereas the first, psychological part is far more persuasive. With the exception of the girl's jump into the water which is well motivated psychologically but equally effective as a novellesque action, the novellesque in this story is not good, and what is good in this story is not novellesque.

What is the "eine Begebenheit" in "Der Mann von funfzig Jahren"? Flavio is supposed to marry his cousin Hilarie. Hilarie is in love with Flavio's father, the major, Flavio with a beautiful young widow, who in turn loves the major. The major and Hilarie become engaged to each other even though not yet publicly. The widow rejects Flavio. Now Flavio and Hilarie fall in love, and finally the major and the widow join hands. This silhouette, which reminds one somewhat of *WN*, is too mathematically perfect to command authenticity. It raises the suspicion that the story is hyperstylized. And so it is. After the opening, which is brisk and novellesque, the author's creative discipline evaporates gradually: tying the knotty problem seems to interest him much more than untying it. Goethe's previously cited remark to Sulpiz Boissereé as he composed *WMW*: "Novellen. Bestimmte Zahl der möglichen Liebesverwicklungen" reflects this greater reliance on invented plots rather than fictional building on actual events.

The genesis of "Der Mann von funfzig Jahren" may provide a clue to the problem Goethe had with its structure and its integration into *WMW*. Off and on he worked on it for about twenty-two years, from 1807 to 1829. It was printed independently from *WMW* in 1818, as part of it in 1821 but only the initial chapter (less than one third of the story), finally published as such in the final version of *WMW* (1829) but in three very uneven parts: the first four-fifths together (Second Book, Chapters 3 to 5), then it skips a short chapter and the beginning of the following one and reappears in Chapter 7, then the reader hears nothing about it for over two hundred printed pages, until finally, toward the end of the novel, a few cursory bits of information provide a nonchalant anticlimax to a story that began so auspiciously, so firmly. We possess numerous schemata for this story. Goethe himself must have felt a bit uneasy about it even in the final text of the novel because, before relating it, he addresses the reader, admits that he had thought of publishing the story piecemeal but claims that its "internal consistency" argued for continued narration; he also asserts that while the "Begebenheit" it narrates appears to be separate from the mainstream of the novel, the reader will recognize at the end of the novel how close is the connection between the two. A good deal of German scholarship has performed veritable acrobatics in order to demonstrate that all these impediments notwithstanding both the internal consistency and the amalgamation with the larger work of these novellesque insertions have been little short of perfect. It is difficult to share that view. Thematic links do not, in themselves, signify artistic integration.

The impetus of the Romantic cult of originality and scholarly reaction against positivism have stifled, especially in the last half century, a proper respect from researchers on the German novella, including Goethe's, for the seriousness with which the "sich ereignete" in Goethe's definition should be regarded. It would be well to keep in mind the observations of Aristotle which, though not referring to novellas, are eminently applicable to the novellesque:

> A poet who writes about something that has really happened
> is no less a poet for that reason....It is probable that much
> that happens occurs against the odds of probability....We
> must prefer the impossible that is credible to the possible
> that is incredible.[3]

The writer of novellas has a lot of room for maneuvering from close adherence to the nucleus of an event that has been recorded, via its artistic completion or truncation, to the periphery of imitation, that is, the invention of an improbable event that becomes probable through the strength of its artistic execution. But the risk of sliding into the non-novellesque is all the greater the farther the writer moves from what Wolfgang Kayser regards as the core of the novellesque,[4] "a real and unique occurrence defined locally and

---

[3]Transposed into English from the German translation of Aristotle's *Poetics* by Olof Gigon (*Poetik.* Stuttgart: Reclam, 1964, pp. 40, 67; see also p. 72).

[4]Translated from *Das sprachliche Kunstwerk,* 6th ed. (Berne and Munich: Francke, 1960), pp. 354-355.

temporally."

In inverse proportion of credibility, the scope of the "sich ereignete" may range from a well-known, major historical event via public, scientific, or scholarly documents, a report of an event by a person directly affected or a witness, to literary sources and realistic inventions by the author. Does it need to be said that boundaries between these categories often are not sharp?

Take the "Beautiful Shopkeeper" novella in the *Unterhaltungen*. It closely follows, but with deftest nuances of translation, omission, and addition, the text of the published recollections (1666) of one of France's great military, diplomatic and court figures, the Marshal François de Bassompierre (1579-1646). Bassompierre's memoirs are written in a straightforward, unpretentious manner and thus invite credibility. From recollections – and novellas – one expects a fine mixture of precision and stylization in selected indications of time and place. This is what we get in Bassompierre and Goethe: "Marschall von Bassompierre – seit fünf oder sechs Monaten – die kleine Brücke [in Paris] – Laden an einem Schilde mit zwei Engeln – Fontainebleau – eine sehr schöne Frau von zwanzig Jahren – Nacht von Donnerstag auf den Freitag," *etc.* But as important is the mediation of the cultural and psychological prerequisites of a specific, past epoch whose *historical* uniqueness enhances the *particular* uniqueness of the episode reported by the Marshal and by Goethe. If you want to reward invention, then Hofmannsthal's neo-romantic adaptation is, of course, 'superior' to Bassompierre and to Goethe. But ignoring the difference in historical consciousness, as Hofmannsthal does, transferring the neoromantic complexes of fin-de-siècle nineeteenth century to these two figures bursting with vitality, the Marshal and the shopkeeper, dissecting and subjectivizing the lapidary, honest, nonanalytic style of the late Renaissance which Goethe maintains with clean dignity – all this is such a violation of authenticity that as a total literary text Hofmannsthal's is vastly inferior to Goethe's.[5]

---

[5]For a full-scale treatment of the novellesque elements of the "Beautiful Shopkeeper" story, see my *Novellistische Struktur. Der Marschall von*

When the author makes use of a source that itself is literary, his access to the "sich ereignete" is even more indirect. The original version of the story of the procurator in the *Unterhaltungen* is already a blend of the novellesque and the moral tale, communicated with remarkable concentration. Goethe used the first printed version from the fifteenth century ("Le sage Nicaise ou l'amant vertueux," last story in the *Cent Nouvelles nouvelles*, author unsure, written about 1462, printed about 1486), that is, the version coming closest to the original occurrence whatever it was. He quadrupled the story in length but preserved the basic structure. In "Die pilgernde Törin" Goethe likewise kept very close to the printed French version ("La Folle en pélerinage," 1789) whose technique, we are told, is looser, more psychological, more veiled than Bassompierre's stories but is still part of the older novellesque tradition. Goethe's translation is regarded as a very fine achievement: he has respected the novellesque integrity of the events with admirable "Fingerspitzengefühl" and has not succumbed to the temptation of interpreting explicitly. In his beautiful tribute to the story, Erich Trunz at the same time defines some of the subtle essence of the novellesque:

> Es ist wie im Leben selbst: man erfährt nur, was man selber
> sieht und hört. Es ist in diesem Falle zu wenig, um genau
> Bescheid zu wissen, aber genug, um den psychischen Verhalt
> zu erschließen. Mit feinem Takt verschleiert die Pilgernde
> ihre Erlebnisse, und doch gibt sie aus innerer Not manches
> davon frei. In dieser Verhaltenheit, diesem Schleier liegt der
> Reiz der Novelle...Der psychologische Tiefblick ist auch in
> dieser Novelle. Aber er wird nicht vordergründig, er wird
> nicht präsentiert...Der Leser muß vieles selbst erschließen.[6]

Bassompierre und die schöne Krämerin (Bassompierre, Goethe, Hofmannsthal), Germanic Studies in America, ed. Katharina Mommsen, no. 46, Bern and Frankfurt, Peter Lang. 1983, 124 pp.

[6]Goethes Werke (see 2., above), VIII, 619.

Farthest from the "sich ereignete" is a story invented by the author with the aim of verisimilitude. To this category belong, predominantly or wholly, the *WN*, "Der Mann von funfzig Jahren," "Nicht zu weit," and the *Novelle*. The — to the best of my knowledge — overwhelmingly invented nature of these stories is, in my judgment, detrimental to the quality of the novellesque in these works. The *WN* and the *Novelle* are so stylized that hardly a reader could believe that they narrate an actual occurrence. "Der Mann von funfzig Jahren" and "Nicht zu weit" start in a most novellesque fashion and then slow down noticeably, the author seems to lose interest, the story oozes away and ceases, like the *WN*, abruptly. The lack of an authentic source seems to aggravate the author's task of untying the knot of the plot. A tendency toward melodramatizing could be the substitute for the lack of a genuine novellesque core.

The unheard-of, the unprecedented, the "unerhörte" in Goethe's novella definition traverses a scale that extends from the unusual — for example, Bassompierre's silent encounters with the beautiful shopkeeper,— to the totally unexpected rendezvous with two cadavers in place of his mistress. Fabricated events, no matter how skillfully manipulated, seem unable to carry through the element of the unexpected, so crucial to the novellesque, with the same authenticity as a core of actual events. Whatever is calculated possesses a planned logic and is therefore typical rather than unique. A novella in which one can predict what this or that person will say or do is unlikely to be a good novella. But a novella author who tries to manufacture surprises by intricate contrivances is likely to achieve results as bad. Sooner or later he will get caught up in his web, like the cleverest but false testimony of a witness in a trial is bound to make a fatal mistake sooner or later.

How about the "Unerhörte" in Goethe's practice? In the first inside tale of the *Unterhaltungen*, the Antonelli story, the unheard-of is, as a matter of fact, very audible but scary and weird: the "fürchterliche Ton." But this phenomenon is blunted as the story moves on or rather declines. First because the horrible noises are attenuated from occurrence to occurrence: the frightful plaintive sounds become shots which become clapping which become heavenly sounds and then vanish completely. Second, because the consequences of these phenomena are too monotonous: three times, after such sounds, the singer faints and so do her companions. Since Goethe followed the original account of a personal experience related by the French actress Hippolyte Clairon, he cannot be blamed, in this case, for the progressive dilution of the "Unerhörte," but it *is* characteristic of some of his work, particularly the later one.

In the second, the "mysterious knocking" story, we experience on less than a page two "unerhörte Begebenheiten": the knocking sound without any ascertainable cause, pursuing a nice-looking, nubile orphan girl serving a noble family, and the outrageous but successful cure:

> Entrüstet über diese Begebenheit und Verwirrung, griff der
> Hausherr zu einem strengen Mittel, nahm seine größte
> Hetzpeitsche von der Wand und schwur, daß er das Mädchen
> bis auf den Tod prügeln wolle, wenn sich noch ein einzigmal
> das Pochen hören ließe.

The knocking ceases. Here the "Unerhörte" is undiluted and remains extremely effective. Goethe wisely refrains, in this as in the Antonelli and Bassompierre pieces, from offering any explanations in the story: he delegates that to the persons in the frame, and even there we are left with a choice of possible interpretations, and only samplings at that.

In the meetings between Bassompierre and the shopkeeper the "Unerhörte" builds up quietly but with pervasive effectiveness: first the almost speechless encounters, the restrained drama where the bending forward of the shopkeeper's wife tells more, and better, than wordy paragraphs; the abrupt alternation between aggression and restraint in an exquisite tradeswoman who immediately insists on spending a night under one cover with the subsequently celebrated Marshal of France, then rejects his caresses in the most self-possessed manner, demands to go to bed with him forthwith and confesses to having so insuperable a desire of joining him that she would have accepted any condition to achieve it. The same woman proclaims unapologetically a double faithfulness to her husband and to her lover. And then she disappears without a trace, leaving her lover two corpses to puzzle about.

The second Bassompierre story contains, on about half a page of print, half a dozen unheard-of features: it is not the adulterous husband who sneaks up to his mistress when he can but a beautiful woman who loves the husband so much that *she* visits *him* regularly; this adulterous relationship takes on the complexion of a second, parallel marriage in that they meet for two years every Monday. The legitimate wife finally discovers them sleeping together but refuses to create a scandal. Trusting her instinct she takes off her veil, covers the feet of the lovers, and leaves quietly. On waking up and seeing the veil, without requiring an explanation, the mistress immediately decides to break off the relationship and not to approach her lover again by a hundred miles. She leaves gifts for the three legitimate daughters which accentuate the fairy-tale potential of the story without jeopardizing, in this case, the extremely effective novellesque.

After the first four stories of the *Unterhaltungen* the novellesque component, including the "Unerhörte," dwindles rapidly. As the baroness correctly states in the frame commentary, the procurator story is primarily a moral tale. The tale about the tribulations of Ferdinand, invented by Goethe, is also a "moralische Erzählung" of some psychological refinement. The *Märchen*, which concludes the Unterhaltungen, is *sui generis*.

We have already touched on the "unheard-of" in the *WN*: the story ends, conventionally enough, with a bride and a bridegroom, but the bridegroom is not the one to whom she had been engaged the morning of the same day. Perhaps it is this awkward combination of the conventional and unconventional that is the fatal flaw in the ending.

The "Pilgernde Törin" of *WMW* is chock-full of unheard-of events and turns. A beautiful, charming young woman tramps companionless along the way. Her clothing components clash (just like those of the beautiful shopkeeper in Bassompierre's story): dusty shoes and shining silken stockings. Her behavior is also strange: her manners are exquisite, she is tactful, intelligent, well read, sings, plays the piano, sews – but nobody knows where she comes from. She is alternately deeply mournful and frivolous, serious and derisive. The "fool" or "simpleton" designation in the title is alternately confirmed and questioned. When father and son compete for her she hints to the father that she expects a child from the son and to the son that she expects a child from the father, and then vanishes never to be seen again. The "Unerhörte" is precise in detail, enigmatic in origin, and perfectly authentic, classical in its objectivity and conciseness. Here the stylization fits the mysterious side of the femme fatale.

The "Unerhörte" in "Der Mann von funfzig Jahren" with its jigsaw pattern is, as mentioned before, too fabricated, too disjointed in treatment and too strung out to be effective.

The initial situation of "Nicht zu weit": a wife and mother failing to appear at her birthday celebration which has been meticulously prepared by her husband and children, because she is gallivanting around in the neighborhood, constitutes, in design and execution, the novellesque "Unerhörte" at its best, as does her being ditched by her beau later on, but the narrator then melodramatizes the "Unerhörte" into a mushy encounter of the husband with an old flame, and the story breaks off there.

In the *Novelle*, the "Unerhörte" (the conflagration in town, the escape of a tiger and a lion and their threat to the princess) turns toward the end into the lyrical rendering of magical legend and presents, as a whole, an uneasy combination of the dramatic, epic, and lyrical, though individual parts are very beautiful.

What is "unerhört" is, be it noted, influenced by the cultural conditioning of the reader. When in the procurator story an elderly husband, during an extended absence, permits controlled infidelity to his beautiful young wife as long as she chooses a sedate, reliable, intelligent, and discreet partner, the Northern reader is likely to view this as "unerhört" whereas the Italian and French reader is likely to find this arrangement historically anchored in the customs of a certain social class (the institution of a "cicisbeo," a "sigisbeé").

To sum up: Goethe has an extraordinary flair for the epic treatment of the "sich ereignete unerhörte Begebenheit," particularly at the beginning of his novellesque stories. Sometimes – and especially when he follows closely a foreign, usually French source – he implements his own definition of the novella successfully in much or all of the story and comes up with superb examples of the genre: in the story of the knocks and the two Bassompierre stories in the *Unterhaltungen*, and in the "Pilgernde Törin" of *WMW*. But in others novellesque discipline and intensity get sidetracked by excessive stylization (*WN, Novelle*) and formal fatigue (Antonelli story, "Der Mann von funfzig Jahren," "Nicht zu weit"). The procurator story stands by itself: it is primarily a moral tale, but the novellesque potential, the humor, wit, and sophistication with which the impending adultery is turned into a moral lesson give it a novellesque spice which benefits the story.

Time and space do not permit us to pursue novellesque elements in all prose, let alone non-prose works of Goethe that clearly do *not* qualify as novellas. "Der Hausball" (1781), "Reise der Söhne Megaprazons" (1792), and "Die guten Weiber" (1800-01) come to mind. The story of the beautiful young Milanese woman in the *Italienische Reise* (Second Roman sojourn, published 1829) is, in subject and narration, embryonically but distinctly and exquisitely novellesque. An early version, in some respects, of the "Schöne Mailänderin," is the fourteen-year-old Wolfgang's first love, the "Frankfurter Gretchen." It provides most of the substance for Book V and the beginning of Book VI, Part I of *Dichtung und Wahrheit* (1811). It comes in four installments, interrupted by the account of the crowning of the Archduke Joseph, but the two events are skillfully intertwined and the execution of the story so careful and elaborate that, with some excisions, it could well be published as a novella. Though we have little historical documentation about the events on which the Gretchen episode is based, it gives every indication of possessing just the right novellesque mixture of "Dichtung und Wahrheit." The "Unerhörte" is represented by the totally unexpected criminal complications into which his association with the "Gretchenkreis" precipitate the adolescent. The coronation enhances the dramatic and epic texture of the story. The account conveys personal authenticity. It is chary of moralistic or didactic digressions, lets the events speak mostly for themselves, is fate oriented, objective and differentiated in approach, has the right blend of distance and empathy, humor and benevolent irony, is interesting and contains clear turning points. The tension proceeds from dilemma (the faked letters and the sweet uncertainties of love) via sudden crises, near-catastrophe (criminal, physiological, psychological), final effect ("Pointe": Gretchen's deposition that her affection for him was sisterly, which infuriates and disenchants the young lover), to the resolution of tension and the "stillen Reiz zum Nachdenken," since a number of points remain in the clair-obscur. Marked stylization, especially in the lack of identification by name of the protagonists and specific locations, is amply justifiable here by the author's understandable reluctance to embarrass his friends in view of the criminal turn of events. Artistic discipline is consistent and there are no signs of auctorial fatigue. The faked letters constitute the "Falke" of the story. While the Gretchen adventure has no novellesque frame, the coronation serves a frame-like function. To be sure, this is not a pure novella either: it has idyllic and fairy-tale elements, which here blend deftly with the novellesque. If you ask me which are the best novellesque stories written by Goethe without close adherence to a model, my answer, "unerhört" as you may find it, is the "Gretchenepisode" in *Dichtung und Wahrheit* and the "Schöne Mailänderin" account in the *Italienische Reise*.[7]

But that does not mean that we need to be apologetic about the high ranking we otherwise give to those novellesque stories by Goethe in which he has, if you want to put it that way, invented the least. Romantics among scholars may be disappointed by that, but, to me, that is a rather narrow view of the matter. In the first place, it is our job to evaluate the quality of literature. Who gets credit for it is a secondary question. No matter who wrote it, a good story is a good story, a poor story is a poor story, and a so-so story is a so-so story. Secondly, just as style has been defined as what we omit, novellesque

---

[7]I have dealt with the first in the next essay: "Die novellistische Struktur des Gretchenabenteuers in *Dichtung und Wahrheit*," and have combined a novellesque analysis of both with the recollections or inventions of *his* "beautiful Milanese woman" by Goethe's father in the third essay of this book: "Autobiography or Fiction? Johann Wolfgang and Johann Kaspar Goethe's 'Schöne Mailänderinnen' and the 'Frankfurter Gretchen' as Novellas."

46

quality is likewise built as much on what you don't say as on what you say. Goethe's self-discipline in safeguarding the original source while translating it – and every translation is an adaptation, a rewriting – is worthy of admiration, not of condescension. Into this artistic self-denial was mixed Goethe's profound empathy and respect for the integrity of foreign cultures. Third, Goethe's weaknesses as a novellesque storyteller are related to his strengths, to his universality, to his existential deference to evolution, genesis, process, systole as well as diastole, which caused long pauses in his creative progress on numerous projects. Since the novellesque is based on a particularly demanding fusion of form and content, structural defects in this genre are more glaring than in others. Fourth, Goethe's historical merits in introducing the Romanic novella into Germany are of the highest order. The surge of the novella, along with the lyric, as the finest literary genre achievement of Germany in the nineteenth century bears witness to his seminal role, even though not all of his novellesque practices should have been followed.

A great deal of lip service has been paid by German literary scholarship to the "indissoluble unity" of form and content, of type and text. But I have not found a corresponding plethora of studies that really, systematically, patiently, textually verify this contention. In undertaking to illuminate the reciprocal relationships between type and text via text analyses viewed in the light of genre hypotheses I have hoped, primarily, to shed light on the nature of novellesque stories. I do not think it is entirely accidental that Goethe provided literary substance for this purpose, for one of his enduring existential concerns was with the polarity between the specific and the general.

Chapter II
Die novellistische Struktur des "Gretchenabenteuers" in *Dichtung und Wahrheit*

Summary

By way of a close look at a profiled episode in Goethe's Dichtung und Wahrheit, *the story of the adolescent Goethe's love affair with the "Frankfurter Gretchen", its distinct novellesque elements are highlighted without gainsaying a degree of epic stylization that dampens the dramatic cutting edge of the happenings recounted. Nevertheless, the novellesque ingredients of the Gretchen adventure detailed in this analysis seem to bear out the conclusion arrived at toward the end of the preceding chapter: that the 'Gretchenabenteuer' is one of Goethe's two best novellesque stories not closely adhering to a model.*

Es gibt Prosa, die man getrost als *Novelle* bezeichnen kann. Das heißt, es gibt Prosastücke, in denen das *Novellistische* so stark ausgeprägt ist, daß es der Prosa seinen Stempel aufdrückt, sie zum Typartigen macht. Es gibt aber auch Prosa – und zu ihr gehört m. E. Goethes Gretchenabenteuer im 5. Buch von *Dichtung und Wahrheit* –, in der das Novellistische *ein* wesentliches Element ist, aber in Verbindung mit anderen gattungsmäßigen Bestandteilen verschiedener Intensität, und wo man besser daran täte, diese "organa" zu durchleuchten, ihre Potenz anzudeuten und ihren gegenseitigen Verwandtschaften oder Getrenntheiten nachzuspüren, als sich auf das einseitige Überwiegen *einer* dieser Komponenten festzulegen, um daraus das Recht herzuleiten, das Ganze als Beispiel des Typus zu etikettieren. Welches Prosastück zur ersten, welches zur zweiten Kategorie gehört, das muß der Einzelanalyse überlassen werden. Aber es sei erlaubt, zu behaupten, dass diese zweite, relativistischere, gemischtere Kategorie zugunsten der ersten, "absoluten" bisher oft verwischt worden ist, obwohl sie ja gerade zur Abgrenzung der ersten unentbehrlich ist.

Ich verlange also nicht den unbedingten Glauben an das Bestehen einer

Gretchen*novelle*. Es soll hier genügen, an Hand einiger weniger Gesichtspunkte von dem Novellistischen *in* der Struktur der Gretchengeschichte zu sprechen. Vorweggenommen sei deshalb sofort, was, besonders auf den ersten Blick, *nicht* novellenhaft, ja anti-novellenhaft an der Gretchenerzählung erscheint: das Andeutende, Halbdunkle, das Stimmungsmäßige und persönlich Betonte, das Gemütliche, Normal-Vernünftige, ja etwas Hausbackene der "Heldin", das Lockere, Unterbrechende der Struktur, die Liebe zum Detail an sich, das Verschlungensein oder manchmal auch nur Nebeneinanderhergehen von mehreren Handlungen, die Abwesenheit des Silhouetten-, Falken- oder Dingsymbolhaften, der einheitlichen verbildlichten Idee. Kurz: das rein Epische (während die Novelle ja zwischen dem Epischen und dem Dramatischen liegt).

Durch das Gretchenabenteuer webt eine freudige Erzählungslust; es hat etwas Spinnendes an sich, ja, es hat viel Märchenhaftes. Das Märchen ist definiert worden als eine "Welt der Einbildung, des Wunderbaren, in der die unbefriedigten Wünsche unserer Welt befriedigt werden", als eine "Mischung von zwei Welten". Ist das nicht genau das, was Wolfgang und Gretchen bewegt? Diese Welt der Einbildung besteht für sie in den glanzvollen, außerordentlichen, wunderbaren Krönungsfestlichkeiten, die sie aus dem Alltag emporheben und ihnen märchenhaft vorgekommen sein müssen. Das Märchenhafte besteht auch in der Liebe zu Gretchen, die tatsächlich (und beinahe tragisch) in die "Welt der Einbildung" gehört, auf die sich seine "unbefriedigten Wünsche" stürzen. Gretchen macht sich zwar über ihre Chancen bei Wolfgang keinerlei Illusionen und bleibt fest auf dem Boden der Realität, aber das Emporheben dieses einfachen Mädchens aus dem niederen Bürgerstand, ohne irgendwelche Anstrengungen oder Ehrgeiz ihrerseits, in die intime Assoziation mit dem jungen Patrizier und Schultheißenkel, der sie liebt und sogar heiraten will, das ist doch "wie im Märchen"! Selbst der glückliche Abschluß des Märchens scheint in Reichweite zu sein – da wird Wolfgang unsanft aus seinem Himmelreich verstoßen, der Traum ist zu Ende – ohne happy ending.

Das Märchenhafte ist nun zwar nicht identisch mit dem Novellistischen, aber mitunter durchaus mit ihm vereinbar. Paul Ernst hat die Novelle sogar die "Schwester des Märchens" gennant. Die historische Entwicklung der Novelle von Boccaccio über Wieland, Goethe, die Romantik und Keller bis zu Hesse birgt viele Spuren dieser Verwandtschaft. Das Märchenhafte und das Novellistische walten nachbarlich zusammen in Goethes *Unterhaltungen deutscher Ausgewanderten*, in der *Neuen Melusine*, in der *Novelle*, und ergänzen sich dank der mehrseitigen Ausrichtung des 5. Buches von *Dichtung und Wahrheit* besonders gut.

Der inhaltlichen Dreischichtung dieses Buches entspricht eine morphologische Dreiteilung: das Gretchenerlebnis ist überwiegend idyllisch, die Krönungszeremonien episch, die Kriminalaffäre dramatisch. Je nachdem Goethe sich einem dieser drei Erlebniskreise zuwendet, wandelt sich die Tönung des 5. Buches ins Lyrische, Epische bzw.Dramatische, oder in eine Kombination dieser Elemente. Die Übergänge von der einen zu der anderen Stimmung sind markant genug, um dem Leser Abwechslung zu bieten, aber doch nicht so schroff und unvorbereitet, daß sie den harmonischen Gesamteindruck stören. Die Gretchenidylle wird, trotz Wolfgangs Verliebtheit, idyllisch-entspannt erzählt; die darauffolgenden und zuweilen damit abwechselnden Reichsfestlichkeiten werden, wenn man so sagen darf, mit entspannter Spannung dargeboten, denn Wolfgang ist bei ihnen ja hauptsächlich interessierter Zuschauer, es steht für ihn persönlich wenig auf dem Spiele; die plötzlich entlarvte, das 5. Buch beschließende Kriminalsache besitzt eine aufwühlende Spannung, die in gewissen paroxystischen Momenten etwas Sturm und Dranghaftes hat (wildes Toben, Bewußtlosigkeit, Krankheit, Selbstmorddrohungen, Hungerstreik, Familienzwist). Schließlich erfolgt die Entladung der Spannung durch Wolfgangs Wut- und Tränenausbrüche und seine langsame Ernüchterung.

Wir dürfen nicht vergessen, daß der Weg vom Idyllischen zum Dramatischen zu Goethes Zeit nicht so weit war wie er uns heute erscheinen mag. Schon Boccaccio gebraucht einen ausgesprochen idyllischen Rahmen, gegen den sich die vorhergehende episch-realistische Beschreibung der Pest und die damit abwechselnden dramatischen Novellen selbst abheben. Ähnlich, wenn auch in anderer Reihenfolge und Betonung, ist die Dreiteilung des 5.

50

Buches: es beginnt mit der dem 18. Jahrhundert zugehörigen ländlichen Idylle, mündet ein in die breite realistische Epik der Kaiserwahl und -krönung, und schließt überraschend mit der Dramatik der Kriminalverwicklungen. Das, was uns heute am Gretchenabenteuer als nicht-novellenhaft vorkommt: das Intime und Malerische, gehört für Goethes Zeitalter und selbst für die nächste Generation – und in Deutschland auch noch später – durchaus dazu; mit Bezug auf die Novelle spricht Mundt von "Darstellung in pittoresken Bildern", Laube von "Genrebildern", Hebbel von "Niederländischen Gemälden", und selbst Heyses "Silhouette" ist aus der Malersprache entnommen, wie ja seine eigene Novellistik überhaupt viel Malerisches-Statisches hat. Das Gedrängte, die Konzentration der Gretchenidylle besteht darin, daß sich Goethe nur auf die wichtigsten Impressionen beschränkt. Trotzdem lag Grund vor, die an Einzelheiten, Entwicklung und authentischen Erinnerungen karge Gretchenidylle etwas aufzupulvern.

Goethe tat das erstens durch die Einfädelung einer Kriminalangelegenheit, in die Wolfgang durch Gretchens Kreis verwickelt wird – die "sich ereignete, unerhörte Begebenheit", welche, bei allen sonstigen Variationen, Goethes gesamter novellistischer Produktion zugrunde liegt. Wenn Hans Franck in seiner *Deutschen Erzählkunst* sagt, daß die konkrete Gestalt des "Unerhörten" in der Novelle eine "Liebesaffäre oder Diebesaffäre" sei, so ist das Gretchenabenteuer die doppelte Probe auf das Exempel, und übrigens in dieser Zweischneidigkeit geradezu frappant mit der Ferdinandnovelle in den *Unterhaltungen deutscher Ausgewanderten* verwandt, wie auch Trunz schon angedeutet hat. In seinem biographischen Schema bezeichnet Goethe den gesamten Erlebniskomplex des 5. Buches mit *einem* Wort: "Ungeheures"; dieses selbe Wort gebraucht er auch im Text des 5. Buches, und es fällt auf, wie forciert er ähnliche Wörter gerade mit Bezug auf das Gretchenerlebnis anwendet, als gälte es, eine ruhige Idylle mit allen Kräften zu dramatisieren. Eine zweite Art der Abwechslung und Spannungserhöhung erreicht Goethe durch die Überleitung zur Krönung Josephs II., die womöglich in diesem Stichwort "Ungeheures" mit einbezogen ist, zum mindesten in ihrer einmaligen Großartigkeit das "Unerhörte" verstärkt.

Die Krönungsbeschreibung ist sowohl episch wie dramatisch. Die historischen Ereignisse werden spannend erzählt, aber mit einer gelassenen, heiteren, unterhaltenden Spannung, und mit einer Breite und einer Freude am bunten Detail, die dem Epischen nahestehen. Aber diese Festlichkeiten haben wiederum doch auch ihre eigene Dramatik, ganz abgesehen von den bereits von Trunz bemerkten novellesken Einschüben, die auf die Krönung Franz I. zurückgehen. Sie sind ja eine farbenprächtige, symbolhafte Inszenierung; Goethe selbst vergleicht diese "Funktionen mit einem Schauspiel, wo der Vorhang nach Belieben heruntergelassen wird". Und die abendlichen, halb-verborgenen Stelldicheins und Spaziergänge Wolfgangs und Gretchens geben den Festlichkeiten noch einen persönlich-dramatischen Beigeschmack, wie umgekehrt Wolfgangs privilegierte Zuschauerstellung, die er auch Gretchen zunutze macht, und überhaupt die allgemeine übermütige Stimmung der Liebschaft zugute kommen. Ein großes und ein kleines, ein Staats- und ein individuelles Drama, sind nicht nur ineinander verschlungen, sondern nähren sich gegenseitig. Der verhaltene aber innige Höhepunkt dieses kleinen Dramas aus "Freundschaft, Liebe und Neigung", wie Goethe es benennt, wird erreicht, als der Autor, um den Leser durch die etwas langwierigen Zeremonien nicht zu ermüden, zum letztenmal auf Gretchen zurückgreift, sie Wolfgang näher als je bringt – "und ich", sagt Goethe, "an Gretchens Seite deuchte mir wirklich in jenen glücklichen Gefilden Elysiums zu wandeln", – es am Abend zum ersten keuschen Kuß kommen läßt, um am nächsten Morgen schon über den glücklichen Liebhaber die Katastrophe hereinbrechen zu lassen. Hier ist der novellistische Umschlag, "diese Wendung der Geschichte, dieser Punkt", in Tiecks Worten, "von welchem aus sie sich unerwartet völlig umkehrt, und doch natürlich, dem Charakter und den Umständen angemessen, die Folge entwickelt". Denn so unerwartet – trotz verstreuter, vorhergehender Andeutungen – und niederschmetternd dieser Zusammenbruch des vermeintlichen Glücks für Wolfgang (und uns) auch ist, so *mußte* dieses Unerwartete doch, rückblickend, früher oder später eintreffen, die gesellschaftliche Übertretung Wolfgangs, sein Verkehr mit gesellschaftlich nicht akzeptablen Freunden *mußte* mal ans Licht kommen, es *mußte* Krach geben – nur übersteigen die Plötzlichkeit, der Umfang und die persönlichen Folgen dieser Katastrophe für Wolfgang unsere nie gestillten, leisen

52

Befürchtungen. Der *Wendepunkt* wird hier wirklich zu einer *Krise* – um Vischers erweiternden novellistischen Begriff zu gebrauchen –, aber nicht zum *Schicksal* wie im *Kohlhaas*. Ein Vergleich dieses Wendepunktes mit verwandten Erscheinungen in anderen novellistischen Erzählungen Goethes: der Ferdinandgeschichte in den *Unterhaltungen*, der "Pilgernden Törin" in den *Wanderjahren*, den "Wunderlichen Nachbarskindern" in den *Wahlverwandtschaften* und der *Novelle*, muss einer anderen Gelegenheit vorbehalten werden. Zu unterscheiden von diesem ganz klar konstruierten äußeren Wendepunkt ist die novellistische Pointe – der innere Wendepunkt – des Gretchenabenteuers: die bestürzte Ernüchterung des leidenschaftlich Verliebten, als er erfährt, daß Gretchens Neigung zu ihm diejenige einer älteren Schwester zu einem Kinde gewesen sei – von dem sechzigjährigen Goethe mit verständnisvoller Ironie erzählt.

Auch dieser sorgsam gewahrte Abstand des Erzählers gehört zu der Tradition der Novelle von Boccaccio und Cervantes über Goethe, Kleist und der Droste zu Paul Ernst und Thomas Mann. Die frühe Novelle ist eher ernst als tragisch. Wolfgangs Liebe zu Gretchen ist echt und stark, und weder der Leser noch Goethe machen sich darüber lustig; aber der Unterschied im Alter, in den gegenseitigen Gefühlen und in Reife bzw. Unreife des Partners gibt dem ganzen Erlebnis doch einen ironischen Unterton. Die Geschichte wird auch taktvoll, gemäßigt, überaus anständig und diskret erzählt; das Extreme – die Wutausbrüche Wolfgangs – kommt erst am Schluß, aber da ist Wolfgang schon isoliert – besser: *wird* isoliert, sozusagen in Quarantäne gelegt, von der Gesellschaft abgeschnitten und unschädlich gemacht. Seine Leidenschaftlichkeit wird überzeugend und unbeschönigt dargestellt, aber die indirekte Erzählungsweise wird nicht aufgegeben, der Dichter behält das epische Heft in der Hand.

Der für die Novelle so wichtige Abstand wird schon bei Boccaccio und meistenteils auch bei Goethe durch die Einführung eines Rahmens konkretisiert. Wenn auch die direkten Beziehungen zwischen Erzählung und Rahmen bei beiden recht lose sind (im Gegensatz zu späterer Novellistik wie der *Hochzeit des Mönchs*, dem *Schimmelreiter* oder dem *Ketzer von Soana*), so erfüllt dieser Rahmen bei dem Italiener und dem Deutschen dieselbe

Funktion: er "bewahrt", wie Bernhard von Arx es anläßlich der *Unterhaltungen deutscher Ausgewanderten* formuliert hat, "eine Welt vor äußerer und innerer Bedrohung". Das gilt auch für die Darstellung des Gretchenerlebnisses: die "symbolischen Ceremonien" der Krönung, dieser großartige Ausdruck einer übrigens nicht ungefährdeten Gesetzmäßigkeit, der Tradition, hinter der Gretchen zeitweilig beinahe verschwindet, sind das Gegengewicht gegen die ungesetzmäßigen und gesetz*losen* Komponenten des 5. Buches, gegen die Liebe des blutjungen Patriziersohnes zu einem älteren, einfachen Mädchen aus dem "falschen" Stadtteil und ihre Verwicklung in kriminelle Machenschaften. Das persönliche Schicksal bekommt hier eine gesellschaftliche Färbung. Zeichnet sich die neuere Novelle dadurch aus, daß sie von ihrer edlen Herkunft her den "feinen" Novellenton beibehält, im Inhalt aber von der überwiegend aristokratisch-patrizischen Atmosphäre Boccaccios zu deren problematischen Berührung mit dem *Nur* – oder sogar *Unter*bürgerlichen hinabsteigt, so ist das 5. Buch, welches unter Beibehaltung des gesellschaftlichen Tones das Aristokratische, Patrizische und Kleinbürgerliche miteinander verbindet bzw. gegeneinander ausspielt, eine charakteristische Etappe auf dem Wege vom *Decamerone* zu *Kleider machen Leute, Aquis Submersus*, Hofmannsthals *Erlebnis des Marschalls von Bassompierre* und Bergengruens *Drei Falken*.

Das Erzählen mit bewußtem Abstand entspricht Goethes klassizistischer Ausrichtung in der Periode der Entstehung von *Dichtung und Wahrheit*. In allem, was die Krönungsfeierlichkeiten angeht, werden Örtlichkeiten und Personen genau gennant; in allem aber, was im Gretchenabenteuer ihn persönlich angeht, werden fast nur fingierte und umschreibende Namen gegeben (Pylades, seine Schöne, Gretchen, die Mutter, die Vettern, ein Aufseher, der Freund usw.), und präzise Ortshinweise fehlen meist ebenfalls. Die Ausdrucksweise ist, ohne Hinsicht auf Person und Stand, gleichgeschaltet, nivelliert; die indirekte Rede wird bevorzugt. Das Repräsentative, Abstrahierende, ja Typische dämpft das Intime-Großartige-Dramatische, entpersönlicht es. Es ist nicht so sehr die Geschichte *seines* Jugendabenteuers als *des* Jugendabenteuers. Goethe gehört durchaus zur Tradition der Novellistik mit didaktisch-moralischen Zwecken, oder, wie bei Boccaccio, jedenfalls Zugaben dieser Art. Von den *Unterhaltungen* bis zur *Novelle* schreibt Goethe "moralische Erzählungen", aber er weiß wohl, wie seine italienischen und spanischen Meister, daß in der gelungenen novellistischen Erzählung das Lehrhafte und Menschenverbessernde nicht aufdringlich werden darf. Die Krönungsfestlichkeiten sind ein ausgezeichnetes Beispiel der natürlichen Verquickung des Unterhaltenden und des Belehrenden. Ja, selbst das Liebesverhältnis ist didaktisch: Gretchen gibt Wolfgang weise moralische Ratschläge, wohingegen Wolfgang sie über das Zeremoniell der Krönung aufklärt. Abgesehen von Gretchens Warnungen wird das Moralische indirekt aber doch unmißverständlich ausgedrückt: der junge Wolfgang gab sich einer Täuschung hin, *also* wird er ent-täuscht; er tut etwas Verborgenes, *ergo* wird er bestraft. An diesem Grundsätzlichen ändert auch das Mißverhältnis zwischen seinem geringen Vergehen und den überraschend weitgehenden Folgen nichts.

Im weiteren und wichtigeren Sinne aber befaßt sich das Gretchenabenteuer, wie überhaupt die Novellistik Goethes, mit dem Problem der Selbstüberwindung, und das Gretchenerlebnis ist tatsächlich im sinnvoll gesehenen Leben Goethes eine markante Etappe auf dem Weg zur Selbsterkenntnis. Hans Wolff hat sicherlich recht, wenn er als Verbindungsstück zwischen den einander zeitlich so nahen *Wahlverwandtschaften* einerseits und *Dichtung und Wahrheit* andrerseits Goethes steigendes Interesse für das Problem der Persönlichkeit und seinen Glauben an die Prädestination anführt; dafür wäre, meine ich, auch das schmerzliche aber nicht tragische Ende des Gretchenerlebnisses ein eindrucksvolles Beispiel.

Zusammenfassend: Einzelauslegungen und Einreihungsversuche bleiben, wie alle Interpretationen, trotz allem Bemühen nach Objektivität subjektiv gefärbt. Jedes einzelne der von mir besprochenen Elemente, oder selbst mehrere, mögen in anderen Erzählungsformen vorkommen, ja vorherrschen, aber Anzahl, Intensität und Verbindung dieser Formen deuten doch unverkennbar auf Goethes novellistische Gestaltung seiner ersten Liebe hin. Diese aus der Textanalyse gewonnene Einsicht würde, glaube ich, bestätigt werden durch den Vergleich mit anderen Werken, Lektüren und Interessen

Goethes aus dieser novellistisch betonten Schaffensperiode, die mit den *Unterhaltungen deutscher Ausgewanderten* beginnt und in den ursprünglich als Novelle geplanten *Wahlverwandtschaften* kulminiert, denen nur zwei Wochen später die Aufnahme der Arbeit an *Dichtung und Wahrheit* folgt. Ich schliesse mit drei Minimalfolgerungen: 1. Wir besitzen noch viel zu wenige gründliche Kunstanalysen von dichterischen Autobiographien, 2. wir brauchen nicht nur Betrachtungen über die Novelle, sondern auch über das Novellistische, und 3. bei der Durchforschung der Novellenproduktion Goethes sollte die novellistische Ausrichtung des Gretchenerlebnisses berücksichtigt werden.

Literatur:

Bernhard von Arx: *Novellistisches Dasein. Spielraum einer Gattung in der Goethezeit.* Zürich 1953.

Johannes Klein: *Geschichte der deutschen Novelle.* Wiesbaden 1954.

Henry H.H. Remak: "Manon Lescaut und die Gretchenepisode in Dichtung und Wahrheit: Quelle, Parallelen, Kontraste", in *Goethe.* Neue Folge des Jahrbuchs der Goethe-Gesellschaft, XIX, 138-154, 1957.

Erich Trunz: Anmerkungen zu *Dichtung und Wahrheit*, Goethes *Werke*, IX, 599-768, besonders 670-681. Hamburg 1955.

Benno von Wiese: *Die deutsche Novelle von Goethe bis Kafka.* Düsseldorf 1956.

Chapter III
Autobiography or Fiction?   Johann Wolfgang and Johann Caspar Goethe's "Schöne Mailänderinnen" and the "Frankfurter Gretchen" as Novellas

Summary

    Cultural/compensatory motivations of Goethe's attraction to the novellesque as an organic phenomenon of the Romanic orbit in general and Italy in particular. Its precipitate in the Italienische Reise *(1786-1788; 1813-1829). "Novella" vs. "novellesque" :definitions, structural elements originating in natural, oral, entertaining (in a deeper sense) interaction between people. Quality raising: the literary novella. The narrator. Gaps of indeterminacy promote authenticity. Function of the listener/reader. Genres: their fundamental, existential ingredients but elastic combinations.*

    The Italienische Reise: *its novellesque substratum. Goethe's indebtedness to the Italian novella (Boccaccio, Luigi da Porta, Bandello, Batacchi, Casti) and to other sources including his own experience of Italian life.*

    The novellesque as the structural component of Goethe's account of his relationship with the 'beautiful Milanese': (October 1787 to April 1788) the "one event" ("eine Begebenheit") that has actually occurred ("sich ereignete"); its "unheard of" characteristics ("das Unerhörte").

    Comparison of this autobiographical/novellesque story with Goethe's novellesque account of his first love adventure with the "Frankfurter Gretchen" in the fifth and sixth books of his fictional autobiography, Dichtung und Wahrheit: *examples of the 'literarization' of personal experience into a novellesque story. Differences and convergences between the two stories: the novellesque "Wendepunkte" (turning points); narrative control/distancing; crisis and catastrophe; transparency of language vs non-transparency of events; the "sich ereignete."*

    Finally, comparison (convergences/differences) of the 'Beautiful Milanese' story of Johann Wolfgang with Johann Caspar's (his father's) account of his own alleged love adventure with a beautiful Milanese woman during his Italian journey in 1740 (Viaggio per l'Italia).

Two lyrical fruits of the "Erlebnis" of the "Schöne Mailänderin": "Amor als Landschaftsmaler" and "Cupido, loser, eigensinniger Knabe", with particular attention to the "sich ereignete Begebenheit" and the "Unerhörte".

Recapitulation of the essay's thrust.

Conclusion: if the "Frankfurter Gretchen" and "Die schöne Mailänderin" episodes were published without their narrative interruptions, they would be recognized as among the best of Goethe's novellas.

Goethe's *Italienerlebnis*, of which the *Italienische Reise* is just the centerpiece, was the most comprehensive and decisive extra-cultural (non-German) experience of his life. In this total matrix, the quasi natural marriage of substance and form achieved in Italian language, literature, art, music, style, landscape, and architecture – the very element that makes a civilization out of a culture and in which he found Germany wanting – represents the cohesive force. In French culture, which Goethe absorbed equally well and in its totality, he could observe a similar bonding, but it had a more cerebral quality to it than the Italian fusion *con amore*. His German heart found its passionate Italian counterpart more to his liking than the sophisticated French *affaires de cœur*.

In this magnetism the art form of the novella plays a significant though not preponderant role. Compared to the ups and downs of German literary taste through the centuries this most continuous of all distinguished prose forms, at least up to the end of the XIXth century, originating in the Romanic and then spreading to the Germanic cultural areas, constituted the principle of stability within variety that enticed Goethe.

The microcosm of the novella offered to a denizen like Goethe a demanding, refined, dramatic, semi-public, semi-private prose mold at a time when the political retardation of Germany was not in a position to develop a

58

macrocosmic art form, a national epic in prose.[1] Since there were no "unerhörte Begebenheiten" of national public range to celebrate, they were moved to the personal range where Germany was as eligible as any other culture. The novella privatizes the latent dynamic energies of national cultures. The cool, controlled, matter-of-fact account of 'unheard of' events true to life happening to a person are embryonically capable of collective expansion when the culture is ready for it. In the course of centuries of experience with the genre, the Romanic orbit had learned how to handle with assurance micro-existential reversals. This engrained tradition could serve as a stepping stone toward the ultimate tackling of macroexistential upheavals in a literature such as the German one, with neither the pluses or minuses of established conventions. The microdramatic/existential could lead to the macrodramatic/universal, given cultural maturity and cohesion on a national scale. This generic constellation made the novella attractive to receptive spirits like Goethe in its equilibrium of foreign and domestic, public and private elements, of passionate substance in a disciplined, even severe vestment, of unpredictability, irrationality, and violence caught in a classical structure that maintains distance and human dignity. The transparency of the language compensates for the opaqueness of the events. The visual element so congenial to novellesque stories (silhouette, falcon, symbol) is based on the joy of seeing, so natural to the Mediterranean setting and always primary to this particular son of the north. The positive stance of Italian culture toward life, toward reality, corresponds to Goethe's vitalism that has minority status in German literature.

It is not my task – and not in my competence – to trace the impact of Italian novellas on Goethe's primary works, although I suspect there is a lot yet to be discovered if one proceeds subtly and indirectly. Rather I have tried to present the cultural affinity of the Italians for the novellesque as part of the

---

[1] The next several observations are English paraphrases of my remarks in German contained in the section "Romania und Germania" of my "Die Novelle in der Klassik und Romantik", Chapter IV of this book, p. 113-114.

matrix into which the episode of the beautiful Milanese woman in the *Italienische Reise* fits.

But, it may be argued, the Italian Journey is not a novella, nor is it a novel which, like *Wilhelm Meisters Wanderjahre*, may contain as insertions a number of novellas. It is a continuation of his autobiography: *Aus meinem Leben.Dichtung und Wahrheit*, only subsequently published as a separate work. The answer, necessarily brief, to this objection is that Goethe himself has balanced out, from the beginning, "Dichtung" with "Wahrheit": an inevitable consequence of depicting events long since past, a compromise fortified not only by considerations of tact and courtesy suffusing a period and a culture a far cry from our present-day cult of indiscretion, invasion of privacy, and 'leaks', but also responding to the esthetic liberty, the artistic potential a poet wants to reserve for himself in whatever he puts down.

This, however, still leaves the question with what justification and to what extent generic considerations are applicable to a chronologically arranged mixture of fact and fiction. What is the difference between "novella" and "novellesque"?

Research use of the word "novella" in two meanings, that of a particular story and of the entire genre, is understandable but has also done a lot of mischief. It is understandable because the term "drama" e.g. can also mean a particular play and the general type. But it has also led to the seemingly ineradicable phenomenon of scholar after scholar declaring that such and such a work is not a novella because it does not manage to squeeze into it every major characteristic of the novellesque, and worse, that there is no such genre or type because no pure examples can be found of it. Of late this nominalist position has been invigorated by the deconstructionist tendencies engulfing, at least in the higher regions, much of academic criticism deeply suspicious of anything normative.[2]

Nevertheless I am, frankly, amazed by the persistence of this

---

[2]Despite these strictures I will, from time to time, use "the novella" myself for "the novellesque", mostly for stylistic reasons.

ahistorical secular agnosticism which seems to disregard the existence of a genre or sub-genre for at least 650 years. History and especially continuity in history make many theoreticians acutely uncomfortable. The comprehensive and systematic analysis of specific texts as to their normative as well as unique features is frowned on. The notion of cohesive works is deemed to be illusory; texts are admitted to the sanctum of theory either as eclectic and incidental props for comprehensive theories or are treated like infinitely variable collages, like telescoped bundles of complexes.

As long as thirty years ago, in 1957, I proposed what seemed to me then – and still does – a sensible approach to the terms "novellesque" and "novella."[3] Hope springing eternal, I will pick up where I left off yesteryear, for just like on this occasion my debut in *Novellenforschung* consisted of investigating an episode in Goethe's autobiographical writings as to its novellesque components. That time it was young Goethe's involvement with his first love, the "Frankfurter Gretchen" in *Dichtung und Wahrheit*; this time it is "die schöne Mailänderin", the beautiful Milanese woman in the *Italienische Reise*,[4] but I intend to go back and forth, like riding on a rainbow,

---

[3]See Chapter II in this book: "Die novellistische Struktur des Gretchenabenteuers in *Dichtung und Wahrheit*." Two of my studies preceding that analysis in time, though not directly concerned with the novellesque, do provide a basis for investigating the same episode: "Goethes Gretchenabenteuer und Manon Lescaut: Dichtung oder Wahrheit?", in *Formen der Selbstdarstellung*, Festgabe für Fritz Neubert, Berlin, Duncker & Humblot, 1956, pp. 379-395, and "Manon Lescaut und die Gretchenepisode in *Dichtung und Wahrheit*: Quelle, Parallelen, Kontraste", in *Goethe*. Neue Folge des Jahrbuchs der Goethe- Gesellschaft, XIX, 1957, pp. 138-154.

[4]The *Italienische Reise*, based on notes taken during and recollections of Goethe's journey to Italy (September 3, 1786 to June 18, 1788) was elaborated from the end of 1813 on. The first part appeared in 1816, the second in 1817, the third, which contains the story of the lovely woman from Milan, not until 1829. The present essay fulfills a 'promise' made in Chapter I: "Goethe and the

between these two stories, carved by Goethe out of his autobiographical fiction, to reinforce their novellesque and other characteristics without gainsaying their differences.

What is the relationship between novellesque and novella?[5] There are prose texts one can safely term novellas. In them the novellesque components are so pronounced that they give the particular text an overall normative imprint. There is, however, also prose in which the novellesque is a discernible or even principal element, but in coexistence or intricate linkage with other generic factors of varying intensity and effectiveness. Only a comprehensive and systematic analysis of the text, the weighing of these elements against each other, can show whether the most accurate overall classification of the work in question is novella or anecdote or short story or tale (Erzählung, conte) or legend or novel, or whether we deal with major or minor novellesque elements in genres such as autobiography, autobiographical fiction, memoirs, diaries, journalistic reports or stories, ballads, fairy tales, or whatever. Both types or, if you prefer a less categorical denomination, both dimensions are widespread and an organic part of literary creation and interpretation, but I dare say that the second approach that addresses itself to the novellesque components in works that primarily belong to other genres or types has rated little attention. There has been too much "either/or" and not nearly enough "both/and", "more/less".

I realize the reader is all eager to get closer to the beautiful Milanese woman, but I must ask him to suspend his desire just a little longer for the sake of stern scholarship. For I have to lay my cards on the table and tell you what I understand by the novellesque. I will, however, refrain from arguing the pro's and con's of my hypothesis. That would carry us too far in this context. It is, like all premises, open to challenge. All I can say is that I have tested and modified it over and over again, for thirty years, in teaching and writing,

---

Novella", specifically on p. 44-45.

[5]This paragraph is a free paraphrasing of the introductory sentences of Chapter II (see note 3 above). See also Chapter I, "Goethe and the Novella", p. 22.

against more than sixty texts, mainly but not only German, that qualify by dint of designated nomenclature,[6] previous scholarship, or my own reading as novellesque to some marked degree, and found it sufficiently relevant and empirically productive to justify its utilization as a structural model. However, the theory will not supersede the text; the particular work will either confirm, partially confirm, question, or defy the model, and may, in conjunction with other texts, alter the keys.[7]

Here are my criteria in nutshells. The keystone remains Goethe's "one unheard-of event that has actually happened" – the "sich ereignete unerhörte Begebenheit"[8] –, central not because Goethe said it but because it goes to the heart of the novellesque. Like a news story, whether transmitted orally or in writing, it must be crisp, factual, and objective; even the inevitable subjective factor must be objectified in presentation. The writer must be as persuasive to the reader as the teller is to the listener: the oral origin of the novella *told, not read* should show up, even in the sophisticated literary versions, in the immediacy and veracity of the dialogue. The audience of a particular novella consists of gourmets: people who savor stories well told, who are demanding, who are critical. The novella has a social function. It must not be boring. Not only must the story itself be newsworthy: whatever you may be willing to put up with when you read, almost everybody will only appreciate a raconteur who relates to you, at a party or in the street, a story that generates tension, surprises, striking formulations, that ends in a climax, that reserves for the last line or lines a punch effect, a well-turned phrase, a clincher – the famous

---

[6]The use of "novella" or "novellesque study" as a printed subtitle is one important piece of evidence in determining the novellesque density of a story but not a conclusive one; the same holds for the absence of generic classification in presenting a text to the public.

[7]See passim in this book.

[8]Conversation with Eckermann, January 29, 1827.

novellesque "Pointe." No listening group has unlimited time and patience – at least not in Romanic countries. It wants to be entertained, but entertained intelligently. Northern and Eastern audiences tend to be more attuned to the written than the spoken word, hence are less intolerant of dreariness as long as they have something to learn from it. Southern publics are much more likely to be good storytellers themselves, waiting for their turn to show off, and they do not want to get frustrated listening to someone who steals their time. The European South has a keen sense for the dramatic in life, but they want this drama to be well constructed, controlled by a connoisseur of his métier, like a good actor.[9] The novella is drama epically mastered, tamed by prose, but this self- disciplining does not dilute tension; on the contrary, it increases the effectiveness of the tension between the unpredictability, the irrationality of the events and the uncanny calmness of the narrator: an effect not unlike the one Kafka has on us. In a novella this tension may build up by way of turning points ("Wendepunkte") from a dilemma to a crisis to a catastrophe or near-catastrophe to a final, decisive turn and, at the very end, an ultimate effect, the "Pointe."

But the novella, as it has developed in literature, has assumed a dimension not endemic to all or perhaps even most newspaper stories and not even necessarily implied by all original novellesque stories of Boccaccio (I intentionally do not call them all novellas because while there is a novellesque content to many of them some of them are closer to being anecdotes, practical jokes, bawdy, burlesque and even grotesque events, moral tales, fairy tales, allegories, etc. than novellas). The literary novella has increasingly raised the expectation that it is not only shocking and entertaining but also significant.

---

[9]It is precisely that ability to dramatize and control his story that 'saves' Goethe from possible imprisonment by Venetian officials when he is suspected of being a spy as he draws the ruined tower of Malcesine on Lake Garda on September 13, 1786 (Goethes *Werke*. Hamburger Ausgabe (HA), Hamburg, Wegner, 1959; *Italienische Reise*: XI, pp. 31-36. All references to the *Italian Journey* in this study will be based on this edition unless otherwise indicated).

Boccaccio could and would, I think, not have called his stories "exemplary novellas" although a few are: Cervantes did. How to convey that significance without overt didacticism and preaching is one of the most difficult tasks of novellas: the secret is not to stultify the reader's prolongation of the novella implemented either by his or her overt reactions to it shared with others of the audience or, later on, with the literarization of the genre, growing silently in his own consciousness. The listener to or reader of a good novella must wonder about what happened, why it happened, how it could have happened differently, and what may have happened afterwards. Animating the reader to carry on, the importance of deliberately leaving, in the novellesque account, as happens so often in newspapers reporting actual events, gaps of indeterminacy rather than playing, unrealistically, the omniscient narrator, – that stimulus which Goethe has described, in his *Unterhaltungen deutscher Ausgewanderten*, as "einen stillen Reiz, weiter nachzudenken"[10] must not be underestimated just because it is so personalized that it cannot be objectively demonstrated. Not only does the narrator of a novella *not* have to include everything he knows: he does not necessarily "understand" all that happened, let alone why it happened: here the reader comes into his own. The important thing is that the author makes it happen, that he has credibility. The happening, or, sometimes against all expectations, non-happening must be allowed to speak for itself as far as possible: something German authors and audiences expect from the drama but often did not and do not from their prose strongly inclined to explicitness, to diffusiveness.

Contrary to a cliché spread rather thoughtlessly in some scholarship, these novellesque criteria are not inventions of prescriptive latter-day Gottscheds. They are building stones and workmanship that respond to existential experience, human needs and compensations, curiosity and anxiety. Whatever the abuses of genre dogmatism in the past, the rise and decline of subgenres and types, and the experimental generic mixes of the present, it is time to remind ourselves that the thrusts of the epical, the lyric, and the

---

[10]HA 6, 167.

dramatic are reflections of basic human nature: they are natural in origin, not mechanical straightjackets. The fundamental ingredients persist; the combinations are wide open.

Before we turn, at long last, to the novellesque ingredients of the story of the beautiful Milanese woman in the Italian Journey, we must identify the novellesque substratum of the work: Goethe's indebtedness to the tradition of the Italian novella, and point out the links, real and potential, between that influence and the composition of the work.

Goethe was familiar with the tradition of the novella from *Il Decamerone* (1348-1353) via the *Canterbury Tales* (1386-1400), the *Cent Nouvelles Nouvelles* (1462-1486), and the *Heptaméron* (1559) to Cervantes' *Novelas ejemplares* (1613) and beyond.[11] It must be kept in mind that the 'classical' non-Italian novella or novellesque collections listed reflect strong Italian influences themselves. Because of the long gestation history of the *Italienische Reise*, any knowledge Goethe had of the Italian novella prior to the appearance of the third part of the work in 1829 might be especially applicable to the story of the "schöne Mailänderin" published in that last installment. Non-Italian novellas and other literary productions of any culture with which Goethe was familiar – and any other experience in his life, for that matter – are, of course, potentially relevant to anything he wrote, but since Goethe's empathy with Italy pervades the account of his Italian journey it makes sense to assume that the Italian novella, as an expression of Italian temperament, lifestyle, and customs, might be especially germane to the *Italienische Reise*. Textual comparisons in depth might well yield new evidence of positive contamination; on this occasion we aim only at listing the principal authors and works Goethe knew, with particular emphasis on specific

---

[11]Convenient summaries of Goethe's documented contacts with all but one of these authors and works may be found in the latest, unfinished edition of *Goethe Handbuch* by Alfred Zastrau, Stuttgart, Metzler, 1961, I: Boccaccio (columns 1291-1293), Chaucer (columns 1625-1626), *Cent nouvelles nouvelles* (column 1606), and Cervantes (columns 1609-1610).

66

encounters and references during his Italian sojourn and readings or mentions that fall into periods of preparation for the publication of the Italian Journey.[12]

Of all Italian writers of novellas and novellesque stories, Boccaccio is the one who accompanied Goethe throughout his life: documented references to him occur in 1765, 1793, 1801/1802, 1807, and 1831. The 1810 to 1812 period of Goethe's life, immediately preceding his active composition of the *Italienische Reise*, contains particularly rich evidence for Goethe's preoccupation with the genre of the novella.[13]

In 1812, he borrowed Luigi da Porta's *Storia di due nobili amanti* (1524). From November 14 to 22 and again on November 25, 1812, Goethe read the novellas by Matteo Bandello (1485-1561), published in 1554 (first three parts) and 1573 (fourth part).[14] In the same period he intensively studied the *Novelle galanti* del Padre Atanasio da Verocchio (1791), actually the work of Domenico Batacchi (1748-1802): We have no less than a dozen references to this activity in February, March, and September of 1811 as well as in June of 1812. On January 15, 1814 Goethe concentrated on Batacchi's novella "La vita e la morte di prete Ulivo"; there is a further reference to him on July 16, 1816.[15] As to the Abbate Giambattista Casti (1721-1803), he occupies a very special place in Goethe's knowledge of Italian novellas as it might pertain to the Italian Journey, because Goethe heard him recite one of his novellas, "L'Archivescovo di Praga", on July 17, 1787, which he called "not very

---

[12]Much of this information has been painstakingly gathered by John Hennig, "Goethes Kenntnis der Schönen Literatur Italiens", *Literaturwissenschaftliches Jahrbuch der Görresgesellschaft*, 21, N.F., 1980, pp. 361-383, which Janos Riesz has kindly called to my attention. Riesz' essay in the same volume has also been helpful.

[13]*Goethe Handbuch*, I, column 827.

[14]Ibid., I, columns 729-730. Bandello furnished the source for Shakespeare's *Romeo and Juliet*, *Much Ado about Nothing*, and, indirectly, *Hamlet*.

[15]Ibid., columns 826-827.

honorable but extraordinarily beautiful," written in ottave rime, three months before meeting the Milanese lady.[16] Around the same time Goethe acknowledges, also in the *Italienische Reise*, the "great pleasure" derived from Casti's recitation; his 'gay and free delivery seemed to render perfect life to the ingenious, excessively brilliant ("genialen") presentations'[17] of his – at that time, unpublished – novellas. (Casti's *Novelle galanti* were printed three years later, in 1790.) Since we have stressed the oral origin and continuing auditive flavor of the novella genre, it is worth noting that Goethe experienced it, on that occasion, as a spoken work of art comprising text and delivery in the Italian manner. Sixteen years later, Goethe had not forgotten Casti: he offered Eichstädt a review of Casti's *Novelle galanti* along with Casti's operatic texts, poems and just published *Animali parlanti*. In 1807 Goethe notes in his *Tag- und Jahreshefte* that Casti's *Novelle galanti* are 'artistically more cohesive and more masterful' in the control of material than Batacchi's, and as late as 1817 he returns to the *Animali parlanti*.[18] It can be concluded, then, that Goethe's affinity for the Italian novella was deep-seated, reasonably continuous, and has a bearing on the composition of the Italian Journey.

We are now ready to turn to the novellesque *Gestalt* of the beautiful Milanese woman. I am by no means the first to draw attention to it. As early as 1902 Otto Waser calls our story a "reizende Novelle",[19] and Herbert von Einem, to whom I may well owe the first impetus in this direction, speaks of the 'novellistische Ausschmückung' of certain parts of the *Italienische Reise*

---

[16]HA 11, 368.

[17]HA 11, 379. See also *Goethe Handbuch*, I, column 1580.

[18]Hennig, op. cit., pp. 376-377.

[19]In *Die Schweiz*, VI, p. 49.

68

and of our specific story as a "zarte Novelle".[20] But, to the best of my knowledge, it has not been analyzed systematically in the light of the novellesque criteria I have adduced.

Leaving aside, for the time being, the first and only mention of the young Milanese woman in the "Correspondence" ("Korrespondenz") part of the Italian Journey, the story proper is entirely limited to the "Report" ("Bericht") sections of the book where it emerges and submerges from time to time. That very fact in itself strongly suggests a double stylizing, a twofold 'literarization', including the 'Novellisierung' of Goethe's actual experiences in Italy. We now know that Goethe subjected even the actual letters he had addressed from Italy to (mostly) Herder and Frau von Stein to significant modifications before they were published as "Korrespondenz"; in the "Bericht" portions he took still much greater liberties with the – by now – semi-historical events.[21] "Bericht", in this particular context, should be taken

---

[20]HA 11, 572-573. Among other recognitions of the novellesque configurations of our story are Emil Staiger (*Goethe*. Zurich and Freiburg im Breisgau, Atlantis, 1956,II,pp.43-44, referring to our "Mailänderin": "In den Briefen äußert sich Goethe darüber, aus Scheu vor Frau von Stein, nur mit der größten Zurückhaltung. Wir sind also angewiesen auf den Jahrzehnte später entstandenen Bericht...einer...von der Wehmut des Versäumten und dem Glück verschwiegener Liebesgewissheit erfüllten Novelle...") and Richard Friedenthal, *Goethe. Sein Leben und seine Zeit* (Munich: Deutscher Taschenbuch-Verlag, 1968) II, p. 312: "...fügt er novellistisch eine Episode mit einer schönen Mailänderin ein."

[21]"Goethe hat viele der von Rom nach Weimar gesandten Briefe vor der Drucklegung verändert,...unzählige Stellen sind gekürzt, miteinander vertauscht oder ganz neu formuliert. Grosse Teile des Textes...hat er...nach erfolgter Benutzung den Flammen übergeben" (Peter Boerner, "Italienische Reise (1816-1829)", in *Goethes Erzählwerk*. Interpretationen. Ed. Paul M. Lützeler and James F. McLeod, Stuttgart, Reclam, 1985, pp. 350-351). Goethe was typically very discreet about his relationships with women after

as a mixture of 'an accurate report' and of a marked epical processing of 'what happened'.[22]

The first installment of our story starts and ends in October 1787; it covers about eight printed pages. The second installment, almost thirty pages later, occurs in December 1787 and amounts to about a printed page and a half. The third installment resumes more than sixty pages later, takes us to February 1788, and occupies one printed page. The final meeting with his lady love happens another thirty-odd pages subsequently, in April 1788, upon his farewell to Rome, claims two pages, and is less than two pages from the very end of the work.

The length of the total story, about twelve printed pages, is relatively short for a potential novella but does not eliminate it from contention: Kleist's *Erdbeben in Chili* and his *Die Heilige Cäcilie oder die Gewalt der Musik* are of similar length, and *Das Bettelweib von Locarno*, clearly a novellesque story, takes just two pages. More serious are the three long interruptions between its parts. They are, however, typical for Goethe's novellesque insertions in longer works, especially in *Wilhelm Meisters Wanderjahre*, and all rationalizations notwithstanding, troublesome in that novel. But in this specific case, as part of a chronologically arranged autobiography, these breaks may be considered organic.

A quick summary of the story. At the beginning of October 1787 Goethe is in Castel Gandolfo. He encounters a pretty young lady and her mother who are neighbors of his in Rome. They in turn introduce him to a friend of theirs, a young Milanese woman. Both young women are very attractive, the Roman lady more Southern, the Milanese woman more

---

the fact (except for Lotte Buff) – and so were they. Angelika Kauffmann destroyed, alas, all letters from Goethe to her except for three accidentally saved (Irmgard Smidt-Dörrenberg, *Angelika Kauffmann. Goethes Freundin in Rom*. Vienna, Bergland, 1968, p. 37).

[22]I am grateful to Victor Lange who has drawn my attention to the import of the "Korrespondenz" and "Bericht" labels.

Northern. Their names are at no time divulged to us. The company plays a kind of lotto, during which Goethe pays as much attention to the new as to the older acquaintance, a fact for which the Roman matron chastises him politely but firmly. The Milanese's brother is employed by a friend of Goethe's, the British art merchant, Jenkins. In a refreshingly open conversation with Goethe the Milanese lady expresses her frustration that the strict supervision meted out to young women in Italy stunts their writing ability (because the family is afraid that the women might use this facility for composing love letters) and excludes them from learning foreign languages such as English which she hears her brother speak fluently. Goethe promises to teach her English and begins immediately. He picks up an English newspaper lying around, finds a sensational news story in it and proceeds to teach her English syntax from it via an amazingly inductive, modern method. The new Héloïse learns as fast from the latter-day Abélard as the historical one, and their inclinations respond to each other quickly although much more chastely than those of the couple of yore. That same evening Goethe learns gradually and to his dismay that his partner is engaged to be married. In Goethean rather than Wertherean fashion he avoids contact with her for a while,[23] but then her impending status as a bride and a spouse gives their relationship a kind of platonic, carefree stability that facilitates a calm and comfortable togetherness pleasurable and profitable to both sides. Here finishes the first installment.

The second installment, two months later, opens with another shock: the Milanese woman's fiancé has broken their engagement, throwing the young woman into a dangerous fever that raises fears for her life. The narrator is

---

[23]Might there be a connection between our story and Goethe's reproduction, without any apparent link with the immediate context and without any explanatory comment, of a letter from an anonymous French reader of *Werther* thanking its author for having led him to the path of virtue in a Werther-Charlotte-like situation? He prints the letter in the interval between the first and the second portion of his account of the adventure with the Milanese woman (HA 11, 443).

deeply affected, but she eventually recovers. End of the second part. Again two months later, in February of 1788, he meets her in the company of his and her friend, the painter Angelika Kauffmann, not only recovered but more beautiful than ever and grateful for Goethe's previously demonstrated, solicitous interest in her recovery. Ends the third installment. And, again two months later, in April of 1788, Goethe pays her a farewell visit just prior to his impending return to Germany. The mood is friendly, delicately intimate, serene until Goethe leaves and discovers that his coach is there but not the coachman. While someone goes to get the coachman and his lovely friend looks out of a low window almost within hands' reach of the traveler, he calls out: "They do not want to take me away from you, you see . . .They know, it seems, how reluctant I am to leave you."[24] "Her reply, my rejoinder, the course of the most winsome dialogue, which, free of all fetters, disclosed the innermost of two but semi-conscious lovers, I will not desecrate through repetition and narration: it was a wonderful, laconic final confession of the most innocent and tenderest mutual affection, accidentally initiated but compelled by inner drives, and that is why I have never forgotten it in mind and heart."[25]

Short as this love story is, there are aspects of it into which we can only enter briefly on this occasion. In the two years of his stay in Italy as described in the Italian Journey, it is unique. There is this charismatic bachelor in his late thirties, the darling of men and women alike, liberated from court and at a safe distance from solicitous friends in small-town Weimar, away

---

[24]"Man will mich nicht von Euch wegführen, seht Ihr', rief ich aus, 'man weiß, so scheint es, daß ich ungern von Euch scheide'" (HA 11, 554).

[25]"Was sie darauf erwiderte, was ich versetzte, den Gang des anmutigsten Gesprächs, das, von allen Fesseln frei, das Innere zweier sich nur halbbewußt Liebenden offenbarte, will ich nicht entweihen durch Wiederholung und Erzählung; es war ein wunderbares, zufällig eingeleitetes, durch innern Drang abgenötigtes lakonisches Schlußbekenntnis der unschuldigsten und zartesten wechselseitigen Gewogenheit, das mir auch deshalb nie aus Sinn und Seele gekommen ist". (HA 11, 554).

72

from the dour north, supremely happy to be in the sunny south and ecstatic to be in Rome – and his self-discipline is such that this is, to the best of our knowledge, the only truly amorous episode he allows himself in twenty months of immersion into art, architecture, nature, science, folk life, and hard work on his own literary projects.[26] It would be a lovely story in any context: in this one its uniqueness stands out to greatest effect – and its climax comes at the very end of the Roman stay. His characterization of the young woman is chary of descriptive physical and psychological details as befits her classical environment, Goethe's classicistic bent, her innate, authentic dignity, and Goethe's discretion. We see her highlighted in brief action scenes like miniature paintings. And we can ask ourselves whether there is some 'deep structural' connection, especially in view of Goethe's consciousness of the North-South polarity pervading the account of his Italian experience, in his giving ultimate preference to the freer, more spontaneous honesty, the wider perspective of the Northern Italian over the, it seems, more formal, perhaps 'prouder' Roman woman. But for our present purposes we need to concentrate on the novellesque dimensions of the event.

One Event – "Eine Begebenheit"

Does the story have unity? Is it focused on one central event, the adventure with the "Mailänderin"? The answer is: yes. The rationale for the four installments, for the long interruptions, is, we have seen, that Goethe presents his Italian journey as a chronicle. Since the four encounters around which the story turns occur in October and December 1787, then in February and April 1788 respectively, they are separated by other events taking place in the meantime. Were the four parts published consecutively, without interruptions, as they easily could be and ought to be, just once, we would have a tight, cohesive story.

---

[26]It is understood, of course, that the author of Erotica Romana, subsequently titled *Römische Elegien*, had happy and fulfilling sensual experiences in Rome.

And are things really *happening* in the story? Analysis of inner evolution, so dear to German authors, must take a backseat to outer action in the novella, just as in a drama. Is there enough real action? The answer is again: yes. Encounter, partnership in playing cards, teacher-pupil relationship, disclosure of her engagement, breaking of her engagement, critical illness, recovery, new encounter in the Venetian Square, a poignant farewell scene: that is certainly enough action for twelve pages although it is all subject to a delicate patina.

"... That Has Actually Occurred" – "Sich Ereignete"

Even though this does not have to be taken literally, there is evidence that the credibility of a novella is strengthened when its nucleus – not, of course, all its details – corresponds to an actual event. What has happened is authentic no matter how shocking or outlandish or 'incredible' it may be.

Did the Milanese woman exist? The question is permitted since for sixty years after the publication of the "zweite römische Aufenthalt" her identity was not known. Indeed she existed. We do have Angelika Kauffmann's portrait of her, also 'lost' for seventy years,[27] as well as Angelika's letter to

---

[27]The iconographic history of the portrait(s) of the 'Milanese woman' painted by Angelika Kauffmann is full of mysteries, hypotheses, theses, countertheses, and inconsistencies. A separate essay of some length, great complexity, and little certainty could be written about it. My own reductive account of it, though trying to stick to the less shaky evidence, is by no means above doubt. On the basis of the conflicting data and assertions I have examined, I am not even certain whether Angelika painted one, two, or more portraits of the "schöne Mailänderin", and when. If there were two, the first was probably composed at the time of the actual encounter between Goethe and his Italian lady, in 1787, while the second one, which is said to be unsigned, dates from between 1790 and 1795.

According to Otto Waser, loc. cit., footnote 19, pp. 49-51, the original painting was discovered in the mid-1890's by the Italian scholar Antonio

Goethe of November 1, 1788, written about half a year after his farewell from Rome and from the Milanese beauty whose formal engagement and nuptials

---

Valeri (Carletta) among the belongings of the Milanese woman's descendants from her second marriage to Francesco Finucci; at the time of Waser's article it was, according to him, the property of the art historian Werner Weisbach. The second one, thought initially to have been a portrait of Lady Hamilton, became, according to Waser (p. 51), part of the pictorial collection of the art connoisseur Jakob Melchior Ziegler (1801-1883), housed in the "Palmengarten vor dem Obern Thor", formerly known as the "Drachengarten", in the Swiss town of Winterthur, and was then inherited by Ziegler's son-in-law, Rudolf Rieter-Ziegler, where it hung in the "Rotes Haus" at the time of Waser's essay.

The beautiful painting located in the Freies Deutsches Hochstift in Frankfurt was acquired by it in 1953. Its description fits the second one though it hails from the estate of Werner Weisbach (whose domicile is given now as Berlin, now as Basel) connected by Waser to the first one! This is just the modest beginning of the perplexities of this iconography, which cannot be pursued farther on this occasion. I am much indebted to Dr. Hans A. Lüthy of the Swiss Institute for Art Research in Zurich, via the intermediary of Professor Hans Wysling of the University of Zurich and the Eidgenössische Technische Hochschule in Zurich, for having initiated me into the bewildering maze of Angelika Kauffmann's portraiture of Goethe's Italian love. Cf. *Führer durch das Frankfurter Goethemuseum*. Freies Deutsches Hochstift, 2d ed., 1955, p. 31; Sabine Michaels, ed., *Katalog der Gemälde*. Freies Deutsches Hochstift, Tübingen, Niemeyer, n.d. (after 1969), p. 69, with illustration and bibliography; Walter Hugelshofer, "Angelica Kauffmann und Goethe in Rom", *Pantheon*, 20 (1962) 109-116, with bibliography and illustrations; M. Liebmann, reply to the preceding essay, *Pantheon*, 21 (January-February 1963) 64, with illustration, etc. etc.

it reports.[28] Goethe himself offers more direct evidence, for in the "correspondence" part of the Italian Journey, under date of "October 8 (1787) but really the 12th"[29] we read the following entry:

> A Milanese woman interested me during the eight days of her stay (in Castel Gandolfo), she distinguished herself very advantageously from the Roman women through her naturalness, her public spiritedness, her fine ways.[30]

That he does not mention her again in the correspondence of the time (addressed mainly to Charlotte von Stein!) contained in the Italian Journey is probably 'proof negative' of his amorous inclination. Her name, we now know though not from Goethe, was Maddalena (or Magdalena) Riggi, born in 1765. She died in 1825, four years before the third volume of the *Italienische Reise*, in which her story appears, was published. Their mutual friend Angelika Kauffmann had died long before, in 1807. We cannot check the historicity of the details of Goethe's relationship with Maddalena as depicted by him in the Journey, mainly because, as noted above, Goethe destroyed the vast majority of the original letters and notes on which he had based the reconstruction of his Italian journey after they had served their purpose. We can only surmise, from the few original documents surviving, that the "Korrespondenz" part of his *Italienische Reise* – in which he records his first encounter with the "Mailänderin" – remains, despite many alterations, close to the "sich ereignete" of 1787 but that his other recollections, in the "Bericht" part of the

---

[28]Text in Eugen Thurnher, ed., *Angelika Kauffmann und die deutsche Dichtung* (Bregenz: Russ, n.d. [1969]), 57.

[29]"Den 8.October, eigentlich den 12ten" (HA 11, 414).

[30]"Eine Mailänderin interessierte mich die acht Tage ihres Bleibens, sie zeichnete sich durch ihre Natürlichkeit, ihren Gemeinsinn, ihre gute Art sehr vorteilhaft vor den Römerinnen aus" (HA 11, 416).

work, are, as already observed, significantly stylized. The 'reporter's' general credibility must, however, be respected. Maddalena's *Gestalt,* as evoked more than forty years after the fact, gives every indication of authenticity.

Having bidden Maddalena farewell, Goethe never saw her again nor corresponded with her. He never went back to Rome though he announced his intention to do so to Angelika. I am almost tempted not to inform the reader that Maddalena wasted little time pining for Goethe, met her future husband on an outing only weeks after Goethe's departure, got engaged to him within two weeks thereafter, married him several weeks later, lived, it seems, in a happy marriage, bore him six sons (one posthumous), got remarried quickly after her husband's death in 1803 and presented her second husband with two more children. Goethe injects this "post factum" knowledge of her (first) marriage into the "Bericht" of his last rendezvous with Maddalena, referring to an "affluent young man" – not named – on "the best terms with the Zucchis" (the married name of Angelika), who, he surmised, seemed to prize Maddalena's charms and to harbor serious intentions toward her.[31] He was none other than Giuseppe Volpato, who was to become a successful manufacturer of ceramics and engravings, son of the well-known copperplate engraver Giovanni Volpato who was a member of Goethe's and Angelika's artistic entourage. In a sense, then, Goethe provided, maybe ex post facto, a replacement for himself before he left and thus perhaps eased his conscience if indeed it needed easing.[32]

---

[31]"Auch konnte ich die Vermutung nähren und den Wunsch, dass ein wohlhabender junger Mann, welcher mit Zucchis im besten Vernehmen stand, gegen ihre Anmut nicht unempfindlich und ernstere Absichten durchzuführen nicht abgeneigt sei" (HA 11, 553).

[32]Goethe hints in his reaction to the breaking of Maddalena's engagement by her fiancé that he was worried about the possibility that his own friendly linkage with the – unbeknownst to him-engaged Maddalena might have led or contributed to this traumatic step: "I counted myself lucky not to have followed up my inclination and to have withdrawn expeditiously from the dear

girl, and ascertained after the most precise inquiries that our mutual sojourn in Castel Gandolfo had not played the slightest role in the pretexts adduced by her fiancé for breaking his vow" ("Wenn ich mich nun einerseits glücklich pries, meiner Neigung nicht nachgehangen und mich sehr bald von dem lieben Kind zurückgezogen zu haben, wie denn auch nach genauster Erkundigung unter den Vorwänden jener Villeggiatur auch nicht im mindesten gedacht worden...") (HA 11, 457).

The story of the discovery of Maddalena Riggi's identity after half a century of prevailing discretion is fascinating and instructive not only in itself but because it illustrates the contribution that philological positivism has made to literary history in general and literary biography in particular in the late nineteenth century. Toward the end of 1890 Otto von Harnack edited, in the *Schriften der Goethegesellschaft V*, a volume entitled *Nachgeschichte der Italienischen Reise. Briefwechsel Goethes mit Freunden und Kunstgenossen in Italien, 1788-1790*. It reveals, for the first time, the actual name of the young Milanese woman and tells us of the happy resolution of her plight through marriage to the young Volpato. But with the typical modesty of the old-time philologist, Harnack did not capitalize on his discoveries, and so it remained for a prominent literary historian of the time, Adolf Stern, to alert a wider reading audience, just a few weeks afterwards, to the solution of the long-time riddle (in *Die Grenzboten*, 49, no. 4, December 9, 1890, pp. 581-583). Stern also called attention to two letters, published by Harnack, one by Angelika Kauffmann addressed to Goethe on November 1, 1788 (see note 22) in which she describes, in her warm, spontaneous way the excursion which resulted in the engagement and marriage of Maddalena and her future husband, and another one from Maddalena's brother, Carlo Riggi, dated January 20, 1789, also to Goethe, in which he also reports her marriage to Giuseppe Volpato as of the preceding July.

A second, mighty corroborative step in further identifying Maddalena Riggi was taken by an Italian Germanist, Antonio Valeri (nom de plume?: Carletta) in the third part, "La Bella Milanese" (pp. 39-56) of his tripartite

78

There is a piquant and very novellesque touch to another "sich ereignete" episode in this love story. As the latter-day though much more restrained Abélard or Saint-Preux sets out to teach his 'New Héloïse' English, he picks, supposedly on the spur of the moment but surely not without some sweet malice, another "sich ereignete unerhörte Begebenheit", viz., *ausgerechnet*, the story in an English-language journal of a desperate girl about to be married falling (but probably jumping) into the water and rescued, it appears, by her bridegroom's rival: a novellesque event surely not unrelated to though not identical with what will turn out to be the situation of his pupil. It is a newspaper story (one of the favorite sources of the "sich ereignete unerhörte" for *Novellisten*) which you will recognize as the source of the novellesque insert in the *'Elective Affinities'* (or perhaps vice versa) entitled "The wondrously strange neighbors' children" ("Die wunderlichen Nachbarskinder").[33]

---

investigation, *Goethe a Roma*, Rome, Societa Editrice Dante Alighieri, 1899. (I am most grateful to the Joseph Regenstein Library of my alma mater, the University of Chicago, possessor of the only recorded copy of this rare and fragile booklet in the United States, for allowing me access to their specimen). Carletta, after duly recording Harnack's and Stern's leads, was the first to derive and expand biographical information on Maddalena Riggi through a diligent study of parish registers and archival protocols. He also rediscovered one of the (probably) two, now famous portraits of Maddalena painted by Angelika Kauffmann (Waser, p. 51) and published the first photograph of her house on the Ripetta, location of the poignant farewell scene between her and Goethe.

[33]Enzo Calani, while pointing out the link between journalism stories ("Berichte") and the novella, states that in Italy journalism does not carry the pejorative flavor it conveys to 'literate' Germans: Introduction to *Italienische Novellen von Boccaccio bis zur Gegenwart*, ed. and tr. Lisa Rüdiger, Bremen, Schünemann, n.d., p. XXX.

The "Unheard Of" – "Das Unerhörte"

The "unheard-of" is much more filtered here than in some novellas translated or adapted by Goethe from foreign sources such as e.g. the two Bassompierre stories in the *'Conversations of German Refugees'* (*Unterhaltungen deutscher Ausgewanderten*) or 'The Fool as Pilgrim' ("Die pilgernde Törin") in *'The Fellowship Years of Wilhelm Meister'* (*Wilhelm Meisters Wanderjahre*). In his own novellesque stories screening is strong, the underlying passion is carefully, perhaps too carefully stylized. But just because there is this even veneer, the bumps stick out more. Maddalena's engagement is as shocking as her dis-engagement, and both are more effective than her more dramatic or melodramatic collapse. The farewell scene, starting out with such easy familiarity in her dress and her charming loquaciousness, also serves to remove his inhibitions, to loosen a deliberate repression verging on the unnatural, especially in Italy, of amorous instincts, to relax and release his emotions now that he is about to leave the land of passion. His off-guard exclamation: "They don't want to take me away from you, they sense, it seems, that I do not want to leave you"[34] is as effective a breakthrough as would be, in a less restrained text, a flamboyant speech or action. And instead of the continuation of the dialogue, we only get a teaser: what she then said and what he replied Goethe won't reveal but he does the non-revealing with so touching and tender a see-through that the effect is nonetheless pervasive.

He had staunchly vowed to himself-and kept to it-not to be diverted while in Italy by anything, not even a woman, from *Bildung* – and now he has to admit that he has been tamed and caught – even if not for good.[35] It is a

---

[34]For the German text, see note 24, this chapter.

[35]"Denn ich war dem Gelübde, mich durch dergleichen Verhältnisse von meinem Hauptzwecke nicht abhalten zu lassen, vollkommen treu geblieben" (HA 11, 422)... "und es bedurfte nicht des Blicks einer klugen Frau um zu gewahren, daß hier was vorgegangen sein müsse und daß ein zeither bis zur trockenen Unhöflichkeit von den Frauen sich entfernender Freund wohl selbst sich endlich zahm und gefangen überrascht gesehen habe" (425).

subtle kind of "Unerhörtes", but in the context it is profoundly moving.

In a much earlier scene, toward the beginning of the relationship, there is a stunning sunset which Goethe would like to watch in the company of his two young beauties. But on the way to them he is detained by women of the older generation and willy-nilly has to gaze in their company at the magnificent spectacle of nature from a pavilion they are occupying while his inner thoughts are directed toward his lovely pupil. The "Unerhörte" enters here through a secondary supporting effect. The delicate, evocative understatements about the couple are supplemented and indirectly invigorated by a dramatization of nature, a profusion of superlatives constituting a remarkable contrast: "the most splendid of views...the incandescent illumination...the cooling blue shadowing of the depth seemed more splendid than ever in oil or watercolor...the last glimpse at the sun...the most beautiful vista...an inestimable view."[36] There is subtle and, in its way, dramatically growing coordination and tension between the overpowering spectacle of nature, the intriguing conversational references to dowry, wedding gifts, and finally a bridegroom with his character assets and foibles. The crescendo of these allusions coincides with the descent of the sun into the distant sea, with an 'inestimable vista through long shadows and the subdued but powerful sidelights' – and as the crescendo and the decrescendo converge, the blow falls upon Goethe's question who the bride is: it is Maddalena. The vanishing of the glorious sun corresponds to his cruel disenchantment. His 'inclination for the pupil secretly loved has been metamorphosed in an instant into the most traumatic of conditions'.[37]

---

[36]"...die herrlichste der Aussichten...die glühende Beleuchtung...die kühlende blaue Beschattung der Tiefe schien herrlicher als jemals in Öl oder Aquarell...den letzten Blick der Sonne...der schönsten Aussicht...einen unschätzbaren Blick" (HA 11, 425-426).

[37]"Die Sonne ging unter...auf eine so grausame Weise belehrt... Neigungen...in die schmerzlichsten Zustände sich umwandeln...meine heimlich geliebte Schülerin" (HA 11, 426-428).

After testing the crux of the novellesque, the "eine sich ereignete unerhörte Begebenheit" against the story of the "schöne Mailänderin", I want to make a reinforcing switch and combine the novellesque analysis of this amorous episode with that of the fourteen-year old Wolfgang's first love adventure: the encounter with the so-called "Frankfurter Gretchen" in the fifth and sixth books of his fictional autobiography, *'Poetry and Truth' (Dichtung und Wahrheit)*.[38] In so doing I hope to achieve several purposes. First, such a comparison will help toward sorting out the specifically Italian components of his experience with the beautiful Milanese woman from Goethe's stylization of another autobiographical love event in *'Poetry and Truth'*, to which both stories belong. Second and more particularly, these accounts are prime examples of the 'literarization' of personal experience into novellesque tales: how does a "sich ereignete unerhörte Begebenheit" become a novella or novellesque story? Third, and still more specifically, how does this happen in the shared context of a profiled, lingering romance lying, in both cases, over forty years back in time, and now re-collected – in the literal sense of the verb – in the period of *Altersstil*? We already know how Goldsmith's *Vicar of Wakefield* helped in shaping the Friederike story, also told forty years afterward,[39] how *Manon Lescaut* did the same for the account of the Frankfurter Gretchen in *'Poetry and Truth'* (and, at least 'in großen Zügen,' how indeed that story is related to other novellesque productions of Goethe from the *Unterhaltungen deutscher Ausgewanderten* via the "Wunderliche Nachbarskinder" in the *Wahlverwandtschaften* to the novellesque inserts in

---

[38]Goethe started formal work on *Aus meinem Leben. Dichtung und Wahrheit* in the fall of 1809. Work on the fifth book of Part I, which contains most of the Gretchen story, was done in 1811; it was printed in September/October 1811. The wind-up of the Gretchen affair at the beginning of Part II, Book 6 was written in the later fall of the same year.

[39]*Dichtung und Wahrheit*, in Goethes *Werke*. (Part II, Book 10), HA 11, 426-429.

Wilhelm Meisters Wanderjahre and the story entitled *Novelle*);[40] now perhaps we can lay up another tier in these *wechselseitige Spiegelungen* by trying to detect the common and un-common features of these two autobiographical novellesque accounts in, originally, the same work.

Let me quickly recapitulate the Gretchen story. Shortly before Joseph the Second, the oldest son of Empress Maria Theresia and Francis I is elected and crowned as Holy Roman Emperor of the German Nation in Frankfurt (March and April 1764), Wolfgang meets, through a friend to whom he gives the name Pylades, a young woman he calls Gretchen, of modest circumstances, very pretty, friendly but of great dignity, with whom the fourteen-year old falls head over heels in love. She prevents him from becoming too embroiled in a prank of forged love letters addressed to a third party and is his moral mentor as well as his friend. He reciprocates by guiding her through the festivities of the election and crowning to which she would not have had access without him. The innocent but tender alliance ends when mutual acquaintances of both are accused of being entangled in a more serious fraudulent affair. This upsets Wolfgang terribly but a long investigation finally proves his innocence as well as hers. She prefers, however, to leave town and the two never see each other again.

There are important traits the two accounts do *not* have in common. When Goethe met Maddalena Riggi he was nearing forty. Gretchen is Goethe's first amorous encounter, a love of early adolescence, with wild dreams including marriage on his part. On hers, there is restrained but genuine affection without illusions. The girl is older, more mature than he, a moral guide, and the social cleavage on top of it makes a lasting connection between them well nigh impossible. Both stories encompass the novellesque ladder from dilemma via crisis and (near) catastrophe to resolution, from tension to distension, but the distribution and accents differ: in the Gretchen episode, the initial dilemma (shall Wolfgang continue to fabricate fictitious love letters for purposes of a practical joke?) occurs just at the very beginning of the

---

[40]See my essays listed in Notes 3 and 4.

relationship with Gretchen and helps to build it since both entertain negative feelings about the prank; there is no gradually intensifying crisis but, at the very end, a completely unexpected catastrophe (at least for him): criminal investigation, involuntary separation. In the Italian Journey, an adult story, the dilemma continues, in one form or another, throughout the "Bericht": Goethe is first caught between the Roman and the Milanese woman, then has to maneuver cautiously when Maddalena is revealed as being engaged and then dis-engaged: the crisis and catastrophe are central to the story but different for the protagonists: Goethe is horrified when he learns his lady love is engaged and is deeply shaken by her subsequent misfortune; but, unlike Werther whose name he invokes on this occasion, he has kept his distance. For her, the breaking of the engagement means far more: social embarrassment if not disgrace in her particular culture, critical illness.

The Gretchen adventure has a characteristic novellesque "Pointe" – a last ironic twist in retrospect: the disenchanting revelation that Gretchen looked at him not as a sweetheart but as a younger brother, which infuriates Wolfgang and promotes his healing. In the more serious story of the Milanese woman and Goethe, mature partners, there is no "Pointe", just a climax of tender intensity – and then farewell for ever. The stakes are higher in the relationship between a man of 38 and a woman of 22 than in the love of teenagers: that is perhaps why it does not come to a kiss in Italy but to a chaste kiss and light but affectionate physical contact in Germany. Although Goethe plays the role of guide and teacher in both accounts – as the coronation guide in the Gretchen episode, as a teacher of English and a man of the world in the story of Maddalena – the didactic and moralizing elements are a good deal more pronounced in the Gretchen episode, with her assuming an active role in both capacities (she is, after all, older and more experienced than Wolfgang), whereas the Milanese woman is a remarkably quick pupil and yearns for a more active educational life but maintains nevertheless a more traditional, passive role consonant with Italian social restrictions imposed on women. But then Gretchen also has more time to lecture Wolfgang and vice versa: her story is three times as long as Maddalena's. There is no equivalent in the Roman adventure of Goethe to the criminal affair terminating the Gretchen episode with traumatic suddenness. And in neither story does symbolism, a notable ingredient of many novellas, play a role worth mentioning. On the whole, the Roman episode is less interlaced with other events, more self-contained and economical than the Gretchen narrative where the lyric/idyllic elements of love, the epic events of the coronation, and the drama of the criminal query cast a wider radius.

The differences having been registered, the points of convergence are surprisingly numerous. There is a striking correspondence in the structure of the two stories. Both consist of four installments, though the three breaks in the Maddalena narrative are much longer.

That the general descriptions of the two lady loves have much in common is worth noting but not too extraordinary in view of the stylization of both stories. Both women are from cultures different from the men's: Gretchen from a lower, Maddalena from a foreign culture, but both are not only lovely and natural but refined, mature, analytic, and eager to improve themselves. There is a complete passage from one of the texts that might as well be in the other one.

> For nothing contributes more to a beautiful union of a young couple that nature has shaped somewhat harmoniously than a girl eager to learn and the young man eager to teach. On that basis a relationship is formed that is as thorough as it is pleasant. She sees in him the creator of her intellectual existence, and he in her a creature that owes her perfection not to nature, chance, or a one-sided desire but to mutual will; and this reciprocal effect is so sweet that we must not be surprised when ever since the old and the new Abélard the most violent passions and as much happiness as unhappiness have sprung from the encounter of two such creatures.[41]

---

[41]"Denn einem jungen Paare, das von der Natur einigermaßen harmonisch gebildet ist, kann nichts zu einer schönern Vereinigung gereichen, als wenn das

It happens to be from the Gretchenepisode, but Maddalena, like Gretchen, envies her partner for being a man: "If I were a boy," says Gretchen, "you and I would, together, learn something decent in universities";[42] and she wants to learn French. She reminds Wolfgang how lucky he is to be from a good family, affluent, and independent.[43] Similarly, Maddalena good-naturedly envies Goethe for being lucky enough to be rich so he can travel to his heart's content whereas she, particularly as a woman, is limited to the station assigned to her by God and His saints.[44] She complains about her stunted education, especially in foreign languages, and says she would love to learn English – which Goethe promptly proceeds to teach her.[45] Both women are, in the best sense of the word, "strebsam"[46] and accept their partner's willingness to instruct them with enthusiasm. Both are very discreet but also very

---

Mädchen lehrbegierig und der Jüngling lehrhaft ist. Es entsteht daraus ein so gründliches als angenehmes Verhältnis. Sie erblickt in ihm den Schöpfer ihres geistigen Daseins, und er in ihr ein Geschöpf, das nicht der Natur, dem Zufall, oder einem einseitigen Wollen, sondern einem beiderseitigen Willen seine Vollendung verdankt; und diese Wechselwirkung ist so süß, daß wir uns nicht wundern dürfen, wenn seit dem alten und neuen Abälard, aus einem solchen Zusammentreffen zweier Wesen, die gewaltsamsten Leidenschaften und so viel Glück als Unglück entsprungen sind." (HA 9, 187-188).

[42]HA 9, 187.

[43]HA 9, 170.

[44]HA 9, 553-554.

[45]HA 11, 423-425.

[46]HA 11, 423 (applied to Maddalena).

spontaneous in their caresses: a touch of the hand,[47] a kiss on the forehead:[48] very little means very much. But both women are capable of spontaneous, uninvited affection: Gretchen lays her arm or even her head on Wolfgang's shoulder when they study together,[49] or innocently fall asleep.[50]　When Wolfgang and his friends drink wine with Gretchen, he wishes she would sit down next to him – but she does not. Maddalena is more determined: when she finds herself at the opposite end of the table from Goethe at mealtime she does not hesitate a moment to walk around it and sit down right next to him.[51] The key terms Goethe uses for Wolfgang's and Gretchen's affinity composed of friendship, love and inclination ("Freundschaft, Liebe und Neigung")[52] are just as applicable to his feelings for Maddalena and, likely, vice versa.

The historic epic event of the coronation has no equivalent in the Maddalena story, but the delicate interaction of lyric/idyllic intimacy with the built-in drama and melodrama of love: broken liaison causing critical illness is common to both.　Wolfgang's forced separation from Gretchen and his violent, life-threatening fever correspond to the adult Goethe's forced separation from Maddalena through her engagement, dis-engagement, and her life-threatening fever. Compared to the Sturm-und-Drang-like paroxysm of Wolfgang's explosions after being torn away from Gretchen, the mature Goethe's parting from Maddalena is subdued and stylized but equally intense.

But there are even more direct correspondences between the male partners' reaction to crisis and catastrophe or near-catastrophe. When Goethe

---

[47]HA 11, 521 (Maddalena).

[48]HA 9, 209 (Gretchen).

[49]HA 9, 175.

[50]HA 9, 197.

[51]HA 11, 425.

[52]HA 9, 209.

hears about Maddalena's engagement he is aghast, cruelly enlightened, seized with "Entsetzen", "auf eine so grausame Weise belehrt",[53] like Wolfgang when told about the criminal inquiry into Gretchen's circle.[54] Like Wolfgang in the Gretchen adventure, Goethe in the Italian Journey finds consolation from disappointed love in drawing and sketching. And after the near-catastrophe, when Maddalena, deserted by her fiancé, has been seized by a fever that raises fears for her life, Goethe gives himself over to pathological imagination, visualizes the formerly happy, joyous, unfettered, open young woman as dimmed by tears, disfigured by disease, prematurely pale and thin and fancies hearing furtive worms gnawing at buildings apparently new and intact;[55] so also does young Wolfgang conjure up the most horrible treatment meted out to his love and her as well as his friends in the course of the judicial examination.[56]

Both narratives contain the famous novellesque turning point or points (Wendepunkte) known (though not clearly defined) since Tieck's time; they corroborate two previous hunches of mine. The first one: if there is only one major turning point it should, for good effect, come toward the end: in the Gretchen episode, it is the totally unexpected criminal case investigation. If there are several distributed throughout the story each individual one may pack less power but they complement and reinforce each other:[57] in the Maddalena Riggi story they are the news of her engagement (see Werther and Lotte!), her dis-engagement, her violent fever, and their farewell which brings them, ironically, closer together than ever. Both accounts also illustrate, however, the

-----

[53]HA 11, 426.

[54]*Dichtung und Wahrheit*, Part I, Book 5 (HA 11, 213).

[55]HA 11, 457-458.

[56]*Dichtung und Wahrheit*, Part I, Book 5 (HA 9, 212-216).

[57]If their aggregate is too powerful they may actually get into each other's way as e.g. in Conrad Ferdinand Meyer's *Die Hochzeit des Mönchs*.

observation made in novella research that, in retrospect, the unexpected turning points may make a higher sense: the social or cultural differences between the lovers in the Gretchen and the Maddalena stories, the time in life (either too young or too set in his life goals) when Goethe encounters these magnetic women give the obstacles to shared happiness erected by the turning points an almost natural inevitability, a phenomenon perhaps related to Goethe's concept of predestination.

A characteristic to which I have previously alluded in my general discussion of the novellesque is the tension between the transparency of language and the non-transparency, in part, of the events, thoughts, and emotions which this language reflects. This 'clair-obscur' enhances the productive charm of our two stories. Is Gretchen's testimony before the investigating committee that she was fond of Wolfgang like an older sister to be taken at face value or did she care for him in an amorous way? Similarly, we have to guess at the depth and intensity of the real feelings of Maddalena for Goethe. We don't even learn why her fiancé dropped her! Gretchen as well as Maddalena control their tenderness; neither of them seem to entertain illusions about a firmer future liaison with their admirers; both remain on realistic ground. But much speculation remains: e.g. how will they – not Goethe – be looking back at these affairs of the heart?

The narrator maintains the same control, even over the outbursts he permits himself, as his women protagonists: the distance, the objectivity demanded by the tradition of the novellesque certainly obtains in both stories, clothed in Goethe's restrained *Altersstil.*

Time and space do not permit a complete comparative canvassing of all novellesque features nor other common motifs of the two episodes such as e.g. that of self-disciplining, *Selbstüberwindung,* a central theme of Goethe's *Novellistik.*

The noteworthy parallels between Maddalena and Gretchen evoke the complexity of the mélange of literary sources with the authentic, "sich ereignete", (here) autobiographical basis of novellesque narrative. A similar intricacy governs, we have seen, the alleged newspaper source of the "Wunderliche Nachbarskinder" novella in the *Wahlverwandtschaften* (1809):

does it go back to the story allegedly gathered from an English journal some twenty years before, in October of 1787, used by Goethe to teach his lovely Milanese friend nouns and verbs of English syntax, or has Goethe inserted, post factum, the novellesque episode of the "Nachbarskinder", twenty years after its publication, into the autobiographical reconstruction of his love adventure with Maddalena Riggi? To what extent is autobiographical writing based on fact, to what extent on fiction, one's own or someone else's? There is, however, yet a third element in this ever more intriguing mesh of fact and intertextuality permeating the story of the "Schöne Mailänderin": Goethe's father's account of his own love adventure with, believe it or not, a beautiful Milanese woman during his journey to Italy in 1740.[58] While Johann Caspar Goethe's "Viaggio per l'Italia" was not published during his (1710-1782) or his son's lifetime, Johann Wolfgang was, as *Dichtung und Wahrheit*[59] shows, familiar with it and took, according to Farinelli,[60] the ms with him to Weimar in 1794, twelve years after his father's death.[61]

---

[58]My attention to this parallel was first drawn by Richard Friedenthal, *Goethe. Sein Leben und seine Zeit*, Munich, Deutscher Taschenbuch-Verlag, 1968, I, 12.

[59]*Dichtung und Wahrheit*, Part I, Book 1 (HA 9, 14).

[60]I, p. VIII (see next note for full bibliographical information on Farinelli).

[61]Several scholars have earned the right to profound gratitude for making available, in excellent editions, all or part of Johann Caspar's lengthy *Viaggio per l'Italia* (undertaken in 1740). We owe the first and so far only edition of the original Italian text, composed by Goethe's father and slightly abbreviated in this edition, to Arturo Farinelli: Johann Caspar Goethe, 'Viaggio in (sic) Italia' (1740), Prima edizione di A. Farinelli per incarico della Reale Accademia d'Italia. I (Text), Rome 1932; II (Inscriptions, Notes, Index), Rome, 1933. I thank the University of Illinois in Urbana for furnishing me this edition. The first German translation of extensive portions of the *Viaggio* is due to Rudolf Glaser, *Goethes Vater. Sein Leben nach Tagebüchern und*

90

First, we must establish the comparability of Goethe Sr.'s *Reise durch Italien* (undertaken in 1740; written up between 1752 and 1771, according to Koppen, p. 17; 'perhaps after June 1761' according to Meier, p. 489) with Goethe Jr.'s *Italienische Reise* (undertaken, as the reader will recall, from 1786 to 1788, written up from 1813 on and published in three installments: 1816, 1817, and 1829); then, we must consider the possibility that the account of Johann Caspar's wooing of his Milanese love, which did not become accessible in its complete text, as translated into German, until September of 1986, might have colored off on Johann Wolfgang's novellesque story of his "schöne Mailänderin".

Any possible evidence of paternal impact on young Goethe faces the psychological obstacle of the prevailing picture of his father as an earnest and erudite but essentially unproductive, pedantic, rather crabby and hypochondriac "Hausgeist" evoked in *Dichtung und Wahrheit*. Even there, the total paternal Gestalt conjured up is decidedly impressive, and the son singles out his father's passion for Italian language and art, a positive foible that surely must be granted some credit for the insatiable nostalgia that finally drove young Goethe to his two-year escapade south. The differences between the two 'travelogues' are pronounced: the father spent seven months in Italy, not two years, and only one month in Rome, not a year; he wrote up his trip

---

Zeitberichten, Leipzig, Quelle und Meyer, 1929, pp. 16-184. His translations leave much to be desired. Erwin Koppen translated and published selected parts of the ms, with a thoughtful introduction and notes, in 1972: *Goethes Vater reist in Italien*. 'Reise durch Italien' von J. Caspar Goethe (Mainz & Berlin, Kupferberg), 139p. The Library of the University of Massachusetts provided me with this edition. To the friendship of Hans Busch I owe the expeditious gift of the most complete German translation published to date (only the copious Latin inscriptions have been preserved in the original language) by Albert Meier: Johann Caspar Goethe, *Reise durch Italien im Jahre 1740* (Viaggio per l'Italia) (Munich: Deutscher Taschenbuch Verlag, 1987), 634 p.

mainly for his own satisfaction and to have something to do; it is much more bookish and dependent, for information and erudition, on contemporary travel guides (Nemeitz, Keyssler); it has no literary pretentions; it maintains an unflinching loyalty to Protestantism and the values of a respected citizen of a "Freie Reichsstadt". Johann Caspar's observations are said to lack his son's artistic touch and 'intensity of intuitive perception, depth of vision and ability of raising what he has seen and experienced to exemplary proportions'.[62] But, given the expected wide differences, the correspondences are surprising. For both father and son, the Italian voyage was the greatest adventure of their lives.[63] When it is said of the father that he brought a capital of recollections from his trip to Italy off which he lived his entire subsequent life[64] the same can be said, if not, to be sure, as exclusively, of his son. The father makes, like his son, many keen, unvarnished comments based on his immediate experience in Italy. The range of his interests may even be greater than his son's.[65] And, after all, there is also plenty of antiquarian erudition – if well presented – in the younger Goethe's descriptions of Italian monuments. Both were in their thirties (Johann Caspar seven years younger than his son, but much more settled in his ways) when they undertook their *Bildungsreise*; both were unmarried. Both were well prepared for the experience, well introduced and had access to privileged and interesting people, yet had open eyes for the people, for commonly shared cultural events such as the carneval (the father for the Venetian, the son for the Roman variety). Both accounts are based on original notes or letters most of which have been destroyed or lost (all of them in the case of Johann Caspar); Johann Caspar's was composed, to the best of our estimates, between twenty-one and thirty-one years, Johann Wolfgang's twenty-five to forty years after the fact; neither of them was originally meant

---

[62]Koppen, "Einleitung", p. 16.

[63]Koppen, ibid., p. 24.

[64]Koppen, ibid., p. 16.

[65]Ibid.

92

for more than a small circle of friends or family.

A much more thorough comparison of the two *Reisen* is needed, but for our present purposes we must concentrate on an analytic comparison of the father's "Liebelei" with his Milanese donna and the son's equivalent.[66] First of all, we have no intention of overstating our case. The personal and contextual differences are evident. Johann Caspar's *Viaggio per l'Italia* consists, all 483 printed pages of it, of 42 "letters" written by Goethe Sr. from Italy (Venice, Padua, Bologna, Rimini, Ancona, Loreto, Rome, Naples, Rome, Florence, Venice, Milan, Turin, and Genoa) to a male correspondent between February 14 and August 20, 1740, plus five appendices of which the fifth (451-483) contains all "letters" exchanged between Goethe Sr. and his lady love. The trysts-by-distance between Johann Caspar and "Maria Giuseffa Merati" of Milan are supposed to have taken place, entirely by correspondence (although, in part, a very unorthodox one), between July 8, 1740 and February 6, 1741. We do not know whether the letters are entirely manufactured or camouflaged, highly stylized transformations of the 'real thing'.[67] Johann Caspar claims, at one point,[68] that he discovered these letters under an old paneling in his Milan inn and that they hail from the preceding, i.e. the 17th century. But they are all dated "740", i.e. 1740. Their style is certainly mannerist rather than rococo or "enlightened". They consist of a seemingly interminable jousting between the

---

[66]Glaser, Farinelli, Koppen, and Meier have not carried the comparison of the father-and-son experiences with their Milanese loves beyond some general remarks. Johann Caspar's entire correspondence with his alleged Milanese flame, including his preliminary remarks (one page and a half) and epilogue (four lines), is now to be found, in German translation, in Meier, pp. 451-483, 575-576 (notes).

[67]Glaser translates the complete amorous correspondence into German (pp. 142-184) and takes it as quite genuine without raising any doubts (p. 143).

[68]Meier, p. 418 (Letter from Milan dated August 2, 1740, to his usual male correspondent).

two potential lovers as to whether she will permit him to pay her a visit –
which never materializes.   The initial contact shows, however, real
imagination: standing at opposite but distant windows they show each other
huge letters accumulating to questions and answers received via binoculars,
such as: (He): "When may I adore you from closer proximity?" (She): "When
I have become a saint." (He): "It is impossible not to adore your beauty, but
if these terms offend you, I will just incline myself before your beauty." (She):
"There is no beauty here and therefore there is no offense." etc. etc.[69] This is
the father's way of achieving proximity to his lady; the son will bring it about
via English instruction. The tone of the jousting between wooer and wooed in
1740 discloses, here and in later exchanges, instances of tart wit that makes
one think that there may have been some autobiographical basis, no matter
how remote, for this Milanese adventure. Why else, Koppen asks, would
Johann Caspar want to have stayed for five full weeks, beginning July 5,
despite its notorious summer climate, in this by no means overly attractive
city?[70] Johann Caspar provides a possible answer in a letter from Milan of
August 2, 1740 directed to his usual male addressee:

> 'The female sex here is considered, as to external looks, as
> the most beautiful in all of Italy...The inhabitants of Milan
> have, on the basis of numerous visits by Spaniards,
> Frenchmen and Germans, a lifestyle different from other
> Italians. In Milan the subservience of women e.g. is less
> customary, since they are watched less strictly and are
> escorted, to boot, by gallants; the girls remain in their
> paternal home until they marry instead of being locked in by
> the walls of a somber convent as is the custom of the jealous
> Venetians and Neapolitans. All in all women and girls enjoy

---

[69]Meier, p. 452.

[70]Op. cit., p. 15.

great freedom here...'[71]

These observations by the father throw a remarkable light on the naturalness and wide perspective,[72] the 'open, inquisitive character',[73] the alertness,[74] the 'open charm' and 'natural gracefulness'[75] that make Maddalena Riggi so attractive to the son.

One may draw other though cautious analogies between the "Liebesgeschichten" of father and son. While the autobiographical 'truth' and the literary potential of Maddalena Riggi are far and away greater than Maria Merati's, both liaisons are literary elaborations of a canvas of, to be sure, widely discrepant factual authenticity. As the son's encounters with the young Milanese woman are divided into four compositional sections, each two months apart (October/December/February/ April), so his father's exchange of letters with his liege lady follows, until just before his departure from Milan, a regular rhythm of two days: July 8 (he), July 10 (she), July 12 (he), July 14 (she) etc. etc. until July 24, when the hiatus between letters gradually increases.

There are a number of passages from Johann Caspar's letters to his lady and hers to him which remind one, *cum grano salis*, of his son's and Maddalena's situation forty-eight years later: his affirmation that, "even if this is hard to believe, you are, in my entire journey through Italy, the first lady, whose...lovely appearance has charmed my heart which, up to this hour, has

---

[71]Meier, pp. 406-407.

[72]HA 11, 416: "...durch ihre Natürlichkeit, ihren Gemeinsinn...".

[73]HA 11, 422: "...von einem offnen, ...gleichsam anfragenden Wesen".

[74]HA 11, 458: "munter".

[75]HA 11, 553: "...mit offner Anmut und ...natürlicher Zierlichkeit".

remained free";[76] the quickness with which the lightning of love has struck the man;[77] the lady's yearning to travel along with the German visitor, if only in her thoughts;[78] the Goethean biographical motif of separating oneself, by a definitive and rather abrupt departure, from a love that threatens to become too engrossing.[79]

What is to be concluded from all this? Not, very probably, a deliberate reliance by the son on his father's Italian 'escapade' as he recreates his own; rather recollections of his father's divergent and yet, in some ways, analogous Milanese love experiences and inventions with which the son must have been familiar. Very discrepant proportions of fact and fiction; no claim that Johann Caspar's Milanese love affair can be called a novella by the farthest stretch of the imagination; great (but far from absolute) variance in artistic *Gestaltung*: certainly. But also coincidences that point to more than themselves, a mixture of the *Erfundene* with the *Sich Ereignete* that has, we surmise, served as one of the many sources, very likely a semiconscious or subconscious one, of the novellesque configuration of the story of Maddalena Riggi, along with the more distinctly involved novella of the "Frankfurter Gretchen."

Before we draw our conclusions, we must turn, if briefly, to the two exquisite lyrical fruits of the "Erlebnis" of the "schöne Mailänderin", "Amor als Landschaftsmaler" and, under the same heading, "Cupido, loser, eigensinniger Knabe!"[80] "Amor" shows us Goethe staring, from the top of a

---

[76]Meier, p. 453. See also his reference to the uncontrollable origin of love as described in Battista Guarini's *Il pastor fido* (Meier, pp. 463, 575).

[77]His 'letter' of July 22; p. 455 (Meier); his 'letter' of July 31; p. 468 (Meier).

[78]Meier, p. 464 (Maria Giuseffa Merati's 'letter' of July 22, 1740); Maddalena Riggi, HA 11, 553-554.

[79]Johann Caspar's 'letter' of August 10, 1740; Meier, p. 473.

[80]"Cupido" appears in *Italienische Reise*, "Zweiter Römischer Aufenthalt", under "Bericht. Januar 1788", HA 11, 478. It is reprinted in "Gedichte und

rock, at a drab, gray canvas of fog. Amor joins him and paints, against the same background, the loveliest landscape and finally

> "............das allerliebste Mädchen,
> Wohlgebildet, zierlich angekleidet,
> Frische Wangen unter braunen Haaren,
> Und die Wangen waren von der Farbe,
> Wie das Fingerchen,[81] das sie gebildet."[82]

We immediately think of his references, in his prose "Bericht" on the "schöne Mailänderin", to the bright brown hair and the clear, delicate skin[83] of Maddalena. The "allerliebste Mädchen" of "Amor" then starts moving toward him, approaching closer and closer, and the poet concludes: "Glaubt ihr wohl, ich sei auf meinem Felsen/Wie ein Felsen still und fest geblieben?"[84]

We agree with Emil Staiger: the narrator sees an objectively dull, nebulous vista transformed, by uninvited love, into a serene perfection that seems objectively unfounded and still entirely objective: from this confusion arises the poem...which, half in jest and half resigned, depicts the agreeable disturbance which the mischievousness of the god of love dares to cause in a (seemingly) secure reality.[85]

The sequel, "Cupido", pursues the same theme: capricious Cupido has

---

Epen", Goethes Werke, HA 1, 237, immediately preceded by "Amor", HA 11, 234-236.

[81]i.e., like Amor's little index finger, "...so rötlich wie eine Rose": HA 1, 235.

[82]HA 1, 236.

[83]HA 11, 422.

[84]HA 1, 237.

[85]Emil Staiger, *Goethe*, op. cit., II, p. 44.

asked for a few hours' shelter but has now set up shop in Goethe's house, staying on for many days and nights, displacing the poet from his bed, burning up his provisions for the winter, upsetting the apple cart, and chasing away all good working intentions. Staiger conjectures that it may have been written shortly after "Amor", when Goethe learned of Maddalena's engagement, and calls attention to a corresponding wording, at the analogous place in the Maddalena action, as occurring in the "Bericht": 'Es wäre wunderbar genug', rief ich aus, 'wenn ein wertherähnliches Schicksal dich in Rom aufgesucht hätte, um dir so bedeutende, bisher wohlbewahrte Zustände zu verderben'; in "Cupido": "...Verbrennet den Vorrat des Winters und senget mich Armen. Du hast mir mein Geräte verstellt und verschoben..."[86]

It is perhaps not an accident that Goethe uses two related pairs of verbs in characterizing, in his prose version, as soon as he meets her, "die Mailänderin von einem offnen, nicht sowohl *ansprechenden*, als gleichsam *anfragenden* Wesen",[87] while in the first sentence of interpretation following "Cupido" he goes beyond "Amor" and generalizes the "Dämon" in the direction of "eine Versammlung tätiger Geister..., die das Innerste des Menschen *ansprechen, auffordern...*"[88] Goethe inserted "Cupido" into *Claudine von Villa Bella*[89] but did not incorporate it into any of his collected lyrics though, as Smidt-Dörrenberg and Trunz note, he remained particularly fond of it.[90] A few months after its presumed conception, on February 9, 1788, he calls it, in the correspondence section of the Italian Journey, his

---

[86]Ibid., II, p. 45.

[87]HA 11, 422. Italics mine.

[88]HA 11, 478. Italics mine.

[89]Published in 1788 in Vol. V of Goethe's Schriften.

[90]Irmgard Smidt-Dörrenberg, *Angelika Kauffmann. Goethes Freundin in Rom*. Mit 15 Bildbeigaben. (Vienna: Bergland, 1968) p. 31; Erich Trunz, "Anmerkungen" to Goethes *Werke*, HA 1, 525.

98

"Leibliedchen".[91] It is particularly striking that, almost forty-one years later, in the very gestation period of the last part of the *Italienische Reise* in which the "schöne Mailänderin" makes her appearance, he seems to intimate that he inserted it into *Claudine von Villa Bella* in such a way as to cover up its specific autobiographical relevance: "Ich habe es jedoch dort zerstückelt, so daß man darüber hinausliest und niemand merkt, was es heißen will."[92] The next day Eckermann remarks:

> "Ich kann das Gedicht nicht wieder los werden," sagte ich, "es ist durchaus eigenartig und drückt die Unordnung so gut aus, die durch die Liebe in unser Leben gebracht wird...Das Gedicht ist wie aus einer anderen Zeit und einer anderen Welt." "Ich werde es auch nicht zum zweiten Male machen", sagte Goethe, "und wüßte auch nicht zu sagen, wie ich dazu gekommen bin; wie uns denn dieses sehr oft geschieht."[93]

Chances are Goethe knew very well 'wie er dazu gekommen ist'! Two days later Eckermann returns to it once again, this time to the musical version by Reichardt:

> "Es ist eigen an diesem Liede", sagte ich, "daß es in eine Art behaglich träumerische Stimmung versetzt, wenn man es sich rezitiert." "Es ist aus einer solchen Stimmung hervorgegangen," sagte Goethe, "und da ist denn auch mit Recht die Wirkung eine solche."[94]

---

[91]HA 11, 518.

[92]*Gespräche mit Eckermann*, neu herausgegeben und eingeleitet von Franz Deibel (Leipzig: Insel, 1908) II, 116-117.

[93]Ibid., pp. 121-122.

[94]Ibid., pp. 132.

The lyrical versions of the Maddalena encounter make it as clear as its novellesque re-creation what gives this "sich ereignete Begebenheit" the flavor of the "Unerhörte". It is not so much the more traditional and almost melodramatic reversals (the jarring news that his lady love is already engaged, then that she has been deserted by her fiancé, followed by her collapse) but a tight contextual rather than absolute "Unerhörtes": the fact that the work-and-formation-oriented self-discipline that the 37-to-39-year old bachelor, so charismatic to women and men alike, has successfully imposed on himself for a year crumbles in minutes when Amor-Cupido, in the shape of a Milanese woman with depth and beauty, wings his/her arrow at him. If we go back once more to the fateful letter Goethe wrote from Castel Gandolfo between October 8 and 12 of 1787 to his Weimar friends, the letter in which, among many other news items, he reports in just one calm sentence, 'without batting an eyelid': "Eine Mailänderin interessierte mich die acht Tage ihres Bleibens, sie zeichnete sich durch ihre Natürlichkeit, ihren Gemeinsinn, ihre gute Art sehr vorteilhaft vor den Römerinnen aus"[95] – a characterization that holds up perfectly to the very end of their relationship –, we find, in its earlier portions, the calm, confident, almost smug restatement of his *Bildungsgelübde* unthreatened by the 'lustige Gesellschaft', including "einige muntere Mädchen, einige Frauen", in this resort "unter einem heitern, köstlichen Himmel": "Wenn man mich außer mir selbst herausbringen könnte, müßten es diese Tage tun, aber ich falle immer wieder in mich zurück, und meine ganze Neigung ist auf die Kunst gerichtet."[96] "Meine ganze Neigung"? And is there perhaps a reason other than social life in general and drawing in particular for the fact that he missed writing home on the last post-day? Our "schöne Mailänderin" turns up after Goethe's long, sustained sojourn in Italy during which, outgoing by nature though he was, he kept to himself and to those who could personally perfect his insights into art and science, as well as to his personal, independent experience of the "Italian way", shunned social

---

[95]HA 11, 416.

[96]HA 11, 415.

obligations, avoided entanglement with women and any other commitments outside his formative priorities – and just a few months before the successful completion of his vows the *ewig weibliche* catches up with him, *schlägt ihm ein Schnippchen*. From a wider perspective, the breakthrough of love via Maddalena signals the re-assertion of the subjective against the reified, abstract, object domination (in perspective and language) in the earlier phases of Goethe's Italian journey which Jane Brown has perceptively analyzed elsewhere.[97]

A quick recapitulation: we started out by imbedding Goethe's novellesque interests in general and the story of the beautiful Milanese woman in particular into the corresponding matrix of Romanic, especially Italian culture for which Goethe had, like his father, a deep affinity through most of his life. Then I surveyed what I see as the indecisiveness, the eclectic nature of contemporary research on the German novella and proposed that working with "novellesque" rather than "the novella" as a generic term does better justice to what I believe is the overwhelming majority of works in which the novellesque combines, successfully or not, with other generic elements. I then laid out, in rapid detail, my definition of the novellesque and, turning to the story of the "schöne Mailänderin", commented on length and installment structure, summed up its "Begebenheiten" and analyzed it in terms of the novellesque 'actual, unheard-of event'. Then we switched, for the screening of other novellesque components, to a two-pronged analysis of the Milanese woman and the Gretchen stories in *Poetry and Truth*, in hopes that a systematic comparison would bring out not only shared and not-shared features of the two opusculi hitherto, I believe, undetected, but throw light on genesis and execution of Goethe's novellesque compositions. Far from exposing all building stones constituting the novellesque we managed, I trust, to touch – not necessarily in that strict order – on the following criteria: dilemma, crisis, catastrophe or near-catastrophe, resolution,

---

[97]Jane Brown, "The Renaissance of Goethe's poetic genius in Italy", in Gerhart Hoffmeister, ed., *Goethe in Italy, 1786* (Amsterdam: Rodopi, 1988), 77-93.

tension/dis-tension (in short, dramatic factors); the proportion of lyric and epic vs. dramatic constituents, turning points ("Wendepunkte"), "Pointe", didactic/moralizing elements, transparency of language vs. gaps of indeterminacy, distant empathy for the events reported objectively in Goethe's *Altersstil*, and striking general analogies between the stories.

For further reinforcement of the autobiographical, intertextual, and, in a very stylized sense, novellesque components of our principal story, we turned to the account Goethe's father gives, almost half a century before his son's, of his love adventure with a Milanese lady, which has just very recently become available, for the first time, in a reliable, complete, scholarly German translation. Finally, we rounded off our journey with the poetic emanations of the Maddalena Riggi experience, "Amor als Landschaftsmaler" and "Cupido, loser, eigensinniger Knabe!", choice exhibits of generic interaction between the novellesque and the lyrical.

The question posed in the title of this essay can now be answered. Of the three prose texts analyzed, Johann Caspar's may have some autobiographical basis, but it is so submerged that, at best, it remains conjectural. Nor does its fictitious treatment: the heavy mannerism, tedious nitpicking, and stagnant action permit us – far from it – to call it a novella. That does not prevent it, however, from providing surprising leads or, at least, analogies to his son's account. In the "Schöne Mailänderin" and the "Frankfurter Gretchen" texts, on the other hand, the autobiographical, as a prime example of the "sich ereignete", and the "unerhörte", plus a number of other significant novellesque elements, enter a complex but happy fusion. If the "Frankfurter Gretchen" and especially the "Milanese Maddalena" stories were printed without the interruptions caused by the necessities of a chronologically arranged autobiography, they would be recognized as being among the most profiled and effective of Goethe's novellas.[98]

---

[98]I wish to thank my sister Hedy and her husband Rob to whose hospitality I owe the completion of this chapter.

Chapter IV
Die Novelle in der Klassik und Romantik

Summary-Outline[1]

Introduction

The breakthrough of German literature in the 1760's, after half a millenary of second-class European status or worse, is illustrated by the dramatic surge, surely quantitative and, though less often, qualitative, of the German novella by the 1830's (Schiller, Goethe, Wieland, Hebel, Kleist, Chamisso, Tieck, Brentano, Arnim, E.T.A. Hoffmann, and again Goethe). In turn the Classicistic and Romantic German novellas continued to leave deep imprints – for better or for worse – on the thriving novellesque culture of German 'Poetic Realism'. There is a commensurate rise of the highest quality in novellesque criticism in German Classicism and Romanticism (Goethe, Friedrich and August Wilhelm von Schlegel, Tieck, again Goethe).

General Definition of the Novellesque ("Allgemeine Begriffsbestimmung")

The unheard-of, authentic event, fateful rather than willed, surprising to the narrator himself. Matter-of-factness, objectivity of narration. The frame as distancing agent. Events must be interesting, hence necessity of tension. Its stages: dilemma –> crisis –>(near) catastrophe –> "Pointe" –> dis-tension –> quiet stimulus to reflection (Goethe's "stiller Reiz zum Nachdenken"). 'Releasing' and 'dissolving' turning points ("Auslösende und auflösende Wendepunkte").

---

[1]This chapter is, at least in intention, a highly concentrated synthesis of the cardinal features of the novellesque in German Classicism and Romanticism and its roots in Romanic cultures. In order to provide meaningful guidance to the reader, especially students who know German but would welcome some help with the argument of this exceptionally comprehensive chapter, I provide a very detailed synopsis rather than a summary. It is partly couched in telegraph style to reduce its already considerable length.

The novellesque as the epic control of the dramatic. Economy, concentration more important than length as touchstones of the novellesque. Careful use of language: the more explosive the 'what' the more disciplined the 'how': basis of novellesque tension, polarity. Aristocratic/upper bourgeois genre. Strong emphasis on tension between intelligence and passion. Rational vs Irrational lead to irony and paradox.

Imagery: concrete, plastic, organic. Object/Symbol ("Dingsymbol"). Silhouette, 'Falcon' ("Falke") of story. Novellesque structure supersedes traditional dichotomy between content and form. In the more musical novellas the "Dingsymbol" becomes the "Leitmotiv". In the Prelude ("Auftakt") to the novellesque tale the macrocosm of the story is often prefigured in the microcosm of the 'full chord' ("voller Akkord").

This chapter limits itself, in the main, to the testing of the central core of the novellesque, the unheard-of event ("die sich ereignete unerhörte Begebenheit") against representative texts of German Classicism and Romanticism.

Theory of the Novella in Classicism and Romanticism ("Theorie in der Klassik und Romantik")

In contrast to the cult of contradictions and incompatibilities between theory and textual reality in contemporary novella research leading to the abandonment, in principle, of any normative endeavor (though that principle is, usually, promptly sidetracked in favor of a heuristic use of "novella" anyway since there is really no viable alternative), which, in turn, arrives at a kind of novellesque chaos theory, this chapter will point to the continuity, with many variations, of the novellesque in primary and secondary texts of German Classicism and Romanticism. Wieland, Schiller, Goethe, Friedrich and August Wilhelm von Schlegel, Schleiermacher, Tieck, Hebel, Goethe again, E.T.A. Hoffmann.

Romanic and Germanic Cultures ("Romania und Germania")

Classicism ("Klassik")

Attraction of German Classicism to Mediterranean cradle of occidental culture (Greece, Rome) and their modern heirs: Italy, France, Spain. Cultural, historical, social, political implications of German Classicism's affinity with the novellesque genre (Goethe, Hebel, Schiller).

Romanticism ("Romantik")

German Romanticism was no less attracted to the novellesque than Classicism, but deepened the exploration of the temporal, historic, uniquely cultural and psychological, the problematics, the contradictory, the passionate, the transitory, the collective. Increasing impact of Spanish literary tradition.

The one unheard-of event ("Eine sich ereignete unerhörte Begebenheit")

Legitimation of the veracity and artistic integrity of the novella. Subjective-artistic modulation of the 'objective' 'report' about a unique event.

One event ("Eine Begebenheit")

If there are several events, one must be the decisive one: it must determine the profile of the story. Differentiated examples: Goethe, Kleist, E.T.A. Hoffmann.

Having actually taken place (Das "sich ereignete")

Reality (or convincing realism) of the core of the event related. Goethe: 'Mostly everything and nothing remains as it was.'

Historic event of some scope. ("Historische Begebenheit grösseren Ausmasses")

Selective historic corroboration of the authenticity of an event of significance/notoriety. Precision of its 'otherness'. Danger of intruding with modern 'Zeitgeist' into this unique singularity (see e.g. Hofmannsthal's reworking of Goethe's 'Bassompierre and the Grocer's Wife' story from the

Unterhaltungen deutscher Ausgewanderten (1795).[2]   *Exemplary amalgamation of the historic and the novellesque: Kleist, Arnim, E.T.A. Hoffmann.*

Public files, legal and scientific documents ("Öffentliche Akten, Wissenschaftliche Dokumente") as sources.

These form the basis and part of the matrix of such novellesque stories as Schiller's 'Criminal because he was deprived of his honor' ("Verbrecher aus verlorener Ehre", 1785). *The story illustrates well Schiller's struggle between, on the one hand, allowing the facts to speak for themselves and letting the reader decide, and, on the other, his urge to humanize the reader by doctoring the 'report'. Hebel's 'Unexpected Reunion'* ("Unverhofftes Wiedersehen") *as the quintessence, on little more than a page, of the novellesque in its purest essence. Relationship of the highly disciplined account to the tenets of classicism.*

The Unheard of ("Das Unerhörte")

Its scale from the unexpected to the sensational/scandalous. The author himself may not fully understand what he has to report. This opens up the possibility of intervention by the supernatural and, in particular, some overlapping with the fairy-tale (e.g. in the second Bassompierre story in Goethe's Unterhaltungen*). Risk of diluting the power of the "unheard-of" by authorial interpretation/moralization and stylization. Examples: Schiller's* "Verbrecher aus verlorener Ehre", *Goethe's* Unterhaltungen deutscher Ausgewanderten, *in which the* "Pochgeschichte" *(the second story in this work) and the first Bassompierre story ("Die schöne Krämerin") are much closer to the pure 'novellesque' (and much more effective) than the more stylized following stories.*

Varying efficacy of the novellesque in other relevant stories by

---

[2]Henry H.H. Remak, *Novellistische Struktur. Der Marschall von Bassompierre und die schöne Krämerin (Bassompierre, Goethe, Hofmannsthal),* Bern/Frankfurt am Main, Peter Lang, 1983 (No. 46. German Studies in America). 124 pages.

Goethe: 'The strange children of neighbors' ("Die wunderlichen Nachbarskinder"), *'The Foolish Pilgrim'* ("Die pilgernde Törin") *– one of the very best novellesque stories in German literature –, 'The Man of Fifty'* ("Der Mann von funfzig Jahren") *from the* Wanderjahre, *the decline of the novellesque as the story progresses in 'Not too far'* ("Nicht zu weit") *from the* Wanderjahre *and in the independent* Novelle *(1828). The "Unheard-of" in its purest form (Hebel's* "Unverhofftes Wiedersehen") *and its climax in Kleist's 'The Marchioness of O..'* ("Die Marquise von O.."), *'The Earthquake in Chili'* ("Das Erdbeben in Chili"), *'The Engagement in Santo Domingo',* ("Die Verlobung in St. Domingo"), *and* "Michael Kohlhaas". *The relationship of the "Unheard-of" in Hoffmann's 'The Lady de Scudéri'* ("Das Fräulein von Scuderi") *to goose-pimple Romanticism* ("Schauerromantik"), *which also characterizes Brentano's 'The story of Decent Kasperl and Beautiful Annerl'* ("Die Geschichte vom braven Kasperl und dem schönen Annerl"), *in which the most genuine novellesque figure is the 88-year old grandmother.*

The "Unheard-of" can also have a humoristic coloring (Arnim's "Der tolle Invalide", *Goethe's* "Prokurator" *story in the* Unterhaltungen, "Die pilgernde Törin," *Kleist's* "Die Marquise von O..").

Melodrama and the "Unerhörte" both are present in Schiller's "Verbrecher aus verlorener Ehre." *Goethe's* Unerhörte, *as previously noted, tends to vary between a decisive introductory chord and overstyled sequences. Hebel's* "Unerhörte" *is of classical/epic, Kleist's of explosive/dynamic but uncannily controlled perfection.* Schauerromantik *and melodrama are recognizable in* "Kasperl und Annerl", "Der tolle Invalide", *and* "Das Fräulein von Scuderi", *but the last two and Kleist's novellas are also characterized by a psychological "Unerhörte" closely tied to novellesque action.*

Other structural elements: Crisis –> catastrophe (or almost-catastrophe); marked turning points for the vast majority of novellas, gradual turning points for several. Irony and paradox. Unanswered questions, sometimes crystallized in the final "Pointe". Visual and acoustic representation of the elementary: Object, profile, image, silhouette, 'falcon'.

Central symbols. Romanticism accentuated colors, especially dramatic ones; weapons, the 'shivery'. Acoustical elements: horrible voices and sounds, occasionally pleasant ones. Music as the acoustic symbol of the 'unheard of'.

Retrospective View of the relationship of Classicism and Romanticism to the novellesque (Rückblick auf die Beziehungen der Klassik und der Romantik zum Novellistischen).

Goethe, E.T.A. Hoffmann, Hebel. Elements promoting or hampering the novellesque. Normalization of the 'angular' by classicism. The dramatic is pushed back by the classical, by didactic-exemplary-allegorical elongations. Unvarnished passions characterize German Romanticism. Greater 'Openness' of Romanticism. But goose-pimple Romanticism, Romantic fatalism (Schiller, Kleist) lead to considerable defects (Arnim) and contrast, in "Kasperl und Annerl", *with its superior parts.*

The supernatural, as long as it is merely adumbrated, is effective: Goethe's Unterhaltungen, *Kleist's* "Erdbeben in Chili", *Hoffmann's* "Ritter Gluck", *but not so when introduced too directly* ("Michael Kohlhaas", "Der tolle Invalide"). *Psychological refinement reinforces the novellesque only as long as it is the direct result of action or is, itself, translated into subsequent action: Schiller, Goethe, Brentano sometimes violate this precinct.*

Mixed Forms of the Novellesque in Classicism and Romanticism (Mischformen des Novellistichen in der Klassik und Romantik)

The anecdote

The anecdote as an unfinished novella. Difference: the anecdote rises and falls with the Pointe, *whereas in the novella the* Pointe *is just one of the significant structural elements, a pointed farewell, with an ironic twist,* after *the dissolving turning point ("auflösender Wendepunkt") of the story. The anecdote turns around a person, the novella around an event. The anecdote is a scene, the novella is a drama or pocket drama. Anecdote = narrative type closest to novella. Goethe, Hebel, and Arnim develop novella from anecdote. Kleist: master of both.*

Moral tale (Moralische Erzählung)

The moral tale is amply represented in the Decameron, Cervantes' Novelas Ejemplares, *and defined by the clergyman in Goethe's* Unterhaltungen. *Secularization of moral tale approaches the novellesque* (Decameron, Schiller, Goethe, Hebel, Kleist, Brentano, Arnim).

Spooky Stories (Gespenstergeschichte, Geistergeschichte, Spukgeschichte).

Compatible with the novellesque as long as seemingly supernatural events may be explained as natural though unheard-of occurrences: Goethe's Unterhaltungen, *Hoffmann's* "Ritter Gluck" *and* "Don Juan".

Fairy tale (Märchen)

The fairy-tale operates in two worlds, the novella in one. The fairy-tale invents, the novella reports. Friedrich Schlegel: the fairy-tale is bizarre, the novella new and striking.

But a mix of fairy tale and novellesque elements occurs already in Boccaccio and continues with Wieland. Both share the mater-of-fact self-assurance of the narrator that what he reports is true. Romanticism lends itself to the mixture of both forms: Tieck, Chamisso, Hoffmann: the novellesque fairy-tales.

Die Geburt der deutschen Novelle in der Klassik und Romantik ist ein Phänomen, das mit denselben Worten bezeichnet werden kann wie der Kern des Novellistischen selbst: »eine sich ereignete unerhörte Begebenheit«. Über ein halbes Jahrtausend lang hatte kaum jemand die deutsche Literatur außerhalb ihrer Sprachgrenzen ernstgenommen. Noch um die Mitte des 18. Jahrhunderts: hundertfünfzig Jahre nach Cervantes' *Novelas ejemplares* ('Exemplarische Novellen', 1613), zweihundert Jahre nach Marguerite de Navarres *Heptaméron* ('Das Heptameron', 1559), dreihundert Jahre nach den *Cent nouvelles nouvelles* ('Hundert neue Novellen', 1462-1486), dreihundertfünfzig Jahre nach Chaucers *The Canterbury Tales* ('Canterbury-Geschichten', 1386-1400) und vierhundert Jahre nach Boccaccios *Il Decamerone* ('Das Dekameron', 1348-1353) – alles

Monumente novellistischer Kunst – war Deutschland auf diesem Gebiet fast buchstäblich eine tabula rasa. Kaum sechs Dezennien später, gegen 1811, liegen von den großen Klassikern (Schiller, Goethe, Hebel) und von Kleist, dem größten Novellisten unter den Romantikern wenn nicht der ganzen deutschen Literatur, Meisterstücke vor, die auf Weltliteraturgeltung Anspruch erheben dürfen. Weitere zwanzig Jahre später, als die historische Romantik abklingt (einen Ausklang der Romantik in der deutschen Literatur gibt es ja überhaupt nicht), gesellen sich Chamisso, Tieck, Brentano, Arnim, E.T.A. Hoffmann und wiederum Goethe zu den Autoren dieser mehr oder minder unangefochtenen Prachtstücke. Darauf folgt die durch Klassik und Romantik noch weitgehend beeinflußte Novellenblüte des poetischen Realismus.

Die Geburt der deutschen Novellen*kritik* ist eine beinahe ebenso »unerhörte« Begebenheit. Heute noch gehört das, was Goethe und August Wilhelm von Schlegel, zum Teil auch Friedrich von Schlegel und Tieck schon kurz vor und nach 1800 über die Strukturelemente des Novellistischen gesagt haben, zu dem Besten, dem Prägnantesten, was je über das Thema geschrieben worden ist. Ein Paradox, das noch der Erklärung harrt: Eine erzromanische Literaturform, die Novelle, südlichem Lebensstil tief verhaftet, jahrhundertelang für Deutschland terra incognita, jedenfalls terra exotica, wird zwischen 1780 und 1830, nach einem dynamischen Spurt innerhalb (sehr vereinfacht gesagt) zweier Generationen, einer klassischen und einer romantischen, eine erzdeutsche Form, nun sorgfältiger, liebevoller, bewußter in Deutschland gepflegt als in ihrer ursprünglichen Heimat, der Romania.

Wir möchten darstellen, wie diese Form, die distinguierteste, bewährteste Prosaform der abendländischen Literatur, sich in Deutschland via Klassik und Romantik durchgesetzt hat, wie ihre charakteristischen Strukturelemente einerseits beibehalten, andererseits der Zeit und dem Autor gemäß verändert worden sind.

Allgemeine Begriffsbestimmung

Was ist das Novellistische? Es beschäftigt sich mit einer sich ereigneten unerhörten Begebenheit. Die Begebenheit muß authentisch sein, sie muß in dem Leser die Überzeugung wecken, daß sie sich wirklich begeben hat.

Das heißt, es ist ein Bericht, der keiner Erklärung oder Rechtfertigung bedarf. Das Geschehnis spricht für sich selbst. Didaktische und moralisierende Interventionen, Interpretationen durch den Erzähler sind nicht novellistisch. Es ist nicht notwendig, ja vielleicht nicht einmal ratsam, daß der novellistische Erzähler versteht, was geschehen ist, noch weniger, warum. Die besten novellistischen Erzählungen (siehe Kleist!) berichten von Ereignissen, die den Erzähler selbst überraschen, bei denen er den Kopf schüttelt. Novellistische Begebenheiten wirken somit eher schicksalhaft als persönlichkeitsbestimmt. Die Authentizität des novellistischen Berichts wird durch Sachlichkeit und Objektivität des Erzählens, durch die Distanz des Erzählers gewährleistet. In einer Anzahl von novellistischen Erzählungen verleiht der Rahmen diesen Abstand. Das Novellistische muß eine interessante Handlung vermitteln; deshalb ist die Spannung für das Novellistische unerläßlich. Die Etappen dieser Spannung heißen Dilemma > Krise > Katastrophe > Pointe > Entspannung > Stiller Reiz zum Nachdenken. Dramatische Umkehr kristallisiert sich in Wendepunkten, besonders dem auslösenden und dem auflösenden.

Das Novellistische ist das episch bewältigte Dramatische. Die Art des Erzählens ist sparsam, konzentriert, straff, geschlossen. Entgegen weitverbreiteten Ansichten spielt die objektive Länge eine weit mindere Rolle als die subjektive Kürze: Kurzweilig ist novellistisch, langweilig ist antinovellistisch. Da die novellistische Erzählung sich inhaltlich auf einen Bericht beschränken muß, nimmt sie in der sorgfältigen sprachlichen und stilistischen Gestaltung der Begebenheit, in dem, wie sie es sagt und durch das, was sie nicht sagt, sondern dem Leser auszugestalten überläßt, ihre künstlerischen Interessen wahr. Je hochpotenzierter die Geschehnisse, desto verhaltener die Darstellung: Diese Polarität ist eine Hauptursache der novellistischen Spannung. Das macht sie zu einer aristokratischen Gattung, einem Genre für Feinschmecker, ursprünglich Adlige und Patrizier, später für aufstrebende, kultivierte Bürger. Die ihr eigene, für die deutsche Literatur außergewöhnliche Betonung der Intelligenz erinnert an ihre romanischen Ursprünge. Die Unstimmigkeit zwischen dieser menschlichen Intelligenz und menschlichen Leidenschaften, die Polarität zwischen Rationalem und

Irrationalem, oder zwischen Intelligenz und schicksalhafter Sinnlosigkeit, gehört zum Zündstoff der Novellistik und führt oft zu Ironie und Paradox. Der bipolare Kontrast zwischen der Durchsichtigkeit der Sprache und der Undurchsichtigkeit der Ereignisse ist entschieden novellistisch.

Das Novellistische ist bildhaft, konkret, plastisch, nicht abstrakt. Das Bild muß für sich selbst sprechen; es wird nicht allegorisch hineingezogen, sondern ist ein organischer Teil der Begebenheit. Es gibt dem Novellistischen das Dingliche, das Profilierte. Die bekannten novellistischen Begriffe: Silhouette, Falke, Dingsymbol sind verschiedene Äußerungen desselben Phänomens. In der mehr musikalisch als visuell ausgerichteten Novellistik wird das Dingsymbol durch das Leitmotiv ersetzt, das hier aber buchstäblich rhythmisch, nicht nur allgemein-motivisch definiert werden muß.

Die Geschlossenheit des Novellistischen gibt jedem seiner Teile den Charakter des Repräsentativen. Der Anfang der novellistischen Erzählung im besonderen soll oder kann den novellistischen Makrokosmos im Mikrokosmos des vollen Akkordes widerspiegeln. Der Begriff der novellistischen Struktur ersetzt und überbrückt den traditionellen Zwiespalt von Inhalt und Form.

Es ist unser Anliegen, die Kardinalelemente des Novellistischen an einigen repräsentativen Primärtexten der Klassik und der Romantik darzulegen. Raumbegrenzung erfordert vorwiegend Beschränkung auf das Zentrum des Novellistischen: die »eine sich ereignete unerhörte Begebenheit«.

Wir beschreiten damit bewußt einen anderen Weg als die neuere Novellenforschung. Sie deutet die Vielfältigkeit der Theorie als Widersprüchlichkeit, belegt diese Widersprüchlichkeit leicht anhand von einzelnen Zügen unzähliger als »Novellen« hingestellter Erzählungen – und kann schließlich doch nicht umhin, mit dem arg attackierten Begriff der »Novelle« zu arbeiten.

Die Versuche klassischer und romantischer Zeitgenossen, eine Begriffsbestimmung des Novellistischen vorzunehmen, sind zahlreich, intelligent und bestätigen auf ihre Art die damalige Entfaltung novellistischer Kunst. Wenn man in der Literaturtheorie nicht gerade nach einer illusorischen Einhelligkeit sucht, fällt auf, wie gewisse novellistische Begriffe und Umschreibungen in beiden Epochen wiederkehren. Dazu gehören Wielands

112

»Simplicität des Plans« und »kleiner Umfang der Fabel«; seine Voraussetzung, daß sich eine Novelle »in unserer wirklichen Welt begeben habe«; Goethes »sich ereignete Begebenheit«; seine Aussage im Rahmen der *Unterhaltungen deutscher Ausgewanderten* (1794/95), »daß jedes Phänomen, sowie jedes Faktum an sich eigentlich das Interessante sei«, und zwar »nicht weil [es] erklärbar oder wahrscheinlich, sondern weil [es] wahr ist«; Friedrich Schlegels Gleichsetzung »Novelle/Empirisch«, seine Bemerkung, die Novelle sei »eine Geschichte, die an und für sich schon einzeln interessieren können muß«, sie neige zum Objektiven und »nichts« sei »dem epischen Stil entgegengesetzter, als wenn die Einflüsse der eignen Stimmung im geringsten sichtbar werden«; seines Bruders August Wilhelm wiederholte Feststellung, daß »die Novelle Erfahrung von wirklich geschehenen Dingen mittheilen soll«; Schleiermachers Assoziation des Novellistischen mit der »Darstellung der äußeren Menschheit«, »der Handlung«, und Tiecks gleichgerichtete Betonung des sich ereigneten Vorfalls, »unpartheiisch« berichtet, als Grundlage des Novellistischen. Eine ähnliche Konvergenz finden wir zwischen Goethes Hervorhebung des Neuen, Interessanten, Unerhörten und der von allen bereits angeführten Kritikern (plus E.T.A. Hoffmann) bemerkten Verwandtschaft des novellistischen Inhalts mit dem Dramatischen. Sie kehrt bei Friedrich Schlegel als »Seltsamkeit«, als »neu«, »überraschend« und »frappant« wieder, bei August Wilhelm als »interessant«, als »seltsame Einzigkeit«, »Energie«, als »merkwürdige Begebenheiten«, als »das Unwahrscheinlichste«, das aber »oft gerade das Wahrste« sei, als »die Leidenschaften [...] der ungeläuterten Natur«, zuweilen als »scandalöse Chronik«; bei Tieck wiederum als »Seltsamkeiten«, als »wunderbar [lies: höchst erstaunlich], vielleicht einzig«. Tiecks berühmtes Postulat des »auffallenden Wendepunktes«, »von welchem aus [die Geschichte] sich unerwartet völlig umkehrt« und »der sie von allen anderen Gattungen der Erzählung unterscheidet«, ist bereits bei August Wilhelm vorgebildet (»die Novelle bedarf entscheidender Wendepunkte«) und steht mit Goethes Novellenbegriff in keinerlei Konflikt.

Von anderen Berührungspunkten müssen wir hier absehen. Demgegenüber gibt es bei Goethe, bei Tieck, bei Schleiermacher und ganz besonders in Friedrich Schlegels weit zerstreuten aphoristischen und fragmentarischen Beobachtungen über das Novellistische auch gegensätzliche, mit sich selbst in Widerspruch stehende Bemerkungen: Sie gehen bei Goethe in Richtung der Tendenz zur moralischen Erzählung, bei Friedrich Schlegel und Tieck in Richtung des Romantisch-Subjektiven, Bizarren, Diffusen und, wie bei Goethe, des Didaktischen. Tiecks eigene novellistische Erzählungen werden diese theoretische Toleranz – meist nicht zu ihrem Vorteil – widerspiegeln: »In der Novelle dagegen vermag ich Dich nicht zu bewundern, / Diese reizende Form hast Du erweiternd zerstört«, sagt Hebbel von ihm.

Romania und Germania
Klassik
Warum eignete sich die Klassik ganz besonders für die produktive Aufnahme der novellistischen Tradition der Romania? (Neben Goethe und Schiller hat auch Wieland Novellen geschrieben, leider keine guten.) Die deutsche Klassik suchte, von Winckelmann bis zu den Humboldts, Anschluß an die Kultur des Mittelmeers: Griechenland und Rom. Griechenland war entfernter und bis 1829 unter türkischer Herrschaft, aber die »italienische Reise« wurde zum Wunschtraum jedes gebildeten Deutschen, der nicht selten auch realisiert werden konnte. Das klassische Erbe Italiens, hauptsächlich in der Kunst, aber auch in der Literatur (Dante, Petrarca, Boccaccio), wurde zum Bestandteil der deutschen Hochkultur. Die Novelle, eine anspruchsvolle Kleinform, jahrhundertelang in Italien, Frankreich und Spanien gepflegt, war ein erreichbares Modell für ein politisch zurückgebliebenes aber kulturell hochentwickeltes Land wie Deutschland, dessen Nationalgeschichte einer epischen Großform kaum Stoff bot. Die »sich ereignete unerhörte Begebenheit« im kleinen, die aber latente Energien größeren Ausmaßes in sich birgt, war für Deutschland gerade das Angemessene. Die Sachlichkeit, die Kühle der Erzählung eines interessanten, dramatischen, umstürzenden Ereignisses im Leben von Einzelmenschen (noch nicht Nationen), die künstlerisch-aristokratische Bewältigung eines individuell umgrenzten Schicksalsschlages, der aber kollektiv erweiterungsfähig ist, die Sicherheit einer jahrhundertelang erprobten romanischen Prosakunst in der Schilderung mikroexistentieller Umwälzungen, die aber bereits einen Schritt zu

makroexistentiellen Veränderungen darstellen mögen, – all das besaß für die literarische Kultur Deutschlands im ausgehenden 18. Jahrhundert die »richtige« Mischung von beispielhaft Fremdem und einheimisch Erschwinglichem, von Privatem und Öffentlichem.

Goethes novellistische Erzählungen beschränken sich noch auf Einzelkrisen. Der militärische, politische und gesellschaftliche Bruch, den die Französische Revolution und der darauffolgende Krieg, teilweise auf deutschem Boden, herbeiführten, bleibt als solcher von den Binnenerzählungen der *Unterhaltungen*, der *Wahlverwandtschaften* (1809) und der *Wanderjahre* (1821, endgültige Fassung 1829) ausgeschlossen, dringt aber bereits in die Rahmenhandlung der *Unterhaltungen* ein. Hier entspricht das Kollektiv-Unerhörte des Rahmens dem Individuell-Unerhörten der Binnenerzählungen. In Hebels *Unverhofftem Wiedersehen* (1811) dient die politisch-militärische Geschichte der großen Welt als Gegenpol zu der unendlich beständigen und gerade deshalb unerhörten Liebesgeschichte eines sich im Tod wie im Leben treuen Paares. Dagegen spielt in Schillers *Verbrecher aus verlorener Ehre* (1785) die Gesellschaft schon eine Kernrolle im novellistischen Geschehen.   Goethe bezieht die Binnenerzählungen der *Unterhaltungen* meist noch aus dem Französischen: Das gilt auch für die "Pilgernde Törin" in den *Wanderjahren*. Die französische Novellentradition beruht aber auf italienischen Vorbildern. Der Rahmen der *Unterhaltungen* bedeutet schon einen erheblichen Fortschritt gegenüber der hochstilisierten Rahmenhandlung Boccaccios. Drei der Binnenerzählungen in den *Unterhaltungen*, darunter die Pochgeschichte, beruhen auf deutschen Quellen oder sind Goethes Erfindung, und die von uns berücksichtigten novellistischen Einschübe in den *Wahlverwandtschaften* und den *Wanderjahren* (außer der "Pilgernden Törin") sowie die *Novelle* (1828) haben sich weitgehend von italienisch-französischen Vorbildern befreit, sind aber in ihrer moralisierenden Stilisierung sicher durch die Lektüre Cervantes' beeinflußt.

Romantik

Das formdisziplinierte Meistern überwältigender Lebenskonflikte und unerklärlicher Zufalls- und Schicksalsschläge, die Behauptung der menschlichen Würde, des Verantwortungsbewußtseins gegenüber unverdientem oder nur halb verdientem Leiden sind sowohl Zentralanliegen des Klassischen wie des Novellistischen. Für die Romantik erwies sich das Novellistische aber von nicht minderer Anziehungskraft. Die deutsche Romantik bedeutet nicht nur einen Bruch mit der Klassik, wie es etwa bei der späteren Romantik in Frankreich der Fall war (Stendhal, Hugo), sondern auch eine andere Sicht der Klassik, ein Ausschöpfen weiterer klassischer Dimensionen. Das Zeitlich-Prekäre, das Historisch-Relativistische, das Fragwürdige wird in seiner Problematik, in seinen Widersprüchen schärfer ausgearbeitet, besonders bei Kleist, aber auch in einem Werk wie E.T.A. Hoffmanns "Das Fräulein von Scuderi" (1819). In jedem der hier exemplarisch behandelten Romantiktexte wird Vergangenheit zu drastischer Gegenwart.

Die magnetische Anziehungskraft Italiens erlitt in der Romantik keine Einbuße, im Gegenteil, aber das Leidenschaftliche, Unberechenbare, das Vergängliche, das sich hinter der klassischen Fassade verbarg, trat in den Vordergrund des Interesses. In der Novellistik wandte sich die Vorliebe von der ihrer klassizistischen Tradition stark verhafteten italienischen Literatur zur spanischen Literatur, die von jeher eine unterschwellige Spannung zwischen rigoroser Disziplin und physischer wie metaphysischer Leidenschaftlichkeit, Aristokratischem und Primitivem, kennzeichnet. Calderón im Drama, Cervantes in der Prosa standen demgemäß im Zentrum des Interesses der Romantik (Tieck, August Wilhelm und Friedrich Schlegel), ohne daß allerdings die besten novellistischen Erzählungen der Romantik sich direkt an bestimmte spanische Modelle halten. Französische Quellen spielen bei Kleist nur eine begrenzte Rolle, aber Arnims "Der tolle Invalide auf dem Fort Raton-neau (1818)" und "Das Fräulein von Scuderi" sind ihnen — etwa ein Dezennium später — immer noch stark verpflichtet. Die »sich ereignete unerhörte Begebenheit« gewinnt kühnere, problematischere Dimensionen — man denke an die Vergewaltigung in Cervantes' "La Fuerza del Sangre" ('Die Macht des Blutes', 1613) und an Kleists "Marquise von O..." (1807/08). Der erstaunliche Prosarealismus, spanische Tradition seit dem ersten Schelmenroman (*La vida de Lazarillo de Tormes* – 'Das Leben des Lazarillo

116

de Tormes', 1554), wurde durch moralisierende Didaktik und Nachdenklichkeit abgeschirmt, die den an solches gewöhnten deutschen Romantiker und Leser aber nicht zu arg störten, da sie seinen eigenen Neigungen entgegenkamen. Die Formdisziplin der klassischen Novellistik lockerte sich, den spanischen Modellen gemäß, in der Romantik. Das Experimentelle setzt sich durch. Die Künstlerschaft wird introvertierter, egozentrischer, bewußter. Die Bildlichkeit wird reicher. Die Verwandtschaft mit Geistergeschichte, mit Märchen und Legende wird enger.

Verglichen mit der Klassik dehnt die Romantik das Kollektivelement in ihren Novellen sprunghaft aus. In Kleists "Michael Kohlhaas" (1810), "Das Erdbeben in Chili" (1810), "Die Verlobung in St. Domingo" (1811), in Brentanos "Geschichte vom braven Kasperl und dem schönen Annerl" (1817), im "Tollen Invaliden" und im "Fräulein von Scuderi" ist das Los des Einzelnen mit dem Geschick von Stadt, Staat, Regierung, Rasse, Volk oder Kirche eng verbunden.

Bei allen Variationen bleiben aber in den besten Prosazeugnissen dieser Richtung der Klassik und der Romantik die novellistischen Grundzüge fest und beständig.

Eine sich ereignete unerhörte Begebenheit

Die weitererzählte Neuigkeit (novella) gehört wohl in allen Kulturen zu den Freuden des gesellschaftlichen Lebens. Die Novelle beruht auf einer Begebenheit, die deshalb, weil sie geschehen ist, unwiderlegbaren Anspruch auf Echtheit hat, aber erzählt, weitergegeben und schließlich niedergeschrieben wird, nicht nur, weil sie authentisch ist (denn das Banale ist auch authentisch), sondern weil sie unerhört, das heißt *merk-würdig* ist. Dieses »Unerhörte«, das den Anstand, das Erlaubte, die sozialen Normen höchstwahrscheinlich verletzt, wird erst einmal dadurch gesellschaftlich legitimiert, daß es eben nun einmal »geschehen« ist, daß es berichtet wird als hochinteressante Tatsache, ohne daß der Erzähler sich auf ein »Für« oder »Wider« einläßt. Damit bewahrt er sich eine weitgehende Stoffreiheit, wenn sie sich auch innerhalb des »sich ereigneten« Bereichs betätigen muß. Der »berichtende« Novellist ist nicht für den »berichteten« Inhalt, wohl aber für die Form des »Berichts« verantwortlich:

Das ist die zweite gesellschaftliche Legitimierung des Novellistischen. Diese Formung geht bei der Klassik in die Richtung der strengen Stilisierung des Objektiven und Subjektiven, bei der Romantik in die Richtung der differenzierten Entwicklung des Subjektiven. Die Kunst des Novellisten ist ein Tanz auf des Messers Schneide: Er muß die objektive Gegebenheit, soweit er sie kennt, respektieren, aber sie durch subjektive Intelligenz einerseits lichten, andererseits ergänzen, das heißt: gestalten, ohne sie ideologisch auszuschlachten. Er muß das »Unerhörte« bewahren, das seinem Stoff das Einmalige, Kitzel und Grusel (innerhalb der Grenzen des Glaubwürdigen) gibt, er muß es aber auch in der objektiven, feinen, verhaltenen Form mitteilen, welche es einer gemischten Gesellschaft von Hörern und später Lesern – in der die Frau eine große Rolle spielt – schmackhaft macht.

Eine Begebenheit

Wir fassen die »eine Begebenheit« als ein in sich geschlossenes, silhouettiertes Ereignis auf, das Ursachen und Folgen hat, die sich auf längere Zeit hin erstrecken können, ohne aber die Schärfe und die Einmaligkeit des Profils zu schwächen. Das Novellistische beschränkt sich entweder auf *eine* Begebenheit, gipfelt in einer solchen oder weist jedenfalls eine *entscheidende* Begebenheit auf.

Solche Begebenheiten sind in den beiden Bassompierregeschichten der *Unterhaltungen* die meteorhafte, kurzlebige aber unvergeßliche Affäre des Marschalls mit der rätselhaften schönen Krämerin und der Ehebruch eines anderen Bassompierre mit einer ebenfalls mysteriösen schönen Frau, die märchenhafte Züge trägt. In der "Pilgernden Törin" kommt ein edles Frauenzimmer als Landstreicherin in die Familie von Revannc. Vater und Sohn verlieben sich in sie, sie verschwindet. Diese drei Geschichten gehören zu den perfektesten novellistischen Versuchen Goethes. Daß sie Übertragungen aus dem Französischen sind, mindert dieses Verdienst wenig. Sie würden sich gerade so gut zu romantischen Novellen eignen: Die Frauen sind in allen drei Fällen mysteriös, leidenschaftlich, ihre Herkunft und ihre Zukunft bleiben ungeklärt. Aber die Behandlung ist klassisch, nüchtern, diszipliniert; Anstand und Leidenschaft halten sich die Waage, zu beiderseitigem Vorteil.

118

In Goethes "Wunderlichen Nachbarskindern" (in den *Wahlverwandtschaften*) entzweien sich die beiden Nachbarskinder, die füreinander bestimmt waren, verlieben, verloben und heiraten sich dann aber doch. Eine vergnügungssüchtige Frau und Mutter läßt in "Nicht zu weit" (der *Wanderjahre*) Mann und Kinder bei ihrer eigenen Geburtstagsfeier sitzen. In Verdruß und Verzweiflung läuft ihr Mann zu einem Gasthof, wo er unerwartet seine »alte Liebe« wiedertrifft. Seine Frau hat auf dem Weg nach Hause Wagenbruch erlitten, währenddessen sie sich von der Untreue ihres eigenen Liebhabers überzeugen muß. Sie kommt niedergeschlagen nach Hause – ihr Mann ist weg. Hier hört die Begebenheit auf. "Die wunderlichen Nachbarskinder" und "Nicht zu weit" haben etwas Ausgeklügelt-Schematisches an sich, das der Klassizistik näher steht als der Romantik.

Die Kleistschen Novellen sind so ereignisreich, daß es nicht leicht fällt, *eine* maßgebende Begebenheit herauszuschälen. Im "Erdbeben in Chili" wird eine Novize, die ein Kind gebärt, durch ein furchtbares Erdbeben sowohl vor der Hinrichtung bewahrt als auch mit ihrem eingekerkerten Geliebten wiedervereinigt, aber aus Anlaß eines Dankgottesdienstes, dem sie beide beiwohnen, von dem aufgestachelten Pöbel getötet. Die verwitwete Marquise von O..., ohne ihr Wissen in andere Umstände gekommen, geht schließlich eine glückliche Heirat mit ihrem »Vergewaltiger« ein. Michael Kohlhaas erhält Genugtuung für seine auf der Tronkaburg mißhandelten Rappen, muß aber selbst dem Staat, dessen Ordnung er gestört hat, durch Hingabe seines Lebens Genugtuung geben. Auf der Insel Santo Domingo verlobt sich während eines blutigen Aufstands gegen die Weißen ein schweizer Offizier in französischen Diensten mit einer Mestizin, die er aufgrund eines Mißverständnisses erschießt, worauf er sich selbst tötet. Die novellistischen Begebenheiten Kleists sind extrem und in dieser Beziehung schon erzromantisch: Dem Leser wird nichts erspart. Die Sprache ist explosiv, also unklassizistisch, aber vollkommen diszipliniert, von einer realistischen Präzision, die in die Zukunft weist.

In E.T.A. Hoffmanns "Ritter Gluck" (1809) trifft der Erzähler in einem Gartenrestaurant, später auf der Straße und in der Oper einen seltsamen, altmodischen, musikbesessenen Fremden, welcher sich als der Komponist Gluck herausstellt. Die Wahl eines Musikers, der zwei Jahrzehnte nach seinem Tod noch am Leben ist und die Geschichte beherrscht, ist zentral romantisch.

Wir kommen zum folgenden Resultat: Die »eine Begebenheit« mag das Geschehen ausschließlich beherrschen oder sie mag das Übergewicht haben. In letzterem Falle stellt sie meist die Ausmündung des Vorspiels, den Höhepunkt der Erzählung dar; sie ist verantwortlich für die Entscheidung des Geschehens. Jedenfalls behält sie ihre grundsätzliche Wichtigkeit für das novellistische Gepräge einer Erzählung der Klassik und Romantik bei.

Das »sich Ereignete«

Für die Glaubwürdigkeit des »sich Ereigneten« gibt es in der Novellistik einen Spielraum, der vom Bericht einer sich ereigneten Begebenheit über die künstlerische Vervollständigung (oder Beschneidung) dieses Geschehnisses bis zur Peripherie der Nachahmung, das heißt der Erfindung einer »wahrscheinlichen« Begebenheit reicht. Das Risiko des Abgleitens in das Nicht-Novellistische ist um so größer, je weiter sich die Handlung von dem entfernt, was Wolfgang Kayser als den Kern des Novellistischen ansieht, »ein [...] >reales< und einmaliges, das heißt örtlich und zeitlich genau festgelegtes Geschehen«. In dem Absatz, der den "Wunderlichen Nachbarskindern" unmittelbar folgt, hat der Erzähler ausgezeichnet das Wesentliche dieser Verarbeitung ausgesprochen. Charlotte verläßt das Zimmer

»[...] höchst bewegt, denn die Geschichte war ihr bekannt. Diese Begebenheit hatte sich mit dem Hauptmann und einer Nachbarin wirklich zugetragen, zwar nicht ganz wie sie der Engländer erzählte, doch war sie in den Hauptzügen nicht entstellt, nur im einzelnen mehr ausgebildet und ausgeschmückt, wie es dergleichen Geschichten zu gehen pflegt, wenn sie erst durch den Mund der Menge und sodann durch die Phantasie eines geist- und geschmackreichen Erzählers durchgehen. Es bleibt zuletzt meist alles und nichts, wie es war«.

Die Mehrzahl unserer Texte sind in der Tat Ausarbeitungen von »sich ereigneten Begebenheiten«. Aus Raummangel können wir uns nur mit einigen

Proben aus der Kategorie: historische Quellen, Akten und Dokumente befassen.

Historische Begebenheit größeren Ausmaßes

Es liegt dem Autor nahe, seinem novellistischen Geschehen durch ein historisches Fundament die Authentizität des Realen zu verleihen. Dazu kommt für den romantischen Novellisten die Sehnsucht nach vergangenen, »ursprünglicheren« Zeiten. Verbunden mit diesem Historizismus ist eine gewisse Genauigkeit der Zeit- und Ortsangaben, die aber wiederum nicht in eine solche Detailfülle ausarten darf, daß das Profil der »einen Begebenheit« verwischt wird. Am Anfang stehen oft einige karge Zeit- und Ortsangaben. Noch wichtiger ist die Vermittlung der historisch-kulturellen, ideologisch-realpsychologischen Voraussetzungen der vergangenen Zeit, eines zurückliegenden Zeitgeschehens. Dieses Epochengefühl authentisiert das novellistische Geschehen durch die Präzisierung seiner Andersartigkeit. Das »schöne Krämerin«-Erlebnis des Marschalls von Bassompierre in Goethes *Unterhaltungen* gehört als klassisch-perfektes Beispiel hierher. Wichtiger noch als die stilisierte Konkretheit gewisser Angaben: »Marschall von Bassompierre – seit fünf oder sechs Monaten – die kleine Brücke [Paris] – Laden an einem Schilde mit zwei Engeln – Fontainebleau – eine sehr schöne Frau von ungefähr zwanzig Jahren – Nacht vom Donnerstag auf den Freitag« ist die Voraussetzung einer psychologischen Ungebrochenheit des Marschalls und der Krämerin, die aus einer härteren Zeit stammen, der Wende des 16. zum 17. Jahrhundert. Die Erzählung wird, in Unkenntnis dieses historischen Bewußtseinsunterschiedes, vollkommen mißverstanden, wenn man, wie Hofmannsthal es in seiner Bearbeitung tut, psychologisch-ethisch-neuromantische Erwartungen des späten 19. Jahrhunderts auf die beiden Hauptgestalten überträgt, wenn der lapidare, ehrliche, sich und andere nicht zerfasernde Stil der Spätrenaissance, den Goethe sauber und würdig bei-behalten hat, nun psychologisch differenziert und subjektiviert wird.

Kleists "Kohlhaas", Arnims "Toller Invalide" und E.T.A. Hoffmanns "Fräulein von Scuderi" sind Musterbeispiele der Integrierung des Historischen in das Novellistische. Die Hauptquelle für den "Kohlhaas" ist Christian

Schöttgens und Georg Christoph Kreysigs *Diplomatische und curieuse Nachlese der Historie von Ober-Sachsen und angrentzenden Ländern* (3. Teil, Dresden und Leipzig, 1731), worin die »Nachricht von Hans Kohlhasen, einem Befehder derer Chur-Sächsischen Lande« aus der Märkischen Chronik von Peter Hafftitz steht:

»Kleists Quelle enthält bereits die Zurückhaltung der Pferde, die Verschleppung des Prozesses durch die sächsischen Gerichte, die Niederbrennung der Wittenberger Vorstadt, das Gespräch mit Luther, das Scheitern der Verhandlungen, den verhängnisvollen Rat Georg Nagelschmidts, das gespannte Verhältnis zwischen Sachsen und Brandenburg, Prozeß und Hinrichtung Montag nach Palmarum« [3].

Das novellistische Gerüst ist, bis auf das Kapselmotiv, ziemlich vollständig in der Erzählung »aus einer alten Chronik« enthalten.

"Der Tolle Invalide" beruht auf einem dokumentarisch überlieferten, novellistischen Unterbau, den Arnim beibehält[4], mitsamt charakteristischen Objekten, Konstanten, die »dingsymbolischen« und einen gewissen psychologischen Wert besitzen. Diesen Unterbau hat Arnim einerseits mit weiteren realistisch-novellistischen Zügen (wahrscheinlich von ihm erfunden oder kombiniert) verstärkt, ihm andererseits aber auch einen nicht-novellistischen, romantischen, idealischen, moralistischen Überbau zugefügt, der mit christlichen und schauerromantischen Allegorien (Feuer, Flamme, Fluch, Teufel, Lilie, Taube, Gnade) überfrachtet ist. Das Resultat ist »ein

---

[3]Helmut Sembdner: Anmerkungen zu Kleist. In: *Sämtliche Werke und Briefe.* München 1965. Bd. II. S. 895-896.

[4]Siehe C.G. Child: Achim von Arnim's "Der Tolle Invalide". In: *Modern Language Notes XII,* 3 (März 1897), S. 188-189; J. Lesowsky: Der tolle Invalide auf dem Fort Ratonneau. In: *Archiv für das Studium der neueren Sprachen LXV* (1911), S. 302-307.

122

unvollständiges Ineinanderaufgehen der beiden Sphären«[5], ähnlich wie ein Jahr zuvor in Brentanos "Kasperl und Annerl".

Ein Vergleich der Vorlagen zum "Fräulein von Scuderi" mit Hoffmanns Text ergibt ein ziemlich typisches Bild der Verarbeitung des »sich Ereigneten« in einer historischen Novelle. Das Problem des Entknäuelns von Quelle und Dichtung ist hier weniger kompliziert als in anderen Fällen, denn der Erzähler hat uns in seinem Erzählungsrahmen selbst (mit einer Ausnahme) zu den Hauptquellen geführt. Verschiedenartige Wirkungen gehen aus von Voltaires kritischer Souveränität und Epochenkenntnis[6], Pitavals Kriminalmodellen[7], Wagenseils biederem Charme[8], Reisebeschreibungen und Zeitromanen. Dazu kommen literarische Einflüsse und eigene literarische Neigungen hauptsächlich romantisch-dämonischer Art, die hier eine geglückte, wenn auch nicht unbedingt harmonische Ehe eingehen. Die dokumentarischen Elemente geben der Struktur der Erzählung die markanten Kerben, die interessanten Konturen, welche sie zu einer gelungenen geschichtlichen Novelle machen, das heißt einer novellistischen Erzählung, die zwischen dem sich Ereigneten und dem Gestalteten steht. Festzuhalten ist, daß das Übernommene keineswegs *per se* novellistisch minderwertiger ist als das Erfundene: Die frei

---

[5]Ernst Feise: Der tolle Invalide von Achim von Arnim. In: *Journal of English and Germanic Philology LIII*, 3 (1954), S. 408.

[6]In seinem *Siècle de Louis XIV*. Berlin 1751.

[7]F. Gayot de Pitaval: *Causes Célèbres et Intéressantes*, Bd. 1 (Den Haag 1734), wohl in deutscher Übersetzung benutzt: *Erzählung sonderbarer Rechtshändel. 1.* Teil. Leipzig 1747. Siehe E.T.A. Hoffmann: *Werke*. Hg. v. G. Ellinger. 15. Teil S. 239. o. J.

[8]Johann Christoph Wagenseil: *De sacri Romani imperii libera civitate Noribergensi commentatio*. Altdorf 1697. In dem zu diesem Werk gehörigen Traktat "Von der Meistersinger holdseliger Kunst" befindet sich Wagenseils Bericht über die Juwelendiebstähle (S. 561 ff.; zitiert nach E.T.A. Hoffmann: Werke, S. 241-243).

erdichtete Olivier-Madelon-Liebesgeschichte gehört zu den schwächsten Bestandteilen der Erzählung.

Öffentliche Akten, Wissenschaftliche Dokumente

Schillers "Verbrecher aus verlorener Ehre", 1785 veröffentlicht mit dem Untertitel »Eine wahre Geschichte«, den der Dichter auch später beibehalten hat, fußt auf den Aufzeichnungen des württembergischen Amtmanns Abel, der den Sonnenwirt Friedrich Schwan (Modell zu Schillers Christian Wolf) festgenommen hatte: sie wurden 1787 durch Abels Sohn Jakob Friedrich, Schillers Lehrer auf der Karlsschule, veröffentlicht. Diese Darstellung weist bereits alle Züge novellistischer Spannungen auf: Familien- und Charakterkonflikte, Wilddieberei, Verwundung, zweimalige Zuchthausstrafe, Festungshaft, Ausbruch aus dem Kerker, Ermordung des Feindes, Eintritt in eine Räuberbande, versuchte aber zurückgewiesene Wiederkehr in die Gesellschaft, Festnahme, Verhör, Bekenntnis und Hinrichtung. Schillers Einleitung spiegelt sein Dilemma zwischen novellistischem Tatbestand und soziopsychologischem Moralisieren wider: An den Gedanken des Helden »liegt uns unendlich mehr als an seinen Taten, und noch weit mehr an den Quellen seiner Gedanken als an den Folgen jener Taten«. Damit begibt sich der Erzähler aber auf das Gebiet des Nicht–Novellistischen. Indem er das Urteil des Lesers durch die Analyse der seelischen, moralischen und sozialen Ursachen der Taten Christian Wolfs zu humanisieren versucht, »beleidigt« er gerade »die republikanische Freiheit des lesenden Publikums, dem es zukömmt, selbst zu Gericht zu sitzen«, und ist damit kein historischer Berichterstatter mehr.

Hebels "Unverhofftes Wiedersehen" weist auf kaum mehr als einer Druckseite alle Merkmale des Novellistischen auf: die eine Begebenheit, das sich Ereignete, das Unerhörte, das Hochpotenzierte, Paradoxe, erzählerische (wie metaphysische) Spannung, Katastrophe, Pointe, entscheidenden auslösenden und auflösenden Wendepunkt, Schicksal gegen Persönlichkeit, disziplinierte Berichtsform, mäßige Länge, epische Bewältigung des Dramati- schen, Intelligenz des Erzählers und Durchsichtigkeit der Sprache a Undurchsichtigkeit der Ereignisse, den vollen Akkord des Anfangs, das

124

Bildhafte (Silhouette, Falke, Allegorie, Dingsymbol, Leitmotiv). Es ist vielleicht kein Zufall, daß diese »schönste Geschichte von der Welt« (Ernst Bloch) sich eng an eine wissenschaftlich belegte Begebenheit des Jahres 1719 anlehnt[9]. Hebel hat nicht nur die stofflichen Umrisse der Vorlage übernommen (Ort, Zeit, Handlung) sondern sich auch an verschiedenen Stellen – selbst wo es nicht notwendig gewesen wäre – wortwörtlich an die Quelle gehalten. Hätte er das getan, wenn er nicht in ihr sowohl stoffliche wie verbale Qualität, latente Literarität entdeckt hätte? Besteht nicht vielleicht eine Verwandtschaft zwischen der verhaltenen, präzisen Prosa einer Akte, die eine geschehene unerhörte Begebenheit dokumentiert, und dieser diszipliniert-klassizistischen, sparsamen, volkstümlich-stilisierten Literaturprosa?

Das Unerhörte

Das »Unerhörte« ist eines der vier Grundelemente des Novellistischen in Goethes Definition. Es bewegt sich in einer Skala, die mit dem »Unerwarteten« anfängt (Bassompierres Begegnungen mit der schönen Krämerin in Goethes *Unterhaltungen deutscher Ausgewanderten*) und bis zu einem derart Unerhörten vordringt (Kleists Novellen), daß man am anderen Ende der Skala von einem beinahe untragbaren Superrealismus sprechen kann ("Das Erdbeben in Chili", "Die Verlobung in St. Domingo"). Die Begebenheiten, die der Erzähler berichtet, müssen ihm selbst unerwartet kommen – das ist die Bekräftigung ihrer »Unerhörtheit«, der schlagende

---

[9]1722 von dem Bergassessor A. Leyel in den "Acta litteraria Sveciae Upsaliae publicata" berichtet. G.H. Schubert erzählt sie in seinen berühmten "Ansichten von der Nachtseite der Naturwissenschaft" (Dresden 1808). Die Zeitung "Jason" brachte ihrerseits Schuberts Fassung" (April 1809) und regte an, daß dieser vielversprechende Stoff von Dichtern behandelt werden solle. Diese Fassung und Anregung bekam Hebel zu Gesicht: Das Resultat ist seine Erzählung. Siehe L. Wittmann: *Johann Peter Hebels Spiegel der Welt. Interpretationen zu 53 Kalendergeschichten.* Frankfurt/Main 1969. S. V-XXII.

Beweis ihrer Glaubwürdigkeit. Die höchste Glaubwürdigkeit des Unerhörten mag dort erreicht sein, wo der Erzähler selbst keinen höheren Sinn in den Geschehnissen sehen kann, wo der Leser damit rechnen muß, daß sie richtungslos sind, wie zum Beispiel im "Erdbeben in Chili".

Schillers Konzept des Unerhörten in seinem "Verbrecher aus verlorener Ehre" ist bereits hochmodern, obwohl die Ausführung teilweise noch im Moralistisch-Sentimentalen des 18. Jahrhunderts steckenbleibt. Zu den angehäuften Missetaten Christian Wolfs kommen außergewöhnliche sozialkritische, psychologische und moralische Konturen: Wolf ist einfacher Bürgerlicher, Sohn eines Gastwirts, noch dazu häßlich; er wird durch Kühnheit und Schlauheit eine Gefahr für den Landesherrn; seine Taten werden, wenngleich nicht entschuldigt, so doch erklärt und humanisiert durch den Mangel an Mitgefühl unter seinen Mitmenschen, die Starrheit des Staates, die Härte der Gesetze. Er will sich, ohne Not, dem Landesherrn stellen, in der Hoffnung, »den Staat zu versöhnen, den ich beleidigt habe« (»Ich weiß, daß ich etwas Unerhörtes begehre«), und ergibt sich schließlich, halb freiwillig, einem ehrwürdigen Oberamtmann – um dann trotz seiner Reue gefoltert und hingerichtet zu werden.

Goethes Prägung des »Unerhörten« als einer der Hauptbestandteile des Novellistischen hat in der Forschungstheorie berechtigten Widerhall gefunden. Wie steht es um Goethes Praxis? Die erste Binnenerzählung in den *Unterhaltungen deutscher Ausgewanderten* nennt der Erzähler »eine Geschichte, die großes Aufsehen erregte«; sie betrifft die Sängerin Antonelli. Der unerklärliche oder nur halb erklärliche »fürchterliche Ton« ist hier das Unerhörte. Dieses Unerhörte stumpft sich allerdings in der Erzählung fortschreitend ab. Die verschiedenen Schallphänomene mildern sich (fürchterliche Klagelaute > Schüsse > Händeklatschen > himmlische Töne), um dann vollkommen zu verschwinden. Auch die Resultate dieser Phänomene sind auf die Dauer zu eintönig: Dreimal fällt die Antonelli (nach einem Klagelaut oder Schuß) in Ohnmacht, auch ihre Begleiter fallen in quasi obligatorische Ohnmacht. Die progressive Verdünnung des Unerhörten durch Stilisierung ist für das Novellistische bei Goethe sehr charakteristisch.

In der nächstecn (Poch-)Geschichte, die nur eine Seite in Anspruch nimmt, erleben wir zweimal Unerhörtes: Das Pochgeräusch ohne erkennbare Ursache, und eine geradezu empörende (aber erfolgreiche) »Kur«:

»Entrüstet über diese Begebenheit und Verwirrung griff der Hausherr zu einem strengen Mittel, nahm seine größte Hetzpeitsche von der Wand und schwur, daß er das Mädchen bis auf den Tod prügeln wolle, wenn sich noch ein einzig Mal das Pochen hören ließe«.

Das Pochen verstummt. Hier bleibt das Unerhörte unverdünnt, unstilisiert, wirksam.

In den darauffolgenden novellistischsten Binnenerzählungen der *Unterhaltungen*, den beiden von Bassompierre berichteten Liebesabenteuern, berührt sich das Unerhörte mit dem Mysteriösen, womöglich Übernatürlichen. In der ersten Geschichte taucht eine agressive Krämerin auf, die schlankwegs darauf besteht, mit dem gefeierten Marschall von Frankreich »eine Nacht[. . .] unter *einer* Decke« zubringen zu dürfen, ihn bei einer Kupplerin trifft, seine »Liebkosungen mit sehr guter Art ablehnt und verlangt, mit [ihm] zwischen zwei Leintüchern zu sein« und »ein so unüberwindliches Verlangen, mit [ihm] zu sein« hat, daß sie »jede Bedingung eingegangen wäre«. Diese Krämerin mit ihrem »kurzen Unterrock von grünwollenem Zeuge« wird aber auch von dem durch Damengunst verwöhnten Marschall als »eine sehr schöne Frau« beschrieben, »mit einer zierlichen Nachtmütze, einem sehr feinen Hemde«, und kurzum hätte er »niemals ein zierlicheres Weib gekannt«. Aber sie kommt nicht zum zweiten Stelldichein. Oder ist sie eine der beiden Leichen, die er im Zimmer des Rendezvous erspäht? Und warum verschwindet sie spurlos? Das – und die beiläufig erwähnte Tatsache, daß ihr »Laden an einem Schilde mit zwei Engeln kenntlich war« –, führt eine Möglichkeit des Übernatürlichen ein, die Hofmannsthal in seiner Bearbeitung des Stoffes weiter (zu weit) entwickeln wird. Aber bei Goethe bleibt dieses Fragezeichen (ohne Antwort) durchaus im Bereich des Novellistischen.

In der zweiten Bassompierregeschichte hinterläßt »eine schöne Frau« ihrem Geliebten drei Geschenke für seine »drei rechtmäßigen Töchter«, »Gaben«, für die sie ihm »die größte Sorgfalt« anbefiehlt und von denen die Abkömmlinge der drei Töchter glauben, daß sie »Ursache manches glücklichen Ereignisses« wären. Sie stellen Elemente dar, die Luise in der Rahmenhandlung an das Märchen von der schönen Melusine und andere Feengeschichten erinnern.

Alle vier dieser exemplarischen novellistischen Geschichten berichten präzise von unerhörten, diesseitigen Begebenheiten; in allen vier besitzt dieses Unerhörte ein übernatürliches Potential. Alle zielen »auf die entschiedene Neigung unserer Natur, das Wunderbare zu glauben«, von welcher in den für die Bestimmung des Novellistischen sehr ergiebigen Rahmenkonversationen der *Unterhaltungen* die Rede ist. Alle hinterlassen den »stillen Reiz, weiter nachzudenken«, der für das Novellistische so bezeichnend ist. Klassisch an der Darstellung dieser übernatürlichen Möglichkeiten in den *Unterhaltungen* ist die Selbstverständlichkeit, die Ruhe, die Sparsamkeit, mit der die mysteriösen Begebenheiten registriert werden, was ihre novellistische Wirkung nur steigert; man vergleiche damit die romantisierte, breite Ausgestaltung des Übernatürlichen in der »Zigeunerin-und-Kapsel«–Geschichte im *Kohlhaas*. Nach diesen ersten vier Erzählungen der *Unterhaltungen* flaut der novellistische Bestandteil, einschließlich des Unerhörten, in den darauffolgenden drei Geschichten rapide ab: Die Prokuratorerzählung ist, wie im Rahmenkommentar richtig festgestellt wird, eine »moralische Erzählung« obgleich nicht ohne novellistische Züge; die Ferdinandgeschichte, ganz von Goethe erfunden, hat wenig Novellistisches, und das *Märchen* ist sui generis.

Bei den "Wunderlichen Nachbarskindern" der *Wahlverwandtschaften* liegt das Novellistisch-Unerhörte in der Tatsache, daß sich Braut und Bräutigam kurz vor der Hochzeit in ihren Brautkleidern präsentieren und um den Segen ihrer Eltern bitten – aber es ist nicht der offizielle Bräutigam, sondern der von ihr scheinbar ohne Gegenseitigkeit Geliebte, dessen Liebe erst durch ihren versuchten Selbstmord erwacht. Die Situation könnte novellistisch sein, ist aber so steif und zurechtgezimmert, daß sie, verglichen mit dem vielversprechenden Anfang der Erzählung, künstlich wirkt.

Die "Pilgernde Törin" in den *Wanderjahren* steckt voll von Unerhörtem. Ein junges, schönes, edles, liebenswürdiges Mädchen zieht ohne Gefolge auf einer Landstraße her. Ihre staubigen Schuhe kontrastieren mit blanken seidenen Strümpfen. Ihr Benehmen ist seltsam ungereimt: Sie besitzt ausgezeichnete Manieren, Takt, Verstand, Belesenheit, Feinheit, singt, spielt

Klavier, näht – aber keiner weiß, woher sie kommt. »Töne tiefer Trauer« wechseln auf einmal in »ein mutwilliges Lied« über, das sie »mit der schönsten Stimme von der Welt lustig und lächerlich vorbrachte«. All dies bereitet auf eine unerhörte und halb-humoristische Situation vor: Vater und Sohn werben um dasselbe Mädchen, sie läßt dem Vater gegenüber durchblicken, sie erwarte vom Sohn ein Kind, der Sohn ist dagegen davon überzeugt, das Kind käme vom Vater – und dann verschwindet sie auf Nimmerwiedersehen.

In der "Pilgernden Törin" ist das Unerhörte so wirksam gestaltet wie sonst kaum in der deutschen Novellistik: Es ist rätselhaft, aber nicht übernatürlich, klassisch in seiner Objektivität und Knappheit.

In dem "Mann von funfzig Jahren" der *Wanderjahre* ist das scheinbar Unerhörte zu ausgeklügelt, zu klassizistisch, es wirkt nicht authentisch.

Die »unerhörte« aber durchaus überzeugende Familiensituation, mit der *Nicht zu weit* einsetzt, droht in ein konstruiertes Melodrama auszuarten, als der verzweifelte Mann im Gasthaus ausgerechnet auf seine frühere Flamme stößt. Das unvermittelte Ende rettet die Erzählung vor der fatalen Möglichkeit einer schematischen Lösung, die das glaubwürdig Unerhörte in Frage stellen könnte. Die Erzählung enthält sehr unterschiedliche Momente: zum einen knappe, realistische, dramatische Situationen voller Überraschungen, zum anderen eine (an den Haaren herbeigezogene) sentimenale Wiederbegegnungsszene.

In Goethes einfach *Novelle* genannter Geschichte bezeichnet der Erzähler via Honorio das um sich greifende Feuer in der Stadt als »einen so unerwartet außerordentlichen Fall« und dann die Entdeckung eines mit knapper Not getöteten Tigers in unmittelbarer Nähe der Fürstin als »seltsames, unerhörtes Ereignis«. Aber die *Novelle* schwingt sich gegen Ende in magische Bereiche, das Unerhörte wird zum Wunderbaren, das Novellistische gerät ins Legendäre.

Zusammenfassend kann man sagen: Goethe hat besonders zu Anfang seiner novellistischen Erzählungen ein ausgesprochenes Flair für das Unerhörte. Dieses Unerhörte wird manchmal durchgehalten, weicht aber in einer Mehrzahl seiner Novellistik der Stilisierung und strukturellen Ermüdungserscheinungen.

Hebels "Unverhofftes Wiedersehen" bietet in seiner ruhigen Gedrängtheit ein klassisch-paradigmatisches Beispiel für das novellistisch Unerhörte: die Wiederauffindung der Leiche eines im Schacht verunglückten jungen schwedischen Bergmanns fünfzig Jahre nach seinem Tode, »in seiner jugendlichen Schöne«, »ganz mit Eisenvitriol durchdrungen«, während seine noch lebende Verlobte »grau und zusammengeschrumpft« ist, aber »die Flamme der jugendlichen Liebe« in ihrem Herzen unversehrt bewahrt hat.

Kein Novellist hat das Unerhörte so intensiv dargestellt wie Kleist, und keiner ist ein größerer Novellist als er. Das Unerhörte der Kleistschen Novellen herauszuschälen hieße soviel wie sie wiederzuerzählen. Der vielleicht berühmteste Anfang irgendeiner deutschen Novelle ist auch der unerhörteste:

»In M. . ., einer bedeutenden Stadt im oberen Italien, ließ die verwitwete Marquise von O. . ., eine Dame von vortrefflichem Ruf und Mutter von mehreren wohlerzogenen Kindern, durch die Zeitungen bekanntmachen: daß sie, ohne ihr Wissen, in andre Umstände gekommen sei, daß der Vater zu dem Kinde, das sie gebären würde, sich melden solle und daß sie, aus Familienrücksichten, entschlossen wäre, ihn zu heiraten«.

Die Vorgeschichte zu diesem »ungeheuren Vorfall« enthält auf den ersten beiden Seiten der Erzählung die Erstürmung der Festung durch russische Soldatan, Feuersbrunst, versuchte Schändung der Marquise durch die »entsetzliche Rotte« auf dem hinteren Schloßhof, ihre Befreiung von den »Hunden« durch einen russischen Offizier, den Grafen F..., der sie in den von den Flammen noch unberührten Flügel des Schlosses trägt, wo die Marquise »völlig bewußtlos niedersank«, und – den berühmten Gedankenstrich, die, in nüchterner Retrospektive gesehen, »Vergewaltigung« der Ohnmächtigen durch denselben Offizier, der daraufhin Anstalten traf, »einen Arzt zu rufen; [er] versicherte, indem er sich den Hut aufsetzte, daß sie sich bald erholen würde; und kehrte in den Kampf zurück«. Und in diesem atemberaubenden Tempo geht es weiter bis zu einer auf der letzten Seite noch ungewissen glücklichen Entwirrung. Das Unerhörte ist hier von Anfang an mehrseitig: physisch, psychologisch, sozial, aber immer geschehnisorientiert.

Das "Erdbeben in Chili" fängt ebenfalls *in medias res* mit einem unerhörten Paukenschlag an:

»In St. Jago, der Hauptstadt des Königreichs Chili, stand gerade in dem Augenblicke der großen Erderschütterung vom Jahre 1647, bei welcher viele tausend Menschen ihren Untergang fanden, ein junger, auf ein Verbrechen angeklagter Spanier, namens Jeronimo Rugera, an einem Pfeiler des Gefängnisses, in welches man ihn eingesperrt hatte, und wollte sich erhenken«.

Erdbeben – Verbrechen – Selbstmordversuch: alles im ersten Satz. Darauf folgt, wie in der "Marquise von O. . .", die Vorgeschichte: Eine Karmeliternovize wird im Klostergarten von ihrem Geliebten geschwängert, sinkt am Fronleichnamstag in Mutterwehen auf den Stufen der Kathedrale nieder, wird erst zum Feuertod verurteilt, dann zur Enthauptung »begnadigt«. Die Fenster in den Straßen, durch die der Hinrichtungszug gehen soll, sind bereits vermietet. All das auf der ersten Seite! Und allein auf der letzten Seite werden ein Mann, zwei Frauen und ein Kind auf furchtbarste Weise totgeschlagen.

Das unverdünnt Novellistische dieser Begebenheiten besteht in der Verbindung zwischen dem Extrem-Unerhörten der Ereignisse, dem Ultra-Realistischen der Beschreibung, dem konsequent Disziplinierten des Berichts und der Bedrohung der weltlichen und göttlichen Ordnung durch diese spezifischen Begebenheiten, die eine metaphysische Spannung erzeugen. Dieses Unerhörte ist nicht nur negativ: Man berichtet auch von »ungeheuern Taten«, von »Römergröße [...] Unerschrockenheit [...] Selbstverleugnung [...] göttlicher Aufopferung«. Das Unerhörte entstammt hier natürlichen Katastrophen (Erdbeben) und menschlich-sozialen Katastrophen (als Verbrechen angesehener Verstoß gegen Religion und Moral, angeordnete Exekutionen, Selbstmordversuch, Nutznießung der Katastrophe durch asoziale Elemente, fanatische Niedermetzelung edler Menschen), aber auch unerhörter menschlicher Bewährung in der furchtbarsten Lage (Don Fernando, Donna El- vira, Josephe, Jeronimo).

Die gleiche extreme Spannung zwischen Positivem und Negativem, aber innerhalb ein und derselben Persönlichkeit und somit noch ungewöhnlicher und romantischer, existiert im *Michael Kohlhaas*. Die Hauptfigur wird bereits im ersten Satz der Novelle eingeführt als »einer der rechtschaffensten zugleich und entsetzlichsten Menschen seiner Zeit«, im vierten Satz als »Räuber und Mörder«.

In der "Marquise von O. . ." sind die Begebenheiten auch unerhört, obschon – bis zur öffentlichen Heiratsaufforderung – privater als im "Kohlhaas"; aber im großen und ganzen handeln alle Personen konsequent. Im "Erdbeben in Chili" sind der Fanatismus von Kirche und Bevölkerung einerseits, die freimütige Liebe der durch die Gesellschaft getrennten Helden andererseits von vornherein deutlich genug eingezeichnet, um brutale Grausamkeiten, Löwenmut und Selbstaufopferung von Anfang bis Ende folgerichtig erscheinen zu lassen. Aber im "Kohlhaas" erleben wir allmählich und systematisch die Entwicklung eines achtbaren, redlichen, gerechten und geduldigen »guten Bürgers« zum fanatischen Zerstörer all derer, die seine Feinde sind oder die er mit seinen Feinden in Verbindung bringt. Der Schlüssel zu beidem, so wird uns versichert, liegt zwar in seinem Wesen, und so bleibt es bis zu seinem Ende, trotzdem bildet das Überhandnehmen des Revolutionären über das Bürgerliche hier den Kernteil des Unerhörten, das sich physisch und psychisch, religiös, politisch und sozial ausdrückt.

In der "Verlobung in St. Domingo" liegt der Ursprung des Unerhörten in einem furchtbaren Rassenkonflikt, der alle menschlichen Gefühle unterdrückt, Meuchelmorde rechtfertigt und selbst bei einem edlen Menschen wie Gustav dazu führt, daß er aus Mißtrauen seine Braut erschießt und Selbstmord begeht.

Nach Kleist erscheinen Novellen anderer Autoren verhältnismäßig zahm. Dabei ist aber in Rechnung zu stellen, daß das Unerhörte bei Kleist pathologische, ja monströse Züge annimmt, die nicht als Norm sondern als Extreme gelten dürfen. Im "Fräulein von Scuderi" kommt E.T.A. Hoffmann ihm ziemlich nahe. Unerhörte Ereignisse und Entdeckungen reißen nicht ab: Haus- und Klostereinbrüche, Überfälle, Vergiftungen (fünf!), Enthauptung, Verhaftungen, Verhöre, Folterungen, Anschläge, Juwelenmorde. Das Juwelenmotiv gibt dem Unerhörten hier ein schauerromantisches Gepräge.

Brentanos "Geschichte vom braven Kasperl und dem schönen Annerl" bringt eine Parade unerhörter Begebenheiten; sie wirken nicht nur schauerromantisch sondern ausgesprochen melodramatisch und literarisch

132

minderwertig. Ein echteres, psychologisch Unerhörtes liegt in der unvergeßlichen 88jährigen Alten, Kaspars Großmutter und Annerls Patin, in der sich primitives, vollkommen in sich ruhendes Gottesvertrauen, trockener fatalistischer Realismus und eine gewisse Altersverwirrung mischen, aber auch in dem Ehrenfimmel Kaspars, der, direkt oder indirekt, zu mehreren Katastrophen führt.

Inwieweit ist das Unerhörte in der klassischen und romantischen Novellistik völlig ernst zu nehmen? Angesichts der Intelligenz und der Distanziertheit des Erzählens, die für die Novelle so charakteristisch sind, würde es Wunder nehmen, wenn das humoristische Element fehlte. In Arnims "Tollem Invaliden" verspricht das Adjektiv im Titel einen heiteren Einschlag, und der Leser wird nicht enttäuscht. Die Erzählung beginnt mit dem Brand des Holzbeins des am Kamin sitzenden, von neuartigen Feuerwerken träumenden Kommandanten von Marseille, Graf Dürande. Eine zufällig anwesende Bittstellerin, Rosalie, versucht, »das Feuer mit ihrer Schürze zu löschen«:

»Bald drangen [Leute] von der Gasse herein, auch Basset war erwacht; der brennende Fuß, die brennende Schürze brachte alle ins Lachen, doch mit dem ersten Wassereimer, den Basset aus der Küche holte, war alles gelöscht, und die Leute empfahlen sich«.

Eine kleine Katastrophe, die leicht hätte eine große werden können, aber als Humoreske endet, bereitet auf eine größere Katastrophe vor, die nach Hangen und Bangen auch positiv endet: Ein Unerhörtes im kleinen Rahmen weist auf ein Unerhörtes im größeren Rahmen, die Verbindung zwischen beiden wird durch Rosalie hergestellt.

Die Heirat zwischen dieser deutschen Frau (Rosalie) und dem französischen Sergeanten Francoeur ist »eine seltne Liebe«, die »den Teufel in ihn gebracht« hat. Zum Beispiel warf Francoeur »neulich [...] den kommandierenden General, der in einer Affäre den Rückzug des Regiments befahl, vom Pferde, setzte sich darauf und nahm mit dem Regimente die Batterie fort«. – »Ein Teufelskerl«, rief der Kommandant, »wenn doch so ein Teufel in alle unsre kommandierende Generale führe [...]; ist Ihre Liebe solche Teufelsfabrik, so wünschte ich, Sie liebten unsre ganze Armee«. Die schlagfertige, erfrischende Antwort des Kommandanten humorisiert und normalisiert das Unerhörte; sie bereitet auf die spätere Reintegrierung des rebellischen »Teufels« vor, dem es leicht an den Kragen hätte gehen können. Dies nur als Modell des glücklichen Ineinandergreifens des Humoristischen und Novellistischen in einem besonderen Fall des Unerhörten, den man durch weitere Beispiele aus der Klassik und der Romantik (Prokuratorgeschichte, "Die pilgernde Törin", "Die Marquise von O. . .") ergänzen könnte.

Zusammenfassend sei bemerkt, daß Schillers Unerhörtes im "Verbrecher aus verlorener Ehre" einer gewissen Melodramatik nicht entbehrt, daß moralistisch-bürgerliche Gesichtspunkte des ausgehenden 18.Jahrhunderts in der Handlungsführung eine prägnante Rolle spielen, daß aber andererseits auch das Novellistisch-Unerhörte, das Überraschend-Überzeugende zu seinem Recht kommt (zum Beispiel im knappen Verhör des Räubers durch den Oberamtmann am Ende der Erzählung, ein klassisches Stück novellistischer Prosa).

Goethes Lenkung des Unerhörten ist sehr ungleich: Ungemein wirksam im Reinzustand, aber häufig versandet dieses Element nach einem dezidierten Einsatz; es wird überstilisiert. Hebels Unerhörtes ist von klassisch-epischer Vollkommenheit. Die Reinform des Dramatisch-Unerhörten erscheint gleich am Anfang bei Kleist: Seine Dynamik des Unerhörten ist bedingt durch die Spannung zwischen Unvorhersehbarem von Satz zu Satz, unerhörten Begebenheiten, Ultrarealistik, explodierender Leidenschaft und, abgesehen von seinen Superlativen, hochobjektiver, hochanalytischer Sprache. Seine unerhörten Begebenheiten sind Naturkatastrophen, gesellschaftliche Katastrophen und menschliche Katastrophen, welche die menschliche und die göttliche Ordnung in Frage stellen.

Bei den drei fast gleichzeitig entstandenen berühmten novellistischen Erzählungen der Romantik ist das gediegene Unerhörte in *Kasperl und Annerl* psychologischer Art (aber von novellistischer Bedeutung, weil es zu überraschenden Handlungen führt), während die Begebenheiten selbst überwiegend der Schauerromantik verpflichtet sind. Schauerromantische und melodramatische Einflüsse sind auch bei Arnim und Hoffmann erkennbar, aber "Der tolle Invalide" und "Der Fräulein von Scuderi" vertreten eine weit höhere Stufe des psychologisch verfeinerten, immer auf die Handlung bezogenen Unerhörten als Brentanos Erzählung, ohne die Vollkommenheit, die Präzision, die pausenlose, sprachlich streng gemeisterte Geladenheit der unerhörten Begebenheiten, aus denen sich das Psychologische ergibt (nicht umgekehrt), Kleistscher Novellen zu erreichen.

Andere Strukturelemente

Die Beständigkeit der novellistischen Strukturelemente, der »geprägten Form, die lebend sich entwickelt«, bewährt sich in Klassik und Romantik, auch wenn man über das Zentralpostulat der »sich ereigneten unerhörten Begebenheit« hinausgeht. Krise und Katastrophe, ob tatsächlich eingetreten oder gerade noch vereitelt, gehören zur unentbehrlichen Instrumentierung der hier betrachteten Erzählungen. Markante Wendepunkte kennzeichnen ebenfalls die allergrößte Mehrzahl; allmählichere Wendungen bestimmen die Antonelligeschichte, die Prokuratorerzählung und den "Ritter Gluck". Die besten Novellen der Klassik und Romantik führen zu Ironie und Paradox, lassen Fragen offen – mehrmals dargestellt durch eine Pointe im letzten Absatz. Das Dingliche, Elementare, Profilierte, Bildhafte, Silhouettierende, Falkenartige setzt sich visuell oder akustisch durch, oft als Zentralsymlbol; visuell als Kleidung und Bedeckung: Halstuch, Schürze, Schleier, altmodisches Kostüm, Leintücher; als Ladenschild; als Feuer; als Tiere: Pferde, Tiger, Löwe; als »lebendiger« Leichnam. Die Romantik betont das Farbige (weiß, rot, schwarz, gold) und Farbendramatische: Flaggen, Feuerwerke, Juwelen; Waffen (Pistolen, Gewehre, Kanonen), das Schaurige (Amulett, Richtschwert). Das Akustische erscheint als furchtbare Stimmen und Töne, Schüsse, Ohrfeigen, Händeklatschen, unheimliche Pochgeräusche, aber gelegentlich auch als angenehmer Klang. Die Romantik erhebt Musik im "Ritter Gluck" zum akustischen Sinnbild des Unerhörten.

Rückblick auf die Beziehungen der Klassik und der Romantik zum Novellistischen

Goethes Entdeckung der romanischen Novellentradition, die Leidenschaften in strenge literarische Formen gießt, entsprach seiner Neigung zum Ausgleich. Die Gesichertheit der klassischen Formen fängt die

Unberechenbarkeit und Unverständlichkeit der Schicksalsschläge auf, sie hält die menschliche Würde aufrecht. Die Form zwingt zu Abstand und Objektivität. Sie findet ihren novellistischen Ausdruck gern in einer Rahmenhandlung, vom *Decamerone* und von den *Canterbury Tales* über den *Heptaméron* bis zu Goethes *Unterhaltungen* und Hoffmanns *Serapionsbrüdern* (1819-1821). Geschlossenheit und Sparsamkeit in Stil, Rhythmus und Tempo sind ihr eigen. Die Durchsichtigkeit der Sprache ist Ausgleich für die Undurchsichtigkeit der Ereignisse. Das Bildliche (Silhouette, Falke) entspricht der Freude am Sehen, welche die Mittelmeerklassik auszeichnet. Das Beste in Goethes Novellistik und die Formvollendetheit und Knappheit von Hebels "Unverhofftem Wiedersehen" gehören in diese Tradition. Die positive Haltung der Mittelmeerkulturen zum Leben, zur Realität, ihre Vitalität kommen der Novellistik, die sich auf ihr aufbaut, zugute (zum Beispiel in den beiden Bassompierregeschichten). Die Stilisierung und Abstrahierung des Klassizistischen, die Bezähmung von Extremen, die Gleichförmigkeit der Gestaltung schränken andererseits die Wirkung des Novellistischen ein. Die sich ereignete unerhörte Begebenheit wird abgeschirmt, in normative kulturelle Formen einbezogen, das Profil wird geglättet, Ecken werden abgerundet. Das Dramatische weicht dem Epischen. Dazu kommt in der deutschen Literatur, besonders in der Prosa, eine gewisse Gestaltungsmüdigkeit, die oft nach einem wirkungsvollen, disziplinierten, dramatischen Anfang eintritt. Der Autor hält nicht durch. Das ist in Goethes Novellistik auffallend. Didaktisch-exemplarische Tendenzen der klassischen deutschen Aufklärung (Schillers "Verbrecher", Goethes Prokuratorgeschichte) und ihre allegorischen Neigungen ("Die wunderlichen Nachbarskinder", *Novelle*) sind dem Novellistischen abträglich.

Leiden und Leidenschaften stehen auch im Zentrum des novellistischen Interesses der deutschen Romantik; sie werden nun aber weniger stilisiert, sie schlagen durch. In manchen Beziehungen wird der Realismus, die Unmittelbarkeit der sich ereigneten unerhörten Begebenheit dem Leser in der romantischen Novellistik direkter, intensiver, präziser vermittelt als in der Klassik. Diskordante Töne werden nicht ausgemerzt. In den besten Fällen (Kleist, weite Partien von Arnim und E.T.A. Hoffmann, Teile von Brentano) ergibt die größere Offenheit der Romantik für Leidenschaften eine vortreffliche Verstärkung des novellistischen Effekts.

Die zusätzlichen Möglichkeiten, welche die Romantik für die Literatur erobert hat, sind aber dem Novellistischen nicht immer zugute gekommen. Die modische Schauerromantik, der romantische Fatalismus, von denen wir selbst bei Kleist einige Spuren entdecken, besonders in der "Verlobung in St. Domingo", und die wir schon bei Schiller, wenngleich gemäßigt, vorfinden, führt im "Tollen Invaliden" zu erheblichen Schwächen (Mutterverdammungsmotiv) und kontrastiert mit anderen, ausgezeichneten novellistischen Partien von "Kasperl und Annerl". Das aus dem 18. Jahrhundert übernommene melodramatische Moment (zum Beispiel Oliviers und Cardillacs Herkunft im "Fräulein von Scuderi") läßt einen Teil dieser vortrefflichen historischen Novelle schablonenhaft wirken und verdirbt dem Leser die Freude an längeren Partien von "Kasperl und Annerl". Das Übernatürliche, das die Romantik wiederentdeckte, wirkt, solange es indirekt angedeutet, dem Nach-Denken des Lesers überlassen wird, durchaus im Einklang mit den vom Novellistischen offengelassenen Fragen, die den Leser weiter beschäftigen sollen. Damit sind beispielsweise die Antonelli- und Pochgeschichten, Bassompierres Krämerin- und Schleierabenteuer in den *Unterhaltungen*, Kleists "Erdbeben in Chili" und Hoffmanns "Ritter Gluck", die solche Fragen anregen aber nicht ausdrücklich behandeln, durchaus novellistisch. Das direkt in eine novellistische Erzählung eingeführte Übernatürliche aber ist prinzipiell, wenn auch nicht immer in der Praxis, unvereinbar mit dem »sich Ereigneten«: Die Episode mit der Zigeunerin im "Kohlhaas" und Rosalies Verfluchungs- und Erlösungsmotiv im "Tollen Invaliden" lassen das erkennen. Das Psychologische, für dessen Vertiefung die Romantik verantwortlich ist, verträgt sich mit dem Novellistischen, solange es nicht Selbstzweck ist, solange psychologische Analysen in novellistische Handlung einmünden oder aus novellistischen Handlungen entspringen: Schillers "Verbrecher", Goethes "Wunderliche Nachbarskinder" oder der Berichterstatter in "Kasperl und Annerl" gehen mitunter darüber hinaus. Diese Erwägungen bringen uns zu den »Mischformen der Novelle« in der Klassik und Romantik.

Mischformen des Novellistischen in der Klassik und Romantik

Es gibt eine Kombination von Strukturelementen, die das Novellistische bilden; wenn sie in einer Erzählung überwiegt, nennt man diese Geschichte eine Novelle. Es kann aber kaum eine Erzählung geben, die nur aus diesen Bestandteilen besteht. Somit sind in den meisten Novellen auch andere typologische Elemente vorhanden. Nur vier von ihnen können hier kurz gestreift werden – soweit wie möglich in bezug auf unsere Auswahl von Texten.

Anekdote

Eine Anekdote, könnte man sagen, ist eine unausgeführte Novelle. Sie reproduziert und gestaltet, wie die Novelle, eine sich ereignete merkwürdige Begebenheit, eine Neuigkeit. Sie hat, wie das Novellistische, eine streng umrissene Form. Sie bedarf, wie die meisten Novellen, einer Pointe. Mit dieser Pointe aber steht oder fällt die Anekdote. Ohne eine gelungene Pointe ist sie nichts. In der Novelle dagegen ist die Pointe nur eins von einer Anzahl von bedeutsamen Strukturelementen[10]. Die Pointe *ist* die Anekdote: Alles ist auf sie zugespitzt. Sie ist geistesgegenwärtig, kaltblütig, entscheidend. In der Novelle ist die Pointe ein letzter, überraschender, oft ironischer Kommentar *nach* dem auflösenden Wendepunkt, ein charakteristisches Adieu, nicht das Ziel des Berichts. Die Anekdote dreht sich um eine Episode, die Novelle um einen Lebensabschnitt, manchmal sogar um ein scharf profiliertes Leben. In der Anekdote tritt die Person hervor, in der Novelle tritt sie hinter der Begebenheit zurück. *Ein* persönlicher Zug charakterisiert die Anekdote; eine *Persönlichkeit* die Novelle. Der Inhalt einer Anekdote ist merkwürdig, schlagend; der Inhalt einer Novelle unerhört. Die Anekdote hat die Anlage zu einer Szene, die Novelle zu einem Drama. Die Anekdote ist kurz, eine Novelle im allgemeinen länger.

---

[10]Einige dieser und der folgenden Formulierungen und Anregungen zu den Vergleichen als solchen verdanke ich Johannes Klein: *Geschichte der deutschen Novelle von Goethe bis zur Gegenwart.* S. 8-30.

Von allen mit dem Novellistischen verwandten Formen steht die Anekdote, seit Boccaccio, der Novelle wohl am nächsten. Die ersten vier Erzählungen in Goethes *Unterhaltungen*, Hebels "Unverhofftes Wiedersehen" und Arnims "Toller Invalide" sind aus Anekdoten hervorgegangen und werden von manchen noch als solche angesehen. Die Verwandtschaft zwischen Anekdote und Novelle zeigt sich nirgends überzeugender als bei dem unübertroffenen Meister beider Typen: Kleist.

Moralische Erzählung

Diese alte Form, welche bereits im *Decamerone* vertreten ist, in dem Adjektiv von Cervantes' *Novelas ejemplares* steckt und die im 18. Jahrhundert aufgelockert wurde, wird von dem alten Geistlichen im Rahmenteil der *Unterhaltungen* als Einführung zu den Binnenerzählungen so umrissen:

»Soll ich wiederholen, mein Fräulein, daß [der wohldenkende Mensch] [...] kleine Fehler und Mängel lustig findet und besonders mit seiner Betrachtung gern bei Geschichten verweilt, wo er den guten Menschen in leichtem Widerspruch mit sich selbst, seinen Begierden und seinen Vorsätzen findet, wo alberne und auf ihren Wert eingebildete Toren beschämt, zurechtgewiesen oder betrogen werden, wo jede Anmaßung auf eine natürliche, ja auf eine zufällige Weise bestraft wird, wo Vorsätze, Wünsche und Hoffnungen bald gestört, aufgehalten und vereitelt, bald unerwartet angenähert, erfüllt und bestätigt werden? Da, wo der Zufall mit der menschlichen Schwäche und Unzulänglichkeit spielt, hat er am liebsten seine stille Betrachtung, und keiner seiner Helden, deren Geschichten er bewahrt, hat von ihm weder Tadel zu besorgen noch Lob zu erwarten«.

Diese Säkularisierung der moralischen Erzählung kommt dem Novellistischen entgegen und könnte gut zur Charakterisierung vieler Geschichten des *Decamerone* dienen. Schillers "Verbrecher", Goethes Antonelli- und Prokuratorgeschichten in den *Unterhaltungen*, "Nicht zu weit", *Novelle*, "Unverhofftes Wiedersehen", "Die Marquise von O. . .", "Kasperl und Annerl" und "Der tolle Invalide" weisen verschiedenste Abstufungen dieses Typs auf, der dem »Charaktergemälde« eng verwandt ist.

Gespenstergeschichte, Geistergeschichte, Spukgeschichte

Dieser Typus ist mit dem Novellistischen vereinbar, solange die überirdischen Erscheinungen als »unerhörte« aber irdische Phänomene erklärt werden könnten. Die Antonelli- und Pochgeschichten in den *Unterhaltungen* und der "Ritter Gluck" (auch Hoffmanns "Don Juan", 1814) gehören diesem Genre an. Verwandt mit ihm, aber ohne die ausdrückliche Zuspitzung auf schaurige Begebenheiten, sind die »Fantasiestücke« der Romantik à la E.T.A. Hoffmann: sie sind, was für realistische Details auch immer in ihnen enthalten sein mögen (siehe zum Beispiel "Rat Krespel", 1817), den Gesetzen dieser Welt nicht unterworfen und daher nicht novellistisch.

Märchen

Auf den ersten Blick scheinen das Märchenhafte und das Novellistische scharf voneinander getrennt zu sein. Das Märchen wirkt, wie Johannes Klein es formuliert hat, in der Sphäre der Einbildung, des Wunderbaren, in der die unbefriedigten Wünsche unseres eigenen Lebensbereichs befriedigt werden. Es operiert gleichermaßen in zwei Welten, während sich das Novellistische trotz seiner Betonung des Außerordentlichen in unserer Welt bewegt. Das Ziel des Märchens ist das Glück. Der Erfolg liegt oft in der Lösung eines Rätsels durch die richtige Formel. Das Märchen fabuliert. Die Novelle zielt nicht auf Lösungen. Novellistische Begebenheiten werfen indirekt Fragen auf, die eine Novelle selten beantwortet. Sie fabuliert nicht, sie berichtet[11]. In den Rahmenbemerkungen der *Unterhaltungen* unterscheidet Karl, der hier sicherlich für Goethe spricht, scharf zwischen dem Novellistischen (ohne es so zu nennen) und dem Märchenhaften:

»Die Einbildungskraft ist ein schönes Vermögen, nur mag ich nicht

---

[11]Mein Vergleich beruht teilweise auf Kleins Abgrenzung von Novelle und Märchen (S. 15/16). Kleins anregende und nützliche Unterscheidungen zwischen Novelle einerseits, Roman, Erzählung, Anekdote, Schwank, Facetie, Legende, Märchen, Kurzgeschichte, Skizze, Ballade, Versnovelle und Drama andererseits sollen hier ausdrücklich erwähnt werden.

gern, wenn sie das, was wirklich geschehen ist, verarbeiten will. Die luftigen Gestalten, die sie erschafft, sind uns als Wesen einer eigenen Gattung sehr willkommen; verbunden mit der Wahrheit, bringt sie meist nur Ungeheuer hervor [...]«.

Friedrich Schlegel differenziert zwischen beiden: »Wie die Novelle in jedem Punkt ihres Seins und ihres Werdens neu und frappant sein muß, so sollte vielleicht das poetische Märchen [...] unendlich bizarr sein«.

So die Theorie, aber in der Praxis liegen die Dinge doch etwas komplizierter. Von Musäus (1782ff) über Goethes "Märchen" in seinen *Unterhaltungen* bis zu den *Kinder- und Hausmärchen* (1812 ff.) der Brüder Grimm und weit darüber hinaus, von der Aufklärung über die Klassik bis zur Romantik gehört das Märchen zu den beliebtesten, besten und differenziertesten Gattungen der deutschen Literatur. Schon bei Boccaccio sind manche Erzählungen märchenhaft. Eine der frühesten deutschen Erwähnungen der Novelle in Wielands *Don Sylvio von Rosalva* (1764) nennt »die arabischen und persischen Erzählungen, die Novellen und Feenmärchen« in einem Atem. In seiner eigenen Anmerkung grenzt Wieland die Novellen nur von den »großen Romanen ab«, und oft sind bei ihm das Märchenhafte und das Novellistische vermengt. Gemeinsam sind dem Märchenerzähler und dem Novellisten (und damit dem Leser) das selbstverständliche Vertrauen in die Erzählung eines »sich Ereigneten« (obwohl sie sich auf zwei verschiedenen Ebenen abspielt), und eine Abneigung gegen moralisierende Exkurse. Die Experimentierfreudigkeit der Romantik mußte notwendigerweise zur Vermischung ihrer bevorzugten Prosaformen, des Novellistischen und des Märchenhaften, führen. Tiecks *Der blonde Eckbert* (1797), Chamissos *Peter Schlemihls wundersame Geschichte* (1813) und E.T.A. Hoffmanns humoristisches, novellistisches Märchen *Der goldene Topf* (1814) gehören zu den typischsten und einflußreichsten Novellenmärchen der Romantik. Von diesen dreien ist Schlemihl, trotz des treffsicheren Themas, eine mißglückte Mischung: zu rührselig, zu moralisierend, zu langweilig. Er wird weder dem Märchenhaften noch dem Novellistischen gerecht. *Der blonde Eckbert* ist die geschickteste aber, trotz ihres psychoanalytischen Kitzels, auch oberflächlichste der drei Erzählungen, und der beschwingte, heitere, witzig-fantastische *Goldene Topf,* ein Säkularmärchen mit sekundärem novellistischem Einschlag, bei weitem das beste Werk.

Literaturhinweise

Die meisten der im Text oder in den Anmerkungen nicht bereits belegten Zitate sind zu finden in dem unentbehrlichen Kompendium: *Theorie und Kritik der deutschcn Novelle von Wieland bis Musil,* Hg. v. Karl Konrad Polheim. Tübingen 1970. Weitere Belege:

> Goethe: Zahlreiche Bemerkungen über das Novellistische (ohne daß das Wort je fällt) in den Rahmengesprächen der *Unterhaltungen deutscher Ausgewanderten*; zu den Quellen der Binnengeschichten in den »Unterhaltungen« siehe: Goethes *Werke.* Hamburger Ausgabe. Bd. 6. München 1960. S. 599-612.
>
> E.T.A. Hoffmann: *Werke.* Hg. v. G. Ellinger. Berlin o.J. 7. Teil, 3. Band der *Serapionsbrüder.* S. 130, 185/186.
>
> Wolfgang Kayser: *Das sprachliche Kunstwerk.* Bern, München 1960. S. 354-355.
>
> Friedrich Schlegel: *Schriften zur Literatur.* Hg. v. W. Rasch. München 1972.

Nicht im Text angesprochen aber allgemein wichtig sind noch folgende Titel:

> Ernst Behler: "Die Zeit der Romantik". In: *Handbuch der deutschen Erzählung.* Hg. v. K. K. Polheim. Düsseldorf 1981. S. 115-129, 571-573.
>
> E.K. Bennett: *A History of the German Novelle.* Cambridge [2]1970.
>
> John M. Ellis: *Narration in the German Novelle.* In: *Anglica-Germanica.* Hg. v. L. Forster u. S. Prawer. Cambridge 1974.
>
> Nino Erné: *Die Kunst der Novelle.* Wiesbaden 1956.
>
> Gerald Gillespie: "Novella, Nouvelle, Novelle, Short Novel?" In: *Neophilologus* 51 (1967), S. 117-127, 225-230.
>
> A. von Grolman: *Novelle.* In: *Reallexikon der deutschen*

Literaturgeschichte. Hg. v. P. Merker u. W. Stammler. Bd II. S. 510-515. Berlin 1926-1928.

Hellmuth Himmel: *Geschichte der deutschen Novelle*. Bern 1963.

Arnold Hirsch: *Der Gattungsbegriff »Novelle«*. In: *Germanische Studien*. Hg. v. E. Ebering. Berlin 1928. Nachdruck Nendeln/Liechtenstein 1967.

Dines Jørgen Johansen: *Novelleteori efter 1945*. Copenhagen 1970.

Johannes Klein: *Geschichte der deutschen Novelle von Goethe bis zur Gegenwart*. Wiesbaden [4]1960.

Ders.: "Novelle". In: *Reallexikon der deutschen Literaturgeschichte*. Hg. v. W. Kohlschmidt u. W. Mohr. Berlin [2]1965. S. 685-701.

Herbert Krämer (Hg.): *Theorie der Novelle*. Stuttgart 1977.

Josef Kunz: "Die deutsche Novelle zwischen Klassik und Romantik". In: *Grundlagen der Germanistik*. Hg. v. H. Moser. Berlin 1971.

Ders.: (Hg.): *Novelle*. Darmstadt [2]1973.

Judith Leibowitz: *Narrative Purpose in the Novella*. In: *De Proprietatibus Litterarum. Series Minor*. Hg. v. C. Van Schooneveld. Den Haag 1974.

Fritz Lockemann: *Gestalt und Wandlungen der deutschen Novelle*. München 1957.

J.H.E. Paine: *Theory and Criticism of the Novella*. In: *Studien zur Germanistik*. Hg. v. A. Arnold u. A. Haas. Bonn 1979.

Karl Konrad Polheim: Novellentheorie und Novellenforschung. 1945-1964. Stuttgart 1965.

Ders.: "Gattungsproblematik". In: Handbuch der deutschen Erzählung. Hg. v. K. K. Polheim. Düsseldorf 1981. S. 9-16, 556-557.

Henry H. H. Remak: "Der Rahmen in der deutschen Novelle: Dauer im Wechsel". In: *Traditions and Transitions*. Studies in Honor of Harold Jantz. Hg. v. L. Kurth u. W. McClain. München 1972. S. 246-262.

Frank Ryder: "Introduction". In: F. Ryder (Hg.): *Die Novelle*. San Francisco 1971. S. XIII-XXVIII.

Walter Silz: "Geschichte, Theorie und Kunst der deutschen Novelle". In: *Der

Deutschunterricht 11 (1959), S. 82-100.

Martin Swales: *The German Novelle*. Princeton 1977.

Benno von Wiese: *Die Deutsche Novelle von Goethe bis Kafka*. Bd. 1: Düsseldorf 1956, 1971; Bd. 2: Düsseldorf 1965.

Ders.: *Novelle*. Stuttgart ⁷1978.

Gero von Wilpert: "Novelle". In: G. v. Wilpert: *Sachwörterbuch der Literatur*. Stuttgart ⁵1969. S. 526-529.

Chapter V
Theorie und Praxis der Novelle: Gottfried Keller

Summary

Ironic contrast between the decline of the novella as a primary genre in the XXth century and the simultaneous surge of novella scholarship. Misconceptions at the base of the attacks against normative/typological approaches to the novellesque. This essay will test the differentiated relationship between the typical and the individualistic elements in three major novellesque stories by Gottfried Keller: "The three righteous combmakers" (Die drei gerechten Kammacher, 1855-1856), "Romeo and Juliet in the Village" (Romeo und Julia auf dem Dorfe, 1855), and "Clothing makes People" (Kleider machen Leute, gestation period: 1860-1874). The major structural novellesque components chosen are the "one event" ("eine Begebenheit"), the "having actually occurred" ("sich ereignete"), the "unheard of" ("das unerhörte"), often with a marked ironic/paradoxical texture, "crisis > (near) catastrophe" ("Krise" > "Katastrophe"), and the novellesque "profile" of the story ("Falke, Silhouette") developing materially into the "object symbol" ("Dingsymbol") or musically into the "Leitmotif" ("Leitmotiv"). Each of these originally physical elements may move in the direction of the metaphysical ("metaphysische Pointe") without losing its material tangibleness: possible comparisons with analogous orientations in Goethe, Kleist, Conrad Ferdinand Meyer, Storm, Hauptmann, Hofmannsthal, Thomas Mann, Bergengruen, and Musil.

In conclusion, Keller is a signal example of a writer who, with all of his strong inclinations toward the epical, toward spinning a yarn, and the lyrical, toward visual intoxication and moralizing, all of which may impair the effect of the novellesque, nevertheless stuck to the dramatic foundation of the novellesque, disciplined rather than diluted by the epic form.

———————

Die Novelle darf sich nicht mehr über Mangel an Aufmerksamkeit von seiten der Wissenschaft beklagen. Jahrzehntelang fristete sie, von sporadischen, oft tüchtigen Einzeluntersuchungen abgesehen, ein recht bescheidenes Dasein im Schatten ihrer großen, im Lichte stehenden Schwester: des Dramas. Ein kümmerlicher Trost war das noch kläglichere Schicksal ihres Vetters, des Romans. Generationen hindurch stammte die einzige Gesamtdarstellung der deutschen Novelle von einem englischen Gelehrten (E. K. Bennett, 1934) – ein ironisch-paradoxer Zug, der ganz gut zu dem Wesen der Novelle paßt. In den 1950er Jahren aber ist aus dem Mauerblümchen eine Ballschönheit geworden, um die sich die renommiertesten Herren der Forschung eifrigst bewerben[1], und zwar gleichzeitig (wieder ein paradoxer,

---

[1]Um den Umfang dieses Beitrages zu beschränken, wird auf die meisten bibliographischen Angaben verzichtet. Eine verläßliche Aufführung der wichtigsten derzeitigen Sekundärliteratur zur Novelle findet sich bei Fritz Martini, "Die deutsche Novelle im bürgerlichen Realismus", *Wirkendes Wort X* (1960), No. 5, 257-278. Nachzutragen wäre hauptsächlich die zweite, verbesserte und erweiterte Auflage von E. K. Bennett, *A History of the German Novelle,* Cambridge 1961 (hrsg. von H. M. Waidson). Es sollte nicht vergessen werden, daß Hans Heinrich Borcherdt schon vor über 35 Jahren die Hauptmerkmale der Novelle festgelegt hat (*Geschichte des Romans und der Novelle in Deutschland.* I. Teil. Leipzig, 1926, S. 5-9). Eine ausführliche, aber sehr subjektive Übersicht über die Kellerforschung von den späten 1930er Jahren bis 1957 gibt Wolfgang Preisendanz in *Germanisch-Romanische Monatsschrift,* N. F., VIII (1958), S. 144 bis 178. – Den folgenden Damen und Herren meines Novellenseminars möchte ich meinen aufrichtigen Dank aussprechen für empfangene Anregungen: Käthe Dietrich, Walter Francke, Stephen Gilmour, David Halvorson, Maurice Heidinger, John Jacobson, Michael Means, Emma Nashan, Patricia Riesenman, Arnold Salip, Phyllis Smith, Frank Stanich, Paula Teich, Joseph Voyles, Carol Williams und Sibylle Wilson.

146

von Johannes Klein und Walter Silz hervorgehobener Zug) mit dem Niedergang der Novelle als lebendig-geübter Form im 20. Jahrhundert. Sie ist nicht mehr zeitgemäß. Die Kurzgeschichte hat sie abgelöst, aber nicht ersetzt.

Woran liegt das späte, aber nun um so raschere Aufblühen der Novellenforschung? Die Novelle ist erzählende Prosa und hat, wie (obgleich weniger als) der Roman, unter der etwas deklassierenden Verwandtschaft mit der Unterhaltungsliteratur, einer beliebten aber kaum respektablen »Gattung«, gelitten. Die schon bei Kleist deutlich erkennbaren Beziehungen der Novelle zur Journalistik – ein Begriff, der in Deutschland einen noch negativeren Beigeschmack hatte als anderswo – hat ihrer literarwissenschaftlichen Salonfähigkeit gewiß nicht genützt. Das trotz Hofmannsthals Protest deutsche Beharren auf dem Unterschied zwischen »Dichtung«, die etwas Sakrales an sich hat, und »Schriftstellerei«, von der etwas nüchtern Berechnendes, unromantisch Berufliches ausgeht, hat bis vor kurzem Roman und Novelle (mit Ausnahmen, natürlich) zu Stiefkindern der Forschung gemacht, denn der Lyrik und dem Drama wohnt eben, so wurde angenommen, *per se* das »Dichterische« eher inne als der Prosaerzählung. Nun ist es anders geworden. Liegt es vielleicht daran, daß man in der Novelle eine in der deutschen Literatur sonst seltene Verbindung von (romanischer) Formvollendung und (deutscher) Inhaltsschwere, (romanisch) Straffem und (deutsch) Beschaulichem, von (romanischer) Handlungskraft und (deutschem) Ideenreichtum, (romanisch) Physischem und (deutsch) Metaphysischem entdeckt hat?

Ein großer prinzipieller Gewinn darf und muß von der heutigen Novellenforschung erwartet werden. Unsere Sekundärliteratur fordert seit Jahren die Erfassung der Dichtkunst von der Sprache, der Form aus. Es wird etymologisiert, semantisiert, skandiert, rhythmisiert, syntaktisiert, strukturisiert, zyklisiert. Im einzelnen haben die Resultate oft überraschend viel, wenngleich etwas trockenes Neuland gewonnen, aber die Integrierung von dem Einmaligen des Einzelwerkes und dem Typischen des Historischen hat sich selten herstellen lassen. Die Novelle eignet sich besser als irgendeine andere literarische Form zum Brückenschlagen zwischen Inhalt und Form, Idee und Kunst, Geschichte und Interpretation.[2] Der Formkern der Novelle hat sich jahrhundertelang bewährt. Er steht mit dem Inhalt in ständiger polarer Wechselwirkung, die eine Entwicklung des Ideellen zwar keineswegs ausschlließt, ihr aber Kunstgrenzen setzt. Über diese Grenzen hinaus ist die Erzählung keine Novelle mehr.

Gerade hier hat sich in der Forschung ein zähes, um so bedauerlicheres Mißverständnis eingeschlichen. Es wird eingewandt: was tut es, ob dieses oder jenes Werk eine Novelle ist? Was hat das mit ihrer Qualität zu tun? Es *hat* etwas damit zu tun. Die Novellenstruktur ist kein von oben erlassener Ukas, keine schulmeisterliche Vorschrift, sondern ein gesundes, gewachsenes, gediegenes *organon,* eine geschichtlich fundierte Kunstforderung, eine Norm, wie sie Wellek für die Bewertung des einmaligen Kunstwerkes im Rahmen der Literaturgeschichte verlangt, und wie es unserer Generation obliegt, sie systematisch für die verschiedenen literarischen Kunstformen und Geschichtsperioden auszuarbeiten.[3] Wir dürfen *nicht* sagen: 'weil diese sich novellistisch gebende Geschichte das »Gesetz« der Novelle verletzt, ist sie zu Minderwertigkeit verurteilt', aber wir *dürfen* aus Erfahrung sagen, daß bei in dieser Richtung tendierender Prosa, welche die erprobten Grundmerkmale »novellistischen Erzählens« in von Wieses klug-bescheidener Formulierung nicht beachtet, die Gefahr groß ist, daß trotz aller möglichen Teilqualitäten ein unausgeglichenes, auseinanderklaffendes Gesamtwerk entsteht, ein Mischmasch (siehe z. B. die *künstlerischen* Mißtöne im *Ketzer*

---

[2]»Es lag dem Verfasser daran, die mit modernen Mitteln der Strukturforschung gewonnenen Ergebnisse fruchtbar zu machen für eine Betrachtung des Geschichtlichen. Die als Baumschulen aufgereihten Interpretationen beginnen langweilig zu werden, man sehnt sich wieder in die Wälder.« (Wolfgang Kayser, Vorwort zu *Das Groteske*, Oldenburg, 1957, S. 10).

[3]Da die Novelle eine romanische Kunstform ist, die sich seit Goethe aber gerade im deutschen Sprachgebiet zu hoher Blüte entwickelt hat, so mögen solche Novellennormen vielleicht auch für die europäische Literaturgeschichte grundlegende Erkenntnisse vermitteln.

von Soana oder der *Hirtennovelle*). Das bedeutet durchaus nicht, daß eine nach allen Regeln der Novellistik gebaute Novelle nun *eo ipso* gut ist; danach wären Heyse oder Emil Strauß die größten Novellisten, danach wäre C. F. Meyer ein größerer Novellendichter als Gottfried Keller. Die ausgezeichnetsten Novellen sind eine Verschmelzung von Typischem und Individuellem, deren Rezept in keiner Literaturapotheke, in keinem Lehrbuch oder Aufsatz zu holen ist, und die gewiß nicht vorausgesagt werden kann; aber das berechtigt den Novellisten nicht, wahllos unvereinbare Bestandteile zu mischen, wie es das »Genie« einem eingibt. Das würde auch beim Drama oder der Lyrik meist schlecht ausgehen.

Was hier folgt, ist ein bloßer Ansatz zur Novellenforschung aus einem solchen, normativen Blickwinkel heraus. Es soll an Hand von drei Kellerschen Novellen gezeigt werden, wie sich das typisch *Novellistische* in drei *Novellen* auswirkt; wie der unwiederholbare Künstler das wiederholbare Kunstgesetz gestaltet; wo das einmalig Subjektive sich von dem typisch Objektiven entfernt, und mit welchen Ergebnissen. Daran soll, unter jeder Norm, ein Ausblick auf *nach*kellersche Novellistik unter diesem Standpunkt geknüpft werden, um zu sehen, inwieweit Keller selbst normativ gewirkt haben mag. Ob bei solchen Vergleichen ein direkter oder indirekter Einfluß, oder reiner Zufall vorliegt, kann in diesem Rahmen nicht erörtert werden; das Phänomen als solches ist hier ohnehin wichtiger als die Ursache. Es soll also ein verbindender Mittelweg eingeschlagen werden zwischen den Novellenforschern, die das geschichtlich-Strukturelle an einer Unmasse von einzelnen Novellen messen wollen und darin ersticken, und denen, die auserlesene Meisternovellen als solche interpretieren und verständlicherweise die Einmaligkeit der Konfiguration des Einzelwerks schärfer unter die Lupe nehmen als das Normative. Wir glauben mit Auerbach, Wellek u.a., daß es möglich und wünschenswert ist, normative Werte aus den qualitativ besten oder charakteristischsten Werken einer Gattung und Periode zu entnehmen und die Variationen dieser Normen an diesen selben − und verwandten − Werken zu erproben. Daß eine solche Methode eine subjektive Auswahl einschließt, stört uns nicht, denn sowohl Literaturgeschichte wie Literaturkritik verfahren selektiv. Eine solche Auslese erwirbt *objektive Fundierung* durch die *wiederholte subjektive Auswahl* aufeinanderfolgender Generationen; was in so verschiedenen Zeiten gutgeheißen wird, wenn auch aus differenzierten Blickwinkeln, mit Variationen und Einschränkungen, das muß *objektiv gut* und deshalb *maßgebend* sein.

Wir setzen also voraus, daß Keller ein guter Novellist ist, daß *Kleider machen Leute, Die drei gerechten Kammacher* und *Romeo und Julia auf dem Dorfe* gute novellistische Erzählungen sind[4], und daß wir gewisse Grundzüge des Novellistischen als geschichtlich gesichert, als normative Vergleichspunkte ansehen dürfen[5]: *eine Begebenheit / sich ereignete / unerhörte* (ironisch-

---

[4]Wir leugnen durchaus nicht, daß man auch drei andere novellistische Geschichten von Keller hätte auswählen können; aber irgendwo muß man einmal anfangen. Unsere drei Novellen sind, glauben wir, Meisterwerke (ein leider abgedroschenes Wort), jede in ihrer Art: *Kleider machen Leute* mit ihrem märchenhaften, optimistischen Einschlag, als Gegensatz *Die drei gerechten Kammacher* mit ihrer pessimistich-grotesken Tönung, und *Romeo und Julia auf dem Dorfe* als Darstellung von Lebenslust und Lebenstragik in einmaliger menschlicher Eindringlichkeit: die Krönung der Kellerschen Erzählkunst. Wir halten es hierbei mit Keller, der die Gesetze der Novellistik an »mustergültigen« Novellen abgelesen sehen wollte. Daß er von der schulmäßigen Novellistik wenig hielt, ist uns bekannt. Letzten Endes ist ausschlaggebend, was er tat (d.h. wie er erzählte), nicht was er, aus Prinzip oder Augenblickslaune, hie und da über die Novellengattung zu sagen hatte; es war verhältnismäßig wenig und erlaubt kaum stichhaltige Schlußfolgerungen. Weit wichtiger ist – wenn es sich zeigen ließe –, daß er empirisch und instinktiv, ohne künstlich-schultheoretischen Einfluß, in seinen novellistischen Werken die gewachsene Struktur der Novelle einhielt; das wäre ein unverdächtiger Beweis für ihre normative Geltung.

[5]Damit soll keineswegs der Möglichkeit oder gar Notwendigkeit einer fortgesetzten Debatte über das Zutreffen dieser Gesichertheit widersprochen werden. Auch Geschichtliches wird von verschiedenen Augen verschieden gesehen. Aber selbst der objektivste Forscher muß sich schließlich, will er

paradoxe) <–/Neigung zur *Katastrophe/Falke–> Silhouette, Dingsymbol* (Leitmotiv)[6].

Eine Begebenheit

Der Begriff der »einen Begebenheit« deckt sich, streng genommen, mit keiner der drei Kellerschen Erzählungen. In *Kleider machen Leute* wird der arme, frierende Schneider von einer hochherrschaftlichen Kutsche mitgenommen; er wird in einem Gasthaus von den Honoratioren der Stadt als Graf angesehen und behandelt; er trifft Nettchen, verliebt sich in sie, macht mehrere Fluchtversuche, verlobt sich mit ihr, wird von den Seldwylern bloßgestellt, flieht wieder, wird von Nettchen gerettet, heiratet sie, lebt »zehn oder zwölf Jahre«[7] in Seldwyla und danach in Goldach. Das ist eine Reihe von Begebenheiten. Besteht man strikt auf *einer* Begebenheit, so muß man das Seldwyler Spiel »Kleider machen Leute« als das entscheidende Ereignis betrachten; beabsichtigt als vermeintliche Katastrophe für Wenzel, erhärtet es Nettchens Liebe zu ihm und führt zum happy ending. Zu eng allerdings sollte der Begriff der »einen Begebenheit« nicht gefaßt werden, sonst paßt er nur auf die Anekdote und Kurzgeschichte. Wenn man in Rechnung stellt, daß die

---

allgemeine Folgerungen ziehen, auf eine Hypothese stützen. Der Sinn der Arbeit liegt gerade in ihrer Überprüfung, Bestätigung oder Veränderung.

[6]Die vom Verfasser ausgearbeiteten Erörterungen der wichtigen Begriffe des Wendepunkts und der Pointe bei Keller müssen hier aus Raumgründen ausgelassen werden. Siehe dazu das Kapitel: "Wendepunkt und Pointe in der deutschen Novelle von Keller bis Bergengruen" in diesem Buch. Der bei der früheren Novelle so bedeutsame Rahmen büßt bei der späteren so sehr an Geltung ein und spielt überdies in den *Leuten von Seldwyla* eine so geringe Rolle, daß wir (trotz C. F. Meyer und Storm) von einer Behandlung hier absehen. Wir verweisen den Leser auf das Kapitel:"Der Rahmen in der deutschen Novelle: Dauer im Wechsel."

[7]Gottfried Keller, Sämtliche Werke, I, München, 1953, S. 839.

ganze Handlung von *Kleider machen Leute* sich fast ausschließlich um die Verhüllung und Enthüllung des Schneiders als Grafen dreht und sich von November bis Fastnacht abspielt, so kann man schließlich doch noch von »einer Begebenheit« sprechen, mit kurzem Vor- und Nachspiel.

Aber in den *Kammachern* und *Romeo und Julia* wäre selbst diese biegsame Auslegung der »einen Begebenheit« nicht mehr haltbar. Die erste Hälfte der Erzählung von den Kammachern erstreckt sich jahrelang über das ein-, zwei- und dreiträchtige Arbeiten und »Leben« (Vegetieren?) der Gesellen, das pointiert begebnislos ist; was wirklich zählt, nämlich ihre Geschäftspläne,, spielt sich hinter der Maske der »Gerechtsamkeit« ab. Der zweite Teil dagegen dreht sich um »*eine* Begebenheit«: das Wettrennen, mit einem knappen Nachspiel, traurig für Jobst und Fridolin, ironisch für Dietrich.

Romeo und Julia zerfällt ebenfalls in zwei Hälften. Die erste ist hier alles andere als begebnislos: sie schildert den entscheidenden Lebensabschnitt zweier Familien, den Abstieg von Wohlstand und (allerdings nicht ganz fleckenloser) Solidität zu Armut und Verfall, skandiert durch einschneidende Ereignisse: Furcheneinreißen, Auktion, Streit, Prozeß, Umzug nach der Stadt (Manz), Hauerei zwischen den Vätern, Steinwurf, Irrenhauseinlieferung (Marti). Die zweite Hälfte aber widmet sich wieder »*einer* Begebenheit«, den letzten 24 Stunden Salis und Vrenchens.

Man könnte auf Grund des Vorhergehenden folgende Hypothese aufstellen: die moderne Novelle *beschränkt* sich entweder auf *eine* Begebenheit oder enthält jedenfalls eine *entscheidende* Begebenheit (oft: gipfelt in ihr): Fastnachtsspiel *(Kleider)*, Wettrennen *(Kammacher)*, die letzten 24 Stunden eines »Hochzeitspaares« *(Romeo und Julia)*. Diese Hypothese würde, so glauben wir, durch Analyse weiterer »exemplarischer« Novellen bestätigt werden: *Die Hochzeit des Mönchs, Die Versuchung des Pescara, Die Reise nach Tilsit* (Titel = Begebenheit), *Der Schimmelreiter* (Deichbau und Deichbruch), *Bahnwärter Thiel* (Tobiäschen wird von der Eisenbahn überfahren), Hofmannsthal-Goethe-Bassompierres *Erlebnis des Marschalls von Bassompierre* (die Nacht mit der schönen Krämerin), *Tristan* (Gabrieles Spielen der Wagnerschen Tristanpartitur), *Der Ketzer von Soana* (Francescos Besuch beim Berghirten), *Der Schleier* (die Entdeckung des

Ehebruches), *Ein Landarzt* (Krankenbesuch), *Mario und der Zauberer* (Vor- und Verführungskunst Cipollas), *Die drei Falken* (die Versteigerung der Falken).

sich ereignete

Trotz der Reichweite der Novelle vom Dramatischen zum Märchenhaften muß sie wie eine sich ereignete *Geschichte* (d.h. etwas, was *geschehen* ist) erzählt werden; ob sie wirklich geschehen ist oder auf einem wahren Geschehnis fußt (wie es z. B. bei *Romeo und Julia* der Fall ist) ist weniger wichtig als daß sie bei aller Seltsamkeit mit solch selbstverständlichem Anspruch auf Wahrhaftigkeit berichtet wird, daß es dem Leser gar nicht einfällt, die Frage nach dem wirklichen Geschehen zu stellen. Daß der Hintergrund der Novelle ein realistischer, nicht breit ausgeführter sondern kräftig angedeuteter sein soll, daran hat sich seit Boccaccio, Cervantes, Goethe und Wieland nichts geändert. Es ist diese Forderung im mündlich-gesellschaftlichen Ursprung der Novelle enthalten: um eine intelligente, feinschmeckerische, etwas abgebrühte Gesellschaft zu unterhalten, erzählt man im allgemeinen keine Märchen oder Idyllen (mit denen man sich leicht lächerlich machen würde) sondern gibt sich den kühl-objektiven Anschein des Berichtenden.

So sind trotz des märchenhaften Einschlags von *Kleider machen Leute* und der idyllischen Durchtränkung *Romeo und Julias* beide »sich ereignete« Geschichten; bei den *Kammachern* erreichen Ironie und Satire manchmal den Punkt, wo der Leser die Absicht, das Konstruierte, das Moralisierende etwas zu deutlich merkt, aber auch sie wird als »heutzutage sich ereignet« erzählt.

unerhörte (ironisch-paradoxe)

Das »Unerhörte« als Bestandteil des Novellistischen bewegt sich auf zwei Ebenen. In der »Urnovelle« handelt es sich nur um eine unerhörte Begebenheit, ein frappantes außerordentliches Ereignis. Das hat die moderne Novelle beibehalten *müssen,* sonst gleitet sie in die *Erzählung.* Ein Schneider, der sich als Graf ausgibt (genauer: es sich gefallen läßt, als Graf angesehen zu werden und diese passive Rolle auch *außerordentlich* überzeugend spielt); Kammacher, die sich in einen Wettlauf um die Hand einer Jungfer verwickeln;

ein blutjunges, unverheiratetes Paar, das auf einem gestohlenen Heuschiff »Hochzeit« feiert – das sind die ungewöhnlichen, aber keineswegs unglaublichen Ereignisse, auf die damals wie heute mit dem Ausruf: »Das ist ja unerhört!« reagiert werden würde. Wie »eine Begebenheit« darf auch »unerhört« nicht zu kraß aufgefaßt werden: es bedeutet im Grunde eine »noch nicht gehörte« oder *so* – in dieser Fassung – noch nicht gehörte Neuigkeit, etwas spezifisch-schlagend-(oft)Skandalöses, aber nicht immer etwas einzigartig Unwiederholbares: jahraus – jahrein gibt es betrügerische Personifizierer *(Kleider)*, »wettlaufende« Liebeskonkurrenten *(Kammacher)* und »wilde« Hochzeiter *(Romeo und Julia)*.

Im Zuge der modernen Verfeinerung und Vertiefung der Novelle (was sie übrigens nicht immer als *Kunstwerk* verstärkt) verbindet sich dieses begebnishaft »Unerhörte« mit einem psychologisch unerhörten, meist ironisch Paradoxen. Denn es ist nicht so unerhört, daß in *Kleider machen Leute* der Schneider den Grafen markiert, als daß er seinem ganzen Wesen nach wirklich mehr Graf als Schneider *ist*. Und noch unerhörter vielleicht ist, daß das geprellte, dem Skandal und der Lächerlichkeit preisgegebene Fräulein aus dem besten Bürgerstand trotz allem ihre Karten auf den Schneider setzt – und gewinnt[8].

In den *Kammachern* ist der Wettlauf als solcher kaum so unerhört wie die geradezu schauerlich-groteske Diskrepanz zwischen dem märchenhaften Motiv des Wettbewerbs dreier armer »Schneiderlein« (lies: Kammacher) um die Hand der »Prinzessin« (lies: Züs) und der Realität: den drei Gesellen (besonder den zwei älteren) blutet das Herz, an einer solchen, ihnen ganz ungemäßen Konkurrenz teilzunehmen, sie beschwören die dummkluge, blutlos unmenschliche »Prinzessin«, sie damit zu verschonen; sie haben furchtbare Magenschmerzen, und schließlich machen sich die beiden älteren durch ihren verzweifelt verbissenen, in Schlägerei ausartenden Wettlauf ganz unmöglich,

---

[8] "Das rein menschliche... ist im Einfachen und Natürlichen gerade das Außerordentliche und Wunderbare." (Benno von Wiese, *Die deutsche Novelle von Goethe bis Kafka,* Düsseldorf, 1956, S. 240.)

sie vernichten sich gegenseitig, einer erhängt sich, der andere verkommt: das ist das (erweitert) Unerhörte. Und man kann noch einen Schritt weiter gehen und sagen, daß der seltsame, beunruhigende Widerspruch zwischen dem äußerlich friedfertigen, gutbürgerlich arbeitsamen, symmetrischen Benehmen der Kammacher und ihrem leidenschaftlich verhaltenen Konkurrenzneid, der schon vor dem Wettrennen in eine grausig-groteske, kreischende Nachthemdszene ausbricht, der Geschichte eine gewisse paradoxe Grundstimmung verleiht.

In *Romeo und Julia* ist das Unerhörte nicht so sehr die wilde Hochzeit auf gestohlenem Brautbett als die Tatsache, daß, wie der Schneider im innersten *doch* ein Graf, so auch Vrenchen und Sali nicht nur dem Schein sondern dem *Sein* nach *wirklich* Eheleute sind; das Paradoxe, daß ihre von der Gesellschaft, den »guten Bürgern« nicht anerkannte Verbindung gerade deshalb, *weil* sie von den beiden gutbürgerlich ernst genommen wird, in den Tod führen muß. Erweitert man den Begriff des Unerhörten für diese Geschichte, so ist der Abstieg der beiden wohlhabenden Bauersleute zu Armut, Spelunkendasein, Hehlerei, Schlägerei und Irrenanstalt gewiß »unerhört«, aber ebenso außergewöhnlich, ja »wunderbar« ist das Unberührtsein der Kinder von diesem radikalen Verkommen der Eltern.

Auch in dieser Beziehung ist Keller, wie uns scheint, charakteristisch für die Entwicklung der modernen Novelle, in der das Unerhörte psychologisch verfeinert und erweitert wird, aber ohne damit das für die Novelle unerläßliche Unerhörte der Begebenheit (d. h. das Dramatische) zu opfern. Im *Pescara* gesellt sich zu dem (unerhörten) Versuch, den Feldherrn des Kaisers zum Verrat zu bringen, der noch außergewöhnlichere, paradoxe Umstand, daß der vom Tode gezeichnete Held fast bereits außerhalb der Versuchung steht. Im *Schimmelreiter* erhalten der Deichbruch und der selbstgewollte Sturz des Deichgrafen ins Wasser ein »unerhört« ironisches Merkmal dadurch, daß Hauke zeitlebens den Aberglauben der Menschen- und Tieropfer zur Sicherung des Deichs bekämpft hat, nun aber selbst, in einer im Grunde eher heidnischen als christlichen Geste, sich als freiwilliges Sühne- und Götterberuhigungsopfer in die Fluten wirft. Das Unerhörte verdichtet sich hier weiter zu einer alles durchdringenden, unheimlichen Stimmung, dem Kampf auf Leben und Tod zwischen Chaos und Ordnung, Heidnischem und Christlichem, Aberglaube und Glaube, Masse und Deichgraf, Übergott und Gott.

Das Unerhörte im *Bahnwärter Thiel* ist nicht nur das Überfahren des Tobiäschens, der Doppelmord und die Einlieferung des Bahnwärters in eine Irrenanstalt, sondern daß diese grausigen Taten und Ereignisse einen scheinbar in jeder Beziehung durchschnittlichen, ja sogar unterdurchschnittlichen Menschen betreffen oder von ihm ausgehen. Wenn man aber diesen anscheinend ganz farblosen Mann näher kennenlernt, so wird die unerwartet intensive, leidenschaftliche Mystik seines Unterbewußtseins zum Unerhörtesten der Geschichte. Ähnlich ist das Unerhörte im *Mario und der Zauberer* und in Bergengruens *Drei Falken* nicht nur, daß ganz unerwartet ein Zauberkünstler niedergeknallt oder ein Falke befreit wird, sondern daß diese Handlungen durch, wie es aussieht, ganz primitive, unbedeutende Männer erfolgen. In beiden Fällen hat das Unerhörte eine ironisch-gesellschaftliche Färbung: die befreiende Tat kommt nicht aus der Aristokratie, dem Bürgertum, von den Gebildeten, sondern aus dem (unverbildeten) Volke. Das Unerhörte in Hofmannsthals *Bassompierre* ist nicht nur das plötzliche Verschwinden der Krämerin, sondern der geheimnisvolle Widerspruch zwischen ihrer kleinbürgerlichen Stellung und sexuellen Willfährigkeit einerseits, ihrer großartig-aristokratishcen, skrupulösen Persönlichkeit andererseits. In Manns *Tristan* wird das Unerhörte (Verführung durch Musik) verfeinert zum Paradoxen durch den Umstand, daß ein Impotenter durch ästhetische Sympathien und von Wagner geborgter musikalischer Sexualität die Verführung erfolgreich durchführt.

Krise –> Katastrophe

Die Neigung der Novelle zu Krise und Katastrophe ist oft vermerkt worden, allerdings mehr im einzelnen als im ganzen. Die drei Novellen Kellers enden entweder in einer Katastrophe *(Kammacher, Romeo und Julia)* oder vermeiden sie gerade noch *(Kleider machen Leute). Aquis Submersus, Die Hochzeit des Mönchs, Der Schimmelreiter, Bahnwärter Thiel, Bassompierre, Der kleine Herr Friedemann, Tristan, Tod in Venedig, Der*

156

Amokläufer, Hirtennovelle, Ein Landarzt – sie alle enden in »Katastrophen«. Gelegentlich wird die Katastrophe gemildert durch einen dem Schicksal abgerungenen halben Sieg: Pescara stirbt, aber rettet Mailand; der Schimmelreiter stirbt, aber sein Deich besteht; Ansas ertrinkt, aber Indre wird gerettet und trägt ein Kind *(Die Reise nach Tilsit)*. Selten hat die Katastrophe einen positiven Charakter *(Mario)*. Die in Cervantes' beispielhafte Tradition fallenden moralisch-novellistischen Erzählungen neigen eher zu versöhnlichen Abschlüssen *(Der Schleier, Die drei Falken)*.

Falke-Silhouette –> Dingsymbol –> Leitmotiv

Von allen Novellenkonzepten scheint dasjenige der »Silhouette«, des »Falken« das unumstrittenste, grundsätzlichste zu sein. Aber auch hier hat der »Erfinder« des Begriffs – wie Tieck bei seinem »Wendepunkt« – bei allem Verdienst Unklarheiten gelassen. Heyse verlangt, »die zu erzählende, kleine Geschichte [soll] eine starke, deutliche Silhouette habe[n], deren Umriß, in wenigen Worten vorgetragen, schon einen charakteristischen Eindruck mache, wie der Inhalt der Geschichte des *Decamerone* vom »Falken« in fünf Zeilen berichtet sich dem Gedächtnis tief einprägt[9].« Der Novellenerzähler solle sich zuerst fragen, »wo der >Falke< sei, das Spezifische, das diese Geschichte von tausend anderen unterscheidet[10].« Das bedeutet nichts anderes, als daß die Novelle eine präzise, geraffte Handlung haben muß, etwas Auffallendes, schwer zu Vergessendes, was sich in wenige Worte fassen läßt. Worin nun aber das Auffallende, Eigenartige liegt, darüber scheint sich Heyse weniger klar gewesen zu sein. Ist es der Umriß der Gesamthandlung? Ist es die »äußere Zufallswendung, die aber die Charaktere tiefer entwickelt[11]?« Oder weist das Bildliche, Objekthafte der Begriffe »Silhouette« und des »Falken«

---

[9]Paul Heyse, *Jugenderinnerungen und Bekenntnisse,* 3. Auflage, Berlin, 1900. S. 348.

[10]Paul Heyse, *Deutscher Novellenschatz,* München, o. J. (1871), I. S. XX.

[11]*Ibid.*

nicht schon darauf hin, daß ein konkreter Gegenstand die Novelle zusammenhält, ihr das Straffe, Einleuchtende, Reale mitteilt, was ihr einen spezifisch-unvergeßbaren Charakter gibt? So genügt das *eine* Wort des »Falken«, um der Erzählung des Boccaccio (9. Geschichte des 5, Tages) ihre »Silhouette« zu geben; dieselben Funktionen erfüllen die drei »Ringe« (3. Gesch. des 1. Tages), die »Hühner« (5. Gesch. des 1. Tages), die abgeschnittenen »Haare« (2. Gesch. des 3. Tages), der »Krug« Wein (2. Gesch. des 6. Tages), das »Faß« (2. Gesch. des 7. Tages), »Mörser« und »Chorrock« (2. Gesch. des 8. Tages), die »Truhe« (8. Gesch. des 8. Tages), usw. Die spätere Entwicklung dieses »Falken« zu einem Dingsymbol wird gelegentlich bei Boccaccio schon vorweggenommen; so hat der Falke in der Geschichte von Federigo degli Alberighi, Frau Giovanna und deren Sohn je nachdem aktive und passive Symbolkraft für das Schlichte aber Edle, Ungebrochene, für Freundschaft, Treue und Liebe, für würdig ertragene Armut, für unstillbare Sehnsucht, Rettung, und Tod. In den »beispielhaften« Novellen von Cervantes wird diese Symbolkraft weiter entwickelt – man denke an das »Glas« des *Licenciado Vidriera*, an »Blut« und »Kruzifix« in der *Fuerza de la Sangre*. Ansätze zu moderner Leitmotivtechnik finden sich auch schon bei Boccaccio, z.B. das eindeutige »Den-Teufel-in-die-Hölle-schicken«-Motiv der 10. Novelle des 3. Tages, oder das schon mit feinen Nuancen durchgeführte Nachtigallenmotiv der 4. Geschichte des 5. Tages.

Wo stehen Kellers drei Novellen in der Entwicklung: Handlungssilhouette –> Falke –> Dingsymobol –> Leitmotiv? *Kleider machen Leute* hat einen »Umriß, [der] in wenigen Worten vorgetragen« werden kann, etwa: »Ein Schneider wird als Graf angesehen und behandelt, und gewinnt die Hand eines reichen, schönen, guten und energischen Mädchens.« In den *Drei gerechten Kammachern* wäre die Silhouette schon problematischer: »Drei Kammacher bewerben sich um eine Jungfer. Der Außenseiter gewinnt sie, während die beiden andern zugrundegehen.« Aber das ließe etwas weniger als die ganze erste Hälfte der Erzählung außer acht, in der die Kammacher mit verbissener Friedfertigkeit um das Geschäft wetteifern und Züs zwar vorgestellt, aber noch nicht von den Gesellen umworben wird. Hier ist, wie schon vorher angedeutet, wenn auch kein Bruch,

158

so doch ein Einschnitt in der Erzählung, welcher eine einheitliche Handlungssilhouette schwächt. In *Romeo und Julia* vollends haben wir es mit einer sich über zwölf Jahre erstreckenden Familientragödie zu tun, deren erstes Drittel durch den Niedergang von Manz und Marti und deren letztes Drittel durch »Hochzeits« -tag und -nacht Salis und Vrenchens bestimmt wird, während das (etwas kürzere) zweite Drittel einen Übergang zwischen beiden Handlungen bildet, in dem Sali und Vrenchen bereits das Übergewicht erhalten, die Väter aber noch eine wichtige Rolle spielen. Eine einheitliche Handlungssilhouette »in wenigen Worten vorgetragen« kommt hier nicht mehr in Frage.

Wir möchten folgende Hypothese aufstellen: je mehr sich die Handlungssilhouette auflöst, desto stärker muß der Autor darauf bedacht sein, das konzentriert Charakteristische der Novelle durch andere novellistische Mittel aufrechtzuerhalten. Zu diesen gehören bildliche »Falken« (Allegorien oder Dingsymbole) und musikalische »Falken« (Leitmotive). Da die Handlungssilhouette in *Kleider machen Leute* noch einheitlich und schlagend genug ist, kann sich Keller hier mit allegorischen Falken begnügen: Fingerhut (= Schneider), Pelzmütze und mit Samt ausgeschlagener Radmantel (= Graf). Auch sonst ist das Nur-Allegorische hier stark vertreten: Gasthof zur Waage, Gasthaus zum Regenbogen, Zur Fortuna (Wohnung des Amtsrats), sonstige Häuserbenennungen, Schlittengalions, usw.

In den *Kammachern,* deren novellistische Handlung eigentlich erst in der zweiten Hälfte (Wettlauf um Züs) beginnt, fehlt es an *einem* »Falken«, aber nicht an ironischen Allegorien und Dingsymbolen: die Kämme (in denen sich Dienstmädchenromantik und prosaischer Nutzen mischen), die im Frühling wiederauferstandene, blau getünchte Wanze (frühlingshaft-menschliche Wanderlust eines parasitischen Lebewesens, = Kammacher), Züs' Schnepper (Symbol ihrer geizigen Parasitennatur: sie hat selbst kein »Blut«, aber saugt es gern aus anderen) und ihre Nippsachen (Allegorien ihrer prätentiösen Sammelwut, tote Attrappen, äußerer Ersatz für das ihr fehlende »Leben«), besonders der Tempel mit dem auf seinem innersten Grunde versteckten, ihr unbekannten Liebesbrief (ihre Unfähigkeit, in ein wahres Herzensgefühl zu schauen): »... Eine falsche Schöne bekam das nicht zu Gesicht, was sie nicht zu sehen verdiente. Auch war es ein Symbol, daß sie es war, welche das törichte, aber innige und aufrichtig gemeinte Wesen des Buchbinders nicht verstanden[12].« Symbolhaft ist auch das Wettrennen (unsinnig-lächerlicher Akt bornierter aber friedfertiger, vernünftiger Männer um eines unechten, im Grunde wertlosen Besitzes wegen, ganz ähnlich wie das sinnlose Prozessieren von Manz und Marti in *Romeo und Julia)*. Leitmotivisch wirkt die ironische Wiederholung von »gerecht« und der Gebrauch der Ziffer »drei«. Wir tun Keller wohl aber kein Unrecht an, wenn wir zugeben, daß in den *Kammachern* Handlungssilhouette, Allegorien, Dingsymbole und Leitmotive kaum ausreichen, um der auf der Grenzlinie zwischen Erzählung und Novelle stehenden Geschichte den prägnanten novellistischen Zug zu verleihen; trotz prachtvoller Einzelheiten hat sich Keller doch vielleicht zu sehr mit Katalogisieren, Kommentieren und Fabulieren aufgehalten und dieser Erzählung etwas bizarr-Gesuchtes mit auf den Weg gegeben, das selbst ihre großartige, ironisch-humorvolle Bitterkeit nicht ganz überbrücken kann.

Mit nur allegorischen Falken ist es in der weit ausgreifenden Novelle *Romeo und Julia* nicht mehr getan; fast alle erheben sich hier zu symbolischer Bedeutung, von noch halb-allegorischen bildlichen Motiven (die Zipfelmützen der Bauern weisen auf den Zipfelstreit wie auch die Narrenkappe Martis hin, die von der Bäuerin mitgenommene Bettstatt Vrenchens auf ihr späteres »Brautbett«, nämlich das entwendete Heuschiff; die von Sali »mit ins Bett« genommenen Brautschuhe Vrenchens sind ein erotisches Präludium zu ihrer späteren Vereinigung) zu Dingen und Wesen eindringlichster und umfassendster Symbolik: der Acker (das Solide, Fundamentale, Beständige, Ernährende – die Erde, Recht und Unrecht), das Wasser (das ebenso fundamental Fließende, Abgründige, Wechselnde, Unwiederbringliche, Unwiderrufliche; täuschendes Vorspiegeln des Erwerbs [das Fischen Manz', Martis und der Seldwyler]; das Erotische; das Säubernd-Sühnende; Leben und Tod). Acker und Fluß zusammen markieren die Pole der Existenz Salis und Vrenchens, ihr Geschick führt vom Acker erst zum sie trennenden, dann ins

---

[12]Keller, *op. cit.*, I, S. 755.

sie vereinigende Wasser; beide sind (je zweimal) die Stätten ihrer Liebesbezeugung: Acker – Wasser – (Brücke *darüber*) – Acker – Wasser (*darin*). Der Steinhaufen auf dem Ackerzipfel ist das Monument der Gemütsversteinerung, der künstlichen Trennung, der menschlichen Verwilderung, der Störung des Gleichgewichts zwischen Natur und Ordnung. An der Grenze des Allegorischen steht die Ansiedlung »zahlloser... feuerrot[er] Mohnblumen« auf diesem »ungerechten Steinhaufen[13]«: das Wachsen der Liebesleidenschaft (Mohn – Opium) auf steinigem Grund (Väter). Diese Dingsymbole (Acker – Wasser – Steinhaufen – Mohnblumen) werden durch ein menschliches Symbol, den schwarzen Geiger, verbunden, der von der »rotbekleideten Steinmasse« *seines* Ackers dem Pärchen zuruft, er »würde gewiß noch erleben, daß sie vor ihm den Weg alles Fleisches gingen[14]«, und sie an der Spitze der grotesk-schauerlichen »Hochzeits«-prozession wirklich den Weg bis dicht an den Strom führt. Er verkörpert das Unrecht der Väter, von dem die Kinder sich so schwer lösen können wie von der Gegenwart des Geigers; die Gefahren und Freuden der Gesetzlosigkeit; illegitime Liebesleidenschaft, der er seine Geburt und gesellschaftliche Verfolgung, seine Bitterkeit aber auch freien Lebensgenuß verdankt, und in die er nun Sali und Vrenchen hineinzuziehen versucht. Und er ist der Tod, der auf die Liebenden wartet, ein halb schreckhafter, halb freundschaftlicher Tod. Leben und Tod verbindet auch das Fisch- und Fischenmotiv: erst die illusorisch-verzweifelte Ersatztätigkeit der Väter, halb Erwerb, halb Spiel, dann, für Sali und Vrenchen, das übermütig todeslustige Symbol der Absage an die herrschende soziale Ordnung im Namen ihrer eigenen höheren Ordentlichkeit, des unbeschwerten, menschliche Gravität abstreifenden, kreaturhaften Liebesspiels im Medium des unendlich Flüssigen und Leichten, Symbol des Traumes einer Metamorphose, des »stirb und werde«: »Fische fingen wir

---

[13]*Ibid*, S. 675.

[14]*Ibid*.

damals, jetzt werden wir selber Fische sein und zwei schöne große[15].« Noch eine symbolische Szene verbindet Leben, Spiel und Tod: das Hineinsperren der »großen blauen« Fliege in den seines Inhalts entleerten, mit Gras verstopften Puppenkopf, der (man beachte die Symbolverstärkung) »feierlich auf einen *Stein*«gesetzt und mit einer »*roten Mohnblume*«bedeckt wird und nun gleich »einem weissagenden Haupte« darin tönt, »und die Kinder lauschten in tiefer Stille seinen Kunden und Märchen, indessen sie sich umschlungen hielten[16]«. Ein prophetisches Vorspiel wiederum nicht nur zum »lebendigen Begräbnis« von Vrenchens Vater[17], sondern auch zu den später »lebendig von der Gesellschaft begrabenen«, sich ohne Ausweg sehenden »Kindern«: was erst Spiel ist, wird später bitterer Ernst (ihre kindlichen Liebesspiele werden später ebenfalls leidenschaftlicher Ernst).

Diese existentielle, bildkräftige Symbolik *Romeo und Julias* kehrt in rhythmischen Abständen wieder, verstärkt sich selbst und gegenseitig, wirkt also, obgleich nicht in sich selbst musikalisch (wie später bei Thomas Mann), doch leitmotivisch. Fügen wir nun noch die hochentwickelte Farbensymbolik (schwarz, rot, blau, braun) und die nicht, oder nur halb, bildlichen Ausdrücke hinzu, die leitmotivisch auftreten (wild, feurig, verwirrt, ehr-, ratlos), dann ergibt sich in *Romeo und Julia* eine Dichte, eine Dramatik, eine Tiefe der umfassenden Symbolik, die aus dem Stoff zu einem Roman eine geschlossene Novelle webt – eine, wir wagen es zu sagen, in ihrer Vollendetheit gleichzeitig beispielhafte und unerreichbare Novelle. Nur Storms *Schimmelreiter* ist ihr darin vergleichbar. Wie Keller in *Romeo und Julia* Abstieg und Kontinuität zweier Generationen in entscheidenden Lebensabschnitten entwickelt, so zwingt Storm sogar drei Generationen und das *ganze* Leben der zweiten (Hauke Haiens) in den Rahmen der Novelle; und wieder ist es die Kraft und vielfältige Grundsätzlichkeit seiner Dingsymbolik, die dem Novellistischen

---

[15]*Ibid.*, S. 704.

[16]*Ibid.*, S. 655.

[17]*Ibid.*, S. 681.

den Ausschlag gibt: das Dämonisch-Elementare, Schicksal, Nacht, Tod und Nichts (die See), das Menschlich-Ordnende (der Deich), die Mischung von beiden (Hybris und Ratio) in Hauke und den ihm zugeordneten Lebewesen: Möwe (christliches Motiv der Bezähmung des Wilden) und Hund (Haukes »christliche« Rettung des zum heidnischen Opfer ausersehenen Tieres), die schwachsinnige Wienke (deren unzertrennliche Gefährten Möwe und Hund sind), Symbol der von der See erlangten Sühne für die ihr durch den Deichbau entgangenen Menschenopfer, der Schimmel (dämonisch-germanischer Streithengst, Wotanspferd, von Hauke halb aus »christlichem« Mitleid, halb aus elementarem Verbundenheitsgefühl gerettet, für Mitmenschen und Leser Symbol seiner Hybris); die Stormschen Varianten zu Kellers schwarzem Geiger (die, wie der Geiger, ebenfalls ganz gutmütige »Hexe« Trins, der teuflischere »Slowak«). Auch hier sind diese Symbole rhythmisch verflochten und werden durch abstraktere »Leitmotive« ergänzt: das Todes-, das Opfer-, das Händedruckmotiv.

Man darf gewiß nicht Dasein und Zahl von Dingsymbolen als solche ohne weiteres zum entscheidenden Prüfstein für den Wert einer Novelle machen. Und doch muß es auffallen, daß unter den besseren modernen deutschen Novellen, denen die Handlung selbst nicht die nötige novellistische Straffheit (wie noch bei Kleist) gibt, die weniger hervorragenden im Allegorischen stecken bleiben (*Aquis Submersus, Die Versuchung des Pescara, Der Ketzer von Soana)*, die besten aber durch überzeugende Dingsymbolik zusammengehalten werden *(Bahnwärter Thiel)* oder durch eine Verbindung von Dingsymbolik, Leitmotiv und Stimmungseinheit: Hofmannsthals *Reitergeschichte, Der kleine Herr Friedemann, Tristan, Der Tod in Venedig, Mario und der Zauberer.* Daß die bewußte Anwendung rezeptmäßiger Dingsymbolik auch ein künstlich-unlebendiges Werk zeitigen kann, zeigt Emil Strauß' meist überschätzter *Schleier;* daß straffe Handlungssilhouette, das Falkenhafte, Dingsymbolik und Sprachmeisterschaft *doch* noch ein zwar edles, aber zu sauberes, zu konstruiertes novellistisches Werk hervorbringen, beweisen Bergengruens *Die drei Falken.* Der Novellist muß zu allem Fingerspitzengefühl und technischem Können noch eine sowohl horizontal umfassende wie vertikal durchdringende Daseinsperspektive besitzen. Aber auch das genügt noch nicht: er muß letzten Endes das Etwas haben, was »imstande ist, aus einem Literaten einen Dichter zu machen«, die »Bürgerliebe zum Menschlichen, Lebendigen und Gewöhnlichen. Alle Wärme, alle Güte, aller Humor kommt aus ihr, und fast will mir scheinen, als sei sie jene Liebe selbst, von der geschrieben steht, daß einer mit Menschen- und Engelszungen reden könne und ohne sie doch nur ein tönendes Erz und eine klingende Schelle sei[18].«

Kellers Kenntnis des Novellistischen war ganz undogmatisch, aber desto verankerter in seinem gesunden Wesen. Sie gründete sich praktisch-empirisch auf ihm vertraute, für ihn mustergültige Novellen, instinktiv auf seinen künstlerischen Takt, die Gradlinigkeit seines Charakters und Schaffens. Daß gerade er, bei seiner starken Neigung zum Epischen und Lyrischen, zu Fabulieren, Moralisieren und Bildrausch – (Elementen, die der sparsam-strengen Novelle gefährlich werden können), *doch* den dramatischen, durch das Epische nur gebändigten Grundzug der Novelle erkannte und ihm treu blieb, das lassen, so hoffen wir, die obigen Ausführungen durchblicken, die sich alle auf wesentlich dramatisch-straffe Hauptlinien der Novelle beziehen: *eine sich ereignete unerhörte Begebenheit, Neigung zur Katastrophe, Falke, Silhouette, Dingsymbol.* Diesen erprobten Begriffen gab er neue Schattierungen, Erweiterungen, Tiefen (so wird die Verbindung zwischen dem Unerhörten und dem Ironisch-Paradoxen betont; Allegorie wird Dingsymbol, Dingsymbol wird Leitmotiv). Zu diesen novellistischen Prinzipien tritt Keller als Mensch und Dichter schlechthin. Seine »Bürgerliebe«, seine warme, aber von der Intelligenz unbestechlicher Menschenkenntnis überwachte Vitalität, sein Gefühl des Wahren und Beständigen und seine unbeirrbare Sensitivität für das Falsche und Gespreizte, seine unbedingte Ehrlichkeit und Charakterfestigkeit, sein Wissen um die enge Verwandtschaft von Tragik und Humor im menschlichen Leben, und die Frische und Echtheit seiner Sprache, die in der deutschen Prosa ihresgleichen sucht – diese Werte erst, in

---

[18]Thomas Mann, "Tonio Kröger", in *Erzählungen,* (Frankfurt), 1960, S. 338.

Verbindung mit seiner novellistischen Ader, weisen ihm in der Geschichte der deutschen Novelle des XIX. Jahrhunderts einen in jeder Beziehung zentralen Platz zu, eine beispielhafte Stellung nicht im Sinne dürrer Regeln, sondern organischer Struktur.

Chapter VI
Wendepunkt und Pointe in der deutschen Novelle von Keller bis Bergengruen

Summary

A "turn" ("Wendung") or "turning point" ("Wendepunkt") as one of the principal hallmarks of the novellesque has been identified since the earliest novella research by German Romantics (August Wilhelm von Schlegel, Ludwig Tieck) up to more recent one but its exact location or locations has been left murky (see introductory paragraph and Notes). It is here proposed to distinguish between two fundamentally novellesque turning points: 1) the actual trigger of novellesque action (not synonymous with the beginning of the story), the circuit breaker, the release ("Auslösender Wendepunkt") that unleashes the forces determining the novellesque core, and 2) the dissolving, final novellesque turn ("Auflösender Wendepunkt") after which the novellesque action quickly runs toward the end. The final, decisive turning point is not synonymous with the ultimate punch line ("Pointe") that is transferred from the genre of the anecdote, a terse, pointed observation, an ironic-paradoxical last twist bringing, like the effective last lines of a scene or act in a drama, an unexpected stimulus in the last moment, leading to the 'quiet mulling over' the story ("einen stillen Reiz, weiter nachzudenken[1]") which the Baroness in Goethe's "Conversations of German Emigrés" (Unterhaltungen deutscher Ausgewanderten, 1794-1795) *considers essential to the enjoyment of listeners after a novellesque-like story has been told.*

Finally, there is what has been termed the "metaphysical twist" ("metaphysische Pointe"), a usually unarticulated but implied, suggested, or possible intrusion of metaphysical intervention or fate sealing the story,

---

[1]*Goethes Werke*, Hamburger Ausgabe, Wegner, 1960 (1951), VI, 167.

166

raising questions but not elaborating on them, leaving them rather to post-story-telling reflections of the reader/listener and thus contributing to the readers' role as co-creator, collaborator of the story, a very novellesque trait: for the principal teller of the story ought to refrain from explicit interpretation which should be left to the audience.

Authors who are tested against these hypotheses include, besides Keller: Schiller, Kleist, C.F. Meyer, Storm, Hauptmann, Sudermann, Hofmannsthal, Emil Strauss, Bergengruen, Thomas Mann, Kafka, and Wiechert.

Einer Anregung August Wilhelm von Schlegels folgend hat Tieck bereits am Ende der 1820er Jahre im Zuge seiner Bemühung, die Novelle genauer zu umschreiben, den Masstab des Wendepunktes definiert.[2] Er ist für ihn "diese Wendung der Geschichte, dieser Punkt, von welchem aus sie unerwartet völlig umkehrt, und doch natürlich, dem Charakter und den Umständen angemessen, die Folge entwickelt."[3] Tieck gebührt das Verdienst, nicht nur die Tatsache dieses Wendepunktes, sondern auch seine bezeichnenden Merkmale ("unerwartet . . . völlig umkehrt . . . und doch natürlich"), welche die Verwandtschaft zwischen Novelle und Drama

---

[2]In Anbetracht des uns zur Verfügung stehenden Raumes verzichten wir auf ausgedehnte Literaturangaben; wir begnügen uns mit Stichproben charakteristischer Interpretationsrichtungen.

[3]A. W. von Schlegel hatte von "entscheidenden Wendepunkten" gesprochen, deren "die Novelle bedarf, so dass die Hauptmassen der Geschichte deutlich in die Augen fallen" *(Vorlesungen über Schöne Literatur und Kunst* [1803/4], III. Teil: *Geschichte der Romantischen Literatur,* hrsg. von J. Minor, in *Deutsche Literaturdenkmale des 18. und 19. Jahrhunderts* XIX [Stuttgart, 1884], S. 245.) – Ludwig Tieck, *Schriften,* XI [Berlin, 1829], S. lxxxvi.

präzisieren (die Peripeteia), ein für allemal erkannt zu haben. Er hat aber im Unklaren gelassen, *wo* in der Erzählung dieser Wendepunkt liegt, und die seitherige Novellenforschung hat wenig getan, diese strukturell wichtige Frage zu klären. Tieck erweckt den Eindruck, als läge der Wendepunkt gegen den Anfang hin oder wenigstens im ersten Teil der Erzählung; von Grolman sagt, er müsse in der Mitte liegen.[4] Bei anderen ist der Begriff noch verwischter,

---

[4]Adolf von Grolman, "Goethes *Novelle*", *Germanisch-Romanische Monatsschrift* IX (1921), S. 183. – Als Beispiel eines solchen Wendepunktes in Goethes Ferdinandnovelle *(Unterhaltungen deutscher Ausgewanderten)* gibt Tieck den sich öffnenden Schreibtisch an. Dieser Vorfall liegt im ersten Drittel der Erzählung. Gleich danach erhebt Tieck dann aber auch "die Reue und Besserung des Jünglings, die in eine Zeit fällt, dass sie fast unnütz wird" (1xxxvii) zu einem gleichwertigen Wendepunkt (s.a. Hellmuth Himmel, *Geschichte der deutschen Novelle,* Bern, 1963, S. 35-38). Dieser liegt kurz vor der Mitte der Geschichte. Tieck verwässert den Wendepunktbegriff weiter, indem er "das sonderbare Verhältnis der Sperata im *Meister"* und "dessen Folgen" dazu rechnet (1xxxvii). Nach dieser Pluralisierung des Wendepunktes kehrt Tieck wieder zur Einzahl zurück: "In jeder Novelle des Cervantes ist ein solcher Mittelpunkt" *(ebd).* Damit trübt er die Sachlage wieder; die scheinbare Auswechselbarkeit der Termina "Mittelpunkt" und "Wendepunkt" hat zu dem Vorurteil geführt, der Wendepunkt müsse etwa in der Mitte der Geschichte liegen (siehe z. B. bei Silz). Von diesen unbedachten Ausflügen kehrt Tieck dann wieder zum Ausgangspunkt zurück: "... nur wird (die Novelle) immer jenen sonderbaren auffallenden Wendepunkt haben, der sie von allen anderen Gattungen der Erzählung unterscheidet" (1xxxvii). Handelt es sich nun um *einen* Wendepunkt oder um Wendepunkte? Wo liegen sie? Sind sie 'äusserlich' oder 'innerlich', faktisch oder moralisch/ethisch? Wie drastisch ist eine solche Wendung? Ist der Begrifff des Mittelpunktes, der Mitte ein 'geographisch-chronologischer' (d. h. = in der Mitte des Ablaufs der Geschichte) oder ein ideologischer (d. h. = der Schwerpunkt der Geschichte)? Ist er identisch mit "Wendepunkt"? All das bleibt ungeklärt, bis in die

168

oder wird übergangen.[5]

---

späteste Literatur. Himmel z. B. erkennt die laxe Terminologie Tiecks und erklärt dann, der Wendepunkt müsse im "Mittelpunkt des Zeitablaufs der Erzählung" stehen, "weil sonst keine 'Umkehr' der Geschichte Raum hätte" (S. 36, 37). Warum *muss* eine Umkehr die Hälfte der Erzählung in Anspruch nehmen? Weitere Verwirrung wird angestiftet durch Himmels Befürwortung eines von Theodor Mundt vorgeschlagenen, zweiten Mittelpunktes (!), eines "Kreismittelpunktes", der mit dem "zentralen Konflikt" gleichbedeutend ist (S. 37) und sich vom chronologischen 'Wende- und Mittelpunkt' unterscheidet. Den Mundtschen Mittelpunkt nennt Himmel auch "Mittelpunkt des Geschehens" (S. 38), aber diese Bezeichnung wäre für den räumlich-zeitlichen Mittelpunkt des Handlungsablaufs ebenso geeignet. Der Leser – jedenfalls dieser – wird ganz konfus, wenn auch mit diesem scheinbar festliegenden, räumlich-zeitlichen Mittelpunkt der Erzählung jongliert wird: "Da eine Erzählung in der Zeit abläuft, wird man unter Mittelpunkt jenen Punkt verstehen, der die Gesamtstrecke harmonisch teilt, wonach sich der erste zum zweiten Teil wie 618:382 verhält" (!?) [S. 492].

[5]Für Heyse fallen die Begriffe "Falke", "Silhouette" und "Wendung" zusammen (*Deutscher Novellenschatz*, München o.J. [1871], I, S. XX; *Jugenderinnerungen und Bekenntnisse*, 3. Aufl., Berlin, 1900, S. 348). Dasselbe gilt noch für Koskimies, für den der Falke ein "scharfer, plötzlicher Wendepunkt" ist (Rafael Koskimies, "Die Theorie der Novelle", *Orbis Litterarum*, XIV, 1959, S. 74). Koskimies betont allerdings die epische Tönung der zeitgenössischen Novelle (besonders seit Tschechow) gegenüber der dramatischen und lässt es offen, ob die einzelnen Novellen – je nachdem, ob sie dramatischer oder epischer sind – *einen* Wendepunkt (peripeteia) oder Wendepunkte aufweisen. Da die episch impressionistische Ausrichtung Koskimies' folgerichtig zu einer Minderbewertung des (dramatischen) Wendepunktes führt, dürfen wir von ihm keine eingehende Präzisierung des Wendepunktbegriffes erwarten. Indem er aber einen "klar umrissenen" Wendepunkt von einer "epischen Schlusswendung und -lösung" unterscheidet

(S. 74-75), gibt er jedenfalls, trotz einer gewissen Unbestimmtheit, einen wertvollen Fingerzeig.

Johannes Klein setzt "Wendepunkt" dem "unerhörten Ereignis" und dem "Mittelpunkt" gleich ("Wesen und Erscheinungsformen der deutschen Novelle," *Germanisch-Romanische Monatsschrift* XXIV [1936], S. 81-100). "Auf die äussere Stellung kommt es dabei nicht an. Das Ereignis kann auch am Ende stehen" (S. 83).

Für Hermann Pongs *(Das Bild in der Dichtung,* II [Marburg, 1939], S. 179-180) und Fritz Lockemann *(Gestalt und Wandlungen der deutschen Novelle,* München, 1957, S. 14). ist "Wendepunkt" gleichbedeutend mit "Pointe". Darüber hinaus identifiziert Lockemann, wie Klein, den Begriff "Wendepunkt" mit der "unerhörten Begebenheit" (S. 18), dann mit "konzentrierter Form" (S. 19), unterscheidet zwischen einem ersten Wendepunkt (Einbruch des Chaos) und einem zweiten (Einbruch der Ordnung) – es könne aber auch umgekehrt sein (1. Wendepunkt = Ordnung, 2. Wendepunkt = Chaos) [S. 16] –, lässt dann jedoch mehrere Wendepunkte zu *(ebd),* spricht herablassend von denjenigen, für die der Wendepunkt "veräusserlicht, *nur* (Kursivschrift von mir – HR) eine Sache der Form" ist, "die sich damit vom Gehalt scheidet" (S. 19), und endet triumphierend: "So ist die Geschichte der Novelle die Geschichte ihrer Wendepunkte" (S. 20). Das ist zuviel des Guten.

Manfred Schunicht ("Der 'Falke' am 'Wendepunkt'", *Germanisch-Romanische Monatsschrift,* N. F. X, [1960] S. 47) spiegelt die in der deutschen Novellenforschung weit verbreitete Angst vor einer formalistischen Zwangsjacke wider, eine Besorgnis, die es zu keiner ernsthaften Analyse des Wendepunktbegriffs kommen lässt. Man fürchtet, nicht weltanschaulich genug zu sein. Der Wendepunkt, schreibt Schunicht (S. 52), sei "auf solch unauflösbare Weise mit Tiecks Weltansicht verflochten, dass es immer problematisch bleibt, diesen Begriff für eine Interpretation der Werke anderer Novellisten zu beanspruchen ... Es ist müssig, in den Werken anderer Novellisten nach Wendepunkten zu suchen" *(ebd.).* Gestützt auf diese

Unsere eigenen, von den Texten ausgehenden Analysen führen zu der Beobachtung, dass die Novelle des 19. Jahrhunderts zwei Hauptwendepunkte aufweist: einen gegen den Anfang liegenden, zeitlich primären, aber qualitativ sekundären, der überhaupt erst die eigentliche Handlung in Fahrt bringt und den wir den *auslösenden* Wendepunkt nennen wollen, und einen zweiten, wichtigeren, spezifisch *novellistischen* Wendepunkt, den letzten, entscheidenden, unerwarteten und doch glaubhaft-natürlichen Umschlag, die dramatische Peripetie, nach der die Novelle schnell ihrem Ende entgegengeht: wir wollen ihn den *auflösenden* Wendepunkt nennen. In den massgebenden Novellen wird dieser novellistische, auflösende Wendepunkt sowohl äusserlich wie innerlich entscheidend sein, während der auslösende Wendepunkt zufälliger, äusserlicher erscheint. Erst im Rückblick vom auflösenden Wendepunkt (und dessen unmittelbaren Folgen) auf den auslösenden erkennt man, dass auch der die Handlung entfesselnde Wendepunkt nicht immer so

---

Selbstsicherheit sucht Schunicht auch garnicht, lässt sich überhaupt auf keine konkreten Beispiele aus der Novellistik ein, die womöglich das 'Weltanschauliche' gefährden könnten.

Sehr enttäuschend ist auch Ilse Wortigs *Der 'Wendepunkt' in der neuen deutschen Novelle und seine Gestaltung* (Diss., Frankfurt a.M., 1931, 56 S.). Sie verfliesst in vielfältigen weltanschaulichen Unterscheidungen und kümmert sich wenig um die immanente Struktur der Novelle. Es wird, wie später bei Himmel, nebelhaft von einem "im Mittelpunkt des Geschehens stehenden Wendepunkt" gesprochen (S. 12); weiter geht die konkrete Erläuterung des Begriffs nicht. Ihre Beispiele sind der Novellenliteratur des XX. Jahrhunderts entnommen.

Benno von Wieses gehaltvolle Übersicht *(Novelle,* Stuttgart, 1963, 89 S.) räumt dem Wendepunkt eine gewisse Bedeutung ein, bezeichnet es aber als "töricht", "dieses kompositorische Prinzip allzu sehr zu betonen und nun überall ängstlich nach dem 'Wendepunkt' in jeder Novelle zu suchen" (S. 15; s.a. S. 11, 17). Im Grunde warnt von Wiese nur von Auswüchsen, die bei der wissenschaftlichen Behandlung jedes Problems unerwünscht sind.

rein zufällig ist, wie es zuerst den Anschein hatte.

Sehen wir uns auf diese Gesichtspunkte hin Kellers drei novellistische Erzählungen *Kleider machen Leute, Romeo und Julia auf dem Dorfe* und *Die drei gerechten Kammacher* an, danach auf Keller folgende Novellen.

Der auslösende Wendepunkt in *Kleider machen Leute* ist, ganz am Anfang, die Aufnahme des Schneiders in die herrschaftliche Grafenkutsche, eine Wendung, ohne welche die gesamte Handlung der Geschichte ungeschehen geblieben wäre; der auflösende Wendepunkt ist die überraschende, unter den Umständen "unerhörte" Entscheidung Nettchens, der reichen, putzfreudigen, verwöhnten Bürgertochter, dem seiner Schande und scheinbar völligem Ruin entgegengehenden armen Schneider *doch* nachzufahren, anstatt sich von dem triumphierenden, standesgemässen Bewerber Melchior Böhni nach Hause begleiten zu lassen. Diese äussere Entscheidung wächst aus dem inneren Instinkt der Frau, dass der 'Schneider' eben doch, rein menschlich gesehen, ein 'Graf' ist, und wird wenig später durch die Bekräftigung der Verlobung und das happy ending bestätigt. Erst im Rückblick auf den auslösenden vom auflösenden Wendepunkt her erkennen wir, dass das Mitnehmen des armen Schneiderleins in der Grafenkutsche wohl nicht *rein* zufällig war: der Kutscher hätte Strapinski vielleicht nicht aufgefordert, wenn er in ihm nicht etwas unschneiderhaftes, grafenähnliches, feines gewittert hätte, etwas, was eben doch in die Kutsche passt.

In *Romeo und Julia* ist der auslösende Wendepunkt das Einreissen der Furche des fremden Ackers durch einen der beiden scheinbar ehrenfesten Bauern; der auflösende Wendepunkt ist der überraschende, geradezu 'unerhörte' Beschluss der 'Kinder', nach der Liebesnacht zusammen in den Tod zu gehen: diese äussere-innere Entscheidung ist eine unmittelbare Folge des physiologischen Wendepunktes in Sali, des Durchbruchs der sinnlichen Leidenschaft. Die Schlägerei zwischen Manz und Marti auf der Brücke, der Händedruck zwischen Sali und Vrenchen zu gleicher Zeit, der Steinwurf, durch den Sali Vrenchens Vater in die Irrenanstalt bringt — all diese Ereignisse stellen keinen novellistisch-auflösenden Wendepunkt dar, weil sie bereits bestehende Tendenzen nur verstärken, keinen entscheidenden Umschlag, keinen innerlichen Durchbruch blossstellen. Erst im Rückblick vom auflösenden auf den auslösenden Wendepunkt sehen wir, dass die kompromisslose Leidenschaft der Kinder, der unwiderstehliche Wunsch des Besitzens bereits von den Vätern vorgezeichnet worden ist, wenn auch auf einer anderen und weit unmenschlicheren Ebene: durch ihr Furcheneinreissen zu Anfang der Geschichte, in ihrer darauf folgenden leidenschaftlichen Sturheit, in ihrem Wettrennen zum Untergang. Der handlungsauslösende Wendepunkt, obgleich bei solch soliden Bauern immer noch unerwartet und 'unerhört', wird allerdings auch durch die wenig verbrämte, hartgesottene (aber wohl ziemlich 'normale') Selbstsucht der Väter vorbereitet, die in dem unmittelbar vorhergehenden Gespräch keinen Finger rühren, dem schwarzen Geiger zu seinem Heimatsrecht zu verhelfen.

Der auflösend-novellistische Wendepunkt in den *Kammachern* ist die unerwartete Eroberung Züs' durch Dietrich, der Durchbruch des Allzumenschlichen bei diesem weiblichen Tugendbold, der all ihre feinen Pläne (jedenfalls die bewussten) zunichte macht und das Schicksal der anderen Bewerber besiegelt. Der auslösende Wendepunkt liegt hier ausnahmsweise genau in der Mitte der Geschichte (aber zu Beginn des eigentlich novellistischen Teils der Erzählung): es ist die Wettlaufsidee des Meisters und Züs' Entschluss, ihre eigene Hand mit dem Sieg in diesem Wettlauf zu verknüpfen. Im Rückblick vom Ende der Geschichte (indifferente Grausamkeit der Gesellschaft) auf den auslösenden Wendepunkt hin ersieht man, dass die Idee des Wettlaufs den sadistisch-unmenschlichen Neigungen des Meisters und Züs' entspricht.

Auch hier erweisen sich die Kellerschen Novellen, wenn nicht als Norm, so doch als guter Ausgangspunkt für die Strukturanalyse späterer Novellen, in der sich die Variationen häufen, ohne aber das Prinzip als solches zu entwerten. Der novellistisch-auflösende Wendepunkt in *Aquis Submersus* ist das leidenschaftliche Wiedersehen zwischen Johannes und Katharina, während und wegen dessen ihr Kind ertrinkt; im *Schimmelreiter* ist es Haukes Krankheitsschwäche, die ihn zu einer für ihn ganz 'unerhörten' Vernachlässigung seiner Pflicht als Deichgraf führt (oberflächliche Reparatur am Deich); im *Bahnwärter Thiel* ist es (äusserlich) die Ermordung Lenes und des 'Balgs' durch den friedfertig-passiven, unterdurchschnittlichen Bahnwärter, innerlich das dieser Tat vorhergehende Versprechen Thiels angesichts seiner ersten Frau, den Tod des Tobiäschens an der Stiefmutter und ihrem/seinem Kind zu rächen; in Sudermanns *Reise nach Tilsit* Ansas' Geständnis, dass er seine Frau ertränken wollte; in Emil Strauss' *Schleier* das – statt Rache – sich einstellende Schuldgefühl der Gattin, die ihren Mann im Schlaf mit seiner Geliebten ertappt; in Bergengruens *Drei Falken* Ceccos Freilassen des Falken (freiwillig spontane Aufgabe seiner scheinbar einzigen Lebenschance, wohlhabend und umworben zu werden); im *Kleinen Herrn Friedemann* Gerdas höhnisches Zurückstossen des von ihr halb ermutigten, halb verfolgten Friedemanns; im *Tristan* Gabrieles Verführung durch den impotenten Spinell und den potenten Wagner; im *Tod in Venedig* Aschenbachs Entschluss, *nicht* abzureisen, in *Mario und der Zauberer* Marios befreiender, gänzlich unerwarteter Pistolenschuss.

Die beträchtlichen Variationen innerhalb dieses novellistisch-auflösenden Wendepunktbegriffs bei und nach Keller sollen keineswegs bestritten werden. So liegen in der *Versuchung des Pescara* der äusserliche und innerliche Wendepunkt (Pescaras tödliche Verwundung in der Schlacht von Pavia) *vor* Beginn der Erzählung. In manchen Novellen sind innerlicher und äusserlicher Wendepunkt nicht simultan, z.B. im *Bahnwärter Thiel*. In anderen bleibt der auflösende Wendepunkt äusserlich, d.h. setzt keinen innerlichen Umschwung voraus (z.B. in C.F. Meyers *Hochzeit des Mönchs* die Durchbohrung Antiopes, in Hofmannsthals *Erlebnis des Marschalls Bassompierre* das Rendezvous mit einer Leiche). In Thomas Manns novellistischen Erzählungen büsst der Wendepunkt an "Unerwartetheit" dadurch ein, dass er psychologisch und impressionistisch etwas vorbereitet wird: so im *Friedemann*, im *Tristan*, im *Tod in Venedig,* selbst im *Mario;* trotzdem bleibt der Einschnitt erkennbar. Es liesse sich, glauben wir, zeigen, dass das ungefähre Zusammenfallen eines äusserlichen und innerlichen Wendepunktes gegen das Ende einer novellistischen Erzählung, welches wir bei Kellers drei Novellen beobachtet haben, so eng mit der dramatisch-"unerhörten" Struktur der Novelle, mit ihrem Wesen und ihrer Wirkung in Einklang stehen, dass eine Verletzung dieser Norm oder dieses Usus' leicht (nicht notwendigerweise) zur künstlerischen Schwächung der novellistischen

Erzählung führen kann. Das gilt unseres Erachtens z.B. für die Verwischung *des* novellistisch-auflösenden Wendepunktes durch Anhäufung von Wendepunkten bei C.F. Meyer, oder für das Zusammenfallen des auslösenden mit dem auflösenden Wendepunkt (Begegnung mit Agata) in Hauptmanns *Ketzer von Soana*. Doch muss man mit allgemeinen Folgerungen vorsichtig sein: so ist im *Herrn Friedemann* die Koinzidenz dieser beiden möglichen Wendepunkte (Friedemanns erste Begegnung mit Gerda ist bereits schicksalshaft-fatal) durchaus gelungen. Mann sichert sich aber dadurch, dass er in dieser Erzählung je einen weiteren, auslösenden wie auflösenden, dramatischen Wendepunkt an den strukturell erprobten Stellen beibehält: das Fallenlassen des kleinen Johannes durch die betrunkene Amme ganz am Anfang (Auslösung) und das Zurückstossen des unglückseligen, obwohl (weil?) verstandenen Liebenden durch Gerda auf der vorletzten Seite (Auflösung).

Pointe

Die Novelle ist aus der Anekdote entstanden.[6] Bei Kleist noch lassen sich leicht diejenigen Anekdoten, die lediglich Anekdoten sein können (z.B. die *Kapuziner-, Unzelmann-,* oder *Bach*anekdote) unterscheiden von denjenigen, die Ansätze zum Novellistischen zeigen (z.B. die *Kapitän von Bürger*anekdote, *Franzosen-Billigkeit)* oder sogar unausgeführte Novellen sind (z.B. *Der verlegene Magistrat).* Die Anekdote verlangt eine Pointe; sie steht oder fällt mit dem letzten Satz, ja manchmal dem letzten Wort. Das mit dem Novellistischen in enger Beziehung stehende Dramatische braucht ebenfalls diese Pointe zu einem wirkungsvollen Aktschluss (vgl. Schillers "Der Lord lässt sich entschuldigen, er ist zu Schiff nach Frankreich" oder "Dem *Fürsten* Piccolomini"). Das Novellistische schliesst ja überhaupt das Pointierte, Präzise, Falkenhafte, auch das Intelligent-Witzig-Ironisch-

---

[6]Heinrich Henel bezeichnet die deutsche Novelle als den "Zusammenschluss von zwei oder mehr... 'Anekdoten'" *(Wächter und Hüter,* Festschrift für Hermann J. Weigand, New Haven, 1957, S. 117).

Unterhaltende des Begriffs "Pointe" ein.

Dieser pointierte, auf die letzten Worte zugespitzte Abschluss, wirkungsvoll-ironisch, noch im letzten Augenblick etwas Neues bringend, (im kleinen) auch unerwartet, auf die Novelle ein letztes schlagartiges Licht werfend, findet in Keller seinen Meister. "Aber in Seldwyla liess er nicht einen Stüber zurück, sei es *aus Undank oder aus Rache.*"[7] (*Kleider*). "Dietrich der Schwabe allein blieb ein Gerechter und hielt sich oben in dem Städtchen; aber er hatte nicht viel Freude davon, denn Züs liess ihm garnicht den Ruhm, regierte und unterdrückte ihn und betrachtete sich selbst als *die alleinige Quelle alles Guten.*" (*Kammacher*). "Man nehme an, die jungen Leute haben das Schiff entwendet, um darauf ihre *verzweifelte* und *gottverlassene* Hochzeit zu halten, abermals ein Zeichen von der um sich greifenden *Entsittlichung und Verwilderung der Leidenschaften.*" (*Romeo und Julia*). In all diesen Pointen spiegelt sich die subjektive Stellungnahme des Erzählers wider, die auf die ganze vorhergehende, meist objektiv oder recht objektiv vorgetragene Geschichte ein oft ironisches, manchmal pathetisches Licht wirft, und zwar in mehr oder weniger ätzenden Worten.

Bei der unerhört ausgeglichenen, "sowohl ... als auch" bestimmten Erzählungskunst Thomas Manns, die den Leser bis zum letzten Augenblick im Schwebezustand hält, wird diese Pointe besonders wichtig, da sie uns die ersehnte Stellungnahme des Autors zu vermitteln scheint. Noch im letzten Satz steht die Partie im *Tristan* unentschieden. Spinell macht zwar vor Anton Klöterjahn Jr. kehrt, aber bewahrt doch Haltung; erst das allerletzte Wort scheint zu entscheiden; "Er ging, gefolgt von dem Jubilieren des kleinen Klöterjahn, mit einer gewissen behutsamen und steif-graziösen Armhaltung über den Kies, mit den gewaltsam zögernden Schritten jemandes, der verbergen will, dass er innerlich *davonläuft.*"[8] In *Mario* bekennt der Autor in

---

[7]Die ausschlaggebenden Worte in diesem Zitat und in den folgenden sind von mir unterstrichen.

[8]Wir sagten "*scheint* zu entscheiden", denn bei Thomas Mann mag selbst die Pointe noch problematisch bleiben; schliesslich *hat* Spinell über die

seiner Pointe klar Farbe (ein bedeutsames Symptom seiner politischen Entwicklung): "Ein Ende mit Schrecken, ein höchst fatales Ende. Und ein *befreiendes* Ende dennoch – ich konnte und kann nicht umhin, es so zu empfinden." Die ironische Pointe im *Tod in Venedig* ist eine Umkehrung der kellerschen in *Romeo und Julia:* "Und noch desselben Tages empfing eine *respektvoll erschütterte Welt* die Nachricht von seinem Tode." Pathetisch-ironisch ist die Pointe der Geschichte selbst (vom Rahmen abgesehen) in der *Hochzeit des Mönchs:*"'Jetzt schlummert der *Mönch* Astorre neben seiner *Gattin* Antiope.' Und ein fernes *Gelächter.*" Ähnlich endet der *Kleine Herr Friedemann:* "Bei dem Aufklatschen des Wassers waren die Grillen einen Augenblick verstummt. Nun setzte ihr Zirpen wieder ein, der Park rauschte leise auf, und durch die lange Allee herunter klang gedämpftes *Lachen.*" Pathetisch-ironisch ist auch der Abschluss des *Bahnwärters Thiel:* "Noch bei der Einlieferung hielt er das braune Mützchen in Händen und bewachte es mit *eifersüchtiger Sorgfalt und Zärtlichkeit"* und derjenige des *Landarztes:* '*Einmal* dem Fehlläuten der Nachtglocke gefolgt – es ist *niemals gutzumachen.*"[9]

Ohne zu versuchen, Kellers Pointen als die allein seligmachenden für die Novelle hinzustellen, gibt es doch zu denken, dass das deutliche Abweichen von Kellers pointierten Abschlüssen symptomatisch für Strukturschwächen, für verwässerte oder unorganische Tendenzen mancher novellistischen Erzählung ist. C.F. Meyers lyrisch-malerisch-allegorisches Ende des *Pescara:* "So glich er einem jungen, magern, von der Ernte erschöpften und auf seiner Garbe schlafenden Schnitter" weist auf die Vermengung zu vieler, mit dem Novellistischen nicht in Einklang stehenden Elemente hin, die seiner Novelle die Schwäche zu grossen Reichtums geben. Die deutsche Novelle steht überhaupt in dauernder Versuchung, das Pointiert-

---

Klöterjahns einen Teilsieg davongetragen: den von ihm geförderten Tod Gabrieles.

[9]Die Pointe *kann* positiv gehalten sein: "Am anderen Morgen ... ritt ich über den *Hauke-Haien-Deich* zur Stadt hinunter" *(Der Schimmelreiter).*

Konkrete mit lyrischen, malerischen, allegorischen und didaktischen Elementen zu verdecken. Der wenigstens bündige, obgleich unterpointierte Schluss von *Aquis Submersus:* "Hier endete die Handschrift" wird geschwächt durch das vorhergehende konventionelle, allegorisch-didaktische, überpointierte: ". . . aber aus dem dumpfen Brausen des Meerers tönete (*sic!*) es mir immerfort, gleich einem finsteren Wiegenliede: Aquis submersus – aquis submersus!" Der *Ketzer von Soana* muss das Unerhörte der novellistischen Erzählung krampfhaft ins Symbolisch-Metaphysische erheben: "Sie stieg aus der Tiefe der Welt empor und stieg an dem Staunenden vorbei – und sie steigt und steigt in die Ewigkeit als die, in deren gnadenlose Hände Himmel und Hölle überantwortet sind." *Der Schleier* moralisiert, didaktisiert und allegorisiert Goethes kompakten Novellenkern zu Tode ("Der Hund . . . sprang neben der Frau auf die Bank und blickte durch den offenen Bogen in die Weite, dem Lichte der aufdrängenden Sonne entgegen").[10] Wiechert verpastoralisiert, verzuckert und verweint eine schön, *zu* 'schön' geschriebene Novelle: "Aber (der Krieg) hat das einfache Holzkreuz nicht berührt, das zu Häupten Michaels aufgestellt worden ist und das nach dem Willen des Lehrers Elwenspök die Worte trägt: Michael – einer Witwe Sohn." *(Hirtennovelle)*. Bergengruen *(Die drei Falken)* verpasst einen pointierten Novellenschluss: "Es blieb still. Niemand klatschte Beifall." durch die unnötig zergliedernde, zu pathetische Zugabe: "Aber allen bebte das Herz in Ehrfurcht, in Scham oder in Erhebung." Nicht alle unpointierten Abschlüsse sind schwach. Der letzte Satz des Rahmens der *Hochzeit des Mönchs:* "Aller Augen folgten ihm, der die Stufen einer fackelhellen Treppe langsam emporstieg" erfüllt das goethesche Desideratum für die Novelle, dass sie zum stillen Nachdenken

---

[10]Der zweite Teil dieses Schlussatzes findet dann wieder zum nüchternen Novellenton zurück: "und als scheuten sie sich, das Tier etwas merken zu lassen, fingen sie miteinander zu sprechen an." Der Vergleich beider Satzteile macht den Kitsch des Satzbeginns besonders schmerzhaft.

178

Anreiz gebe.[11]

Metaphysische Pointe (Ironie-Paradox)

Während die novellistisch-auflösende Pointe *ein* letztes, abrundendes Licht auf die Erzählung wirft, so fasst die (meist unausgesprochene) metaphysische Pointe die konzentrierte, allgemeine Bedeutung der Geschichte, die Quintessenz, den Zusammenstoss zwischen Geschick und Menschenwollen, in einer (meist von dem Leser zu formulierenden) geschliffenen, prägnanten, überraschenden, oft ironisch-paradoxen "Spitze" zusammen. Auch hier hat Keller, die kleistsche Tradition fortsetzend, Einschneidendes geleistet.

Die Gesamtpointe von *Kleider machen Leute* ist, dass der Betrüger, der falsche Graf, das Schneiderlein, doch im Grunde ein 'echter' Graf, ein feiner Aristokrat ist, dass die von ihm Betrogenen betrogen sein *wollen,* ihm die Rolle aufdringen, um ihn dann zu verurteilen, und dass diejenigen, die den Betrug aufdecken, die schlechtesten von allen sind und dafür am Ende bestraft werden. In den *Drei gerechten Kammachern,* der didaktischsten der drei novellistischen Erzählungen, verurteilt Keller ausdrücklich die "blutlose Gerechtigkeit" der drei verbissen gleichgerichteten Streber[12] als etwas Unmenschliches, das zu unmenschlicher Behandlung der "Gerechten" selbst führt, zu Verkommen, Irrsinn und Selbstmord. Es ist ironisch und paradox, dass die 'unmenschlichen' Kammacher schliesslich durch ihre menschlichen Schwächen der 'Unmenschlichkeit' Züs Bünzlins zum Opfer fallen, der nun aber ihrerseits menschliche Schwäche ein Schnippchen schlägt, indem sie sich von Dietrich erobern lässt – ausgerechnet demjenigen der drei Kammacher, den sie *nicht* heiraten wollte, der einzige, der diesen verrückten, wohl

---

[11]*Unterhaltungen deutscher Ausgewanderten,* Hamburger Ausgabe, 4. Aufl., 1960, VI, 167.

[12]Goethe: "Der Mensch kann nur mit seines Gleichen leben und auch mit denen nicht, denn er kann auf die Länge nicht leiden, dass ihm jemand gleich sei" *(Goethe Handbuch,* Stuttgart, 1955. S. 1593).

symbolischen Lebenswettlauf (an dem sich keiner der Läufer gern beteiligen will) *nicht* mitmacht, und der ihn gewinnt. Aber auch ihn, den 'Gerechten', ereilt das gerechte Geschick des Pantoffelhelden unter der Zungenfuchtel von Züs. Gewiss eine der paradoxesten und misanthropischsten Gesamtpointen der Novellenliteratur.

Romeo und Julia wimmelt geradezu von ironisch-paradoxen metaphysischen Pointen, erwachsen auf dem alttestamentarischen Boden der Vätersünden, die an den Kindern heimgezahlt werden. Hier handelt es sich nicht um Eltern, die ihre Kinder zu retten versuchen, sondern um Kinder, die das Beste an der Vergangenheit der Eltern für sich zu retten gewillt sind. Die Kinder wollen das Alte, Solide, die Väter das 'Neue', Unsolide. Was früher die festbürgerliche, ungetrübte Wirklichkeit war, das ist jetzt für Kinder ein Traum, der so natürlich, vollkommen und ihrer Anlage und Herkunft gemäss *wirklich* ist, dass sie nicht mehr in die 'wirkliche' Welt zurückkönnen. Die sture Gleichgerichtetheit der Eltern führt die Väter, in tödlicher Umklammerung (siehe als deren allegorischer Ausdruck die aussichtslose Schlägerei auf der Brücke zwischen Manz und Marti), in eine gemeinsame Lebenskatastrophe; die gleichgerichtete, kompromisslose, entsagungsunfähige, sinnliche aber die Gesellschaftsordnung bejahende (nur die besondere, sie umzingelnde Gesellschaft verneinende) Leidenschaft der Kinder zwingt sie ebenso unwiderstehlich, in letzter Umarmung, in den Tod. Was die Kinder den 'früheren' Eltern gleichstellt (die alte Solidität und Ehrbarkeit) stösst sie ebenso sicher in den Tod wie das, was sie von den 'späteren' Eltern trennt: Freundschaft und Liebe. Die Ausgeglichenheit ihrer sinnlichen Gefühle und gesellschaftlichen Bestrebungen wird Sali und Vrenchen zum Verhängnis. Wären sie darin ärmer gewesen, wären sie am Leben geblieben. Wäre es ihnen hauptsächlich auf Ehrbarkeit angekommen, hätten sie sich getrennt. Wäre es ihnen nur auf sinnliche Erfüllung angekommen, hätten sie sich dem schwarzen Geiger angeschlossen. Die Verbindung von Liebe und Ehrbarkeit, von, krass gesagt, Liebe und *Eigentums*liebe, welch letztere auch den Vätern zum Verhängnis wird, wirkt tödlich. Dass Kinder (die noch kaum gelebt haben) Selbstmord begehen, ist (obwohl es nicht selten vorkommt) an sich schon paradox; der Selbstmord eines Siebzigjährigen wäre sinnvoller. Die

180

Gesellschaft – ein Organismus, der seine Berechtigung aus dem Prinzip der Geselligkeit, der gemeinsamen Bestrebung und Hilfe bezieht – steht, mit wenigen Ausnahmen, dem Menschen verständnislos, indifferent, feindlich, die Katastrophe befördernd und geniessend gegenüber.

Schon passiv ist die Gesellschaft teilweise für den Streit der Väter verantwortlich, denn Manz und Marti begehen die grössten Dummheiten, um von ihren Mitbürgern nicht als dumm angesehen zu werden. Selbst wenn die Gesellschaft ausnahmsweise Sympathie zeigt (die Bäuerin, die Wirtin), verstärkt sie die unwiderstehliche Illusion der 'Hochzeiter' und führt sie damit näher zum Tod als einzigem Ausweg. Die Gesellschaft als solche ist mitschuldig am Tod dieser Jugendlichen, die doch das Zeug zu künftigen Stützen der Gesellschaft haben – ja, sterben, weil sie sich der gesellschaftlichen Ordnung zu verbunden fühlen, um in wilder Ehe leben zu können. Diese Gesellschaft, in der jeder für sich selbst zu stehen scheint, sich nur zu Schadenfreude mit anderen zusammentut, in der Mensch und Mensch *nicht* kommunizieren, lässt gleichgültig die einzigen Menschen der Erzählung, die menschliche Verbindung miteinander haben und in höherem Sinne streng moralisch sind, in den Tod gehen, und verdammt sie dann, im Namen ihrer selbstgefälligen, hohlen Moral – und wird von dem Erzähler mit ruhiger, umso beissenderer Ironie selbst verdammt. Das Glück scheint überhaupt nur ausserhalb der Gesellschaft – die doch gegründet ist, dem menschlichen 'Glück' Fortdauer zu verschaffen – möglich zu sein: unter dem wilden Völkchen des schwarzen Geigers, in der Irrenanstalt (erst dort gewinnt Marti Heiterkeit und Zufriedenheit zurück!) oder im Tod. Da das Zigeunerleben für Sali und Vrenchen nicht in Frage kommt, bleibt diesen lebenslustigen und lebensfähigen jungen Leuten nur die eine Möglichkeit des Glücks: der Tod. *Romeo und Julia auf dem Dorfe* ist vielleicht *die deutsche Tragödie:* der Aufstand des elementaren Naturgefühls gegen den Gesellschaftskodex *und* das zähe Hängen an gesellschaftlicher Ordnung und Ordentlichkeit verbinden sich zur Herbeiführung der Katastrophe.

Das sind die aus tiefster, ehrlichster Menschenkenntnis und Menschenliebe stammenden, ironisch durchtränkten, paradox gestalteten metaphysischen Pointen Kellers. Nur *ein* Wert thront über ihnen: die Liebe.

Auch sie wird in den bitteren *Kammachern* in Frage gestellt, aber das ist wenig gegen ihren Triumph über schwerste Hindernisse in *Kleider machen Leute* und *Romeo und Julia auf dem Dorfe*.

Die ironisch-paradox gefärbten metaphysischen Pointen der gehaltvollsten nachkellerschen deutschen Novellen können hier nur kurz angedeutet werden. Im *Schimmelreiter* wird dem 'christlich' -sozialsten Haupt der Gesellschaft, dem Deichgrafen, der sich für sie aufreibt, der sich gegen Sektiererwesen und Heidentum wehrt, von dieser selben pro forma christlichen, in der tragenden Unterschicht aber abergläubischen Gesellschaft ihr eigener Aberglaube angehängt. Er wird zu einem Dämonen gestempelt.[13] Nachdem er unter grossem Risiko heidnische Menschen- und Tieropfer verdammt und verhindert hat, stürzt er sich selbst, als ein halb-heidnisches, halb-christliches Sühneopfer, ins Wasser. Im *Pescara* stellt sich der in der Form un-, ja antichristliche Feldherr als der wahrste Handlungschrist heraus, während der Vertreter des kompromisslosen Christentums (Moncada) unmenschlich (d.h. unchristlich) ist, und der Heilige Vater sehr unheilig christliche Ethik politischen und materiellen Plänen unterordnet. Im *Bahnwärter Thiel* rächt sich der friedfertige, passive, religiöse Vater durch eine im Namen seiner schwächlich-vergeistigten ersten Frau begangene brutale Gewalttat an seiner brutalen zweiten Frau. Er rächt sich für die fahrlässige Tötung seines ersten Kindes durch die Ermordung seines zweiten Kindes. Er versucht, das Gleichgewicht zwischen Geist und Körper, das durch seine sexuelle Hörigkeit zu weit zugunsten des Körpers verschoben worden ist, durch eine körperliche Tat wiederherzustellen. Im *Mario* ist die intelligente, gebildete Zuhörerschaft zur Tat gegen den von ihr halb verabscheuten, halb bewunderten Künstler-Sadisten-Diktator Cipolla unfähig. Die Befreiung kommt durch die unverbildete, instinktive, primitive Menschenwürde des Kellners. In den *Drei Falken* erweist sich, wie in *Kleider machen Leute*, der

---

[13]Nicht *ganz* zu Unrecht. Hauke *hat* etwas Dämonisch-Elementares, einen Anflug von nicht-christlicher Hybris, die zu dieser Kristallisierung Anhalt und Vorwand gibt.

von der Gesellschaft scheel angesehene, auf der untersten Respektabilitätsstufe stehende Aussenseiter doch im Grunde als der echte Herzensaristokrat. Auch hier würde es sich verlohnen, die Hypothese zu erhärten, ob die Abwesenheit oder Oberflächlichkeit einer ironisch/paradox betonten metaphysischen Pointe in oft hoch (zu hoch) eingeschätzten Novellen *(Aquis Submersus, Hochzeit des Mönchs, Ketzer von Soana)* nicht symptomatisch ist für strukturelle und gehaltsmässige Schwächen dieser novellistischen Erzählungen.

Chapter VII
Vinegar and Water: Allegory & Symbolism in the German Novelle between Keller and Bergengruen

Summary

Utilitarian rather than adulatory approach toward metaphor, allegory and symbol. Definition of terms: non-absolute differentiation. Critical application to three major novellas roughly contemporary with each other: Conrad Ferdinand Meyer's "The Tempting of Pescara" (Die Versuchung des Pescara, 1887); *Gottfried Keller's "Romeo and Juliet in the Village"* (Romeo und Julia auf dem Dorfe, 1856), *and Theodor Storm's "The Rider of the White Horse"* (Der Schimmelreiter, 1888). *"Image-falcons" ("Bild-Falken"), "object symbols" ("Dingsymbole"), "musical falcons" ("Leitmotive"). Further critical application to Gerhart Hauptmann's "Railguard Thiel"* (Bahnwärter Thiel, 1887), *Emil Strauss' "The Veil"* (Der Schleier, 1920), *Bergengruen's "The Three Falcons"* (Die drei Falken, 1937), *Gerhart Hauptmann's "The Heretic of Soana"* (Der Ketzer von Soana, 1911-1917). *Very brief consideration of Hofmannsthal's "The Adventure of the Marshal de Bassompierre"* (Das Erlebnis des Marschalls von Bassompierre, 1899/1900) *and of his "Story of a Horseman"* (Reitergeschichte, 1899) *as well as Thomas Mann's "Little Mr. Friedemann" ("Der kleine Herr Friedemann", 1897), "Tristan"* (Tristan, 1902), *"Death in Venice"* (Der Tod in Venedig, 1911-1913), *and "Mario and the Magician"* (Mario und der Zauberer, 1930). *The future (?) of the symbol (a signal? a token?): Kafka's "A Country Doctor"* (Ein Landarzt, 1918), *Musil's "The Blackbird"* (Die Amsel, 1928). *Retrospective glance at the German novella of the XIXth century.*

"I cannot feel satisfied with a literary criticism which substitutes, for the conception of the writer as 'man speaking to men,' the conception of the writer as an imagination weaving symbolic patterns to be teased out by the intellect . . ." Nowadays we tend to "find significance in what the work suggests rather than what it says"; we "direct our imagination towards types and figures rather than towards their actualization."[1]

"We have, not without some ridiculous excess, pinnacled the effigy of Coleridge over the intense inane where supreme critics breathe the incense burnt in our temples."[2]

"A work of art is not just an abstruse message hidden in code. By indulging our trade in the seclusion of university seminars and almost never encountering writers, we have forgotten how fallible, how pressed by time and greed and love, how eccentric and fanciful and disorderly, how tempted by plagiarism and mystification, how unlike engineers striving for symbolic structure and functional imagery inspired writers can be."[3]

"Criticism is a secondary activity and should avow it. It does not have to substitute its own intellectual subtlety for the lack of it in the creator."[4]

By this time the reader may feel like A.J. Liebling, who, writing in the favorite learned periodical of American scholars, *The New Yorker,* talks about inviting his favorite aunt for dinner only to be stuck by her hatpin. Or, to come closer to home, like a big-hearted Texan pressing a black-widow spider to his bosom.[5] But I have taken precautions. I have barricaded myself behind

---

[1]Helen Gardner, *The Limits of Literary Criticism* (London: Oxford University Press, 1956), p. 39. My attention to this quotation was called by Henri Peyre, "Seventy-Five Years of Comparative Literature: A Backward and a Forward Glance," *Yearbook of Comparative and General Literature,* VIII (1959), 24-25.

[2]Peyre, "Seventy-Five Years of Comparative Literature," *Yearbook of Comparative and General Literature,* p. 20.

[3]*Ibid.,* p. 25.

[4]*Ibid.*

[5]This essay was originally delivered as one of five lectures at a symposium on "Literary Symbolism" held in the fall of 1963 at the invitation of the

quotations from two very respectable people, one of whom, for increased protection, is an English lady. To add an indubitably American touch to this cosmopolitan phalanx, I need only refer to a healthy explosion, "Metaphor: A Little Plain Speaking on a Weary Subject," by one of the most irritating and, I think, invigorating gadflies operating from an English Department in this country, Morse Peckham, who has assailed "the most common position to-day, the position that carries with it the richest critical and academic status and self-approval," namely that "poetry is a means of discovering a 'truth' which is accessible to no other way of thinking, and that the technique of such thinking is metaphor."[6] You should not miss his more serious than hilarious discussion of Monroe Beardsley's splendid metaphor, the chocolate kilowatt.

What is needed in the study of symbolism today is less subtlety and more sanity, more discrimination and less *cultismo,* more plain speaking and less mystification, more communication and fewer monologues within what John Livingston Lowes has called our "own solemn troops and sweet societies."[7] Let us make a modest effort to make certain, at least, that the other fellow knows what we are trying to say, an undertaking fraught, to be sure, with the danger of giving him the opportunity of discovering whether we are right or wrong.

I have felt the urge to do a little plain speaking myself at the outset of my disquisition in order not to appear as sailing wrapped from top to bottom in the flag of symbolism, an attire in which I would feel uncomfortable. I want to confess that the metaphorical, the allegorical, the symbolistic approaches to literature are, to me, only one, two, or three ways of getting at what matters in a literary work, and that I bear no grudge against the psychological, the ideological, the sociological, yes, even the biographical approach, where the nature of the work justifies their use. I agree with Georg Christoph

---

Department of Germanic Languages at the University of Texas in Austin.

[6] In *Connotation, I (Winter, 1962), 29.*

[7] *The Road to Xanadu* (New York: Vintage, 1959), p. vii.

186

Lichtenberg and Hugo von Hofmannsthal that 'the whole man must move together,' not just aesthetic man.[8] The best defense for the symbolistic approach would be, and, I think, *is*, that it is most appropriate to *the whole man* (in its wider, non-generic meaning).

Nor, once we have decided that metaphor, allegory, or symbol hold the key or one of the keys to a work, should we fall prey to upgrading the obvious. It is obvious that Werther will indulge in metaphors other than those used by Lotte or Albert (and, let it be said *en passant,* the fact that neither Lotte's nor Albert's metaphors are as numerous or as rich as Werther's – to tell the truth, they tend to be trite[9]– does not detract one whit from Lotte's and Albert's significance in the story). It is obvious that Faust will speak a language different from that of Mephistopheles, Settembrini from that of Naphta. Secondly, let us be resolutely *critical* in our review of image patterns. Even the greatest writers will sometimes resort to hackneyed, misplaced, or excessive allegories, to ill-digested symbolism, or greenhouse metaphors. It almost takes courage these days, certainly on the part of a *Germanist*, to assert that Goethe, yes, Goethe himself, allegorized portions of *Faust II* to a tedious death and that nine out of ten paladins of their excellence would be less than charitable with them if they were not hallowed by Goethe's name. Neither Goethe nor Hauptmann nor Thomas Mann have wholly escaped the fatal German error equating *Prosaliteratur* with *Bildung,* the *Symbol* with the stillborn *Bildungssymbol.* It almost takes courage, and exposes one to the suspicion of being low-powered, to wonder aloud what the *artistic* worth is of

---

[8]Lichtenberg, *Gedankenbücher,* ed. Franz H. Mautner (Frankfurt and Hamburg: S. Fischer, 1963), p. 47. Hofmannsthal, "Die Briefe des Zurückgekehrten," in *Prosa II* (Frankfurt: S. Fischer, 1951), p. 325 ("The whole man must move at once").

[9]I owe this information to an oral communication of Frank G. Ryder, expanding on his "Season, Day, and Hour: Time as Metaphor in Goethe's *Werther,"* *Journal of English and Germanic Philology,* LXIII, No. 3 (July, 1964), 389-407.

some of the most dazzling exhibitions of learning in symbolic garb by Thomas Mann;[10] it almost takes courage to ask where the point of diminishing returns in "imagistic" writing is reached in Proust or in Joyce or in Faulkner. It is – to end with a positive contention rather than a critical note likely to be misunderstood as gratuitous impertinence – it is the unique combination of a highly economical, deceptively concrete, yet bottomless (and very personal) symbolism, on the one hand, and an immaculate, puritan, miserly control of language, a combination of depth and leanness, of abyss and discipline, that make of Kafka *the* towering novelistic figure of our time.

If I address myself to allegory and symbolism in certain German *Novellen* today, the preceding caveats notwithstanding, it is because symbolism is, I feel, particularly indigenous to this genre, and because this genre in which German literature of the nineteenth century and, occasionally, the twentieth century has reached the level of world literature is most inadequately known among devotees of other literatures and, indeed, among those of comparative and world literature.

Before coming to grips with particular *Novellen* I must define my terms. In an epoch when the preoccupation with metaphor, allegory, and symbol has become the badge of the "establishment," the ticket to the intellectual country club, there has been a striking dearth of intelligible definitions. I do not claim to give you a universally acceptable definition; indeed, I feel quite incapable of providing it. All I can hope to do is to give you a clear understanding of what my own definition is. I feel quite justified in choosing from the various possibilities those most suited to my particular

---

[10]What Robert Champigny says about myth applies to the symbol: "A myth is anti-poetic in so far as it imposes an elaborate semantic structure" ("The Swan and the Question of Pure Poetry," *L'Esprit Créateur,* I [Fall, 1961], p. 148). J. Christopher Middleton persuasively argues the same in "Two Mountain Scenes in Novalis and the Question of Symbolic Style", in *Literary Symbolism,* ed. Helmut Rehder, Austin and London, University of Texas Press, 1965, 83-106.

task, to the tradition, time, authors, and subjects I am talking about. I do not postulate – far from it – that metaphor, allegory, and symbol have meant or must always mean what I take them to mean in my context.

I consider metaphor, allegory, and symbol to be three related but distinct terms. Metaphor I deem to be the analogy of apparently disparate empirical phenomena, the linguistic concatenation of two or more observable things or events belonging to different areas of human activity and experience. A metaphor, whether simple or compound (one or more forms of resemblance), normally starts with and ends in concrete manifestations of human endeavor.

For purposes of this investigation, allegory is the conscious stylistic disguise of one thing as another, usually the substitution of a person, an image, or an event for a concept; the intentional, rational conversion of a specific abstraction into a specific concretion. Allegory, like metaphor, is no more and no less than a manner of speaking.

The symbol, in my context, is a concrete object or, more rarely, a living being, organic part of the story, which suggests, however, one or more abstract, invisible elements or ideas giving the story a broader, more universal dimension – a *Hintergründigkeit* – whether these rapports were intended by the poet or not.

The symbol is *capable of* linking up the general with the specific, the universal with the temporal, the eternal with the accidental, the infinite with the finite, the (in philosophical terms) realistic with the nominalistic.[11] A successful, that is poetic, symbol will *intimate* this nexus through context; it will not articulate it, for "it is the essence of poetry to be ambiguous."[12]

-----

[11] We refer here to Andrew O. Jaszi's deeply probing analysis of "Dauer im Wechsel," "Idee und Erscheinung," in his "Symbolism and the linguistic Paradox: Reflections on Goethe's World View", in *Literary Symbolism,* 63-82.

[12] Andrew Jaszi, *ibid.,* p. 78.

"When the soul *speaks*, alas, the *soul* speaks no longer."[13]

The metaphor, then, states a specific though unexpected relationship explicitly: x = y; the allegory indicates a specific relationship implicitly: x (= y); the symbol implies an unspecified range of relationships: x = (a + b + c.....). The metaphor remains on the same, usually pragmatic level; the allegory proceeds, in the intention of the author, from the abstract to the concrete, obliging the reader to retrace the author's steps inversely to get at its meaning; the symbol tends to be born as a particular concretion which the reader may develop and create into an abstraction or abstractions, going in the same direction, most likely, as the author did.[14]

Nature and purpose alone of these three poetic elements do not permit us to pronounce judgement on them in the hierarchy of poetic values. It is their utilization in a particular work that is decisive. Yet they possess varying ranges of poetic usefulness. Of the three, the allegory is likely to be the least rewarding to the modern author and reader. It may be ingeniously elaborated or subtly camouflaged, it may test the detective flair of the reader, but it may be little more than a show of erudition on the part of the author, an exercise of learned virtuosity, a test of the reader's *Belesenheit.* In practical use allegory, at least in the German *Novelle,* tends to be artificial, static, and trivial. The metaphor is more rewarding because it shows the creative power of the poet explicitly (or reveals its weakness), because it does not hide behind a façade of secretiveness, and because, due to the unexpectedness of linking elements and areas hitherto thought to be unrelated, it creates in the reader the desire to

---

[13]"*Spricht* die Seele, so spricht, ach! schon die *Seele* nicht mehr" (Schiller, "Sprache," in *Votivtafeln,* Werke [Munich: Knaur, 1959], I, 200). I owe this reference to the kindness of Professor Friedrich Wilhelm Wodtke.

[14]Alfred Zastrau, thus, is mistaken when he states that allegory in Sulzer's definition ("... represents abstract concepts, through the senses, to perceptive cognition" ["daß sie abgezogene (abstrakte) Vorstellungen dem (sic!) anschauenden Erkenntnis sinnlich darstellt"]) cannot be differentiated from symbol *(Goethe-Handbuch,* 2nd. edition, [Stuttgart: Metzler, n.d.], p. 136).

follow up, on his own, this new relationship. The symbol seems the most productive of the three because it does most toward making the thoughtful and sensitive reader a cocreator; it is the most dynamic of the three.[15] It thus imposes a much greater obligation on author and reader; a trite symbol is a greater crime than a trite metaphor or a trite allegory, and an undiscriminating interpretation of a symbol is a graver misdeed than an undiscriminating interpretation of an allegory or a metaphor.

Neither the inherent handicaps of the allegory nor the inherent greater promise of the metaphor and the symbol are factors decisive enough to block the achievement of a great allegorist or ensure the success of a mediocre poet or symbolist. I am well aware and appreciative of the vitality and power of metamorphosis of the allegory as proved, for example, on the contemporary stage. I am well aware that the most significant symbolism, though intellectually rich, *may* be artistically poor. Nevertheless, empirically speaking, my context, the German *Novelle* in the period investigated, justifies qualitative differentiation in the literary potentiality of allegory and symbol.

Being already out on a limb, I might just as well go out a little farther yet and ask whether we can make some sort of prediction – based on hindsight – on the relative merits of intentional vs. unintentional symbolism. Here it might pay to consult the poets themselves. Browning, without exactly recommending the intentional approach, certainly does not rule it out:

> "But Art – wherein man nowise speaks to men,
> Only to mankind – Art may tell a truth

---

[15]I am encouraged to find, after the completion of this study, that Blake's understanding of poetry, as interpreted by Northrop Frye, tends in the same direction: "He ... defends the practice of not being too explicit on the ground that it 'rouses the faculties to act.' ...He expected the critic's response to be also a creative one ... His aim is ... to transfer to others the imaginative habit and energy of his mind" ("The Road to Excess," in *Myth and Symbol* [Lincoln: The University of Nebraska Press, 1963], pp. 3-4).

Obliquely, do the thing shall breed the thought,
Nor wrong the thought, missing the mediate word.
So may you paint your picture, twice show truth,
Beyond mere imagery on the wall–
So, note by note, bring music from your mind,
So write a book shall mean beyond the facts,
Suffice the eye and save the soul besides."[16]

Nor does Goethe, and yet his constitution seems to point strongly to the nonintentional approach; to him, symbolic representation, as the core of poetry, "articulates something particular without thinking of the general or pointing to it. Whoever absorbs this particularity in its vitality receives concurrently the general, without realizing it, or realizing it but later on...[17] Everything that happens is symbol, and in representing itself perfectly it points to the rest."[18] This definition is eminently applicable to the best tradition of the German *Novelle*. The *Novelle* takes a unique occurrence, disciplines it but does not adulterate it, an occurrence in which the particulars are perfectly

---

[16]*The Ring and the Book* (Boston: Houghton, Mifflin and Company, 1895). My attention was first called to this quotation by J. L. Salvan in his article on symbolism in the *Dictionary of World Literature* (New York: Philosophical Library, 1943), p. 567.

[17]". . . die Natur der Poesie . . . spricht ein Besonderes aus, ohne ans Allgemeine zu denken oder darauf hinzuweisen. Wer nun dieses Besondere lebendig faßt erhält zugleich das Allgemeine mit, ohne es gewahr zu werden, oder erst spät" (Goethe, *Maximen und Reflexionen,* Hamburger Ausgabe, 14 vols. [Ha"mburg: Christian Wegner, 1960], XII, 471).

[18]"Alles, was geschieht, ist Symbol, und, indem es vollkommen sich selbst darstellt, deutet es auf das Übrige" (Letter to Carl Ernst Schubarth dated April 2, 1818, *Goethe-Briefe,* ed. Philipp Stein [Berlin: Otto Elsner, 1905], VII, 168).

viable in themselves, are not strained or stretched to represent the general, but provide food for thought tending toward the general, Goethe's "quiet enticement to meditate further."[19]

Subsequently Walther Killy, in his book with the provocative title: *German Schmaltz (Deutscher Kitsch[20])* did nothing but rephrase Goethe's definition in distinguishing between what he calls "pseudosymbolism," an obtrusive device contrived by the writer and dependent upon explicatory pointers, and genuine symbolism, which is a component of what happens, part of the matrix of the story – in short, something that makes sense itself.

I would thus venture to say that the symbols more likely, in the words of Browning, to "suffice the eye" as well as "save the soul," to "twice show truth," are the ones whose range and depth are imperfectly realized by their vessel, the author, elementary rapports welling up in the poet, demonstrating their basic nature through the very unconsciousness of their eruption, intuited rather than worked out.[21]

Let us try to test and illustrate these generalities through specifics. We choose as our main exhibits three works by three writers contemporary with each other, all three considered first-rate: *The Tempting of Pescara (Die*

---

[19]" . . . stillen Reiz, weiter nachzudenken" *(Unterhaltungen deutscher Ausgewanderten,* Hamburger Ausgabe, VI, 167.) Cf. Benno von Wiese's sane distinctions between allegory and symbol, based on Goethe's theory (alas, not always practice), in his "Bild-Symbole in der deutschen Novelle," *Publications of the English Goethe Society,* New Series, XXIV (1955), 132-133.

[20]Walther Killy, *Deutscher Kitsch* (Göttingen: Vandenhoeck and Ruprecht, 1962), p. 21.

[21]J. Christopher Middleton characterizes this kind of symbolism as "open-ended" and rightly warns against the frequent assumption that the poet who "makes meaning" is expected to "know it" (*Literary Symbolism,* p. 103). "The making of meaning does involve a kind of unknowing" (*ibid.,* p. 104).

Versuchung des Pescara), by Conrad Ferdinand Meyer (1887), *Romeo and Juliet in the Village (Romeo und Julia auf dem Dorfe),* by Gottfried Keller (1856), and *The Rider of the White Horse (Der Schimmelreiter),* by Theodor Storm (1888) – authors, incidentally, practically unknown to the Western World outside German-speaking areas, classics who have not even reached first base on their way toward world literature.

These stories are quite unlike each other: Meyer unfolds, against a flamboyant cinquecento tapestry, the story of a general tempted to betray the emperor; Keller describes the bourgeois decline of two peasants and the gaily and sadly beautiful love of their children ending in their deaths; Storm relates the superhuman (in more ways than one) struggle of a lone giant of a dike-reeve against outside chaos (the sea) and a stubborn, obstructionist society. The unlikeness of the stories is irrelevant here, since we are inquiring into the quality of allegorism and symbolism, not their historical or sociological appropriateness.

Meyer's *Novelle* is not five sentences old when he calls our attention to a fresco opposing a Bacchic feast to the feeding in the desert, which itself contrasts "a small and hardly visible" Christ in the background to a merry company of Lombardian reapers in the foreground.[22] This is a visual reference to the mixture of the worldly and the divine in the story, a graphic representation of the disproportionateness between the dominating worldly and the minuscule divine and Christian elements, even in the Pope himself. But this is not all yet. The happy reapers are there for a purpose. After they have been specifically connected and restricted to a happy reaping episode in the life of Pescara and his wife,[23] and further limited by Pescara to an allegory of death,[24] the last sentence of the *Novelle* describes Pescara, just dead, as

---

[22]Conrad Ferdinand Meyer, *Sämtliche Werke* (Munich: Droemer, 1953), p. 590.

[23]*Ibid.,* p. 654.

[24]*Ibid.,* p. 664.

194

resembling "a young, gaunt reaper, exhausted by the harvest and sleeping on his sheaf."[25] In the German original, thanks to a participial construction, "reaper" is the last word in the story, which thus begins and ends with this simile. If you bother to work out the equation, it refers not just clearly, but obviously, to the proximity of life and death, of the worldly and the religious – the merry and the grim reaper. If you don't work it out, the episodes make little sense at all; they are extraneous to the story.

Without respite, the next sentence on the first page of the *Novelle* refers us to a detail of this fresco, a flirting girl who allows a youth to embrace her and to shove a roasted fish between her "dazzling shining teeth."[26] The fish, in this context, is a further visual reference to the juxtaposition of *ecclesia* and *la dolce vita*.

Additional pictorial reinforcement comes in this chapter: another painting, this time of Pescara himself playing chess with his wife, Victoria Colonna. She fixates him with a searching, interrogative glance, while touching the queen with hesitant fingers; he, a "warrior of earnest and toilsome features, hides a smile in the severely drooping corner of this mouth".[27] The picture will be explained by the subsequent plot: Pescara's wife, tempted by the possible reward of an Italian queenship (for herself) if she can talk her husband into treason, yet slowed down by her own compunctions, wonders (like everybody else in the story) what he will do next; the grave features of the general and his drooping mouth indicate his fatal injury, as yet unknown to his wife, which makes a mockery of her ambitious attempt. Hence his smile.

To make sure *we* understand, Meyer sees to it that at the very end of this chapter the conveniently summoned moon casts it beams precisely on this chess-game painting: "What will you do, Pescara? – He was pale like death,

---

[25]*Ibid.*, p. 680.

[26]*Ibid.*, p.590

[27]*Ibid.*, p. 596.

with a smile in the corners of his mouth."[28]

The preceding examples (with one exception) all have this in common: they are extraneous elements that would have no relevance, no place in the story except as consciously introduced illustrations with a specific, limited meaning yielded by hindsight: x (= y). Bacchus and reapers represent the joy of life, Christ and (as it will turn out) again the reapers, the *memento mori*. The fish likewise juxtaposes the world and the spirit, life and death. The chess game again allegorizes life and death, the temptation of life and the knowledge of death.

The fact that Meyer had to resort to the awkward and repeated use, the artificial insemination of paintings illustrates the manipulated nature of this insertion; as a matter of fact, he will have to use three more allegorical paintings in the rest of the story to make his point: the painting, allegedly by Leonardo da Vinci, showing, among other things, a serpent swallowing a child[29] (an allegory of disaster, engineered by smart and treacherous "snakes," in store for the adolescent Duke of Milan); then a verbal painting from Dante's *Inferno*, showing the two "traitors," Brutus and Cassius, hanging head down, suspended from Lucifer's hands (an allegory of the wages of treason beckoning to Pescara);[30] finally, the altar painting in the convent, *Saints' Wounds (Heiligenwunden)*, showing a mercenary thrusting his spear into Christ's body[31] (an allegory of the death-inflicting wound Pescara himself received at Pavia, responsible for a turn of his mind toward practiced Christianity).

To this we can safely add the living picture of Pescara slumbering on a seat flanked by two sphinxes and facing a fountain (death facing the flow of

---

[28]*Ibid.*, p. 606.

[29]*Ibid.*, p. 638.

[30]*Ibid.*, p. 652.

[31]*Ibid.*, p. 662.

life, whose beginning and end are bathed in mystery).[32]

This is by no means the extent to which these motifs are used: the chess-game motif (*spielen* means both "playing" and "toying") continues throughout the story. Pescara is said to be toying with Italy like the cat with the mouse,[33] he toys also with his confidants (Bourbon and Del Guasto), Bourbon toys with Morone and the Duke of Milan, etc.; the whole *Novelle* could be compared to a chess game. The death motif is further illustrated, visualized, and repeated (spear wound, Pescara's self-personification as "death,"[34] the death [by treason!] of Julia, [35] the men responsible for Pescara's actual death [Bläsi] or plotted death [Moncada], the murder of Pescara's father [again Moncada], and finally the somewhat anachronistic appearance, in the last chapter, of Pescara as "Death the Strangler,"[36] who hardly harmonizes with the lyrical "Death the Reaper" in the same chapter). But pursuing each allegory and leitmotif to its legitimate end in this story would leave little else: it would merely confirm, with embracing fullness, the cumulative, over-saturated nature of Meyer's allegories – the very weaknesses which Killy has diagnosed as the difference between what he calls pseudo-symbol and symbol.

Let there be no rejoinder that the culprit here is not only allegory but symbol, that the reaper, the fish, the snake, possessing double characteristics, must be classified as symbols. An allegory may refer to one abstraction or to a frozen contrast between two abstractions, or to one abstraction first and another one subsequently. It is univalent, regardless, not ambivalent or multivalent; it deliberately refers to one specific abstraction at *one* time.

The one symbolic exception to the previously cited gallery of

---

[32]*Ibid.*, p. 639.

[33]*Ibid.*, p. 617.

[34]*Ibid.*, p. 637.

[35]*Ibid.*, p. 641.

[36]*Ibid.*, p. 673 ("der Würger Tod").

allegories is, I think, Pescara's smile. This smile does not have a set value. It is subject to a range of interpretations. It is the quintessence of his pragmatic wisdom of life. In this particular situation, it seems to reflect an affectionate and amused understanding of his wife's quandary, a knowledge of the absurdity of the commotion of which he is the center, a philosophic acceptance of a tough break, a smile at the irony of fate offering him everything when he is nearing nothing, a detached view of Pescara the living by Pescara the already dead, and just a touch of bitterness (drooping mouth), all this against the "serious and severe" expression of a man loyal to others (king, friend Bourbon, wife) and to himself, repelled and yet somewhat attracted by the invitation to an allegedly patriotic treason. This is not an erudite picture whose key is available only to the educated, and too easily at that; this is a basic and yet complex human reaction; this is a symbol which is part of the main.

With this gratifying exception, the initial impression of static, univalent allegorization is confirmed in and by the rest of the story. The bilious Guiccardin prefers vinegar to oil, but deserves credit for providing me with the allegorical part of my title.[37] After he talks about the conspiracy, lightning and thunder furnish an operatic flourish, and, to add insult to injury, we are being informed that this is an omen.[38] The same lightning must serve again to dazzle and warn Victoria Colonna, who is rationalizing the treason.[39] But after her long prayer the heavens brighten.[40] The tempter, Morone, clad in a black coat, steps out from and steps back into the night.[41] As Pescara nears the fateful decision in his choice between loyalty and treason, midnight

---

[37]*Ibid.*, p. 597.

[38]*Ibid.*, p. 612.

[39]*Ibid.*, p. 614.

[40]*Ibid.*

[41]*Ibid.* p. 619.

198

strikes from the clocktower, and once again Meyer puts the dot on the *i:* "The twelfth strike – irrevocable."[42] After Pescara's heart attack "the hanging lamp is extinguished,"and with these words the chapter ends.[43] To Moncada's question about his goal, Pescara replies by dipping his hand into the brazier and opening it: "Dust and ashes."[44] As the defeated Duke of Milan enters his palace, the canopy over his throne collapses, and we are told that this is a bad omen.[45] And when, little later, the Duke of Bourbon smashes his goblet against the marble floor, this not only means but we are explicitly informed that it *does* mean that he is renouncing his claim to the Duchy of Milan.[46]

These thickly sprinkled and rather disconnected allegories are bordered by two personalized allegorizations; Italy – arbitrary,[47] fantastic, unreliable, but acting with heart as well as with head, disorganized but likeable, grotesque but human – is personalized by Morone (!), *Morone buffone;* Spain – cold, calculating, fanatic, intelligent, cruel, consistent, well-organized, born to rule but inhuman – by the *monkish Moncada* (!). Even though these humanized countries exhibit various characteristics, the equation remains the same everywhere: $x = y$.

We cannot here take the time to investigate thoroughly the similes in the *Versuchung des Pescara.* They seem about as shopworn as the allegories discussed above. Two examples: the rumor of Pescara's impending desertion

---

[42]*Ibid.,* p. 657.

[43]*Ibid.,* p. 658.

[44]*Ibid.,* p. 672.

[45]*Ibid.,* p. 673.

[46]*Ibid.,* p. 675.

[47]See Benno von Wiese, *Die deutsche Novelle von Goethe bis Kafka* (Düsseldorf: Bagel, 1956), I, 265.

is compared to the fountains of Italian *piazzas:* both are equally public.[48] Aside from the relative staleness of the comparison itself, a little thinking shows that the comparison is very superficial. A fountain runs evenly, steadily; rumors in cities and inns circulate with much more uncertainty, with unpredictable pauses. The limpidity of the water is hardly a suitable simile for the opaque substance of treason. On the same page, Italy's advances to Pescara are described as follows: 'Italy throws herself into his arms . . . he will caress, subjugate, and discard her . . ., oh he will play with her like the cat with the mouse.'[49] It is certainly possible to caress, conquer, and abandon a woman or, stretching the metaphor, even a country; it is likewise possible to toy with someone, as the cat with the mouse, but have metaphor and simile mixed up in the same exclamation is not only unnecessarily cumulative but borders on the absurd. A mouse does not throw itself into the arms of a cat; a cat does not have arms; a cat does not caress a mouse; a woman throwing herself into someone's arms is everything but a mouse. The first metaphor, by itself, would be quite dashing, except that Italy, the woman, is not animated by patriotic passion only, but by all kinds of ulterior motives in making advances to Pescara. The second, cat-and-mouse, simile, is appropriate neither to Pescara nor to Italy. Both juxtaposed in the same sentence are frightfully ill-matched. The mediocrity of the imagery confirms the mediocrity of the allegory.

I am certainly not the first one to have seen these weaknesses, although even those who have detected them appear anxious to soften the unmistakable verdict.[50] But, worse than that, even the *critical* observers

---

[48]Meyer, *Sämtliche Werke,* p. 617.

[49]*Ibid.*

[50]Benno von Wiese, while admitting weakness, nevertheless credits Meyer, in *Pescara,* with "a high degree of novellesque ability" ("einen hohen Grad novellistischen Könnens," *Novelle* [Stuttgart: Metzler, 1963], p. 68). H. M. Waidson refers to *Pescara,* along with *Michael Kohlhaas, Die schwarze*

continue to speak of the *symbolic* power of these images.[51] As I hope to have shown, the imagery I have dealt with, excepting one instance, is allegorical, not symbolical, univalent rather than ambivalent or multivalent, static rather than dynamic, extraneous rather than intrinsic, intentional rather than organic.

This is not to say that allegorization, sparsely and deftly or humorously used, cannot be a real asset to the *Novelle*. Take Keller's delightful story, *Clothing Makes People (Kleider machen Leute,* 1873/4).[52] The title being what it is, clothing is bound to be involved in the imagery of the story – it is a "natural." The thimble stands for the "tailoresque" part of the hero; fur-cap, velvet-trimmed coat, and gloves for the aristocratic bearing of Wenzel Strapinski, the dark-haired darling of fate. Note that these are functional attributes, objects that serve practical purposes while serving as specific allegories. They are used economically, and always with a sense of humor. It is true that there are places in the story where Keller accumulates whole mountains of allegories:[53] houses with allegorical names: the House of the Golden Dragon, of the Swiss Sword, of the Unicorn, of the Bird of Paradise, of Old Independence, of New Independence, of Civic Virtue A, of

---

Spinne and *Romeo und Julia,* as one of the "characteristic masterpieces of the nineteenth-century Novelle" (in the revised edition of E. K. Bennett's *A History of the German Novelle* [Cambridge: University Press, 1961], p. 241).

[51] Johannes Klein, *Geschichte der deutschen Novelle von Goethe bis zur Gegenwart* (Wiesbaden: Steiner, 1960), p. 48; von Wiese, *Die deutsche Novelle,* I (1956), pp. 252, 267; von Wiese, *Novelle,* p. 68.

[52] There seems to be a connection between the typifying intent of a *Novelle* and a corresponding richness in allegories: *Kleider machen Leute, Die drei gerechten Kammacher, Aquis Submersus, Der Ketzer von Soana, Der Schleier.*

[53] From here on I expand, now and then, on pointers contained in chapter five of this book: "Theorie und Praxis der Novelle: Gottfried Keller."

Civic Virtue B, of "Zum Wiedersehen 1 und 2,"[54] and others, but these are affectionate take-offs on Swiss history and bourgeois virtues, and even when the sun breaks through as an allegory of Strapinski's ascending fortune[55] the humorous coloring of the situation is unmistakable.

We recently proposed the hypothesis that the looser the silhouette of the *Novelle*, represented by the unified occurrence of *one event* (the *eine Begebenheit* of Goethe's famous definition of the *Novelle*[56]), the greater the necessity of the author to save, by other means, the concentration indispensable to the *Novelle*.[57] Among the most effective of these means are image - "falcons" ("Bild-Falken"), object-symbols (*Dingsymbole*) and musical "falcons" (*Leitmotive*). We further suggested, and venture to broaden this into a more general hypothesis at this time, that when the silhouette of the action is still relatively unified and striking but needs some reinforcement through images, the use of allegory may be adequate to meet this purpose (witness *Kleider machen Leute*); but when the *Novelle* threatens to burst its classic boundaries (as it does in the *Versuchung des Pescara*) to the extent of jeopardizing the *Gestalt* of the genre as such, the accumulation of allegories – Meyer's remedy – will not do. On the contrary, allegorical proliferation, as in the *Versuchung,* may have the effect of scattering attention in all direction, of offering too many disconnected and univalent images – of further weakening the structure of the *Novelle*. A quantitative corrective is likely to prove impotent. A qualitative compensation is much more likely to do the job, and that is the upgrading of the allegory to a symbol – in the *Novelle,* normally an object-symbol. Being more pervasive, more encompassing, more flexible,

---

[54]Gottfried Keller, *Sämtliche Werke* (Munich: Droemer, 1953, 2 vols.), I, 818.

[55]*Ibid.,* p. 812.

[56]Goethe to Eckermann, January 25, 1827: "Was ist eine Novelle anders als eine sich ereignete unerhörte Begebenheit?" (*Eckermanns Gespräche mit Goethe,* ed. Ernst Merian-Genast [Basel: Birkhäuser, 1945], I, 210).

[57]See our chapter five, "Theorie und Praxis der Novelle: Gottfried Keller."

it can link a whole story through no more than one or two principal symbols; being multivalent, it is better suited to hold the *Novelle* together than univalent allegory. It is true that the appropriateness and the quality of the symbol then become much more decisive for the story than the relevance and persuasiveness of one of several or many allegories. This would fit into the high degree of workmanship, of artistic responsibility that characterizes the best products of the German *Novelle*. At the same time, as soon as conscious efforts to create symbols are involved, the symbol may become a rational construct lacking in life, in veracity, which is precisely what will happen to certain well-known examples of the genre by Gerhart Hauptmann, Emil Strauss, and Werner Bergengruen. In the finest *Novellen,* symbols, though subject to rational polishing, must be functional and, as it were, instinctive by birth.

For possible illustrations of this hypothesis let us look at what are probably the best two German *Novellen* of the second half of the nineteenth century, Keller's *Romeo and Juliet in the Village (Romeo und Julia auf dem Dorfe)* and Theodor Storm's *Rider of the White Horse (Der Schimmelreiter).*

Romeo und Julia is not devoid of allegory, and this allegory is not necessarily bad. To be sure, when the two peasants, locked in a fatal struggle that paralyzes them as surely as two drowning persons clasping each other, meet on a "narrow, tottering bridge," under lightning and thunder, there is too direct a connection, I am afraid, between the "rumbling rancor" of the thunder and of the protagonists, the "heavy raindrops" and their tears; the setting of the scene, not the scene itself, has something Hollywoodish.[58] Compare it to the deluge at the conclusion of the *Schimmelreiter:* what is a theatrical and dispensable stagesetting in Keller becomes, in Storm, a necessary and organic, cataclysmic showdown between the forces of evil and good, chaos and civilization, the sea and man – Armageddon.

---

[58]Keller, *Sämtliche Werke,* I, 668-670. Here I cannot be quite as forbearing as Walter Silz in his *Realism and Reality: Studies in the German Novelle of Poetic Realism* (Chapel Hill: University of North Carolina Press, 1956), p. 87.

But other allegories in *Romeo und Julia* and the *Schimmelreiter* are quite effective. Colors have a powerful impact in *Romeo und Julia:* the redness of the lonely poppy in the abandoned field where the children play[59] and later on, amidst "innumerable poppies," love each other in earnest,[60] the cherry-redness of the skirt of one of the "gypsies," [61] the sturdy, unpruned rose bushes developing on their own around their place of amusement,[62] the comparison of Vrenchen to a purple rose [63] or a red carnation,[64] the "necklace and belt of small red berries" of the five-year-old girl,[65] intensified – similar to the poppy motif above – to a "sextuple necklace of rowan-berries" of another one of these "bohemians,"[66]– and I have not exhausted the instances – all of these stand for one and the same thing: the "surging blood"[67] of the two lovers, particularly of Vrenchen, their desire for union. At first reading this allegory is functional and unobtrusive, at second and third readings one detects its (still functional) richness, and at tenth reading one wishes there were a little less of it. But who reads a work ten times except a professor? Is it fair to judge a *Novelle* not written for petulant scholars but for a non-

---

[59]Keller, *Sämtliche Werke*, I, 654, 655.

[60]*Ibid.*, pp. 675, 677.

[61]*Ibid.*, p. 698.

[62]*Ibid.*, p. 697.

[63]*Ibid.*, p. 699.

[64]*Ibid.*, p. 693.

[65]*Ibid.*, p. 654.

[66]*Ibid.*, p. 698.

[67]*Ibid.*, pp. 700, 703. See also Ernst Feise, "Kellers *Romeo und Julia* und Stifters *Brigitta:* Aufbau und Gehalt," in *Xenion: Themes, Forms, and Ideas in German Literature* (Baltimore: The Johns Hopkins Press, 1950), p. 160.

204

professional, yet sensitive and intelligent audience, by our highly specialized, academic standards alone? Be that as it may – and I am asking a question which is not a rhetorical one – the "red" allegory in *Romeo und Julia* is effective because, though univalent, it is richly suggestive, yet simple and common.

Nevertheless, the story could quite conceivably have proceeded without it; the allegory is, no matter how warm and rich, an added touch. It reminds one of the ash tree ("Eberesche") in the *Schimmelreiter* which stands, in lone grandeur, by the side of the old dikegrave's house, "visible from afar";[68] the tree vaults over the handshake, signifying, for all intents and purposes, the engagement of Elke, only child of the old dikegrave, and Hauke, the dikegrave-to-be; it rustles over the married but childless Elke;[69] beneath it the eerie white horse, one of the key symbols of the story, makes his first appearance;[70] from the tree Hauke takes his last departure, Elke catches the last glance of her husband.[71] The ash tree is, clearly, allegorical; it represents the continuity of the Volkerts, then of the Haien family, the dike-reeve dynasty. It occurs at least nine times in this role. Before Hauke's final departure – appropriately, perhaps too appropriately – "the old ash-tree creaks, as if it were to burst asunder."[72] The ash tree does not clash with the North Sea landscape; it is rare but not foreign; it represents a basic organism; it is picturesque, it is visually impressive. But it is nevertheless quite unusual, the highest tree in the village, a distinction perhaps too obvious; only survivor of three ash trees planted by Elke's great-grandfather, it is, let us admit it, a stage prop with a very specific assignment, nicely, cleverly reinforced throughout the

----

[68]Theodor Storm, *Werke* (Munich: Droemer, 1953), p. 902.

[69]*Ibid.*, p. 926.

[70]*Ibid.*, p. 935.

[71]*Ibid.*, p. 967.

[72]*Ibid.*

story; it is expendable. In comparison, the heap of stones separating the fields of Manz and Marti in *Romeo und Julia* is structural, endemic;[73] it would roughly correspond to the dike in the *Schimmelreiter*.

What images in these two stories *are* centripetal, elementary symbols?[74] In *Romeo und Julia*, field and river, functional manifestations of two of the four traditional elements of life: earth and water. The well-tilled soil is the very foundation of rural existence, the staff of life for the two peasants, Manz and Marti, the nutrient of civilization. It stands for more than the prosperity of its owners; it guarantees the continuity of the society which seems as unshakable as the creases of the knee-breeches of those tilling this good earth.[75] But there is untilled earth between the tilled areas of earth, a wild plot of land covered with weeds and stones, a symbol of neglect and disorder, and, as it turns out, of intentional or, at least, tolerated injustice to its déclassé owner. The growth of the stone wall separating the once good neighbors becomes, like the Berlin Wall, the visible token of the inhumanity of man toward man, the separation of families and lovers, the grotesque sundering of what belongs together; it is, alas, nothing but the monumental reflection of the rigid disposition of the bearers of the breeches which Keller describes as "chiseled in stone"[76] on the first page of the *Novelle*.

---

[73]Udo Kultermann includes in his excellent analysis of "Bildformen in Kellers Novelle *Romeo und Julia auf dem Dorfe*" *(Der Deutschunterricht,* VIII, No. 3 [1956], 86-100) a discussion of stone symbolism.

[74]See Susanne K. Langer's observations on "charged" symbols, basic phenomena, and objects (a sunset, a cross, a ship) inherently loaded with symbolic meaning *(Philosophy in a New Key* [New York: Pelican, 1948], pp. 231-232). Reginald Phelps notes Keller's "liking for symbolism . . . of a rather simple kind" ("Keller's Technique of Composition in *Romeo und Julia auf dem Dorfe,"* Germanic Review, XXIV, No. 1 [1949], p. 42).

[75]Keller, *Sämtliche Werke,* p. 651.

[76]*Ibid.*

206

This, then, is already a polar symbolism reaching to the roots of mankind's existence and troubles. But Keller goes it one better yet; for this negative symbol, trapped and staring out from in between two positive, life-giving symbols, becomes, in turn, the source of the positive potentialities of disorder. Again, as early as the first page, Keller tells us that "a world of tiny winged creatures hummed undisturbed above" this "fallow waste," enjoying the opportunities of irregularity.[77] The earth has caught up with the stones, has grown over them in magic profusion, equilibrium is being restored, bright red poppies shoot out of the desert – allegories, if you wish, blossom on symbols, life and love arise from stone. For it is on this very forsaken field that Sali and Vrenchen find each other, first at the ages of seven and five, in playful love; it is on the top of the stony crest that they see each other, once a year, during the period of their enforced separation; it is there that they spend their first happy day together as adolescents before the final break between their parents; it is there that they first kiss each other; it is along this crest that they walk "quietly, happily, and calmly"[78] like a promised couple; it is there that the exuberant music of a "wild wedding" ceremony fades into the distance[79] and they take the decision to marry and die without benefit of clergy.[80] The soil carries them from childhood to wedding, which equals death.

The other pole of their existence is the river. Their destiny takes them from the land that first brings them together, separates them, then unites them again, to the water that first separates them,[81] above which, on a shaky bridge leading across, they seal their first, fleeting union with "hands moist and cool

---

[77]*Ibid.*

[78]*Ibid.*, p. 674.

[79]*Ibid.*, p. 702.

[80]*Ibid.*, p. 703.

[81]*Ibid.*, p. 668.

from the water and the fish,"[82] on which they celebrate their wedding night, and in which they die as one. As indispensable to existence as the soil, it represents the flowing rather than the solid, the liquid and unfathomable instead of the firm, change rather than continuity, the irretrievable and irresistible rather than the stable, the dynamic rather than the static. I should not have said it "represents"; it *is*, or rather it *becomes*.[83] The water symbol here derives an ironic depth from its ambiguity: as life-giving soil here, in the shape of a contested field, gives rise to ruin and ultimately death, so life-giving water becomes the place and means of ruin (the illusory fishing expeditions of Manz, Marti, and the Seldwylers) and of death.[84] Liquid, the biological source of life, the distinct quality of the erotic and procreative, becomes the medium of a death as immaculate as its victims, cleansing them of any possible stains, a means of expiation if sin occurred. Ironically enough, self-righteous public opinion will equate this voluntary submergence only with the theft of the hay barge which has to serve the two lovers as their nuptial couch, with what Keller, sarcastically, calls "rampaging immoralism" and "barbarization of passion."[85]

This is symbolism at its best. Not at its only, but at its best. Mark that the story makes perfect sense as a story, is, with very occasional lapses, natural and unforced and convincing without any symbolic interpretation at

---

[82]*Ibid.*, p. 670.

[83]Professor Jaszi's relevant comments, in the discussion following the delivery of this paper, have called my attention to the danger of backsliding into "static" verbs ("represents"), more appropriate to allegorism, when trying to describe the nature and power of the symbol.

[84]For pertinent observations on the water motif, see Helmut Rehder, *"Romeo und Julia auf dem Dorfe:* An Analysis," *Monatshefte,* XXXV, No. 8 (December, 1943), 442 ff. Also Feise, "Kellers *Romeo und Julia . . . ,"* *Xenion,* p. 158.

[85]Keller, *Sämtliche Werke,* p. 705.

208

all.[86] The search into its symbolism adds implied dimensions but does not disqualify or invalidate or truncate findings that do not penetrate all these layers. This is the kind of symbolism that is not dependent upon *a* key, *a* formula, an intricate combination accessible only to the highly sophisticated mind, or perhaps invented by it, as Mr. Peyre has suggested.[87]

I insist that the most complex symbolic interpretation is not necessarily the "right" one. Complexity *may* be superficial, *may* mean muddled thinking, unable to separate the chaff from the wheat, waning artistic strength. Excess of symbolism and allegory is a greater offense than too little or none, for it camouflages mediocrity. The best *Novelle* is the one that does justice to the polarities and ironies of human existence without sacrificing the functional concreteness, the "truthfulness" and the limpidity of storytelling inherent in the genre.

Examined by these demanding standards, Storm's *Schimmelreiter* will be found fully comparable to Keller's *Romeo und Julia* in the organic quality of its main symbols: horses, sea, and dike. The sea, seen throughout the story from the land, is the demonic-destructive,[88] the rebellion of the elements, fate, night, death, nothingness rushing tigerlike to tear up the defense which human order, Christian civilization have thrown up against the onslaught of chaos: the

---

[86]"I believe that the proper and perfect symbol is the natural object, that if a man uses 'symbols' he must so use them that their symbolic function does not obtrude; so that a sense, and the poetic quality of the passage, is not lost to those who do not understand the symbol as such, to whom, for instance, a hawk is a hawk" *(Literary Essays by Ezra Pound,* ed. T. S. Eliot [London: Faber and Faber, 1954], p. 9).

[87]Peyre, "Seventy-Five Years of Comparative Literature," *Yearbook of Comparative and General Literature,* p. 25.

[88]The life-giving properties of water (e.g., fishing) are here dwarfed by its life-taking nature; see not only Hauke's and Elke's fate but also the death of Trine Jans' son in the shipwreck.

dike. These constituents of existence are humanized in the dominating creatures of the story: Hauke Haien and his *Schimmel*. The acquisition of the raggety, ill-treated horse seems a Christian act, a bad bargain intentionally concluded by a compassionate man expressing thanks for the completion of his plans for a new dike. This down-in-the-dumps horse fattens up, however, into a vigorous steed that flies through the air like Odin's horse. There was more method than madness in Hauke's acquisition of an essentially sound but run-down animal. Rider and horse develop a reciprocal magnetism evolving into fusion, an elementary attraction that reinforces Hauke's own demonic instincts, becomes a living symbol of his *hybris* at war with his *ratio* as the sea rages against the dike outside him. We ask ourselves whether chaos has not planted its own seeds beneath the rational upper layer of Hauke. Will chaos, which does not only exist outside but inside, will the sea have the last laugh, after all, a "horse-laugh," as it has already come back at Elke and Hauke by "casting a curse" on their only child? For Wienke, too, exemplifies this mixture of heathen and Christian elements, a mixture which manages at once to be complex and perfectly natural, for in this Germanic territory along the North Sea the fringes remain pagan to this very day: the pagan and Christian elements are intertwined and superimposed. The pagan undertow of this coastal area would be inclined to cast Wienke off as a creature that is not viable, an underprivileged being eligible for sacrifice like a bastard dog or a gipsy child. But father and mother accept and love her in the spirit of Christianity as they have saved the horse, the dog, and the sea gull. Yet the child herself has unbreakable ties with the elementary, she belongs to another world, she has a strange attraction to and for the demonic (Trine Jans, the sea), she is forever accompanied by creatures which themselves are animalic in origin but domesticated, humanized by man, hybrid beings: sea gull and dog.

No matter how far we descend into this abyss, uncharted depths remain. The ultimate act of the dikegrave, his voluntary jump into the raging sea, preserves its secret, too, for it may be interpreted as a Christian act of contrition for his *hybris,* a last gesture of love and loyalty to wife and daughter, already drowned, or as a more pagan than Christian attempt to placate the sea by offering it the human sacrifice of life which he had stubbornly withheld from it until this time. And the sea understands, and respects the bargain: the Hauke-Haien dike is left intact, the dike which in itself is a symbol of rational order, of selflessness – and of pride amounting to *hybris*.

When the author has succeeded in creating, in two or three symbols, a fusion of rational and irrational, of the unique and the permanent, of action and meaning, an entity whose components make sense as integral parts of the story, make sense also in their polar relationships, but whose interlacing, whose various combinations seem inexhaustible though none does violence either to the story or to the universe against which the story moves, then the author has achieved the well-nigh impossible. Keller and Storm have done it in these two stories that belong to world literature. They could not have done it without the universal power of the symbol.

In *Railguard Thiel (Bahnwärter Thiel)*, by Gerhart Hauptmann (1887), we have, perhaps, the last contemporary German *Novelle* in which the object-symbol fulfils adequately – in this case, admirably – its centripetal role, in its logical and emotional magnetism as well as its organic imbeddedness in the story. Hauptmann has captured a symbol of technology, the railroad, and has given it universal yet very concrete meaning. It is the monster that arises, as the tiniest black dot, on the farthest point of the horizon, almost invisible, that grows, first very slowly, soon with frightful speed, that descends upon us like an envoy of chaos,[89] rattles, snorts, roars, screams toward us like a modern version of Odin's wild hunt, like a technological *Schimmelreiter*, grazes us with its wings of disaster: the apocalypse of the day of judgement. On Thiel's day of judgment, which becomes also that of Lene and of the "brat" (*der Balg*[90]), it no longer grazes us, it runs right into us, into Tobias, bouncing him and us around like a rubber ball.

The rails, it has been remarked, grasp Thiel's existence as

---

[89]von Wiese, *Die deutsche Novelle*, I, 271.

[90]Gerhart Hauptmann, *Bahnwärter Thiel* (Stuttgart: Reclam, 1962), p. 43.

hypnotically, as octopuslike as the animal scent of his second wife, Lene.[91] He does not really understand their meaning. The emperor who once traveled from Berlin to Breslau along the rails guarded by Thiel remains invisible to him. All he derives from passing trains, even before his son is killed by one of them, are grave injuries caused by a wine bottle casually thrown out or a piece of coal. Nevertheless, the machine is not depicted as a one-dimensional malefactor (as so frequently in German literature of the time, unless it is ignored entirely as being "unpoetic"). His service is faithful in the fullest sense of the word, for it involves not only loyalty to his appointed work, but faithfulness to his former, cleaner, more spiritual existence, "Dienst" not only to the ethos of work, of "Arbeit," the badge of nobility, as Silz has seen so well,[92] of poetic realism, but also "Minnedienst" – "Dienst an Minna," his first wife, his truly better half. The two together keep him clean. His railroad post becomes a religious sanctuary which he defends against the intrusions of his sexual partner, and when this defense collapses outwardly and Thiel half acquiesces in the invasion of his present wife, the hard-working animal, his resentment, his squashed piety are pressed into the depths of his subconscious, only to explode again, after the killing of his son by the railroad (!) train through the neglect of his second wife, as a double murder of revenge and self-cleansing. Hauptmann has given the railroad a soul, not only in the lonely guardhouse altar where Thiel worships Minna, but in the wondrous sounds which, as we all know, emanate from telegraph wires along the rails and from the rails themselves if we bend down and listen to them. He has bedded, finally, the sober and yet so frightfully portentous rails into the equally sober and melancholy stretches of sand and pines of the Mark Brandenburg, whose lonely leanness and beautiful sadness form the nutrient for direct, individualistic communication with the divine, which crosses the tracks as a squirrel.

Since *Bahnwärter Thiel* the overwhelming complexity of

---

[91]von Wiese, *Die deutsche Novelle*, I, p. 273.

[92]Walter Silz, *Realism and Reality*, p. 144.

contemporary life has made it just about impossible for an artist even of the first magnitude to write a representative *Novelle* held together by a truly comprehensive symbol. The attempts to return to the more classic form of the *Novelle* have either been failures or only partly successful. To the failures belongs Emil Strauss' *The Veil (Der Schleier,* 1920), usually grossly overrated.

The veil, in its whiteness, lightness, softness, translucence, and adaptability, its marital and religious connotations, is a lovely feminine symbol, but scarcely appropriate to the twentieth century. Representing, as it here does, the early matrimonial happiness of a noble couple, a wife's silent exhortation of an errant husband and, at the same time, her merciful[93] tribute to a second honeymoonlike, quasi-marital happiness of her husband with his mistress, it is a grand, beautiful, and symbolic gesture totally incredible, alas, stylized, purified so as to make complete constructs of these timelessly impossible and oh so wonderfully generous people.

Although Bergengruen's *Three Falcons (Die drei Falken,* 1937) is better literature than the *Schleier,* the falcon symbol, reminiscent of Boccaccio, is an elegant failure. The boldness, dignity, and *noblesse* of the falcons, their self-restraint and voluntary service, so to speak, superimposed on their love of liberty, are impressive but too remote from the twentieth century and probably at home in none. They are centripetal in the story, but marginal in their existential application to modern life. In order to give them more universal meaning, Bergengruen has tried to make them representative of humanity: as there are noble and ignoble falcons, so there is selfless and selfish humanity, the latter portrayed by a silkdealer couple, a covetous young widow, and one part of Albinelli, executor of the will; the former portrayed by the late falconer, the prior of the monastery of the Holy Ghost, the better part

---

[93]The veil in Brentano's *Geschichte vom braven Kasperl und dem schönen Annerl* and in Keller's *Kleider machen Leute* also carries the connotation of mercy. See B. A. Rowley's introduction to *Kleider machen Leute* (London: Arnold, 1960), p. 25.

of Albinelli, and of Cecco, the limping bastard, natural son of the falconer. All these pieces fall much too neatly into place; the *Novelle* does not spring to life.

For analogous reasons, the allegorism in Hauptmann's *Heretic of Soana (Der Ketzer von Soana,* 1911-1917) – and here I know I go against strongly entrenched opinion – is a failure all the more painful since it comes from a man who started out as a first-rate artist and has much greater ambitions in this story than Bergengruen in his. Hauptmann's would-be symbolism is to take in the Dionysian and the Christian antitheses, though feeble attempts are made to connect them here and there; for example, the shepherd of the Christian flock with a real, heathen goatherd.[94] The result is, unfortunately, a sophomoric kind of allegorism, so direct, contrived, and self-enclosed as to be an insult to the intelligent reader, a "symbolism" all too clearly fed by encyclopedias and reference works – a *"Bildungssymbolik."*[95] The he-goat *(Ziegenbock)* allegorizes the sexually aggressive male, and it is hardly necessary for Hauptmann to have him swallow the priest's breviary to indicate that eros will dispose of Christian asceticism.[96] Even less necessary is the ride on top of the goat the author imposes on the female embodiment of eros, Agata,[97] or the schoolmasterly comment of the goatherd to his visitor as they watch two bucks fight: "Eros! Eros!"[98]

On top of this are piled additional sexual allegories, apparently in the

---

[94]Gerhart Hauptmann, *Der Ketzer von Soana* (Gütersloh: Bertelsmann, 1955), p. 42.

[95]There is no denying, of course, that there are fine and authentic, if somewhat monotonous, southern nature descriptions in this work of Hauptmann.

[96]Hauptmann, *Der Ketzer von Soana,* p. 62.

[97]*Ibid.,* p. 112.

[98]*Ibid.,* p. 16. This is but a striking illustration of the overemphasis on didactic "prodesse" and the slighting of poetic "delectare" in much of German literary prose.

214

belief that intensity can be achieved by accumulation: the far-fetched copulative allegory of a "black thunderstorm resting on the giant dorsal rock of the Monte Generoso (!) like a huge steer resting on a heifer, practicing with panting loins the procreative work of fertilization";[99] a further male-aggressive sexual allegory is the leitmotif of the fishing eagle circling over the same Monte Generoso, an image employed, with slight variation, when Francesco the priest shoots down like a falcon on Agata's lip;[100] there is the sarcophagus, decorated with Dionysian scenes, in which the luscious women of Soana do their laundry, casting inviting glances at their saintly priest (triumph of life over death again, in case you don't know); there is the female erotic allegory of the "young apple trees,"[101] the crack in the tree bark and voluptuous lines of the mountains;[102] and, if you are difficult to please, we have for you, to top it off, the omnipresent waterfall, no doubt indicating passion, accompanying the action from beginning to end. Not one of them is necessary to the story. Each and everyone is dragged in as a stage requisite and pointed at with the index finger: "Here! Don't you see?" The sensuous balsam of Hauptmann's story has so seduced its middle-aged professorial readers, craving, like Faust, sexual rejuvenation, that few of them have bothered to examine the pitifully conventional, ill-matched, and over-done imagery of the story.

———

We can only conjecture what the future of the symbol in the *Novelle* will be, or, in view of the atomization of our life, whether it has a future at all. Archetypal symbolism was the natural way of expression for earlier, highly structured, centripetal societies governed by recognized symbols regulating life. In any modern society seeking a return to primitivistic patterns (fascism, nazism, communism), centripetal symbols stage a forced comeback. In our

---

[99]*Ibid.*, p. 101.

[100]*Ibid.*, p. 136.

[101] *Ibid.*, p. 141.

[102]*Ibid.*, p. 68.

western, centrifugal society (witness, for example, the declining fortunes of mass rallies and national celebrations in this country), centripetal symbols either seem no longer the organic way of expression, or when new symbols (the airplane, the "bomb" missiles) are replacing the old ones, literature has had a hard time catching up with them.[103]

This centrifugal trend has been offset, to an extent, by the rediscovery of the primitive within us, which has resulted in a flourishing archetypal symbolism in contemporary literature and criticism.

Since the symbol is the key factor in the finest achievements of the nineteenth-century *Novelle,* we must ask ourselves, in the light of this prognosis, whether the *Novelle* itself has a future in the twentieth century? It certainly does not have much of a present. It is not the obsession with violence of our present-day literature and, alas, not only literature, that threatens the *Novelle,* which has thrived on violence, nor the absurdity of existence which we find, from one of the earliest and still the finest teller of *Novellen,* Heinrich von Kleist, via Keller's *Die drei gerechten Kammacher* to Hauptmann's *Bahnwärter Thiel.* But can the classic economy of form of the *Novelle,* its lean clarity, its taut explosiveness – still respected and carried, as a matter of fact, to uncanny perfection by Kafka – can it survive the wild experimentation in language (not thought) of today and tomorrow, can the symbol as a unifying factor survive the reckless centrifugal sprinkling about of assorted symbols so fashionable in today's literature, art, and cinema? Only time can tell.

Hofmannsthal's best novellesque efforts *(Bassompierre, Reitergeschichte)* and Thomas Mann's *Der kleine Herr Friedemann, Tristan, Der Tod in Venedig, Mario und der Zauberer* seem to rely less on central symbolism than on a mixture of object-symbolism, allegories (often ironic), leitmotif, and unity of mood. Thomas Mann's symbolism is highly conscious, cerebrally worked out, "expendable," allegoric, in short. But not only –

---

[103] See Langer, *Philosophy in a New Key,* pp. 227, 234. Cf. also Richard Brinkmann, "Abstract lyrics of Expressionism: End or Transformation of the Symbol?", in *Literary Symbolism,* 107-136.

216

certainly in *Tristan* and especially in *Der Tod in Venedig* – is it handled with such exquisite artistic finesse that it creates the poetic texture of his stories, not only does the combination of intellectual "raffinement" and literary tact produce an *aesthetic* pleasure, but it often resides in a twilight zone between allegory and symbol in which Mann's sophistication makes sport of professorial endeavors to establish viable theoretical distinctions. Thus, in *Der Tod in Venedig,* the various "Dance of Death" figures are clearly allegorical, but the nature of death itself, strictly within the context of the story – beauty and decomposition, liberation and humiliation, truth and impudence, authenticity, degradation, self-fulfillment and self-abandonment, etc.– is so complex and "open-ended" that the allegory ends up as a symbol. We cannot venture into this hybrid realm within the frame of this chapter.[104]

We can perhaps anticipate, concurrently with the decline of the symbol, a dramatic reintensification of the story, of the action, compensating the *Novelle* for the tautness lost with the vanishing symbol. Such a shift, a very hypothetical one at this moment, would reverse the trend of the last seventy-five years, in which the symbol has tended to fill the vacuum left by the decline of sharply profiled action formerly guaranteeing some sort of unity to the *Novelle.*

There is another possibility. A dominant image maintains, perhaps fortifies, its central role, but, reflecting the brokenness of contemporary life, evolves from the relative firmness of the "symbol" to the intentional vagueness of a "signal," a "token." In Kafka's *Country Doctor (Ein Landarzt,* 1918),

---

[104]For a point of departure, see von Wiese's "Bild-Symbole," *Publications of the English Goethe Society (see above),* p. 157, and his analysis of "Der Tod in Venedig" in *Die deutsche Novelle,* I (1956), particularly pages 310-324. The synopsis of Haskell M. Block's "Allegory and Symbol: A Reappraisal," *Actes du IIIe Congrès de l'Association Internationale de Littérature Comparée* (['s-Gravenhage: Mouton, 1962], p. 346) points to a detached, comprehensive survey of the distinction and interaction between allegory and symbol in western scholarship since the eighteenth century.

the horses – functional, central, existential, and artistically convincing – seem to run the gamut from the (illusion of the) trusty helpers of man to the envoys of a demonic supreme power unknown to us, unfathomable, irresistible, apparently illogical, working toward ends, if any, we can never know, and with consequences overwhelmingly negative. Musil's *Blackbird (Die Amsel,* 1928) brings a liberating beckon from afar (childhood? death? the supernatural? God?).[105]

In the meantime all we can do is to look back at the golden age of the German *Novelle,* the nineteenth century, from Kleist to Hofmannsthal, and conclude that the few best *Novellen* are those with the most elementary symbolism, be it earth or water, dike or sea, horses or rails, and that straight allegories tend to leave a sour taste in our mouths, like C. F. Meyer's vinegar. Vinegar is good as flavoring, but one cannot drink it straight. Humorous and ironic allegories, from Keller's thimble to Mann's proper names, can complement the earnestness of symbolism; the specific-ironic can season the pervasive-problematic; entertainment and wit can humanize the metaphysical, to give the best *Novellen* that flavor of the unique, unobtrusively and yet compellingly moving toward the universal, that has earned, in the relative absence of great German novels, the nineteenth-century *Novelle* the distinction of representing Germany's finest prose contribution to world literature in that epoch.

---

[105]Benno von Wiese, *Die deutsche Novelle,* II, 299-318.

Chapter VIII
Der Rahmen in der deutschen Novelle: Dauer im Wechsel

Summary

*Continuity and change of the novellesque frame as Wolfgang Kayser describes its function. Oral narrative situation as basis for the frame. The frame as epic compensation for the dramatic substance of the novellesque events told in the inside story (*Binnenerzählung*). Expansion of the frame in the directions of auditors, readers, and narrators. Example: Boccaccio (*Decamerone*), Goethe (*Unterhaltungen*) Brentano (*Kasperl und Annerl*), Storm (*Schimmelreiter*), Musil (*Die Amsel*), Grass (*Katz und Maus*).*

*Contamination between frame and inside story. Advantages: C.F. Meyer (*Die Hochzeit des Mönchs*), Theodor Storm (*Der Schimmelreiter*); drawbacks: Wilhelm Raabe (*Else von der Tanne ; Zum Wilden Mann*); mixed results: Stefan Zweig (*Der Amokläufer*).*

*Frame and novellesque quality: Jeremias Gotthelf (*Die Schwarze Spinne*); Theodor Storm (*Der Schimmelreiter*). Frame-like interruptions by the narrator: Annette von Droste-Hülshoff (*Die Judenbuche*), Robert Musil (*Die Amsel*).*

Aspects of the novellesque frame not addressed in this essay (first #, Section V). The three traditional paths of novella research (theory; ideas; individual interpretations) need to be structurally/typologically systematized.

Tentative conclusions: 1) Emancipation of the frame in the direction of independence: Brentano, Kasperl und Annerl; Grillparzer, Der arme Spielmann; Jeremias Gotthelf, Die schwarze Spinne; Conrad Ferdinand Meyer, Die Hochzeit des Mönchs; Theodor Storm, Der Schimmelreiter; Robert Musil, Die Amsel. 2) Contamination between frame and inside story (Raabe, Else von der Tanne and Zum wilden Mann; Stefan Zweig, Amokläufer and Schachnovelle). 3) Subjectivization of the frame (Boccaccio, Goethe, Brentano, Grillparzer, Gotthelf, Droste-Hülshoff, C.F.

Meyer, Storm, Hauptmann, Stefan Zweig, Musil, Grass). 4) Growing uncertainty of the reporter (from the Decamerone *via the* Unterhaltungen *to* Die Amsel *and* Katz und Maus. *5) Evolution of the frame from the aristocractic in the direction of the bourgeois: Boccaccio, Goethe, Brentano, Grillparzer, Gotthelf, Droste-Hülshoff, C.F. Meyer, Storm, Gerhart Hauptmann, Emil Strauss, Stefan Zweig, Musil, Grass. 6) Decline of the social/communal element of the frame.*

Critical Review of Research. List of secondary literature used.

I

In seinem unverändert frischen und klugen *Sprachlichen Kunstwerk* legt Wolfgang Kayser die Trinität der Ursituation des Erzählens vor uns: einen Vorgang, der erzählt wird; ein Publikum, dem erzählt wird; einen Erzähler, der zwischen beiden vermittelt. «Durch einem technischen Kunstgriff kann diese Ursituation sichtbar gemacht und gesteigert werden: indem der Autor noch einen anderen Erzähler vorschickt, dem er die Erzählung in den Mund legt.»[1]

Das Wort «Novelle» vermeidet Kayser hier; er zieht Varianten des Wortes «erzählen» (Erzählkunst, Erzähler, Erzählung, erzählerisch, das Erzählte) vor. Doch weisen seine Beispiele und seine Definition fast alle in die Richtung des Novellistischen: *Decamerone, Heptameron, Pentameron, Canterbury Tales, Unterhaltungen deutscher Ausgewanderten* (daneben 1001 *Nacht*), Storm, C. F. Meyer.

Der Autor einer Rahmenerzählung schafft sich durch das Publikum, das er sichtbar vorführt, und durch den als Figur festgelegten Erzähler eine eindeutige Perspektive und feste Grenzen, die er nun einhalten muß. Aber durch die mit dieser Technik gegebene Begrenzung erwirbt er nun auch fruchtbarste Möglichkeiten.[2]

Die Funktion und Varianten des Rahmens in der deutschen Novelle an einigen Beispielen typologisch-historisch anzudeuten, beständigen und

---

[1] S. 201. – Der Guggenheimstiftung verdanke ich die nötige Muße, Materialien und Beobachtungen zur vorliegenden Arbeit sammeln zu können.

[2] *Ibid.* (Kayser).

220

unbeständigen Strukturelementen des Rahmens, seiner Kontinuität und Abwandlung nachzugehen, die Kayserschen «Möglicheiten», den Spielraum, welchen der Rahmen dem novellistischen Binnenerzählen läßt, zu überschauen – das ist die Aufgabe dieses Versuchs.

Wie Kayser gehen wir von der ursprünglichen mündlichen Erzählsituation aus. Wenn man einer Geschichte zuhört, die von jemandem erzählt wird, erlebt man diese Geschichte zweidimensional: erstens von ihrer eigenen Geschehnisebene aus (d.h. man versucht, sich in die Zeit, in die Welt zu versetzen, in denen die Geschichte spielt), zweitens aber von der gegenwärtigen Ebene aus, denn der Erzähler sitzt ja vor uns und spricht. Der Erzähler bleibt *unser* Zeitgenosse, noch während seine Erzählung eine vergangene Zeitgenössigkeit erweckt. Wenn er mehr als *eine* Geschichte erzählt, unterbricht er sich, führt uns von der Vergangenheit in die Gegenwart zurück und fängt dann eine zweite Geschichte an, später eventuell eine dritte usw., denn ein wirklicher Erzähler ist ein Viel-erzähler. Die Gegenwartspausen werden somit als immanenter Bestandteil dem Zyklus des Vergangenheitserzählens einverleibt.

Wenn das Erzählte eine gewisse Länge hat, wird der auf Erfolg bedachte Erzähler (und welcher Erzähler ist es nicht?) sich auch innerhalb einer Geschichte unterbrechen. Die Unterbrechung mag vom Räuspern bis zum subtilen Kommentar gehen. Umrahmung und Unterbrechung können nach Belieben verfeinert werden: der Erzähler spricht *jetzt* von einem Ereignis, das ihm in der Vergangenheit mitgeteilt wurde, das also aus einer noch früheren Vergangenheit stammt. Je feiner der Geschmack der Zuhörer (später: der Leser), je größere Ansprüche die <Gesellschaft> von Hörern (später: Lesern) an Erzähler und Erzählung stellt, desto raffinierter wahrscheinlich die Unterbrechungen der Erzählung durch den Erzähler, desto komplizierter die Zeitstruktur der Novelle, desto interessanter der Rahmen.

Der Rahmen einer Erzählung hat demnach einen ganz natürlichen Ursprung in der mündlichen Erzählsituation, deren Grundelemente heute gelten wie vor Tausenden von Jahren. Die Novelle ist aber eine besondere Art der Erzählung, und es fragt sich nun, welche besondere Funktion der Rahmen in einer Novelle ausübt.

Der Inhalt der Novelle ist dramatisch. Die Thematik der Novelle ist weitreichend, aber was auch erzählt wird, es darf nicht langweilig, es muß interessant sein, denn sonst ist es keine «Neuigkeit». Goethes «Was ist eine Novelle anders als eine sich ereignete unerhörte Begebenheit?»[3] ist trotz zahlloser gelehrter Versuche der Novellenforschung seither immer noch die beste Begriffsbestimmung.

Die Form der Darstellung dieses Dramatischen ist aber episch. In dieser Verbindung des dramatischen Inhalts und der epischen Form liegt der Kern des Novellistischen. Auch diese Verbindung beruht bereits auf der ursprünglichen Erzähllage. In einer gesellschaftlichen Situation muß das Pikante, das Frappante, das Unerhörte in einer Weise gesellschaftlich verarbeitet, dargestellt, zivilisiert werden, daß es für eine *gemischte* Zuhörerschaft annehmbar ist (siehe schon das *Decamerone*), daß es interessiert ohne zu beleidigen, ohne die Zuhörer in Verlegenheit zu bringen.[4]

---

[3]Zu Eckermann am 25. Januar 1827 *(Goethes Gespräche,* hrsg. von Flodoard Freiherr von Biedermann. Leipzig, Biedermann, 1910. III, 335. Bei dem in dieser Ausgabe angegebenen Datum vom 29. Januar handelt es sich wahrscheinlich um einen Irrtum).

[4]«... Das kann ich von dem Zirkel erwarten, in dem ich lebe, daß Gleichgesinnte sich im stillen zueinander fügen und sich angenehm unterhalten, indem der eine dasjenige sagt, was der andere schon denkt. ... In Gesellschaft laßt uns nicht vergessen, wieviel wir sonst schon, ... um gesellig zu sein, von unsern Eigenheiten aufopfern mußten, und daß jeder, solange die Welt stehen wird, um gesellig zu sein, wenigstens äußerlich sich wird beherrschen müssen» (Goethe, *Unterhaltungen deutscher Ausgewanderten,* in *Werke,* Hamburger Ausgabe, VI, 137).
In seiner *Hochzeit des Mönchs,* einer der <novellistischsten> Novellen der deutschen Literatur, die auch über einen typologisch bezeichnenden Rahmen verfügt, sagt Conrad Ferdinand Meyer von seinem Helden Astorre: «Der Druck der auf ihn gerichteten Aufmerksamkeit und die sozusagen in der Luft fühlbaren Formen und Forderungen der Gesellschaft ließen ihn empfinden, daß

Die epische Form des Erzählens, die direkten Dialog sparsam gebraucht und
eher berichtet als zitiert, dient diesem Ausgleich, und in diesem epischen
Ausgleich spielt der Rahmen eine besondere Rolle. Dem Einmalig-Unerhörten
der berichteten Begebenheit gesellt er das Beständig-Feste des Rahmens zu,
dem Wechsel die Dauer, dem Irr- oder Wahnsinn den Sinn, dem Häßlichen das
Stilisierte[5], dem Außerordentlichen das Ordentliche, dem Chaos die Ordnung,

---

er nicht die Wirklichkeit der Dinge sagen dürfe, energisch und mitunter häßlich
wie sie ist, sondern ihr eine gemilderte und gefällige Gestalt geben müsse. So
hielt er sich unwillkürlich in der Mitte zwischen Wahrheit und schönem Schein
und redete untadelig» *(Sämtliche Werke,* München, Droemer, 1953, S. 507).
An Paul Heyse schreibt Meyer über dasselbe Werk: «Die Neigung zum
Rahmen dann ist bei mir ganz instinktiv. Ich halte mir den Gegenstand gerne
vom Leibe oder richtiger, gerne so weit als möglich vom Auge und dann will
mir erscheinen, das Indirekte der Erzählung (und selbst die Unterbrechungen)
mildern die Härte der Fabel» *(Briefe C. F. Meyers,* Leipzig, Haessel, 1908, II.
340/341).
Diese Milderung ist in der *Hochzeit des Mönchs* umso mehr am Platze, als
Meyer in Dante einem mürrischen, «herrischen» (Meyer gebraucht diesen
Ausdruck im selben Brief) Erzähler das Wort erteilt.
Die vom Autor vorgeschobene <Autonomie> des Erzählers ermöglicht es ihm,
Dante für die Binnennovelle verantwortlich zu machen, d. h. die für eine
Novelle wichtige Stilisierung einem anderen, weltberühmten Autor in die
Schuhe zu schieben: «Dante hielt inne. Seine Fabel lag in ausgeschütteter
Fülle vor ihm; aber sein strenger Geist wählte und vereinfachte» *(Sämtliche
Werke, 505).*

[5]Das Dazwischentreten als Erzähler macht es C. F. Meyer in der *Hochzeit des
Mönchs* z. B. möglich, durch bewußtes Stilisieren und Distanzieren und
Einschieben einer weiteren Mittelsperson, Donna Olympia, einen transluzenten
Schleier über die heikle Szene zu werfen, in welcher der Mönch Astorre mit
dem Barfüßermönch körperlich ringt und ihn dann besticht, damit der
Barfüßer ihn mit Antiope verheiratet *(Sämtliche Werke, 519).*

der Gewalt die Disziplin, dem Sprengenden des Inhalts das Verhaltene der Form, dem Unmittelbaren das Mittelbare.

Das ist die klassische Funktion des Rahmens. Bei ihr ist es nicht geblieben. Es liegt auf der Hand, daß das Gegenwärtige des Rahmens, im Gegensatz zum Vergangenen der Binnenerzählung, zu persönlichen Verbindungen in beiden Richtungen drängt: in Richtung des Hörers bzw. Lesers und in Richtung des Erzählers. Die Gestalt eines Briefes wird sowohl durch die Persönlichkeit des Adressaten wie durch die des Absenders geprägt. Noch stärker muß das der Fall sein für den Adressaten, der dem Erzähler gegenübersitzt. Der Bericht derselben Art von Begebenheit durch denselben Erzähler wird verschieden ausfallen, je nachdem er sie diesem oder jenem Kreis erzählt. Der Einfluß der Gruppe, an den die novellistische Erzählung gerichtet ist, auf die einzelnen Erzählungen ist gleichbleibend, solange die Gruppe gleichbleibt (*Decamerone*), färbt dagegen merklich und verschieden auf den Ton der einzelnen Erzählungen ab, wenn sich die Zusammensetzung der Gruppe ändert. So ist es kein Zufall, daß in Goethes *Unterhaltungen* die ersten vier, heikleren novellistischen Geschichten in der Abwesenheit der Baronesse erzählt werden, die letzten beiden (vom abschließenden, entschieden nicht-novellistischen *Märchen* abgesehen) aber, welche im Grunde moralische Erzählungen sind (die Prokurator- und Ferdinandgeschichten), in ihrer Anwesenheit. Diese Kolorierung ist eine Mischung gesellschaftlicher Rücksichtnahme auf die kollektive Gestalt des zuhörenden Kreises, auf die verbindende und verbindliche Funktion der erzählten Novelle und auf die individuelle Ausrichtung der einzelnen Zuhörer, an den oder an die, explicite oder implicite, mehr oder minder merklich die einzelne Novelle im Rahmen des Novellenringes gerichtet ist.

Diese halb-kollektive, halb-individuelle Rücksicht auf Hörer- und Hörerinnenkreis steht in der Mitte der Entwicklung der Literatur vom Kollektiv-Stilisierten, auf die Empfängergruppe Ausgerichteten, zum Individuell-Heterodoxen, auf den Erzähler Gezielten. Der Berichterstatter wird vom objektiven Medium zum subjektiven Gestalter, ja zum Inhalt des Erzählten. Cum grano salis könnte man die Entwicklung etwa so darstellen: es (die Erzählung) –> sie (die kollektiven Empfänger) –> er, sie (die individuellen Empfänger) –> ich (der Erzähler). Die Etappen dieses Weges kann man ungefähr am *Decamerone*, an Goethes *Unterhaltungen* und Brentanos *Geschichte vom braven Kasperl und schönen Annerl* ablesen. Im *Decamerone* wird auf die Zusammensetzung des Zuhörerkreises die größte Rücksicht genommen. Die Persönlichkeit und selbst das Geschlecht des Erzählers oder der Erzählerin färbt nur minimal auf Thema und Art der Einzelerzählungen ab. Im Rahmen selbst wird auf das Einzelkolorit der Erzähler und Zuhörer etwas mehr Rücksicht genommen, aber auch da herrscht Stilisierung vor. In Goethes *Unterhaltungen* färbt die Eigenart des jeweils Erzählenden, trotz immer noch selbstbeherrschter Zurückhaltung, bereits stärker auf Art und Ton der Erzählung ab, während sich die Temperamente des zuhörenden, rezensierenden und auslegenden Kreises im Rahmen manchmal bereits leidenschaftlich Luft machen. Trotzdem setzt sich auch im Rahmen der gute Ton nach einigen Krisen weiter durch. In Brentanos *Kasperl und Annerl* ist der Erzähler schon zu einer der interessantesten Figuren der Erzählung geworden.

Innerhalb der auf den unterhaltenden Bericht und disziplinierte Form angewiesenen Formgegebenheiten der Novelle kann sich diese Entwicklung nur relativ abzeichnen, nicht so weitgehend wie im elastischeren Roman. Es handelt sich um feine und feinste Differenzierungen wie z. B. den erzählenden Schulmeister im *Schimmelreiter*, einen aufgeklärten, rationalistischen Erzähler eines Berichts von starkem Realismus und ebenso starken unaufgeklärten, irrationalistichen, dämonischen Zügen, die gerade durch das Wissen um den skeptischen Erzähler größere Beglaubigung erhalten. Ebenso fein nimmt dieser Erzähler Rücksicht auf die nicht ganz einheitliche Zusammensetzung seiner Zuhörerschaft. Vom *Schimmelreiter* führt der Weg zu der weit engeren Verbindung zwischen Erzähler und Binnenerzählung in Musils *Amsel* und Grass' *Katz und Maus,* obgleich auch in diesen beiden Novellen auf den oder die Zuhörer (*sic* – nicht nur den Leser) subtile Rücksicht genommen wird.

Hier bieten sich für den Novellisten, der sich für einen Rahmen entscheidet, biegsame Möglichkeiten, den für die Novelle so wichtigen Ausgleich objektiver und subjektiver Elemente zu erzielen. Wenn die Binnenerzählung trocken berichtet, kann der Rahmen durch subjektivere

Färbung einen gewissen Ausgleich schaffen; sollte die Binnenerzählung sich in einer subjektiveren Richtung bewegen, so kann ein sachlicher Rahmen das nötige Gleichgewicht wiederherstellen.

II

Die Worte «Ausgleich» und «Gleichgewicht» weisen darauf hin, daß wir bisher mit zwei Strukturelementen, der Binnenerzählung und dem Rahmen, operiert haben, die sich deutlich voneinander abheben. Was geschieht, wenn Rahmen und Binnenerzählung mehr und mehr aufeinander abfärben?

Kayser lobt die *Hochzeit des Mönchs* als «meisterhafte Lösung» des Problems der Verbindung zwischen Rahmen und Kernerzählung.[6] Gefühle, Konflikte, Berufe, ja Namen, die in Dantes Erzählung enthalten sind, spielen auch im Rahmen eine Rolle. Ist eine solche Verknüpfung gut *per se?* Gewiß, sie gibt dem Interesse der Binnengeschichte eine weitere Dimension und trägt zur Reichhaltigkeit der Erzählung als ganzer bei. Aber Erweiterung und Verästelung sind dem literarischen Kunstwerk nicht ohne weiteres zuträglich. Mehr ist manchmal weniger. Ein schwerer Rahmen kann die Proportionen einer Novelle belasten, Unstimmigkeiten verursachen, die Klarheit der strukturellen Linien verwischen, den Rahmen zu einem Konkurrenten der Binnenerzählung machen und somit künstlerische Unsicherheit schaffen, die für den novellistischen Effekt so unentbehrliche Konzentration verzetteln. Ein feinfühliger Leser wird sich durch die *zu* klaren Analogien des Meyerschen Rahmens eher abgestoßen als angezogen finden.[7]

Ebenso problematisch ist Kaysers folgende Bemerkung: "Mit der Hörerschaft, die in einer solchen Erzählung leibhaft eingeführt wird, gewinnt

---

[6]*Op. cit.,* 201-202.

[7]Im bereits zitierten Brief an Heyse legt sich der unbestechliche Kritiker Meyer über den Dichter Meyer Rechnung ab: «Hier freilich wird der Verschlingung von Fabel und Hörer zu viel, die Sache wird entschieden mühsam. Ein non plus ultra! M'en voilà guéri!» Und Hans Schmeer weist darauf hin, daß Meyer in späteren Novellen den Rahmen nicht mehr gebraucht (Nachwort zu C. F. Meyer, *Sämtliche Werke,* S. 1109).

der Dichter ein Mittel, um reale Leser zu beeinflussen. Die integrierende Hörerschaft kann dazu dienen, uns vorzufühlen, sie kann uns zeigen, in welcher Haltung wir das Erzählte aufzunehmen haben."[8]

Für diese Bereicherung gilt dasselbe, was wir soeben für die engere Verknüpfung zwischen Rahmen und Binnenerzählung angeführt haben: die Gefahren halten den Vorteilen mindestens die Waage. Denn so diszipliniert das Gefüge der Novelle sein sollte, so soll ja gerade diese Sparsamkeit den Leser anregen, selbst die Novelle in seinen Gedanken weiterzuführen. Die Baronesse in Goethes *Unterhaltungen* verlangt von der Geschichte, die der «geistliche Hausfreund» erzählen soll: «Ihre Geschichte sei unterhaltend, so lange wir sie hören, befriedigend, wenn sie zu Ende ist, und hinterlasse uns einen stillen Reiz, weiter nachzudenken.»[9] Das Mit- und Nachwirken des Hörers und Lesers ist einer der allergrößten Reize der Novelle; es gehört zum integralen Bestandteil der besten Novellen: Diese Mitarbeit zu unterbinden, unsere persönlichen Reaktionen vorwegzunehmen, «uns vorzufühlen» kann, wenn es sich nicht mit feinstem Taktgefühl verbindet (wie es in den *Unterhaltungen* glücklicherweise durch wirkliche Unterhaltungen, verschiedene Standpunkte geschieht), als ein Eingriff in die Rechte des Lesers angesehen werden, als eine Beleidigung seiner Intelligenz, eine Abschnürung seines Mitwirkens, ein ungebührliches Geltendmachen der eigenen Interpretation des Autors, die, wenn nicht mit größter Sparsamkeit und Klugheit geübt, mit dem Wesen des Objektiv-Novellistischen unvereinbar ist.

So muß Kaysers Feststellung, daß Meyer und Storm «die Technik der Rahmen-erzählung zur Meisterschaft entwickelt» haben, mit Vorsicht aufgenommen werden.[10] Gerade, weil «ein großer Teil des erzählerischen Werks von Theodor Storm und fast das ganze erzählerische Werk von C. F.

---

[8]*Op. cit.*, 202.

[9]Hamburger Ausgabe, VI, 167.

[10]*Op. cit.*, 201.

Meyer von dieser Art ist»[11], muß man an der automatischen Überlegenheit einer Schwerpunktverlagerung auf den Rahmen einige Zweifel hegen. Vielleicht ist es doch manchmal nicht mehr als ein «technischer Kunstgriff»[12], eine komfortable und womöglich etwas mechanische Angewohnheit, die mehr mit den Gepflogenheiten des Autors und seiner Vorgänger als mit den Forderungen des Stoffes zu tun hat.

III

Es empfiehlt sich somit, einige novellistische Erzählungen unter die Lupe zu nehmen und zu sehen, wie die Rahmentechnik sich als organischer Teil des Ganzen bewährt. Zwei Beispiele für schlechte Resultate: Wilhelm Raabes *Else von der Tanne* und *Zum Wilden Mann*. *Else von der Tanne* fängt mit Rückblendung an: der Pfarrer Friedemann Leutenbacher zu Wallrode im Elend (!) sitzt am Weihnachtsvorabend des Jahres 1648 in seinem Haus, arbeitet an seiner Weihnachtspredigt und erinnert sich der Ankunft Elses und ihres Vaters in Wallrode zwölf Jahre vorher (1636). Darauf wird dieses Ereignis beschrieben. Zurück zum Pfarrer, der nun über die zwischen 1636 und 1648 verflossenen Jahre nachsinnt. Dann wird die Lebensgeschichte Elses und ihres Vaters *vor* Wallrode (also vor 1636) eingerückt, worauf die Erzählung der Steinigung Elses durch die Dorfbewohner Wallrodes am Tage Johannis' des Täufers 1648 folgt. Schließlich stirbt der Pfarrer selbst. – Das Verhältnis zwischen Rahmen und Binnenerzählung ist eng aber ungeschickt, unruhig, sprunghaft, unübersichtlich.

In Raabes *Zum wilden Mann* können die ersten drei Kapitel als Rahmen bezeichnet werden. Wir lernen den Apotheker Phillipp Kristeller kennen, der seinen beiden Freunden, dem Pastor Schönlank und dem Förster Ulebeule, erzählt, wie er vor mehr als dreißig Jahren Besitzer der Apotheke «Zum wilden Mann» wurde. Die novellistische (eher melodramatische) «unerhörte Begebenheit» vom wilden Mann, deren Einzelheiten ich dem Leser erspare, nimmt die nächsten drei Kapitel in Anspruch. Vom siebten bis zum

---

[11]*Ibid.*

[12]*Ibid.*

16. Kapitel sind wir wieder in der Rahmenatmosphäre, in der aber der «wilde Mann» vom 7. Kapitel ab schon wieder auftaucht und das Heft der Handlung in der Hand behält. Der Rahmen entpuppt sich also als die eigentliche Hauptsache in der Erzählung, der novellistische Kern beschränkt sich im Grunde auf die Vorgeschichte, die Rollen sind vertauscht, die strukturellen Proportionen sind so verschoben, daß das Novellistische, Schauerromantische und Biedermeierische eine unsichere Zwangsheirat eingehen.

Schwieriger liegen die Dinge in Stefan Zweigs *Amokläufer*. Der Rahmen beginnt mit einem sachlich-verhaltenen halbseitigen Rückblick des Autor-Erzählers auf einen Vorfall im Hafen von Neapel im März des Jahres 1912, der dann auf den letzten beiden Seiten der Geschichte eingehender beschrieben wird, ebenfalls mit der ruhigen Sachlichkeit eines Reporters bis auf die letzten vier Zeilen, in denen leider ein durchaus entbehrliches schauerromantisches Füllsel angehängt wird.

Ein zweiter Rahmen beginnt schon auf der ersten Seite der Novelle zu Anfang einer Schiffsreise von Kalkutta nach Neapel. Dieser Rahmen, der die schwüle Atmosphäre auf der «Oceania» und die ersten Kontakte mit dem ‹Helden› der Geschichte, einem Arzt, beschreibt, nimmt etwa ein Sechstel der Gesamterzählung in Anspruch; ihm entsprechen gegen Ende der Erzählung zwei diesen Sekundärrahmen abwickelnde Seiten, die dem Ende des Primärrahmens unmittelbar vorausgehen. Das Ende des Primärrahmens bildet aber auch den endgültigen Abschluß des Sekundärrahmens.

Dazwischen liegt der novellistische Kern (etwa 4/5) der Erzählung, die Beichte des Arztes, der in einen tödlich verlaufenen Abtreibungsversuch einer Holländerin in Indonesien verwickelt ist. Die Proportionen der beiden Rahmen zueinander und zur Binnenerzählung, Länge und Einreihung sind organisch und gelungen.

Der Bericht des Binnenerzählers (des Arztes) ist zu lang (59 Druckseiten), um nicht unterbrochen zu werden. Es gibt denn auch neun bis zehn kurze Unterbrechungen. Soweit diese Unterbrechungen sich auf verständliches Zögern, Stocken, oder selbst den Zuspruch einer Whiskyflasche zurückführen lassen, sind sie ganz in Ordnung. Die meisten Zäsuren fallen aber sinnigerweise mit dem Schlagen der Schiffsglocke zusammen. Die

Erzählung beginnt mit dem Schlagen der Schiffsglocke um halb eins, fährt nach einer Pause mit dem Schlagen der Schiffsglocke um ein Uhr fort, hört mit dem Schlagen der Schiffsglocke um zwei Uhr wieder auf, fängt wieder an, hört auf, die Schiffsglocke schlägt drei, er fängt wieder an zu sprechen und beendet seine Erzählung endlich ohne Mithilfe der Schiffsglocke.

Das ist zu offensichtliche Erzählstrategie, Begleitmusik zweiter Garnitur. Die Novelle ist eine aristokratische Form: einige wiederholte Mißgriffe billiger Art können hier Schaden anrichten, der nicht wiedergutzumachen ist. In dieselbe Rubrik gehört die Tatsache, daß der Binnenerzähler drei bis vier Seiten lang, «geschüttelt von einem heulenden Zorn», seinen Bericht «schrie»[13] – eine novellistische Unmöglichkeit, denn die Novelle besteht ja nicht nur aus der Spannung der Begebenheiten, sondern aus der Spannung zwischene dem Dramatischen der Ereignisse und dem Verhaltenen-Konzentrierten-Sparsamen der Form. Die Unterbrechungen der Binnenerzählung, welche den Hörer-Leser immer wieder in den Rahmen zurückführen, sind zu mechanisch für die feinsinnigen Ansprüche des Novellistischen, und sie stellen keinerlei bedeutsame Zäsuren dar zwischen den verschiedenen Teilen der Binnenerzählung, die unentwegt auf emotionellen Hochtouren läuft. Eine geschickt manipulierte sensationelle Erzählung, aber keine gute Novelle.

IV

Weder die enge Verflechtung von Rahmen und Binnenerzählung *(Else von der Tanne, Zum wilden Mann)* noch eine Widerspiegelung von novellistischem Kern im Rahmen *(Die Hochzeit des Mönchs)*, weder verschiedene Reaktionen der Rahmengruppe auf die Binnenerzählung(en) *(Unterhaltungen deutscher Ausgewanderten, Die Hochzeit des Mönchs)* noch der konventionell eingehaltene, oberflächlich distanzierte, aber im Grunde nicht wirklich profilierte Rahmen *(Amokläufer)* befördern als solche den Erfolg einer Novelle *qua* Novelle. Die Einhaltung eines an sich gesunden Strukturprinzips verbürgt noch nicht die Qualität eines besonderen

---

[13]Stefan Zweig, *Der Amokläufer*, Leipzig, Insel, 1922. S. 68.

230

literarischen Kunstwerks, und die Nichteinhaltung eines solchen Prinzips verhindert nicht in allen Fällen die Existenz eines Kunstwerks. Doch müssen wir, um nicht in einen reinen Nominalismus zu verfallen, voraussetzen, daß gewisse Strukturprinzipien organische Berechtigung haben, daß deshalb der Rahmen in der Novelle innerhalb eines gewissen Spielraums eine organisch-profilierte Rolle zu spielen hat und daß diese Rolle *sui generis* sein, sich irgendwie von der Binnenerzählung abheben muß, um überhaupt eine sinnvolle Funktion zu erfüllen. Hier kommen wir zurück auf eine Beobachtung von Kayser: die Rahmenerzählung entspricht einer Grundforderung, «die das Publikum an die Erzählkunst stellt, ...nämlich das Erzählte zu beglaubigen».[14] Nicht, daß der Rahmen Vorbedingung für eine solche Beglaubigung ist, sondern daß der Rahmen, wenn sich der Autor entschlossen hat, ihn zu gebrauchen, diese Aufgabe irgendwie erfüllen muß. Vier Novellen mögen dies beispielsweise erläutern.

Die Binnenerzählung in Gotthelfs *Schwarzer Spinne* handelt von göttlich-christlichen und teuflisch-magischen Dingen, die trotz der realistischen Kraft des Erzählten an der dichterischen Glaubwürdigkeit einer <sich ereigneten unerhörten Begebenheit> Zweifel aufkommen lassen könnten. Gotthelf distanziert sich von der mythisch-übernatürlichen Blitz- und Donnererzählung dadurch, daß er sie vom Großvater erzählen läßt und daß er den überwiegenden (obwohl nicht ausschließlichen) Ernst, den dramatischen «Teufel oder Gott» der Binnenerzählung mit einem gemütlich-realistisch-humoristischen schweizer Genrebild umrahmt. Gerade genug Kontrast und Distanz, um die Binnenerzählung zu beglaubigen, aber nicht so viel, daß sie eventuell in Frage gestellt werden könnte. Die schwarze Spinne verbindet Rahmen und Binnenerzählung, sie ist in beiden Teilen der Novelle reell, aber im Rahmen doch humoristisch schattiert.

Es ist ein Meistergriff Storms, daß er die ins Übernatürliche schlagende Geschichte des *Schimmelreiters* durch den alten aufklärerischen Schulmeister erzählen läßt, aus dessen intelligentem Mund wir manches

---

[14]*Op. cit.*, 201.

Abergläubische erfahren und <glauben>, gerade weil er selbst Zweifel daran hegt und rationelle Erklärungen parat hat, also uns ähnlich ist. Aber den Ausschlag gibt doch die überzeugende Erzählung und das Gefühl, daß auch er sich dem Transzendental-Heidnischen der Begebenheiten nicht entziehen kann, daß er selbst in ihrem Bann steht, wie sehr er sich auch dagegen sträubt.

Von Zeit zu Zeit unterbricht sich der Schulmeister, um den Leser an die Perspektive zu erinnern und um den rationalen Teil der Erzählung vom irrationalen zu trennen. Zwischen dem Schulmeister und uns hat Storm aber noch zwei weitere Vermittler eingeschaltet. Erstens den Erzähler der ganzen Geschichte («ich»), d. h. den Verfasser der Blätter, die vor mehr als einem halben Jahrhundert (also in den 1830er Jahren) in den «Leipzigern» oder «Pappes Hamburger Lesefrüchten» erschienen. Dieser Verfasser berichtet ein Rahmen-Ereignis, das für ihn selbst Jahre zurückliegt (1820er Jahre), während die Binnengeschichte für den sie erzählenden Schulmeister wiederum mehr als 70 Jahre zurückliegt, so daß auch er sich auf Hörensagen stützen muß. Zweitens Storm selbst, der die Geschichte vom Schimmelreiter als Knabe im Hause seiner Urgroßmutter «vor reichlich einem halben Jahrhundert» las.[15] Da er dieser Blätter seither nicht mehr habhaft werden konnte, kann er sich nicht für «die Wahrheit der Tatsachen verbürgen»[16], fügt aber sogleich hinzu, «daß ich sie seit jener Zeit, obwohl sie durch keinen äußeren Anlaß in mir aufs neue belebt wurden, niemals aus dem Gedächtnis verloren habe».[17]

Der Autor stärkt das Vertrauen des halb mißtrauischen Lesers in die übernatürlichen Schattierungen der Novelle durch die kluge, aber sparsam eingebaute Staffelung des Rahmens. Der dreifache[18], aber ganz natürliche Zeitabstand (1880er Jahre – 1830er Jahre – 1820er Jahre – Mitte des 18.

---

[15]Theodor Storm, *Werke,* München, Droemer, 1953, S. 889.

[16]*Ibid.*

[17]*Ibid.*

[18]Im Grunde handelt es sich um einen vierfachen Zeitabstand, denn der heutige Leser erlebt die Novelle auch von *seinem* Zeitgefühl aus.

Jahrhunderts bis 1756) ruft eine verminderte Erwartung von Genauigkeit im Leser hervor und entwaffnet (auch durch die künstlerische Authentizität des Erzählten) die Skepsis des Lesers gerade dadurch, daß er ihr entgegenkommt. Storm wußte, daß eine übernatürliche Novelle in den 1880er Jahren «ein heikel Stück» war, und er brauchte einen Rahmen, «weil es seine Mucken hat, einen Deichspuk in eine würdige Novelle zu verwandeln».[19]

Ein ausgezeichneter Rahmen, aber ganz ist er Storm auch nicht gelungen. War es nötig, die Begegnung mit dem Schimmelreiter und den Deichbruch im Rahmen zu wiederholen? Hier wiederum ist zuviel Verstärkung abträglich: «so fühlt man Absicht, und man ist verstimmt».[20]

Annette von Droste-Hülshoffs *Judenbuche* hat keinen eigentlichen Rahmen, aber rahmenähnliche Einschnitte, in denen die Droste sich vom Geschehen in der Novelle distanziert und betont, daß sie berichtet, nicht erdichtet. «Es würde in einer erdichteten Geschichte unrecht sein, die Neugier des Lesers so zu täuschen. Aber dies alles hat sich wirklich zugetragen: ich kann nichts davon- oder dazutun.»[21] Später, am Ende der Geschichte, aber noch vor der Pointe (der hebräischen Inschrift am Baume) wiederholt sie: «Dies hat sich nach allen Hauptumständen wirklich so begeben im September

---

[19]Brief an Erich Schmidt vom 3. Februar 1885 (zitiert in Storm, *Sämtliche Werke,* hrsg. von Albert Köster, Leipzig, Insel, 1919-24, VIII, 288. Ich verdanke diese Auskünfte dem kenntnisreichen Stormforscher Clifford A. Bernd). Ähnlich schreibt Storm an Heyse am 29. August 1886: «In Arbeit ferner: *Der Schimmelreiter,* eine Deichgeschichte, ein böser Block, da es gilt, eine Deichgespenstsage auf die vier Beine einer Novelle zu stellen, ohne den Charakter des Unheimlichen zu verwischen» *(Der Briefwechsel zwischen Paul Heyse und Theodor Storm,* hrsg. von Georg Plotke, München, Lehmann, 1918, II, 170).

[20]Goethe, *Torquato Tasso,* Hamburger Ausgabe, V, 99, Vers 969.

[21]*Gesammelte Werke,* IV, 38, Vaduz, Liechtenstein Verlag, o. J. (1948).

des Jahres 1789.»[22] Mehr zu tun ist nicht nötig, denn die Erzählung ist selbst authentisch, realistisch, dokumentarisch genug, um ohne Rahmen bestehen zu können, besonders da man bei Kriminalgeschichten ein gewisses Halbdunkel, nicht ganz aufgeklärte Fragezeichen bereitwillig in Kauf nimmt. Was «sich wirklich zugetragen hat», braucht keine weitere Beglaubigung. Für den berichtenden Novellisten ist es nicht nötig, alles von ihm Berichtete zu verstehen: «Denjenigen», schreibt die Droste, «die vielleicht auf den Ausgang dieser Begebenheit [d. h. den Mord des Försters] gespannt sind, muß ich sagen, daß diese Geschichte nie aufgeklärt wurde...»[23] Diese präzise Unklarheit ist durchaus novellistisch. Sie begünstigt in hohem Maße Goethes <stillen Reiz zum Nachdenken>, ist also auch künstlerisch höchst wirkungsvoll.

Eng verwandt mit der Drosteschen Haltung ist diejenige Robert Musils in seiner *Amsel*. Der Erzähler kommentiert seine Geschichte von Zeit zu Zeit, schüttelt den Kopf, nimmt Vorbehalte, Zweifel, Unsicherheit des Zuhörers (Aeins) und des Lesers vorweg, und stärkt damit das Vertrauen des Lesers auf die Integrität des Erzählers und des Erzählten. Der Erzähler stellt Fragen, die er nicht beantworten kann (oder will): «Mir wurde bewußt, daß ich auf etwas wartete, aber ich ahnte nicht worauf.»[24] «Ich weiß nicht, welches Ende [die Geschichte] finden soll.»[25] «Es war gar keine Nachtigall, es war eine Amsel, sagte ich mir, genau so, wie du es sagen möchtest.»[26] «Das alles hing ganz von selbst zusammen, aber ich weiß nicht wie.»[27] Wenige Schriftsteller

---

[22]*Ibid.*, IV, 63. Einige Texte haben 1788, aber das richtige Datum ist 1789.

[23]*Ibid.*, IV, 37.

[24]Frankfurt, S. Fischer, 1962, S. 71.

[25]*Ibid.*, S. 72.

[26]*Ibid.*, S. 72.

[27]*Ibid.*, S. 73.

haben den Kern des Novellistischen so zentral getroffen wie Musil im vorletzten Staz seiner Erzählung: «Es hat sich eben alles so ereignet; und wenn ich den Sinn wüßte, so brauchte ich dir wohl nicht erst zu erzählen.»[28]

V

Hiermit haben wir höchstens einige der strukturellen Probleme und erzählerischen Funktionen des Rahmens in der Novelle berührt. Der Aufmerksamkeit wert wäre noch vieles andere: Unterschiede zwischen dem Rahmen innerhalb einer Novelle und dem Rahmen eines Novellenzyklus' (z. B. bei Keller), einfacher Rahmen und Schachtelrahmen, Probleme des Ich-Rahmens (wer ist dieses Ich? siehe z. B. *Kasperl und Annerl, Brigitta, Der arme Spielmann, Die Judenbuche, Der Schimmelreiter, Die Amsel, Katz und Maus)*, das mündliche Element im Rahmen, Vergleich zwischen Spannung im Rahmen und in der Binnengeschichte, Qualitätsvergleiche zwischen Rahmen und Binnenerzählung, Rahmendistanz als Humor, als Ironie, als Verfremdungseffekt, der Rahmen als Kommentar über das Novellistische (z. B. Goethes *Unterhaltungen)*, der unvollständige Rahmen (Halbrahmen), Verhältnis zwischen Malereirahmen und Bühnenrahmen einerseits, Novellenrahmen andererseits, der Rahmen als das moralische Sprachrohr des Autors (z. B. Gotthelf, Keller), der Rahmen in erweitertem Sinn (z. B. historischer, geographischer, religiöser, sozialer, ethischer >Rahmen< des Geschehnisses, Stimmungsrahmen bei Storm, Hofmannsthal usw.), Rahmen als Perspektive, der Roman als Rahmen für darin eingestreute Novellen (z. B. *Wilhelm Meisters Wanderjahre)*, Struktur- und thematische Unterschiede zwischen Rahmen- und rahmenlosen Novellen (z. B. bei Kleist: Vortreten des dramatischen Elements), und im allgemeinen eine weitgehende Vertiefung und Erweiterung der Erforschung der Beziehungen zwischen Rahmen und Binnengeschichte als einer Zentralfrage der Novellenforschung, die wir kaum mehr als anschneiden konnten. Wann, wo, und wie wird der Rahmen selbst novellistisch? Vergleiche zwischen der Rahmenfunktion in der deutschen Novellistik und romanischen oder russischen Novellen wären außerordentlich

---

[28]*Ibid.*, S. 82.

fruchtbar.

Trotz der Fülle der Novellenforschung fehlt es uns empfindlich an Studien, die novellistische Strukturelemete in repräsentativen Novellen, gestützt auf eingehende Textstudien, systematisch vergleichen, um zu strukturtypologischen Ergebnissen zu gelangen. Die Novellenforschung bewegt sich hauptsächlich immer noch auf drei Pfaden: dem theoretischen Pfad, der zu allgemeinen Sentenzen führt und sich wenig um konkrete Beispiele kümmert; dem ideologischen Pfad, der Ideen und Motive durch eine Anzahl von Novellen verfolgt, ohne daß diese Ideen und Motive aber als typisch novellistisch gelten könnten, und dem werkimmanenten Pfad – Einzelinterpretationen, oft von ausgezeichneter Qualität, die aber zu keinen Folgerungen über die Novelle als Gattung führen.

Angesichts dieser Lücken können unsere Endbetrachtungen über Dauer und Wechsel des Rahmens in der Geschichte der deutschen Novelle nur einen bedingten, empirischen Charakter tragen. Der Leser möge sie als impressionistische Diskussionsthesen ansehen.

1) *Verselbständigung des Rahmens.* Im *Decamerone* ist der Rahmen (von der realistisch-frappanten Einleitung, dem Pestbericht, abgesehen) noch hochstilisiert, aristokratisch, neutral, während die Binnenerzählungen im Inhalt, nicht in der Form, weniger stilisierte Züge, ja sogar demokratische Anklänge (z. B. den Bäcker Cisti in der zweiten Novelle des sechsten Tages) enthalten. In Goethes *Unterhaltungen*, nicht ganz ein halbes Jahrtausend später, ist die Funktion des Rahmens im großen und ganzen noch wie bei Boccaccio: Aristokraten retten sich vom Zeitgeschehen (französische Revolution statt Pest) in ablenkende, unterhaltende Erzählungen einmaliger Begebenheiten. (Eine bürgerlich-bäuerische Abwandlung derselben Grundsituation finden wir noch im *Schimmelreiter:* in furchtbarem Wetter wird im Wirtshaus durch Erzählen der Geschichte vom Schimmelreiter Zerstreuung gesucht). Aber trotz der Beibehaltung einer gewissen Stilisierung dieses Kreises wird die Rahmenhandlung bei Goethe sowohl zeitgeschichtlich wie psychologisch gegenüber Boccaccio vertieft. Die Akzentverlagerung auf den Rahmen kann sich im 19. Jahrhundert auf zweierlei Art auswirken. Sie kann bedeuten, daß die Rahmenerzählung selbständiger wird, sich trotz

gewisser Querverbindungen in Charakter und Ton mehr oder weniger deutlich von der Binnenerzählung abhebt, Kontrast und Kompensation darstellt, der Binnenerzählung in inhaltlichem Interesse und künstlerischen Ansprüchen gleichwertiger wird, ohne ihr aber den Rang abzulaufen. So bereits im Quasirahmen von Brentanos *Kasperl und Annerl,* im *Armen Spielmann,* in der *Schwarzen Spinne,* in der *Hochzeit des Mönchs,* im *Schimmelreiter,* und weit später in der *Amsel.*

2) *Vermengung des Rahmens mit der Binnenerzählung.* Der Drang, den Rahmen von formeller Attrappenhaftigkeit zu inhaltlicher und künstlerischer Gleichwertigkeit mit der Binnenerzählung zu promovieren, kann aber auch zu einer Integrierung mit der Binnenerzählung führen, die zu dem entgegengesetzten Resultat, zum Verlust des Rahmens an Profil führt (Raabes *Else von der Tanne* und *Zum wilden Mann,* Stefan Zweigs *Amokläufer* und *Schachnovelle*).

3) *Subjektivierung des Rahmens.* Im *Decamerone* wechseln die Novellenerzähler dauernd, alle *zehn* kommen an jedem der *zehn* Erzähltage einmal zu ihrem Recht, die subjektive Färbung der Einzelerzählung wird kontrolliert und stilisiert, und was davon übrig bleibt, wird noch einmal durch die Reihenhaftigkeit der sich abwechselnden Erzähler normalisiert, entpersonalisiert. In Goethes *Unterhaltungen* gibt es immer noch *mehrere* (aber nicht mehr zehn) Erzähler, nicht mehr hundert sondern nur noch sieben Erzählungen. Die verschiedenen Erzähler haben zwar weit mehr Persönlichkeit als bei Boccaccio, aber ihre Erzählungen (nicht alle sind novellistisch) werden immer noch vom guten, neutralen Ton der Gesellschaft getragen. Im 19. Jahrhundert begnügt sich der Rahmen überwiegend mit *einem* Erzähler (*Kasperl und Annerl,* wo allerdings die Großmutter noch eine Nebenerzählerrolle spielt, *Der arme Spielmann, Die schwarze Spinne, Die Judenbuche, Die Hochzeit des Mönchs, Der Schimmelreiter*). Trotz der Personalisierung des Erzählers und seines größeren Mitschwingens mit der Binnenerzählung bleibt aber das Bestreben des Autors, ihn aus der Binnennovelle herauszuhalten, mehr (*Schwarze Spinne, Judenbuche, Hochzeit des Mönchs, Schimmelreiter*) oder weniger (*Kasperl und Annerl, Der arme Spielmann*) prononciert. Im 20. Jahrhundert scheint der

Berichterstatter weitgehend in den Bericht integriert zu sein: *Der Ketzer von Soana, Der Amokläufer, Die Amsel, Katz und Maus.* Den komplexen Nuancen dieser Integrierung kann hier nicht nachgegangen werden. Man könnte, wieder cum grano salis, die Stellung des Erzählers in der Novelle historisch etwa so darstellen: zehn Rahmenerzähler –> mehrere Rahmenerzähler –> ein Rahmenerzähler –> Erzähler wird in die Binnenerzählung subjektiviert.

4) *Wachsende Unsicherheit des Berichterstatters.* Der Griff zum Rahmen mag als solcher schon, besonders im 19. Jahrhundert, als eine Art Unsicherheit des Autors ausgelegt werden, der sich durch das Dazwischentreten eines anderen Erzählers zu decken sucht. Aber selbst innerhalb der Rahmennovellen bemerkt man eine Entwicklung von der unangefochtenen Selbstsicherheit der Erzähler im *Decamerone* über die bereits angefochtene, aber immer noch entschlossene und entscheidende Präsidentschaft der Baronesse in Goethes *Unterhaltungen* zu der problematischen Selbstunsicherheit des Berichterstatters in der *Amsel* oder in *Katz und Maus,* die dem Verlust des Selbstvertrauens, unserer existentiellen Unsicherheit als Kulturerscheinung des 20. Jahrhunderts zu entsprechen scheint.

5) *Verbürgerlichung des Rahmens.* Die Verbürgerlichung des Rahmens der Novelle gehört zur Verbürgerlichung der Novelle überhaupt. Die Novelle ist im Ursprung eine romanische aristokratische Form, denn wer sonst, außer vielleicht im Winter oder auf Reisen, kann es sich leisten, sich tagelang Erzählungen anzuhören? Die Kunst des Novellistischen (Stilisierung, feinste Wortwahl, Formdisziplin, Urbanität) weist ins Edle, und ob die Form von einem Edelmann oder einer Edelfrau, einem Patrizier oder Bürgerlichen gehandhabt wird, sie bleibt (mit wenigen Ausnahmen: *Die schwarze Spinne*) aristokratisch bis ins 20. Jahrhundert hinein, so skandalös auch der Inhalt sein mag (*Der Ketzer von Soana, Der Schleier*). Dagegen wird die Zusammensetzung des Kreises, in dem sie erzählt wird, darunter die Herkunft des Erzählers, im 19. Jahrhundert notwendigerweise bürgerlich werden müssen, wenn die Gattung überhaupt ihre Lebensberechtigung behalten soll. Boccaccios Rahmen war noch ausschließlich aristokratisch, Goethes in den

Unterhaltungen ist es noch überwiegend, aber C. F. Meyers fürstlicher Rahmen in der *Hochzeit des Mönchs* ist bereits mehr Ausnahme als Regel. Dazwischen liegt die Mischung von herzoglichem und Volksrahmen in Brentanos *Kasperl und Annerl* und die eindeutig bürgerlich-bäuerlichen Rahmen vom *Armen Spielmann, der Schwarzen Spinne, der Judenbuche,* und *des Schimmelreiters.* Im 20. Jahrhundert ist die Verbürgerlichung des Rahmens komplett (*Ketzer von Soana, Amokläufer, Amsel, Schachnovelle, Katz und Maus*).

6) *Verlust des Gesellschaftlichen.* Der Begriff «Gesellschaft» birgt Differenzierungen, die für die Entwicklung der Novelle ganz besondere Bedeutung haben. Im engeren Sinne entspricht «Gesellschaft» dem Bedürfnis nach Zusammensein, Aussprache, Ablenkung, Unterhaltung, Neuigkeiten zu hören und Neuigkeiten zu erzählen. Im weiteren Sinne ist Gesellschaft das Gegenteil von Alleinsein, es ist die Unterstützung, die der weitgehend hilflose Einzelne vom Zusammensein und Zusammenwirken mit anderen Menschen erhofft.

Der Rahmen in der Novelle entspricht genau diesen beiden Grundbedürfnissen des Menschen. Die psychologischen Reaktionen auf die zunehmende Übervölkerung in Westeuropa, namentlich in den Städten, die Beweglichkeit der Bevölkerung, die Entfaltung anderer Kommunikationsarten (Zeitung, Zeitschrift, Buch, Broschüre, Theater, Kino, Radio, Telefon, Fernsehen), das gesteigerte Tempo des Lebens hat dem gesellschaftlichen Beisammensein, dem «Neuigkeiten hören und erzählen» einen Dämpfer aufgesetzt. Man hat weder Zeit noch Lust, in Ruhe künstlerisch geformte Neuigkeiten zu hören. In der Blütezeit der cocktail parties entbehrt der novellistische Rahmen einer vitalen Grundlage. Der Abstieg des Rahmens in der Novelle entspricht dieser Entwicklung; er zeichnet sich bereits in dem Papiersurrogat für den lebendigen Erzähler, nämlich der <Herausgeberfiktion> (Kayser, Seite 202; Kanzog, Seite 340) ab, die bereits in Storms *Aquis Submersus* gezwungen und in Hauptmanns *Ketzer von Soana,* schwankend mit der mündlichen Erzählsituation vermengt, gänzlich unauthentisch wirkt.

Der weitere Sinn der «Gesellschaft» als der sozial gegliederten, wirtschaftlich tätigen und politisch organisierten Gesamtheit eines Volkes spiegelt sich im Grundinhalt der Binnenerzählung in einer Rahmennovelle. Diese Binnengeschichte (oder die ganze Novelle, wenn sie keinen Rahmen hat) handelt überwiegend vom Konflikt zwischen Einzelmensch und gesellschaftlichen Normen, oft durch das Fatum ausgelöst und kompliziert, aber selten ganz unfreiwillig. Wer auch immer in diesem Konflikt gewinnt oder verliert, die kommunalen und individuellen Werte als solche waren anerkannt. Die Kollektivisierung und Zentralisierung, die politische Synchronisierung und Mechanisierung des 20. Jahrhunderts bieten vielerorts nicht mehr die Vorbedingungen für die prinzipielle, zum mindesten künstlerische Gleichwertigkeit dieser Begriffe. Andrerseits hat Literatur, die häufig einen Oppositionsstandpunkt einnimmt, oft mit Enttäuschung, Haß, Ekel, Gleichgültigkeit, Ironie oder Zynik auf diese Entwicklung reagiert und sich auf eine anti-kommunale, selbstanalytische Position zurückgezogen. Damit wird auch die novellistische Binnenerzählung hinfällig, die auf der Annahme einer dramatischen Spannung zwischen beiden ungefähr gleichbedeutenden Werten beruht.

Die disziplinierte, formell vollendete Struktur der Novelle widerspricht ebenfalls dem Zug des Jahrhunderts. So steht der Verlust des Rahmens in der Novelle, im engeren und im weiteren Sinn, symbolhaft für den Verlust einer kulturellen und existentiellen Tradition des Abendlandes in unserer Zeit. Das Grundproblem – die Spannung Mensch - Gesellschaft – ist heute noch akuter als damals, aber die Novelle ist im 20. Jahrhundert wahrscheinlich nicht mehr die ihr angemessene dramatisch-epische Form. Es ist sicherlich kein Zufall, daß die deutsche Novelle gerade im 19. Jahrhundert, als das Kommunale und das Individuelle sich die Waage hielten, ihren Höhepunkt erreichte.

Solange wir uns noch oder wieder um wirkliches Gleichgewicht dieser beiden Werte bemühen und nicht um Unterjochung des einen durch den anderen, wird die deutsche Novelle des ausgehenden 18. und 19. Jahrhunderts uns viel zu sagen haben. Einschließlich des Rahmens: denn Rahmen bedeutet Spielraum für den Einzelnen, aber gesellschaftlich bedingten, nicht unbegrenzten, bedeutet Spannung und Ausgleich von Kraft und Form.

240

Stand der Forschung.

Kenntnis über den derzeitigen Stand der Novellenforschung im allgemeinen vermitteln das Realienbuch von Benno von Wiese (1963; 4. Auflage 1969), die Übersicht von Klein im *Reallexikon,* 2. Auflage, 1963-1965, der Forschungsbericht von Polheim (1964; 1965) und der von Kunz herausgegebene Sammelband *Novelle* (1968).

Was die Rahmenforschung insbesondere anbetrifft, so spielt sie innerhalb der wissenschaftlichen Bemühungen um die Novelle eine überraschend untergeordnete Rolle. Der hier folgende Abriß der Rahmenforschung ist eingeteilt, soweit möglich, in einschlägige Arbeiten zur Novellenforschung, die nichts oder wenig zum Rahmen als einem Strukturelement der Novelle zu sagen haben, solche, deren Beitrag uneinheitlich, aber bereits höher einzuschätzen ist, und schließlich diejenigen, welche besonderes Gewicht auf den Rahmen als Strukturkomponente der Novelle legen.

Bastiers (1910) umfangreiche, vernünftig angelegte und weitgehend typologische Arbeit nimmt vom Rahmen keine Notiz. In der <klassischen>, ausgezeichneten Studie von Hirsch (1928) wird der Rahmen in dem überwiegenden systematischen Teil nicht berücksichtigt, im Gegensatz zu den Einzelanalysen. In der allgemeinen Einleitung («The Novelle as a literary genre») zu Bennett/Waidsons Buch (1934; 1961 – S. 1-19) ist keine Rede vom Rahmen, obgleich im Kapitel über die klassische Novelle der Rahmen als ein grundlegendes Formelement der Novelle bezeichnet wird (S. 26). Petsch (1934, S. 254-255; wiedergedruckt bei Kunz, Hrsg., 1968, S. 193-194) begnügt sich mit *einer,* allerdings feinsinnigen Seite über den Rahmen. In Pongs' weitläufigen Ausführungen über die Novelle (1939: S. 97-296, davon S. 97 bis 109 mit einigen kleinen Änderungen nachgedruckt in Kunz, Hrsg., 1968) wird dem Rahmen nur sporadische Aufmerksamkeit geschenkt (S. 97, 124/125, 172, 185, 191, 225). Seine Interpretation des Rahmens, dessen prinzipielle Wichtigkeit er anerkennt, aber auf die er nicht näher eingeht, ist zu elastisch, zu zerfließend: «...das beständige Umspannthalten des Stoffes durch den Geist des Erzählers, der auf Symbolisierung gerichtet ist» (S. 97). Pongs' allgemeine Ausrichtung ist nicht strukturell, sondern existentiell-metaphysisch

(Konflikte und Polaritäten), tragisch, dämonisch, unbewußt.

In Silz' Synthese, «The Nature of the Novelle and of Poetic Realism» (S. 1-16) in *Realism and Reality* (1956) fällt nur *ein* wenig besagender Satz über den Rahmen, während es in seinen Einzelanalysen zu trefflichen Bemerkungen über den Rahmen kommt (z. B. im *Armen Spielmann*, S. 69-70). In den jeweiligen Syntheseversuchen, die von Wiese seinen beiden Novelleninterpretationsbüchern vorausschickt (1956, 1962) wird der Rahmen ganz kurz abgetan (S. 27 und 13); jedenfalls aber wirft er die wichtige Frage auf, inwieweit die Verwendung des Rahmens zur Verdoppelung der Erzählerperspektive führen mag (S. 13, 1962). In seinen Einzelanalysen (*Armer Spielmann, Hochzeit des Mönchs*) wird von Wiese dem Rahmen dagegen gerechter. In seiner kleinen Novellensynthese von 1963 (revidierte Auflage, 1969) spielt der Rahmen eine etwas größere, aber immer noch sehr bescheidene Rolle (S. 10, 33-36, 56-57).

Steinhauer (1958, 1969, 1970) hat für Novellendefinitionen nichts übrig und schenkt dem Rahmen keine Beachtung. Koskimies (1959; wiedergedruckt in Kunz, Hrsg., 1968, S. 408-409) betont die prinzipielle Bedeutung der Rahmenerzählung in der klassischen Novellenkunst, aber sagt wenig mehr darüber. Bei Martini (1960; wiedergedruckt in Kunz, Hrsg., 1968) findet man nützliche, aber vereinzelte Bemerkungen über den Rahmen (S. 362, 367, 371). Valencys erfrischende und intelligente Einführung zu einer Novellensammlung des 13. bis 16. Jahrhunderts (1960) spricht selten vom Rahmen, weist aber bereits darauf hin, daß im *Heptameron* von Marguerite de Navarre die Erörterungen über die erzählten Geschichten und die Persönlichkeiten im Rahmen weit interessanter und künstlerisch gediegener sind als die Geschichten selbst (S. 17). Im systematischen Teil des Buches von Himmel («Vorgeschichte und Theorie der deutschen Novelle», S. 9-41) kommt der Rahmen nicht vor (1963); allerdings ist die geschichtlich-aneinanderreihende Einstellung Himmels dem Herausschälen von Strukturelementen nicht günstig. Auch in den vielen Einzelanalysen ist vom Rahmen kaum die Rede. Das auf hohem und hohlem Roß trabende, prätentiöse Buch Malmedes (1966) entledigt sich des Rahmens als eines «längst als entbehrlich eingesehenen Wortes» (S. 45). Thieberger (1968/9) nimmt in seiner umfangreichen und gehaltvollen Studie vom Rahmen so gut wie keine Notiz und hat überhaupt wenig generell-typologisches über die Struktur der Novelle zu sagen. Ryders (1971) ausgezeichnete Einleitung zu seiner Novellensammlung schließt den Rahmen als ein charakteristisches Element der Novelle aus.

Obgleich Pabst (1949, 1953, teilweise wiedergedruckt in Kunz, Hrsg., 1968) eine der Hauptstützen der Nominalisten ist, welche von strukturellen Dauerelementen der Novelle wenig halten, trifft man bei ihm auf besonders feinsinnige und eingehende Bemerkungen über Rahmenfunktionen, hauptsächlich allerdings aus romanischer Sicht (S. 316-324 in Kunz, 1968). Was er über die Distanzschaffung und – verkürzung des Rahmens, über den Rahmen der Erinnerung und den Rahmen der Ernüchterung, über die Zerstücklung des Rahmens und die Zertrümmerung der Distanzen, und über den erweiterten Rahmenbegriff (Widmungsbriefe, Prologe, Avertissements) der älteren Literatur zu sagen hat, ist kenntnisreich und anregend. Pabsts «Nachtrag 1966» (bei Kunz) läßt durchblicken, daß er heute vielleicht nicht mehr ganz so nominalistisch urteilen würde wie in seinen einflußreichen Schriften der 1940er und 1950er Jahre. Klein (1954) zerfasert seinen Ausblick auf die Novelle in so viele inhaltliche und ideologische Einzelrichtungen, daß weder die Struktur als solche noch der Rahmen insbesondere zu ihrem Recht kommen. Es bleibt aber zu beachten, daß er der 4. Auflage seines Novellenbuches (1960) ein Kapitel über die Formengeschichte der deutschen Novelle zugefügt hat. Dort gibt er eine zwar kurze, aber gute Übersicht mit konkreten Beispielen über den Rahmen: gesellschaftlicher und künstlerischer Ursprung, verschiedene Rahmenformen, Verhältnis zwischen Rahmen und Binnennovellen, sogar Rundfunk als Rahmenfunktion (S. 31-35). In seiner späteren Untersuchung zum Thema («Novelle» im *Reallexikon*, 2. Aufl., 1963-1965) hält er den Rahmen für «soziologisch wichtig» (S. 693) und macht eine Anzahl prinzipiell geordneter Bemerkungen zum Rahmenproblem (S. 692-694). Ähnlich wie Klein ist Kunz' *Geschichte der deutschen Novelle* (1954; 2. Auflage 1960) historisch, analytisch, thematisch orientiert; den novellistischen Erzählformen wird aber einige Beachtung geschenkt, und es kommt zu treffenden Vergleichen zwischen den novellistischen Rahmen Boccaccios und Goethes (Spalten 1795-1802), dazu Tiecks (Spalte 1813-1814) und schließlich Gotthelfs und Kellers (Spalten 1857-1859). In seiner *Deutschen Novelle zwischen Klassik und Romantik* (1966) und seiner *Deutschen Novelle im 19. Jahrhundert* (1970) bietet er nichts systematisch Wertvolles über den Rahmen, dagegen enthält seine sehr vernünftige Einleitung («Theorie der Novelle», S. 1-23) zu dem von ihm herausgegebenen, höchst wertvollen Sammelband über die *Novelle* (1968) einen wohl ausgewogenen, kurzen Kommentar über die ethische und ästhetische Funktion des Rahmens (S. 6-8). (Über Kaysers bündige aber gehaltvolle, prinzipielle Bemerkungen zum Rahmen gibt der Text meiner Arbeit Aufschluß.)

Erné und Lockemann billigen dem Rahmen grundlegende Bedeutung in der Novellistik zu. Ernés (1956) Feuilletonformat (aber warum soll Intelligenz nicht Charme haben?) und Lockemanns (1957) zu einseitige Chaos-Ordnungsausrichtung und seine (wie bei Klein) erdrückende Menge von Novellenanalysen sind der wissenschaftlichen Anerkennung ihrer Gedanken abträglich gewesen. Trotzdem gebührt ihnen in der Rahmenforschung ein hervorragender Platz (Erné: S. 30-52; Lockemann: S. 11-16, siehe auch Lockemann in Kunz, Hrsg., 1968, S. 329-345). Erné betont die Parallele zwischen gesellschaftlichem Rahmen und architektonischer Komposition, Rahmen als Distanzbedürfnis, Erzähler als Kontrastfigur, und gibt einleuchtende Beispiele aus verschiedenen Literaturen. Lockemann unterscheidet zwischen Zweckrahmung und legitimierender Rahmung, geschlossenem und offenem Rahmen, sieht die Rahmennovelle als Prototyp der Novellenform und die gesellschaftliche Ordnungsfunktion des Rahmens als grundlegend. Er geht in seinen Anforderungen und Definitionen fraglos manchmal zu weit. Substantiell und förderlich ist die Übersicht und Zusammenstellung der Sekundärliteratur über die «Rahmenerzählung» von Kanzog (1968), die sich allerdings nicht auf die Novellistik beschränkt. Das Typologisch-Strukturelle kommt bei dem historisch-chronologisch ausgerichteteen Schema auch hier nicht sehr zur Geltung.

Es scheint somit für die Rahmenforschung in der Novellistik bezeichnend, daß an systematisch-strukturellen Überblicken ein großer

244

Mangel, an weitverstreuten, vereinzelten prinzipiellen Bemerkungen und eingehenden Analysen des Rahmens in Einzelwerken dagegen kein Mangel herrscht. Diese wissenschaftlichen Lücken erklären neben der übertrieben skeptischen Einstellung Polheims zum Bestehen spezifisch novellistischer Strukturelemente die Tatsache, daß in seinem konzentrierten und überaus nützlichen Forschungsbericht über die Novelle von 118 enggedruckten Druckseiten (1964, 1965) kaum sechs sich mit der Rahmenforschung auseinandersetzen (1964: S. 230-231, 254-258; 1965: S. 23-24, 47-51. Der Hauptwortlaut beider Ausgaben ist der gleiche; die Hinzufügungen 1965 beschränken sich auf Vorbemerkung, Anhang, Register und Druckanordnung).

Berücksichtigte Sekundärliteratur: Bastier, Paul. *La nouvelle individualiste en Allemagne de Goethe à Gottfried Keller.* Essai de technique psychologique. Paris, Larose, 1910. – Bennett, E. K. und Waidson, H. M. *A History of the German Novelle* (1934). 2d edition: Cambridge (England), University Press, 1961. – Erné, Nino. *Kunst der Novelle.* Wiesbaden, Limes, 1956. – Himmel, Hellmuth. *Geschichte der deutschen Novelle.* Sammlung Dalp 94. Bern und München, Francke, 1963. – Hirsch, Arnold. *Der Gattungsbegriff «Novelle».* Germanische Studien 64. Berlin, 1928, Nachdruck: Nendeln/Liechtenstein, Kraus, 1967. – Kanzog, Klaus. «Rahmenerzählung», in *Reallexikon der deutschen Literaturgeschichte,* 2. Auflage, Band III, Berlin, de Gruyter, 1968, S. 321-343. – Kayser, Wolfgang. *Das Sprachliche Kunstwerk* (1948). 6. Auflage. Bern und München, Francke, 1960. – Klein, Johannes. *Geschichte der deutschen Novelle von Goethe bis zur Gegenwart.* Wiesbaden, Steiner, 1954. – id., *Geschichte* usw., 4., verbesserte und erweiterte Auflage, *ibid.,* 1960. – Klein, Johannes. «Novelle», in *Reallexikon der deutschen Literturgeschichte,* 2. Auflage, Band II, Berlin, de Gruyter, 1965. S. 685-701. – Kunz, Josef. «Geschichte der deutschen Novelle vom 18. Jahrhundert bis auf die Gegenwart», in *Deutsche Philologie im Aufriß,* 2. überarbeitete Auflage, Band II, Berlin, Erich Schmidt, 1960, Spalten 1795-1896. – Kunz, Josef. *Die deutsche Novelle zwischen Klassik und Romantik.* Berlin, Erich Schmidt, 1966. – Kunz, Josef (Hrsg.) *Novelle.* Darmstadt, Wissenschaftliche Buchgesellschaft, 1968. Darin: Josef Kunz, «Einleitung», S. 1-23. Der Band enthält eine Sammlung wichtiger

Bemerkungen und Aufsätze über die Novelle (Wieland, Goethe, Eckermann, Friedrich Schlegel, August Wilhelm Schlegel, Tieck, Schleiermacher, Hebbel, Mundt, Vischer, Heyse, Spielhagen, Storm, Keller, Ernst, Musil, Lukács; Walzel, Jolles, Hirsch, Bruch, Pongs, Grolman, Petsch, Klein, Krauss, Hankamer; Pabst, Burger, Lockemann, Martini, Mackensen, Koskimies, Schunicht, Joachim Müller, Weinrich; Bibliographie: Schriften zur Theorie der Novelle seit 1915 in chronologischer Folge; Alphabetischer Index zur Bibliographie). – Kunz, Josef. *Die deutsche Novelle im 19. Jahrhundert.* Berlin, Erich Schmidt, 1970. – Lockemann, Fritz. *Gestalt und Wandlungen in der deutschen Novelle.* München, Hueber, 1957. – Malmede, Hans Hermann. *Wege zur Novelle.* Stuttgart, Kohlhammer, 1966. – Petsch, Robert. «Die Novelle», in Petsch, *Wesen und Formen der Erzählkunst,* Halle, Niemeyer, 1934, S. 245-261. – Polheim, Karl Konrad. *«Novellentheorie und Novellenforschung* (1945-1963)», in *Deutsche Vierteljahrsschrift für Literaturwisseneschaft und Geistesgeschichte,* Sonderheft, XXXVIII, Oktober 1964, S. 208-316. – Erweiterte Fassung: *Novellentheorie und Novellenforschung.* Ein Forschungsbericht 1945-1964. Stuttgart, Metzler, 1965. – Pongs, Hermann, «Aufsätze zur Novelle», in Pongs, *Das Bild in der Dichtung,* Marburg, Elwert, 1939, II, 97-296. – Ryder, Frank (ed.), «Introduction», in *Die Novelle* (Holt, Rinehart, New York 1971, xiii-xxviii). – Schefski, Harold K., "The Novelle in Russian Literature," M. A. Thesis, Stanford University, Juni, 1970 (ungedruckt). – Silz, Walter. *Realism and Reality.* Studies in the German Novelle of Poetic Realism. Chapel Hill, University of North Carolina Press, 1956. – Steinhauer, Harry, «The Novelle as an Art Form», in «Introduction», *Die deutsche Novelle* (1936). Expanded edition. 1880-1950, New York, Norton, 1958, S. 14-22. – Steinhauer, Harry. «Introduction», in *Ten German Novellas,* New York, Doubleday, 1969, S, ix-xxv. – Steinhauer, Harry, «Towards a definition of the novella», *Seminar,* VI, no. 2, Juni 1970, S. 154-174. – Thieberger, Richard. *Le genre de la nouvelle dans la littérature allemande.* Publications de la Faculté des Lettres et Sciences Humaines de Nice, 2. Paris, Les Belles Lettres, 1968 (1969). – Valency, Maurice, «Introduction» to *The Palace of Pleasure.* An Anthology of the Novella (13. bis 16. Jahrh.), New York, Capricorn, 1960, S. 2-28. –

von Wiese, Benno. *Die deutsche Novelle von Goethe bis Kafka.* Interpretationen. Düsseldorf, Bagel, 1956. – von Wiese, Benno. *Die deutsche Novelle von Goethe bis Kafka.* Band II. Düsseldorf, Bagel, 1962. – von Wiese, Benno. *Novelle.* Stuttgart, Metzler, 1963. – 4., durchgesehene Auflage, *ibid,.* 1969.

Chapter IX
Thomas Mann als Novellist

Summary

*Introduction: Considerations justifying the generic approach to several stories by Thomas Mann as structured novellas: "Little Mr. Friedemann" (*Der kleine Herr Friedemann, 1897*); Tobias Mindernickel, 1898; Tristan, 1902, and "Mario and the Magician" (*Mario und der Zauberer, 1930*). Each of these stories is examined in the light of three fundamental novellesque criteria.*

The One Event ("eine Begebenheit").

It is, in all four cases, a fatal encounter. Mario *demonstrates, in comparison to the three earlier stories, certain twentieth-century characteristics: psychological refinement (but without impairing the dramatic tension) and socio-political pressures.*

That has actually occurred ("sich ereignete").

*Here again, the first three stories differ from the fourth: there is no documentable source for them (which does not necessarily mean that they are not persuasive); their authenticity is broadly cultural and internal. The last story, (*Mario*), once again, stands by itself because it is based, according to Mann's explicit testimony, on the vacation stay of the Mann family in Viareggio (August 13 to September 13, 1926): only the lethal (and very novellesque) ending was invented by Mann or rather by his daughter, Erika. The three layers in* Mario *are 1) the personal and private, 2) the politically charged atmosphere, and 3) the problematics of the artist (Cipolla). While there is evidence that an actual specific occurrence promotes the authenticity of the novellesque action based on it, Mann's artistic genius (like Kleist's) compensates for the absence of the original event in the first three stories; in the last one the actual experience has furnished the novellesque core and helps in making it convincing.*

The Unheard-of ("Unerhört").

*In three of the four stories (*Friedemann, Mindernickel,

Mario*) it is strikingly positioned at the very end: Friedemann's abject and poignant suicide; Mindernickel's fatal stabbing of his dog; the shooting of Cipolla. The shock of the "unheard-of" catastrophe in* Friedemann *and* Mario *has a maximum effect because it seems to come as a complete surprise (except in meticulous retrospect); in* Mindernickel *it is weakened by the triple, preceding episodes of the dog's brutalization by his master; in* Tristan *it is not totally surprising, in view of Spinell's deliberate campaign toward Gabriele's 'salvation' – 'expiation' by way of a musical, Wagner – induced death. But the preparation for it throughout the story is of such ingenious sophistication, such mounting if gradual crescendo crowned by perhaps the most intoxicating passion climax in operatic literature (by proxy) that the final effect of the 'unheard-of' is, if less shocking, still very impressive.*

Conclusion: Goethe's "eine sich ereignete unerhörte Begebenheit", if used with text-oriented differentiation, offers a clearly serviceable approach to Mann's four novellesque stories.

Notes. Critical Bibliography (Note No. 5).

»Die Form gilt uns Deutschen gemeinhin als eine Konvention, als Verkleidung und Verstellung ... (wir haben) eine außerordentliche Angst vor dem Worte Konvention und auch wohl der Sache Konvention.« (Nietzsche, *Unzeitgemäße Betrachtungen* II)

»Mein Vater hat von der Pflicht der Überlieferung, der Bewahrung der Kontinuität ein stark ausgeprägtes Bewußtsein gehabt«. (Golo Mann)[1]

---

[1]*Thomas Mann. Erinnerungen an meinen Vater* (1964). Bonn, Inter Nationes, o. J., S.5.

Zum Versuch, die novellistische Struktur einiger Erzählungen Thomas Manns zu erhellen, diese Vorbermerkungen:

1) Der gattungsstrukturelle Eingang zu Manns Werk ist *ein* Zugang, nicht der einzige; ein wichtig*er*, nicht der wichtig*ste*.

2) Für ihn spricht: Gattung ist, historisch gesehen, das *literarischste* Ordnungsprinzip der Literatur, das eigentlichste. Andere Blickwinkel, ob philosophisch, ideengeschichtlich, thematisch, psychologisch, linguistisch, semiotisch, religiös, politisch, wirtschaftlich oder sozial besitzen ebenfalls grundsätzliche Berechtigung. Einen besonderen Anspruch bezieht eine Methode nur aus der Beschaffenheit des gewählten Textes und aus der Qualität ihrer Ausführung. Das Resultat entscheidet.

3) Text ist die letzte Richterinstanz für Theorie. Die Existenz des Textes, nicht die Theorie, ist das A und O der Literaturwissenschaft. Text/Theorie stehen in einem Verhältnis wechselseitiger Produktivität. Die Theorie entdeckt neue Dimensionen des Textes, der Text neue Dimensionen der Theorie.

4) Die formbestimmte Methode ist ein Stiefkind der Germanistik. Zu oft ist »Form« (»formell«, »Formalismus«) noch gefühlsmäßig durch die Verknüpfung mit dem »Äußerlichen« belastet, während »Bedeutung« und »Sinn« mit »Innerlichem« und »Substanz« verbunden werden. Thomas Mann ist ein hochintellektueller Schriftsteller. In der Literatur über ihn ist die Tendenz, sich auf das Intellektuelle zu stürzen, überwältigend und verständlich. Und doch: wie gern hörte er sich »den Zauberer« nennen! Manns Erzählungen einmal hauptsächlich als ererbte und neugestaltete Formtypen zu prüfen: – da gibt es noch viel Neuland in den Niagarafluten[2] der Thomas-

---

[2]Die zutreffende Formulierung stammt aus Oskar Seidlins Besprechung von T. J. Reed, *Thomas Mann: The Uses of Tradition*, New York, Oxford University Press, 1974, in *Journal of English and Germanic Philology*, LXXV, 1976, S. 268.

250

Mann-Literatur.

5) Mann war ein kulturtraditionell und – kenntnisausgerichteter Schriftsteller, der sich der Novelle als seit der Mitte des 14. Jahrhunderts historisch ausgeprägter und gerade in Deutschland im 19. Jahrhundert hochflorierender Kunstform durchaus bewußt war. Alle vier hier besprochenen Erzählungen sind von Anfang an ausdrücklich als »Novellen« veröffentlicht worden. Mann spricht häufig von der Novellenform, vom »Novellistischen«[3], auch in bezug auf seine eigenen Werke dieser Art. Im *Kleinen Herrn Friedemann* läßt unser Held sogar »die intime Stimmung einer fein geschriebenen Novelle auf sich wirken«[4] – es wäre ganz à la Thomas Mann, wenn dem Autor dabei z. B. die vorschwebt, in welcher dieser Satz steht. All das bedeutet natürlich nicht, daß man von ihm oder irgend jemand anderem einförmige Begriffsbestimmungen des Novellistischen erwarten dürfte.

6) Mann hat zeit seines Lebens annähernd einunddreißig Erzählungen veröffentlicht, davon etwa fünf Sechstel vor dem Ersten Weltkrieg, unter denen die weitaus größte Mehrzahl Anspruch darauf erheben darf, auf ihren novellistischen Gehalt hin untersucht zu werden. Die Literatur über sie strotzt auch von Hinweisen auf »Novelle« und »novellistisch«, aber fast nie unternimmt sie einen halbwegs systematischen Versuch, ausfindig zu machen,

---

[3]Darunter in einem bisher nur teilweise veröffentlichten Brief an mich vom 25. Oktober 1946, in dem er schreibt, daß »Maupassant ... meine Novellistik mitbestimmte.« Siehe *Die Briefe Thomas Manns. Regesten und Register. III: Die Briefe von 1944 bis 1950.* Hrsg. von Hans Bürgin, Hans-Otto Mayer und Yvonne Schmidlin. Frankfurt, Fischer, 1982, S. 303. Diese Sammlung enthält ein Verzeichnis der Briefempfänger aber noch keine Namen- und Sachregister.

[4]Thomas Mann, *Erzählungen.* O. O., Fischer, 1960, S. 81. In diesem Kapitel wird nach dieser Ausgabe zitiert.

was nun wirklich novellistisch an der Geschichte ist. Damit soll hier ein
bescheidener Anfang gemacht werden.[5]

---

[5]»Die gesamte Thomas-Mann-Literatur vermag heute niemand mehr zu
überblicken« (Hans Wysling, »Psychologische Aspekte von Thomas Manns
Kunst«, in: Wysling, *Thomas Mann heute,* Bern und München, Francke, 1976,
S. 7). Dieser Ausspruch des besten heutigen Kenners der Thomas-Mann-
Schriften nötigt uns, mit positiven und negativen Urteilen über die Thomas-
Mann-Forschung sehr vorsichtig zu sein, und das um so mehr als wir, solange
es noch kein umfassendes Mann-Nachschlagewerk gibt, nicht annehmen
dürfen, daß wir seine eigenen Äußerungen über die Novelle als Kunstform
oder das Novellistische als Kunsttendenz nahezu vollständig kennen. Selbst
bei der Interpretation der uns bekannten Aussagen muß ihr Kontext im Auge
behalten werden, und darunter an erster Stelle, daß eine Novelle eine
Erzählung ist, eine Erzählung hingegen keineswegs notwendigerweise eine
Novelle. In: »[On Myself]« (1940), (gedruckt in den *Nachträgen* zu seinen
Gesammelten Werken in dreizehn Bänden, Frankfurt, Fischer, 1974, hrsg.
von Hans Bürgin und Peter de Mendelssohn, XIII, S. 127-169) nennt Mann z.
B. den *Kleinen Herrn Friedemann* eine »Erzählung« (S. 135). Das bedeutet
in diesem Zusammenhang nur, daß er hier einen umfassenderen
Kategorieausdruck benutzt. Wenn er wenig später (S. 137) in demselben
Vortrag von seiner Überzeugung spricht, »daß die Kurzgeschichte, wie ich sie
in der Schule Maupassants, Tschechows und Turgenjews erlernt hatte, mein
Genre sei«, so darf man nicht vergessen, daß er von *Luischen, Enttäuschung*
und dem *Bajazzo* spricht, auf die »Kurzgeschichte« zutreffen mag – ganz
abgesehen davon, daß man auch von Thomas Mann nicht verlangen darf, daß
er immer und zu jeder Gelegenheit die exakteste Terminologie verwendet.
Jedenfalls sollten wir uns Harry Matters zutreffende Bemerkung vor Augen
halten, daß »der Begriff der Erzählung ... eigentlich nichts über die spezifische
Form des Werkes aussagt, denn auch Romane, Legenden und Märchen
gehören zur erzählenden Gattung der Literatur ...« (»Mario und der Zauberer.
Die Bedeutung der Novelle im Schaffen Thomas Manns«, *Weimarer Beiträge,*

252

VI, 1960, S. 593).

Unsere Hauptstütze in der Erfassung der einschlägigen Literatur ist Hans Rudolf Vagets *Thomas-Mann-Kommentar zu sämtlichen Erzählungen*, München, Winkler, 1984. Wert und Nützlichkeit dieses Kompendiums sind nicht hoch genug einzuschätzen. Für jeden Erzähltext, darunter auch den vier von uns ausgewählten, liefert Vaget erklärende Anmerkungen, Entstehungsgeschichte, Selbstdeutungen, Kontext und Rezeption (zeitgenössische Kritik, Deutungsgeschichte). Es handelt sich hier um die beste Art von selektivem, urteilsgelenktem Positivismus. Die Hoffnung, die das einleitende Kapitel, »Thomas Mann der Novellist« (S. 27-47) erweckt, daß die Struktur der von Mann gewählten Kunstform ernstlich erforscht wird, erfüllt sich allerdings auch hier nicht. Vaget betont zwar, »daß das literarische Ansehen des *Novellisten* [Hervorhebung von Vaget] Thomas Manns auf einem festeren Fundament gegründet ist als das des Romanciers« (S. 27), daß die Novelle »sein Genre« ist (S. 30) und daß Mann »sich ... im Anlauf auf die Romanform ... zunächst einmal an die vertraute Struktur der Novelle« (ebda.) hält, bezeichnet alle vier der hier zu besprechenden Erzählungen als »Novellen« und arbeitet durchwegs mit den Begriffen »novellistisch«, »Novellist« und »Novelle«, verrät uns aber nicht, was nun diese Struktur ist oder sein könnte und gebraucht den Terminus »Novelle« meist als gleichbedeutend mit »Kurzgeschichte«, »Kurze Erzählung« und »short fiction«.

Die mir bekannte restliche Thomas-Mann-Literatur ist ebenso zurückhaltend und im Grunde schweigsam. Selbst in Studien, die sich eingehend mit Formfragen beschäftigen, gibt es, mit einer gewissen Einschränkung für *Mario,* kaum einen Versuch, die Novellenform als solche zu beachten. Max Kapp, *Thomas Manns novellistische Kunst. Ideen und Probleme. Atmosphäre und Symbolik seiner Erzählungen* (München, Drei Masken, 1928) enthält kein Wort über *novellistische* Kunst. Ein gehaltvolles Buch wie Hermann Stresaus *Thomas Mann und sein Werk* (Frankfurt, Fischer, 1963) schließt z. B. Kapitel wie »Das epische Formproblem« oder »Die Schriftstellernovellen« ein, beleuchtet das Biographische, das Lyrische, das Epische, gebraucht auch gelegentlich den Ausdruck »Novelle«, geht aber mit kcinem Wort auf novellistische Struktur ein. Andererseits werden in manchen Arbeiten Bestandteile des Novellistischen in Werken Manns hervorgehoben, ohne daß sie mit irgendwelchen Gattungsmerkmalen in Verbindung gebracht werden. Henry Hatfield bemerkt z. B., daß *Friedemann* scharfsinniger, gelassener und reifer ist als seine Vorgänger und in *medias res* einsetzt, bringt aber die Gattung nicht zur Sprache (*Thomas Mann*, Norfolk, Conn., New Directions, 1951, S. 17-18). In Walter Weiss' *Thomas Manns Kunst der sprachlichen und thematischen Integration* (Düsseldorf, Beihefte zu *Wirkendes Wort* Nr. 13, 1964), einer Studie, die Vaget die umfassendste Untersuchung der Merkmale *Marios* nennt (S. 248), ist auf den *Mario* gewidmeten Seiten (80-100) von der »sehr kurzen und knappen Ouvertüre« (S. 81), von der »dramatisch-spannenden Erlebniserzählung« (ebda.), von »Antithetik« (S. 85) und »Leitwörtern« (S. 86-88) die Rede, aber ohne jeglichen Bezug auf ihre novellistische Funktion.

Die drei nennenswerten Ausnahmen in der (nicht?) novellistischen Forschungsorientierung beschränken sich alle auf *Mario*. Es sind Harry Matter (1960, s.o.,diese Anmerkung), Hartmut Böhme, »Thomas Mann: *Mario und der Zauberer.* Position des Erzählers und Psychologie der Herrschaft«, *Orbis Litterarum*, Nr. 30, 1975, S. 268-316, und Gert Sautermeister, *Thomas Mann: Mario und der Zauberer*, München, Fink UTB, 1981.

Matter arbeitet in dem relativ kurzen aber äußerst gehaltvollen Teil VII (S. 590-596) seines Aufsatzes konsequent mit Strukturelementen der Novelle. Er charakterisiert die heute für *Mario* übliche Bezeichnung »Erzählung« unter Fortlassung des Untertitels »Ein tragisches Reiseerlebnis« als »irreführend« und stellt fest, daß »die bewußte Heranführung, die novellistische Technik [*Marios*] in dieser Art einzig unter den Erzählungen« Manns dasteht (S. 593). Der novellistische »Aufbau« wird »überaus streng« genannt (S. 591). Matter verwendet traditionell anerkannte novellistische Kriterien in seiner Analyse *Marios:* die bemerkenswerte Begebenheit, den berichtenden Ton, Abwechslung zwischen indirekter (1. Teil der Novelle) und direkter (2. Teil der Novelle) Rede, zwischen dem Epischen und Dramatischen, die »klar zu übersehende Handlung« (S. 593), Steigerung, einzelne Höhepunkte und Endhöhepunkt (überraschendes Ende), das Neue, Unerhörte, Konzentrierung auf »das eine große Ereignis« (S. 594), Verwandtschaft mit der Rahmennovelle und konstatiert: Goethes »klassische, wenn auch allgemeine Definition trifft auf *Mario und der Zauberer* voll und ganz zu« (S. 593). Matter geht zwar in seiner Studie, die noch andere Schwerpunkte hat, nicht im Einzelnen auf die von ihm wahrgenommenen novellistischen Aufbausteine ein, stellt aber fraglos in den Wogen der Mann-Forschung durch die Unabhängigkeit seiner Auffassung einen herausragenden Felsen dar.

Böhmes Verweise auf die novellistische Tradition sind verstreuter und verschwommener, aber er teilt jedenfalls »der klassischen Novellenstruktur« (S. 286) eine Rolle im Verständnis *Marios* zu und analysiert Faktoren wie Merkwürdigkeit, Unheimlichkeit, Handlung und Handlungshemmung, Peripetie, Schlußwendung, Katastrophe, Schicksal, und ästhetische Geschlossenheit. Er ist meines Wissens nach der einzige, der aus dem Zeugnis Manns, die Niederschießung Cipollas sei eine novellistische Erfindung (siehe Anmerkung 17), die strukturellen Konsequenzen zieht und fragt, ob dieser Schluß auch zur sozialpsychologischen Realität der Erzählung paßt – eine Frage, die für die Bewertung der Verbindung zwischen Ideologie und Ästhetik zentral ist. In diesem Falle wird sie verneint. Er irrt aber, glaube ich, wenn er »die Utopie des »glücklichen Endes« der klassischen Ästhetik der Novelle zuschreibt« (S. 304): so eindeutig ist die Schlußwendung in der Geschichte der Novelle keineswegs. (Böhmes Untersuchung ist in Hermann Kurzke, Hrsg., *Stationen der Thomas-Mann-Forschung*, Aufsätze seit 1970, Würzburg, Königshausen und Neumann, 1985, S. 166-189 nachgedruckt.)

Sautermeister nimmt sich vor, im Gegensatz zu der »federführenden« Forschung, die sich mit einem bloßen »Widerspiegelungsverhältnis« von Politik in Literatur begnüge, »den Zusammenhang zwischen poetischer Konstruktion und gesellschaftlicher Bedeutung in Manns Erzählung erstmals

7) Struktur ist die Synthese von Sinn und Form. Besser: in der Struktur werden Sinn und Form Gestalt. Von diesem Gesichtspunkt aus können novellistische Erkenntnisse Einblick geben in weitgehendere Probleme, Erfolge und Niederlagen künstlerischer Gestaltung im Werk Thomas Manns.

8) Einwand: die Hypothese, daß eine Novelle eine Novelle sei, führt notwendigerweise zum Resultat, daß eine Novelle eine Novelle ist. Man hat bereits gefunden, was man sucht. Was ist damit gewonnen?

Antwort: Natürlich besteht diese Falle. Ein gewisses *parti pris* des unternehmungslustigen Forschers auszumerzen ist weder möglich noch wünschenswert. Aber die Gefahr zu erkennen und sie einzudämmen ist besser als sich durch sie lähmen zu lassen. Nichts halbwegs Wichtiges ist ohne Risiko zu erreichen. Die Klippe des circulus vitiosus läßt sich umschiffen,

---

aufzuschließen« (S. 7) und sieht »die vom *Mario* intendierte Wirkung«, in angemessener Formulierung, in der doppeldeutigen Schwingung »zwischen vertrauter Novellentradition und provozierend zeitgeschichtlichem Gehalt, zwischen stilvoller Geschlossenheit und pochender Offenheit zur politischen Gegenwart« (S. 8). Dieser Vorsatz führt folgerichtig zu dem Abschnitt »Novellistisches Erzählen« als erstem innerhalb des Kapitels »Textimmanente Ästhetik«, in dem er freilich nur drei von zwanzig Seiten beansprucht. Er stützt sich hier, als Arbeitshypothese, auf Benno von Wieses nützliche Novellenmerkmale: Goethes unerhörte Begebenheit, Tiecks Wendepunkt, die »objektive Merkwürdigkeit« eines »als wahr erzählten und als wahr anmutenden, einmaligen Einzelfalls«, formale Geschlossenheit, Notwendigkeit des Geschehens, kunstvollen Aufbau, leitmotivische Verdichtung, eine gewisse allgemeine Gültigkeit, gesellschaftliche Bezogenheit, Unterhaltung (S. 31-33).

Der nächste Abschnitt, »Kunstvoller Aufbau. Leitmotive« (S. 33-40) teilt die Erzählung, in Anknüpfung an »klassisch-novellistische Formprinzipien«, in vier Akte ein, mit je zwei dramatischen Höhepunkten, einem Vorspiel und einem Ausklang. Im übrigen beherrschen andere Gesichtspunkte das anregende Buch.

solange der Forscher bereit ist, seine Hypothese aufgrund seiner Textbefunde abzuändern, so daß Endresultat und anfängliche Voraussetzungen oder Vermutungen keineswegs und unwandelbar miteinander übereinstimmen. Das ist das Ethos aller wissenschaftlichen Forschung. Es steht unseren Lesern immer offen, aus ihrer eigenen Sicht der angeführten Textzeugnisse zu mehr oder minder verschiedenen Interpretationen zu gelangen: ein großer Vorteil der induktiven gegenüber der deduktiven Methode, bei der entgegengesetzte Theorien oft in gleichem Glanz erscheinen. Im übrigen kommt es mir weniger darauf an zu beweisen, daß diese oder jene Erzählung Thomas Manns eine oder keine Novelle ist, als durch das Anlegen gattungsstruktureller Maßstäbe genauer zu erkennen, was an einem überhaupt zum Novellistischen neigenden Erzähltext typisch und was atypisch ist, ob und wie es zu einem Kunstwerk führt: sicherlich eine Kernfrage aller Literaturwissenschaft. Kaum eine Novelle ist 100% novellistisch, und novellistische Elemente gibt es in zahlreichen Texten, die hauptsächlich einer anderen Gattung angehören, z. B. Balladen, Zeitungsberichten, Autobiographien, Märchen, Romanen. Viele Texte sind *besonders* novellistisich: andere sind *auch* novellistisch: beide Typen sind für die historisch-kritische Literaturerkenntnis aufschlußreich.

Wir beschränken uns als ersten Ansatz in zweierlei Weise: einerseits auf die bewährte, aber minimale goethesche Definition der Novelle als »einer sich ereigneten unerhörten Begebenheit«[6], andererseits auf vier novellistische Erzählungen Thomas Manns: *Der kleine Herr Friedemann* (1897), *Tobias Mindernickel* (1898), *Tristan* (1902), und *Mario und der Zauberer* (1930).

Eine Begebenheit

Unter der »einen Begebenheit« versteht die Literatur über die Novelle cum grano salis einen profilierten Vorfall, ein absolut oder relativ geschlossenes Geschehnis. In unseren vier Texten handelt es sich sich eher um

---

[6]Gespräch mit Eckermann vom 29. Januar 1827.

eine Kette von eng zusammenhängenden Szenen, die in einen Höhepunkt/Tiefpunkt einmünden: Auftritte und Endpunkt bilden eine geschlossene Gesamtbegebenheit, die ihrerseits im Rückblick wie ein Scheinwerfer ein gesamtes Lebensbild enthüllt oder auch nur halbdunkle Existenzfragen aufwirft.

Der kleine Herr Friedemann

Nach einem Vorspiel von etwa sieben Seiten, das die ersten dreißig Jahre des »Lebens« des kleinen Herrn Friedemanns überblickt, folgt die »eine Begebenheit«, die über alles weitere entscheidet: Friedemanns fatale Begegnung mit Gerda von Rinnlingen, um deren Konsequenzen in etwa sechs Hauptszenen sich das letzte dreiviertel der Erzählung dreht. Dieses »einmalige« Zusammentreffen, so stellt es sich heraus, ist der Kristallisationspunkt seiner ganzen Anlage, seiner Verkrüppelung, seiner Feinheit, seiner Sehnsucht nach Leben, Liebe und Verständnis. Der Höhepunkt ist ein Tiefpunkt (aber auch eine Befreiung): Friedemanns Verstoßung und Selbstmord. Der unaufgeklärte und gerade deshalb ebenso novellistische Gegensatz dazu ist Gerdas Leben, das auch am Schluß noch zum großen Teil rätselhaft bleibt.

Tobias Mindernickel

Vorspiel: der Zwischenfall mit dem verwundeten Jungen. Dann der Ankauf des Hundes Esau (wieder eine fatale Begegnung) und die vier zwiespältigen Vorfälle, in denen Mindernickel das Tier abwechselnd mitleidig und grausam behandelt. Sie erreichen ihren Höhepunkt/Tiefpunkt in der Erstechung Esaus durch seinen Herrn. Die Begebenheit ist die Erwerbung und auseinderklaffende Behandlung des Hundes, schließlich die Bluttat: diese *eine* Begebenheit enthüllt auf zehn Seiten in ein paar dramatischen Szenen die gesamte Existenz dieses paroxystischen Jammermenschen in ihren Höhen und Abgründen.

Tristan

Wieder ein Vorspiel von etwa neun Seiten. Dann die »eine Begebenheit«: Gabriele und Spinell machen Bekanntschaft. Wieder eine fatale Begegnung: (diesmal für sie, nicht, wie im *Friedemann,* für ihn), deren Folgen wiederum drei Viertel der restlichen Erzählung beanspruchen. Sie verdichten sich in neun Szenen, bis auf die letzte (eine neue Begegnung Spinells mit Anton Jr., diesmal »fatal« nicht für den »Säugling« sondern für den »verwesten Säugling«) alle pointierte Unterhaltungen. Den Höhepunkt/Tiefpunkt stellt Spinells gelungene Verführung, »kraft« von Wagner geborgter Potenz, der zarten Patientin dar, deren unmittelbare und von dem Surrogatverführer gewollte Folge ihr physischer Tod aber ihre künstlerische Wiedergeburt ist. In dieser weitläufigeren Novelle wird durch die stetig stattfindenden Auftritte das ganze Leben der problematischen Dreiuneinigkeit (Klöterjahn-Gabriele-Spinell) aufgerollt.

Mario und der Zauberer

Dreißig Jahre und mehr nach diesen drei klassisch gebauten Novellen wird die »eine Begebenheit« im *Mario* verwickelter. Das Vorspiel zum novellistischen pièce de résistance der Darstellung hat sich hier zu einem selbständigeren, aber doch durch seine geladene Stimmung psychologisch auf die eigentlich novellistische Begebenheit (Cipolla) vorbereitenden Teil emporentwickelt: das Verhältnis ist annähernd 1 : 3. Die novellistische Begebenheit als solche, aus etwa sechs »Kunststücken« zusammengesetzt, die den Szenen in den vorhergehenden drei Novellen entsprechen, ist aber durchaus geschlossen: es ist die Vorstellung. Und es ist zum vierten Mal eine fatale Begegnung, hier zwischen dem Zauberkünstler/Hypnotiseur/Verführer und seinem meist italienischen Publikum, fatal aber diesmal nicht für das Opfer (siehe Friedemann, Esau, Gabriele) sondern, auf überraschend / novellistische Weise, für den geistigen Missetäter: Cipolla, im Gegensatz zu dessen überlebenden Vorfahren: Gerda, Mindernickel und Spinell. Der

Tiefpunkt für das Publikum – für die Menschenwürde – wird hier umgedreht in ein »Ende mit Schrecken, ein höchst fatales Ende. Und ein befreiendes Ende dennoch ...«[7], – in einen Höhepunkt: ein echt novellistisches Paradox. Der äußerst begrenzte Aufschluß über das Vorleben beider Hauptfiguren (Cipolla, Mario) wird wettgemacht, nicht nur durch die grelle Beleuchtung des Existenzproblems des verdächtigen, womöglich unlauteren Künstlers (ein Hauptmotiv des Lebenswerks Thomas Manns), sondern – etwas ganz Neues in Manns novellistischem Schaffen – durch ein feinfühliges Situationsbild der nationalistischen Phase eines ganzen Volkes, der Mischung von gleichschaltender Suggestionskraft autoritärer Mächte und gebildeter sowie unverbildeter Opposition dagegen.

Fazit: der novellistische Umriß der »einen Begebenheit« in den vier Erzählungen ist klar. Die Begebenheit ist in allen vier Fällen das Resultat einer fatalen Begegnung. Ihre Konsequenzen werden in getrennten Szenen und einem erzählerischen Endhöhepunkt oder – tiefpunkt kristallisiert, der im Rückblick auf die gesamte Erzählung das Lebensproblem der Hauptbeteiligten kurz und scharf beleuchtet. Ein Vorspiel läuft dem novellistischen Kern voran.

Auffallend sind die typologischen Unterschiede zwischen den ersten drei, chronologisch nahe aneinanderliegenden Novellen um die Jahrhundertwende und *Mario* etwa drei Jahrzehnte danach. In allen vier steht die anfangs vielversprechende und dann fatale Begegnung der beiden Hauptfiguren (Friedemann – Gerda, Tobias – Esau, Spinell – Gabriele, Cipolla – Mario) im Mittelpunkt des Geschehens. Das Profil des novellistischen Kerns bleibt klar. Aber im *Mario* macht sich das 20. Jahrhundert bemerkbar. Das Vorspiel gewinnt an Selbständigkeit, an Breite. Die Szenen innerhalb der Cipolla*vor*führung, die eine *Verführung* wird, sind weniger scharf voneinander getrennt. Das psychologische Interesse, bei Mann schon immer vorhanden, in den frühesten Novellen *(Friedemann,*

---

[7]*Erzählungen*, S. 711.

Mindernickel) noch in merklich novellistischer Zucht gehalten, im *Tristan* schon weiter entfaltet, wird im *Mario* zu einem bedeutenden Faktor, ohne aber – das sei hervorgehoben – die Spannung des sich Ereignenden, die für das Novellistische unerläßlich ist, zu beeinträchtigen. Diese *tour de force:* Vertiefung und Verbreitung ohne Spannungseinbuße bringt Mann dadurch fertig, daß er im langen Vorspiel des *Mario* dem Psychologischen einen nationalpolitischen, kollektiven Stachel gibt, der bei aller Unterbetontheit der Akzente etwas nicht geheures in sich birgt und nicht nur den Erzähler, sondern auch den Leser (hier eigentlich Zuhörer) nervös macht. Wir sind, wenn wir zum Anfang des eigentlich novellistischen Geschehens gelangen, im vollen Sinne des Wortes gespannt. Das Ineinanderspielen des individuellen und kollektiven Gereiztseins im *Mario* erzeugt einen undefinierbaren, aber um so spürbareren Druck. Die im Vorspiel am Strande und im Hotel noch verstreuten Zwischenfälle, die unangenehme, merkbare, aber nicht eigentlich drohende Gruppenspannung werden nun bei der Cipolladarbietung, die selbst in das Gebiet der hypnotischen Massenpsychologie, das heißt, des Hochdramatischen fällt, zu einem dichtgedrängten Publikum zusammengeballt, andererseits durch eine erhebliche Beimischung von Intelligenz (sowohl von seiten der Zuschauer wie des Künstlers) differenziert, individualisiert, verstärkt, so daß sich diese Mischung unmittelbar auf beiden Seiten in Handlungen umsetzt, ohne die das Novellistische nun einmal nicht auskommt. Wir haben hier ein selten gelungenes Beispiel dafür, daß der Aufstieg des Psychologischen in der Literatur des 20. Jahrhunderts, das Erbe Dostojewskis, nicht notwendigerweise zum Abstieg der äußeren Handlung führen muß.

Hand in Hand mit dem intensiven Hang zum Psychologischen in der Literatur des 20. Jahrhunderts geht, bei Mann ebenfalls mit sehr dezenten Akzenten, die Betonung der gesellschaftlichen Problematik innerhalb der novellistischen Begebenheit: im *Friedemann* und *Mindernickel* von geringer Bedeutung ist sie bereits ein wenn auch untergeordneter Faktor im *Tristan:*

das Problem des hochintelligenten, verfeinerten, passivsterilen, »impotenten«, »unnützen« Künstlers gegenüber dem unkünstlerisch-vitalen, groben, produzierenden – und hier charakterlich überlegenen businessman. In politisch-kulturellem Gewande ist die gesellschaftliche Problematik etwa drei Jahrzehnte später einer der Hauptfaktoren im *Mario,* aber auch da noch in das Eigengesetzliche des Novellistischen integriert.

sich ereignet

Goethe betont in seiner vierteiligen knappen Definition der Novelle, daß die Begebenheit der Novelle »sich ereignet« haben muß. Damit ist natürlich nur der Kern des novellistischen Geschehens gemeint. Was sich ereignet hat, ist *eo ipso* authentisch, so weit hergeholt es auch scheinen mag. Die geschickteste Konstruktion eines Autors kann nie dieselbe Autorität besitzen wie die seltsamen Vorfälle des Lebens. Aber die *Darstellung* eines Begebnisses, sei es auch die genaueste und treueste, selbst eine gerichtliche, kann in ihrer Wortwahl, ihrem Aufbau, ihrem Stil auch bei bestem Willen zur Objektivität nicht der Umbildung der Wirklichkeit entgehen, zumal diese Realität notgedrungen nur lückenhaft bekannt ist. Es ist hier nicht der Ort, in der literarischen Reproduktion und Metamorphose dieses »sich ereigneten« zwischen wahr, wahrhaftig, wahrscheinlich und glaubwürdig, zwischen äußeren und inneren Ereignissen zu unterscheiden. Es sei nur gesagt, daß die empirisch-externe Legitimation des Novellenkerns von der heutigen Forschung nicht ernst genug genommen wird, obwohl wir in der guten Tagespresse tagtäglich Musterbeispiele der Wiedergabe »sich ereigneter Begebenheiten« vor uns sehen, das Fundament ihrer Zuverlässigkeit.

In den ersten drei Erzählungen *(Friedemann, Mindernickel, Tristan)* fällt das ursprünglich »sich ereignete«, soweit wir informiert sind, vollkommen weg. Von irgendwelchen öffentlichen, halböffentlichen oder privaten Geschehnisquellen zu den zentralen Begebenheiten dieser Erzählungen ist so gut wie nichts bekannt. Vaget hat die Wurzeln dieser Werke sorgfältig

262

abgesondert[8]: sie sind halb versteckt (à la Thomas Mann) vornehmlich innerlich erlebter Natur: »Sublimierung seiner erotischen Nöte«, Kunst als Surrogat für das Leben, Selbstkarikierung, Außenseitergefühle, »der Wille zum Glück«, scheiternd an der eigenen physischen und psychischen Unfähigkeit zum Glück einerseits, andererseits an der Verlegenheit, Gleichgültigkeit und Abneigung, ja dem Ekel der »Normalen« und sogar der anderen »Abnormalen« wie Gerda oder anderer Einfriedpatienten dem Außenseiter gegenüber. Daraus entstehen »die geheimen Rachegelüste der im Leben zu-kurz-gekommenen gegen das Leben«[9]. Diese Ressentiments werden entweder an anderen, den »Gesunden«, ausgelassen (Esau, Klöterjahn Sr. und Jr., Gabriele als Ehefrau und Mutter) oder an sich selbst (Friedemann)[10]. Dazu kommen, mindestens so belangreich, kulturpessimistische Einflüsse: Nietzsche, Schopenhauer, Dekadenz, Ästhetizismus des Fin de siècle, Naturalismus, literarische Modelle (d'Annunzio, Hamsun, Tschechow) und, wie üblich bei Mann, parodistische Ausbeutung von Bekannten (z. B. Holitscher im *Tristan*). Hier bewegt sich Mann weitgehend in der für die wesentliche Literatur des 20. Jahrhunderts charakteristischen Richtung: psychologischer Relativismus, inzestuöse Tendenzen: Literatur, nicht »Leben« als Quelle für Literatur. Hier ist für das herkömmlich »sich ereignete« der Novellistik wenig zu holen.

Unerwartet kommt dann drei Jahrzehnte später ein Rückgriff auf gerade dieses wirklich, wenn auch in Umrissen »sich ereignete«, im *Mario*.

----

[8]a. a. O., S. 54-58, 70-72, 85-86.

[9]Vaget, a. a. O., S. 71.

[10]»Was ging eigentlich in ihm vor, bei dem, was nun geschah? Vielleicht war es dieser wollüstige Haß, den er empfunden hatte, wenn sie ihn mit ihrem Blicke demütigte, der jetzt, wo er, behandelt von ihr wie ein Hund, am Boden lag, in eine irrsinnige Wut ausartete, die er bestätigen mußte, sei es auch gegen sich selbst, der ihn mit einem Durst erfüllte, sich zu vernichten, sich in Stücke zu zerreißen, sich auszulöschen...« (*Friedemann*, S. 105).

Hier haben wir ein besonders aufschlußreiches Beispiel dafür, wie ein Novellist vom ersten Rang das traditionelle Element des »sich ereigneten« mit neueren Phänomenen verschmilzt. Was hat sich wirklich ereignet?

Katja und Thomas Mann verbrachten vom 31. August bis zum 13. September 1926 mit ihren Kindern Elisabeth und Michael zwei Ferienwochen bei Viareggio an der ligurischen Küste Italiens, in Forte dei Marmi, »das mit dem Torre di Venere der Novelle identisch ist«[11]. Ortsangaben, Hotels, Personen beziehen sich alle oder meist auf Tatsachen unter fingierten, mehr oder weniger abgeänderten Namen (z. B. hieß Frau Angiolieri in Wirklichkeit Angela Querci[12]). *Mario* ist zuerst in Velhagen & Klasings *Monatsheften*[13] als *Tragisches Reiseerlebnis. Novelle* und noch im selben Jahr (1930) als Buch unter dem Titel *Mario und der Zauberer. Ein tragisches Reiseerlebnis*[14] erschienen; später ist der Untertitel weggefallen. Ursprünglich also spielte das »sich ereignete« im Titel eine größere Rolle als nachher. Was ist nun »wirklich« geschehen?

»Der »Zauberkünstler« war da und benahm sich genau, wie ich es geschildert habe. Erfunden ist nur der letale Ausgang: In Wirklichkeit lief

---

[11]Mann in einem Brief an (Vorname unermittelt) Hopkins vom 27. November 1930, in *Dichter über ihre Dichtungen: Thomas Mann*, II: 1918 - 1943, hrsg. von Hans Wysling und Marianne Fischer, München und Frankfurt, Heimeran und Fischer, 1979, S. 369. Die »Dokumente zur Entstehungsgeschichte« des *Mario* sind zusammengetragen in Karl Pörnbacher, Hrsg., *Thomas Mann: Mario und der Zauberer.* Erläuterungen und Dokumente, Stuttgart, Reclam, 1980, S. 24-31. Siehe dort S. 27.

[12]Brief an Hopkins.

[13]44: Heft 8, April 1930, S. 113-136.

[14]Siehe *Dichter über ihre Dichtungen: Thomas Mann*, II, 366; Pörnbacher, S. 30; Vaget, S. 220.

Mario nach dem Kuß in komischer Beschämung weg und war am nächsten Tage, als er uns wieder den Tee servierte, höchst vergnügt und voll sachlicher Anerkennung für die Arbeit »Cipolla's«. Es ging eben im Leben weniger leidenschaftlich zu, als nachher bei mir. Mario liebte nicht wirklich, und der streitbare Junge im Parterre war nicht sein glücklicher Nebenbuhler. Die Schüsse aber sind nicht einmal meine Erfindung: Als ich von dem Abend hier[15] erzählte, sagte meine älteste Tochter [16]: »Ich hätte mich nicht gewundert, wenn er ihn niedergeschossen hätte.« Erst von diesem Augenblick war das Erlebte eine Novelle ...«[17]

Auf die Niederschießung Cipollas kommen wir unter dem Gesichtspunkt des »Unerhörten« zurück; was wir hier festhalten wollen ist die bewußte, selektive Verdichtung des tatsächlich Gesehenen und Gehörten mit dem zur Novellenform gehörenden Leidenschaftlichen, das aber auch durchaus mit dem Italienischen, also dem »Wirklichen« übereinstimmt.

Was am *Mario* eine Abart der Thomas Mann durch sein ganzes Schaffen begleitenden Künstlerproblematik ist – also ein nicht wahrnehmbar »sich Ereignetes« – und was daran der persönlichen Begegnung mit dem italienischen Faschismus – also dem tatsächlich sich Ereigneten – entspricht, ist gerade in den letzten beiden Jahrzehnten oft diskutiert worden. Es ist eine verwickelte und heikle Angelegenheit, weil die Gefahr besteht, daß der Beschauer von seinem eigenen ideologischen Blickwinkel aus das politisch-antifaschistische Moment im *Mario* über – oder untertreibt, oder aus

---

[15]d. h. zu Hause in München.

[16]Erika.

[17]Brief Thomas Manns an Otto Hoerth vom 12. 6. 1930 (Thomas Mann, *Briefe* 1889 - 1936, hrsg., von Erika Mann, Frankfurt, Fischer, 1961, S. 299-300.) Wiedergedruckt in *Dichter über ihre Dichtungen: Thomas Mann*, II, 367-368; Pörnbacher, S. 26-27; Vaget, S. 222-223.

Sympathie für Thomas Mann und gutem Willen halb instinktiv und halb bewußt eine politische Ehrenrettung versucht: dabei spielen nachträgliche Einsichten eine nicht immer eingestandene Rolle, denn der italiensiche Faschismus begegnete in den 20er und frühen 30er Jahren des 20. Jahrhunderts einer größeren Toleranz und sogar begrenzten Sympathien auch bei solchen, die dem Nationalsozialismus kritischer gegenüberstanden[18]. Eine

---

[18]Vaget legt eine ausgezeichnete, ausführliche und kritische Übersicht über die Entstehung, die Selbstdeutung, den Kontext und die Rezeption (weitgehend nach Ländern geordnet) *Marios* vor (a.a. O., S. 222-249). Kurzke (a.a. O., S. 10-11) ergänzt ihn. Unter den einschlägigen Studien hebt sich Egon Schwarz' »Fascism and Society: Remarks on Thomas Mann's Novella *Mario and the Magician*« *Michigan Germanic Studies*, II, 1976, S. 47-67 durch ihre genaue Textbezogenheit hervor. In manchem stimme ich Schwarz und Vaget zu. Ich glaube, daß man bei allen Äußerungen Thomas Manns den Kontext: Empfänger, Zeit, Taktik und Strategie, seine zuvorkommende Höflichkeit, aber nicht Unwahrhaftigkeit, die Eigenrevision seines Bildes im Sinne späterer Entwicklung in Betracht ziehen muß. Der Brief, den er noch aus Forte dei Marmi am 7. September 1926 an Hofmannsthal schrieb, scheint mir die glaubwürdigste Grundlage für Thomas Manns Absichten zu bieten, soweit sie ihm bewußt waren und soweit sie im *Mario* wirklich ausgeführt worden sind: »Wir haben Licht und Wärme in Überfülle gehabt, und die Kinder waren glückselig am Strande und im warmen Meer. An kleinen Widerwärtigkeiten hat es anfangs auch nicht gefehlt, die mit dem derzeitigen unerfreulichen, überspannten und fremdenfeindlichen nationalen Gemütszustand zusammenhingen und uns belehrten, daß man jetzt nicht gut tut, einen Badeort dieses Landes in der rein italienischen Hochsaison aufzusuchen. Erst seitdem bei vorschreitender Jahreszeit das slawisch-deutsche Element sich ausbreitet, fühlt man sich behaglich. Natürlich hat das eigentliche Volk seine Liebenswürdigkeit bewahrt und steht geistig nicht unter dem blähenden Einfluß des Duce. Im Ganzen aber kann ich nicht sagen, daß dieser Besuch meine Achtung vor den Italienern gehoben hätte, trotz schöner physischer und

266

weitere Schwierigkeit ist, daß das Etikett »Faschismus« aus propagandistisch-ideologischen Gründen, obwohl historisch und wissenschaftlich zum mindesten ungenau, wenn nicht irreführend, ohne Unterschied für die autoritären Ideologien, die Italien, Deutschland und später Spanien in den 30er Jahren regierten, gebraucht oder mißbraucht wird.

Für die, wie ich sie sehe, drei Hauptthemen *Marios:* 1) das

---

intellektueller Gaben. Das eigentlich europäische Niveau halten eben doch Franzosen und Deutsche (wobei ich natürlich Österreich einbegreife). England bleibt in gewisser Weise darunter, Italien in noch gewisserer. Habe ich Unrecht?« (Pörnbacher, a. a. O., S. 24-25; Vaget zitiert einen Auszug. S. 222).

Man kann seine unmittelbaren Eindrücke des »sich ereigneten« etwa so zusammenfassen: a)In der italiensichen Hochsaison macht sich das (faschistisch angekurbelte) Nationalgefühl unangenehm bemerkbar. (Im Text des *Mario* können der Herr im Schniepel und Cipolla als deren Hauptvertreter gelten). b) Das Volk kümmert sich wenig um die Aufgeblasenheiten des Duce. Wie sich das im Text niederschlägt, ist allerdings schwer entscheidbar. Marios befreiender Schuß? Aber es bestehen keine Anzeichen dafür, daß Mario diese spontane Tat aus irgendwelchen anderen ihm bewußten Gründen als der öffentlichen Preisgabe seiner persönlichsten Gefühle und seiner physisch-ekligen Demütigung begeht. Auch die sonstige Opposition gegen Cipolla scheint keine bewußten politischen Wurzeln zu besitzen, eher instinktive Sympathie für den mutigen Einzelrebellen, gemischt mit ebenso instinktiver Anerkennung des Könnens und der unfehlbaren Wirkung des zaubernden Hypnotiseurs (grotesk-symbolische Variante Mussolinis? Hitlers?). Gegen die Primärrolle des italienischen Faschismus spricht, ganz abgesehen von Manns hochdifferenzierten Kommentaren zum *Mario,* schon die Tatsache, daß das Problem ihm kaum unter den Nägeln brannte, denn er hat es erst drei Jahre später auf einer Ferienreise an die Ostsee in Angriff genommen, um am Strande überhaupt etwas tun zu können.

»Persönliche und Private«[19], das aber z. B. auch den Byzantinismus im Hotel einschließt (die Lämpchen- und besonders die Keuchhustenepisoden), den der Erzähler als empörenden Mißbrauch der Macht, als Ungerechtigkeit, als kriecherische Korruption anprangert[20], 2) die politische Atmosphäre und 3) die Künstlerproblematik, scheint mir der angemessenste Generalnenner das Ethische in Verbindung mit dem im weiteren Sinne Moralischen und Politisch/Nationalen: das sind auch die drei Elemente, die in Manns eigenen Kommentaren, wenn auch in verschiedenen Reihenfolgen, immer wieder auftauchen.[21]

Zu welchem Endresultat über das »sich ereignete« in unseren vier novellistischen Erzählungen kommen wir nun? Wie man auch darüber denken mag, die Analyse des »sich ereigneten« im *Mario* sollte uns jeglicher Sorge entheben, daß die Untersuchung von novellistischen Erzählungen auf gleiche Strukturelemente hin zu einer Zwangsjacke führt, die alles Differenzierte unterdrückt. Das Gegenteil ist der Fall: gerade der Vergleich des einmaligen Textes mit dem typologischen Gerüst stellt das Verschiedene mit dem Gemeinsamen heraus und zeitigt Ergebnisse, die weder simplistisch noch atomistisch sind. Die Hauptelemente des »sich ereigneten« im *Mario* stammen zu etwa zwei Teilen aus tatsächlichen, persönlich-privaten Erfahrungen und politischen Nationalbewußtseinserlebnissen, zum dritten Teil aus des Autors permanenter Künstlerproblematik: alle drei verbinden sich in der tragisch-grotesken Hauptfigur Cipollas. Die Fabel der frühen drei novellistischen Erzählungen (*Friedemann, Mindernickel, Tristan*) stützt sich dagegen

---

[19]Siehe Manns »Lebensabriß« (1930) in Pörnbacher, a. a. O., S. 27-29, und sein Brief an Claire Goll vom 21. September 1931, ebda., S. 29.

[20]Erzählungen, S. 662, 663.

[21]Siehe die vorzügliche Zusammenstellung der »Selbstdeutungen« Thomas Manns bei Vaget, S. 223-226.

überwiegend auf Existenz- und Bewußtseinsprobleme des Künstlers und Outsiders, sie ist zum größten Teil erfunden. Die Geschichte der deutschen Novelle zeigt, daß ein ausgesprochener Mangel an einem sich wirklich ereigneten Novellenkern leicht zu einer nicht überzeugenden Novelle führen kann. Das ist eine Beobachtung, kein Gesetz. Kleist z. B. hat es glorreich dementiert. Thomas Manns frühe drei Novellen gehören in die gleiche Ausnahmerubrik. Letzten Endes entscheidet die Textqualität, nicht die Theorie.

Unerhört

Unter den vier Kardinalfaktoren des Novellistischen, der »einen«, »sich ereigneten«, »unerhörten« »Begebenheit« ist das Wort »unerhört« wohl das für die Novelle bezeichnendste. Um dramatisch wirksam zu sein (die moderne Novelle ist die Schwester des Dramas, nach Storm)[22] muß dieses »unerhörte« markant, pointiert, unverwischt sein. Andererseits aber treibt der Motivierungsdrang des Autors ihn zur Vorbereitung, Erklärung, Legitimierung des Unerhörten – zu seiner intellektuellen Verstärkung aber künstlerischen Zerfaserung, d. h. *novellistischen* Schwächung. Bei einem psychologisch wie intellektuell gleich glänzenden Analytiker wie Mann, der aber *vor allem gut erzählen will,* ist die Begegnung dieser an und für sich entgegengesetzten Tendenzen, Erfolg, Teilerfolg oder Mißerfolg ihrer Um- und Verschlingung besonders aufschlußreich.

In drei von den vier Erzählungen ist das unmittelbar Unerhörte unverkennbar und steht, wie bei einem Aktschluß, auf den ja »alles« ankommt, ganz am Ende: im *Friedemann* ist es sein Selbstmord; im *Mindernickel* die

---

[22]»Die heutige Novelle ist die Schwester des Dramas und die strengste Form der Prosadichtung« (Theodor Storm, »eine zurückgezogene Vorrede aus dem Jahr 1881«, in Karl Konrad Polheim, Hrsg., *Theorie und Kritik der deutschen Novelle von Wieland bis Musil,* Tübingen, Niemeyer, 1970, S. 119).

Erstechung des Hundes; im *Mario* die Erschießung Cipollas. Sind die vom Autor entfalteten Begleitumstände dieses Unerhörten seiner Wirkung zu- oder abträglich? Da dem *Friedemann* wie *Mindernickel* und *Tristan* keine, soweit wir wissen, »wirkliche« Begebenheit zugrunde liegt, kommt es in diesen drei Texten ganz besonders auf die Authentizität der Gestaltung an.

Durch den existentiellen Kontext Friedemanns und die Seltsamkeit seiner Partnerin wird das Unerhörte in der Novelle noch unerhörter. Daß ein enttäuschter Liebhaber Selbstmord begeht, ist nur in begrenztem Sinne unerhört, und war es wohl auch Ende der 1890er Jahre kaum noch. Aber wer ist er? Er ist ein Mann des Friedens, dem Gewalthandlungen vollkommen fernliegen. Er ist ein wohlsituierter Kaufmann, dem seine drei unverheirateten Schwestern Ersatz für Ehefrau und Familie bieten. Er ist in der Stadt angesehen und hat an der Börse ein Wörtchen mitzureden[23]. Er liebt seinen Garten, d. h. die heitere, saubere, kultivierte, geordnete Natur. Er liebt die Literatur, Theater und Musik. Er spielt Geige. Er raucht Zigarren. Er ist fein gekleidet. Er hat einen Buckel und hat sich mit seinem Schicksal abgefunden. Er erwartet die Zukunft »mit Seelenfrieden«[24].

Daß all die vermeintlich gelungenen Sublimierungen *dieses* Mannes, die wir mit wohlwollender Genugtuung und dem kostenlosen Mitleid der *beati possidentes* zur Kenntnis genommen haben, am Ende zusammenbrechen, daß »dieser kleine, gänzlich verwachsene Mensch zitternd und zuckend vor (Gerda) auf den Knien lag« und »mit einer unmenschlichen, keuchenden Stimme ... stammelte«, daß er nun, »behandelt von ihr wie ein Hund[25], am Boden lag« und eine »irrsinnige Wut ... betätigen mußte, sei es auch gegen sich selbst ... ein Ekel vielleicht vor sich selbst, der ihn mit einem Durst erfüllte, sich zu

---

[23]*Erzählungen,* S. 85.

[24]Ebda., S. 83.

[25]Man denkt an den Hund Esau im *Mindernickel.*

270

vernichten, sich in Stücke zu zerreißen, sich auszulöschen ... «, daß dieser
hochfeine, wohlbehütete Mann sich schließlich auf dem Bauch an den Fluß
schiebt, daß wir ihn für immer mit seinen Beinen am Ufer, seinem Kopf im
Wasser verlassen[26], diese Mischung des Unerhörten mit vom Erzähler für die
Endszene aufgespartem, endlich durchbrechenden echten Pathos einerseits,
herzzerreißender und gleichzeitig doch etwas lächerlicher Groteske andrerseits:
das ist erznovellistisch und unerhört wirksam. Und von Gerdas Seite wird das
Unerhörte noch weiter angepeitscht. Sekunden zuvor hat sie ihn noch mit
feinem Verständnis und Takt ausgefragt und ihm zugehört, seine
Lebenstapferkeit anerkannt und sich als Leidensgefährtin ausgewiesen – und
nun schleudert sie ihn mit verächtlichem Lachen seitwärts zu Boden[27].
»Unerhört«, aber im Rückblick auf die vorhergehende Darstellung nicht ganz
unerwartet, denn ihre pathologisch-sadistischen Komplexe (kann man sie als
Teil ihres novellistischen Schicksals ansehen?), gegen die ihr vollkommen
normaler Gatte gefeit ist und die sie nun an Friedemann ausläßt, sind schon
vorher von Zeit zu Zeit zutage getreten. Die Unsicherheit, welche die
»wirkliche« Gerda ist (die Antwort kann nur lauten: beide), erhöht die
novellistische Spannung.

Tobias Mindernickel: die Erstechung Esaus ist die Schlußszene in
dem zwiespältigen Verhältnis von Tobias zu Esau. Daß ein Herr seinen Hund
aus freien Stücken ersticht wäre heute wie damals ein unerhörter Akt. Es wäre
schwierig für einen Erzähler, ihn aus heiterem Himmel zu inszenieren, da es
sich um eine sowohl vorsätzliche wie auch impulsive Tat handelt, wohingegen
ein Schicksalseingriff nicht motiviert zu werden braucht (und deshalb reiner
novellistisch ist). Drei Szenen bereiten auf die letzte Wendung vor: die

---

[26]*Erzählungen,* S. 104-105.

[27]Ebda., S. 104.

»maßlose«[28] Verprügelung des *zu* lebenslustigen Hundes durch seinen mißmutigen Gebieter; nochmalige »lange und erbitterte«[29] Verdreschung des Hundes nachdem er, in seiner Daseinsfreude, seinem Herrn entwichen ist; unbeabsichtigte, schwere Verletzung des Hundes, der sich ein von Mindernickel »ungeschickt gehaltenes«[30] Messer in den Leib rennt – dasselbe Messer, mit dem Tobias in der vierten und letzten novellistischen Szene das Tier töten wird. Wir haben somit zwei Verprügelungen und zwei schwere Messerverwundungen, die erste nicht tödlich, die zweite tödlich. Dazu kommen nun noch wiederholt vorangehende, ausdrückliche psycho-pathologische Charakterisierungen der sich ablösenden Phasen von Mitleid und Grausamkeit, von Minderwertigkeitskomplex und Größenwahn in der Persönlichkeit des, wenn man so sagen darf, abwechselnd hündischen Herrn und herrischen Hundes. Summa summarum: fraglos ist der »unerhörte« Höhe- oder Tiefpunkt am Schluß der Erzählung effektvoll aber weniger wirkungskräftig als im *Friedemann* weil angeglichener an vorhergehende Handlungen und Analysen. Dazu kommt, daß Mindernickel eine zu lebensunfähige, zu abseitige Figur ist, um unser Interesse im gleichen Maße zu erwecken wie der kleine Herr Friedemann, der alles getan hat – und nicht erfolglos –, um sein Leben mit Sinn zu erfüllen.

Die Erschießung Cipollas durch Mario ist dagegen ein Musterstück des Unerhörten. Nichts in der Schilderung Marios deutet im Lesen der Novelle darauf hin, daß auf der letzten von vierundfünfzig Seiten der passive, gutmütige, verschlossene Kellner den »Zauberkünstler« niederschießen wird. Wir haben es hier im buchstäblichen Sinne mit einem Knalleffekt zu tun. Aus

---

[28]Ebda., S. 146.

[29]Ebda., S. 148.

[30]Ebda., S. 149.

272

Manns Brief an Otto Hoerth[31] wissen wir nicht nur, daß er diesen Abschluß auf Grund einer spontanen Äußerung seiner Tochter Erika dem Erlebten zufügte, damit daraus eine Novelle würde, sondern auch, daß er, »um sie auszuführen«, »das Atmosphäre gebende anekdotische Detail«, »den Hotelier – und das übrige vorbereitende Ärgernis ... (brauchte). Weder Fuggiero noch der zornige Herr am Strande noch die Fürstin hätten sonst das Licht der Literatur erblickt.« Dank des zufälligen Überlebens dieses kommentierenden Briefes Thomas Manns wissen wir genau, in welchen Stadien aus dem Zauberkünstler – Hypnotiseurerlebnis eine Novelle wurde: a) der dem wirklich Erlebten hinzugefügte/erfundene, novellistisch-unerhörte »Knalleffekt«. b) Ausarbeitung der Hotel- und Strandzwischenfälle im ersten Teil, um die explosive Stimmung anzudeuten, in der nach vierundfünfzig Seiten die wirkliche Explosion, so überraschend sie auch kommt, wenn auch nicht »wahr«, vielleicht nicht einmal vollkommen überzeugend, so doch im Rückblick glaubwürdig ist. Wir haben es hier mit der gegenseitigen Steigerung – nicht der Vorwegnahme – des Unerhörten zu tun: das Unerhörte der Schuß- und Schlußtat als solcher wird vorbereitet durch die gereizte, klimatisch, kulturell – psychologisch und nationalpolitisch bedingte Atmosphäre im Hotel und am Strand, die aber immer noch im Rahmen der zu erwartenden Schattierungen des »Normalen« steht.

Die Schwelle, die von diesen beunruhigenden aber noch nicht hochgespielten Symptomen zum eindeutig novellistisch Unerhörten führt, heißt Cipolla. Als zaubernder Künstler – schließlich ein legitimer Beruf – stünde er noch mit einem Fuß im Bereich des »Normalen«; als unwiderstehlicher Massenhypnotiseur, der sich noch dazu bei Männern und Frauen verschiedenster Anlagen, Herkunft und Berufe durchsetzt (den Erzähler halb oder mehr einbegriffen), wird er immer unheimlicher – und doch tut er einem gleichwohl ein wenig leid, man hegt für ihn doch noch die Sympathien,

---

[31]Siehe Anmerkung 17.

die einem ohne seine Schuld Benachteiligten in einer Gesellschaft der Gesunden zukommen (siehe Friedemann, Tobias, Spinell). Erst der letzte Übergang von phänomenal – betäubender Virtuosität zu immer weniger verdeckter sadistischer Hybris erklärt im Rückblick den Schuß, der im Vorblick fast völlig unerwartet kommt, besonders von seiten des stillen, eher apathischen Marios. Die Steigerung des Unerhörten von einer gereizten, aber noch nicht kritischen Stimmung im Hotel und am Badestrand via den echt/faulen Zauber Cipollas zu allmächtiger Hypnose und, innerhalb von Sekunden, dem kläglichen Zusammensacken der Verzauberung ist eine der höchsten novellistischen Leistungen im Gesamtwerk Thomas Manns.

Tristan stellt unter den vier Erzählungen einen Sonderfall des Unerhörten dar. Die Gesamtthematik des *Tristan*, die so vollkommen in der Gedankenwelt Thomas Manns zuhause ist: Feinheit, Kunst, Krankheit, Dekadenz, Romantik, Musik, Tod <–> Bürgertum, Fleiß, Pflichttreue, Solidität, Materialismus, Robustheit; die so offenbar eine Probe aufs Exempel: Sehnsucht nach der Kunst <–> Sehnsucht nach dem Leben veranschaulicht, läßt darauf schließen, daß die *Idee,* nicht eine wirklich sich ereignete, unerhörte Begebenheit, an der Wiege dieser Novelle stand. Nichts von Selbstmord, Erstechung, Erschießung. Daß eine junge Mutter an der Schwindsucht stirbt, ist nicht unerhört. Wie bringt es der Autor zustande, das Ideell-Unerhörte in überzeugende »natürliche« Fiktion umzusetzen?

»Da ist ein wunderbares Geschöpf, eine Sylphe, ein Duftgebild, ein Märchentraum von einem Wesen. Was tut sie? Sie geht hin und ergibt sich einem Jahrmarktsherkules oder Schlächterburschen. Sie kommt an seinem Arme daher, lehnt vielleicht sogar ihren Kopf an seine Schulter und blickt dabei verschlagen lächelnd um sich her, als wollte sie sagen: Ja, nun zerbrecht euch die Köpfe über diese Erscheinung! – Und wir zerbrechen sie uns.«[32]

Nun, wir können ruhig einige Meter von den »Wolkenpfühlen«

---

[32]*Erzählungen*, S. 232.

abrücken, »die Herr Spinell (Gabriele) dienend bereitet«[33], wir sollten auch Herrn Klöterjahn höher einstufen als das Schreckbild, das Spinell von ihm, aus keineswegs nur lauteren Absichten, entwirft, – und werden immer noch zugeben müssen, daß wir die Nachricht der Verlobung der zarten, hochmusikalischen Gabriele Eckhof mit dem appetitbeherrschten Großkaufmann Anton Klöterjahn mit Kopfschütteln und, wohl möglich, dem Ausruf: »Unerhört!« quittiert hätten. Aber nun weiter. Die uns bereits wohlbekannte fixe Idee Manns, das Verlangen des Künstlertyps, des Außenseiters, des oder der physisch Benachteiligten nach ungebrochenem Selbstbewußtsein nimmt zusätzliche Gestalt an in der Geburt Anton Klöterjahn Jrs. Das kraftstrotzende Baby saugt, möchte man sagen, die begrenzten Lebensreserven seiner Mutter auf. Sie kommt ins Sanatorium »Einfried«, wo nun der feinfühlige aber impotente Mann und Künstler Spinell sie (aus Idealismus? aus Ressentiment?) ihrem Mann und ihrem Kind langsam abspenstig macht und sie mit Hilfe der hochpotenten Musik Wagners, gegen das Verbot ihres Arztes, zur Kunst zurück(ver)führt, worauf sie prompt einen Rückfall in die Schwindsucht erlebt, der zu ihrem Tode führt, ein Sieg Spinells, aber auch wieder ein Pyrrhussieg, denn letzten Endes läßt er sich von Klöterjahn Sr. abkanzeln und läuft vor der ungebrochenen Vitalität von Klöterjahn Jr. davon. Das ist zumindest etwas ausgepicht Interessantes, »unerhört« in einer ganz sonderlichen Mischung des Psychologischen, Intellektuellen, Ideologisch-Kulturellen mit einer trotz oder vielleicht gerade wegen ihrer Hermetik äußerst spannenden Fabel, ein gelungenes novellistisches Kunststück, wie es außer Thomas Mann vielleicht in unserem Jahrhundert bisher nur noch Kafka zuwege gebracht hat.

Schlußfolgerung: das Unerhörte im überlieferten novellistischen Sinn finden wir somit, klar und deutlich markiert, in drei der vier untersuchten

---

[33]Ebda., S 237.

Erzählungen: *Friedemann, Mindernickel, Mario*. Im *Friedemann* und *Mario* ist die Durchschlagskraft des Unerhörten quasi total, weil es beim Vorwärtslesen vollkommen überraschend kommt, am entscheidenden Ende steht, und doch im Rückblick nicht unmotiviert ist. Im *Mindernickel* büßt das Unerhörte aus zweierlei Gründen an Wirkung ein: die Erstechung hat durch die vorangehenden Verprügelungen des Hundes und dessen erste, schwere, unbeabsichtigte Messerverwundung etwas von einem »déjà vu«, und Mindernickel kann nicht das Interesse Friedemanns und Cipollas beanspruchen.

Die unverkennbar intellektuelle Basis von *Tristan* stellt für das eigentlich Literarische und besonders das Novellistische eine Gefahr dar, und das Unerhörte ist auch tatsächlich im *Tristan* verteilter, weniger pointiert als in den drei anderen Erzählungen. Das einzigartige Fingerspitzengefühl Manns bringt es aber noch fertig, durch die aparten Umstände der Vorgänge, kraft seiner fabelhaft motivierten, ausgeführten und trotz allem Raffinement authentischen Spitzfindigkeiten eine für seine Erzählung als Ganzes geltende »Unerhörtheit« zu schaffen.

APPENDIX I

Concise statement on the origin, evolution, and prospects of the German Novella

The novella, which caters to unexpected twists, to irony and paradox, has itself a history full of these traits.[1] Though fed by ancient Oriental, Arabic, Greek, Latin, Provençal, French and Italian story materials, it did not reach directive norms until Boccaccio's *Decamerone* (1348-53), still considered a near perfect prototype of the genre. A characteristic product of *Romania (Cent Nouvelles Nouvelles,* 1440; Marguerite de Navarre's *Heptaméron,* 1558; Cervantes' *Novelas Ejemplares,* 1613), combining Romanic love of living and of dramatic action with an acute sense of form, it has become, since Cervantes, notwithstanding such stellar novellesque authors as Basile, Gozzi, Verga, and Pirandello of Italy, Mérimée and Maupassant of France, a secondary art form in its native habitat.

Its finest sustained flowering since its Romanic debuts occurred in the cultural areas of Europe that used German as the literary language in the 19th century (Kleist, Gotthelf, Stifter, Keller, Storm, Gerhart Hauptmann). In English-speaking areas "novella" usually means, nowadays, no more than a short novel, though specific stories may be excellent samples of the continental genre (e.g., James Purdy's *63: Dream Palace,* 1957). But for all its auspicious beginnings with Chaucer and its vogue in 16th century England, the art form has been domesticated neither there nor in America, where Poe channeled the best efforts of briefer prose into the short story, nor in Russia though she produced one of the impressionist novella-writers most influential in the 20th century: Chekhov.

---

[1]This entry was first published under the heading "Novella" in the *Encyclopedia of World Literature in the 20th Century,* New York, Frederick Ungar, 1969, pp. 466-469. Complete bibliography, p. 291.

In German-writing areas structure and function of the *Novelle* intrigued practitioners (Wieland, Goethe, Tieck, Grillparzer, Hebbel, Storm, Heyse) and critics (Lessing, August Wilhelm and Friedrich Schlegel, Laube, Mundt, and Hettner) of the highest distinction from its naturalization in the late 1700's through the 1800's. While little theoretical consensus had been reached by 1900, the *Novelle* had emerged, next to the lyric poem, as the most distinguished German contribution to Western literature. Not until the 1950's was there a massive breakthrough in Germanic scholarship on the *Novelle*, at the very moment when the genre has been superseded, if not replaced, by the short story and overshadowed by the drama, the radio play (*Hörspiel*), the novel, and lyric poetry.

Even though the theory of the novella has never attained the coherence and general acceptance of the structure of two literary forms closely related to it, the drama and the ballad, its individual ingredients, though weighted very differently, have long been identified: above all, the "unheard-of occurrence that has actually happened" (Goethe), its sharp profile (Heyse's "silhouette" and "falcon"), and its reversal (Tieck's "Wendepunkt") closely related to the "peripeteia" of the drama.

What a novella relates must be unique, or at least very striking, but realistic; it must be dramatic not only in creating tension but also in the objectivity of its presentation. Here the novella comes close to the journalistic news story, and it is by no means accidental that two of the finest German novellas, Kleist's *Marquise von O...* (1810-11) and Keller's *Romeo und Julia auf dem Dorfe* (1856), as well as one of the most successful ones, Zweig's *Amokläufer* (1922), are (in fact or allegedly) based on newspaper stories. The decline of the novella in the 20th century is, in part, attributable to the usurpation by newspapers of human-interest stories.

The novella is, then, originally a news item (genuine or doctored or invented) designed to divert a mixed, refined audience temporarily displaced and disturbed by ill fate (e.g., the plague in the *Decamerone*, war in Goethe's *Unterhaltungen*). The tales are told by various tellers who constitute the frame of the work. This is still the structure of Goethe's *Unterhaltungen deutscher Ausgewanderten* (1794-95); with some modifications, of Conrad

Ferdinand Meyer's *Hochzeit des Mönchs* (1884), which has reduced story and teller to one but preserved the aristocratic nature of the audience; and of Theodor Storm's *Schimmelreiter* (1888) which is likewise content with one teller, has subjected the auditors to a bourgeois metamorphosis but preserved, like Meyer, Goethe, and Boccaccio before him, the original purpose of distracting them from ominous happenings. The purpose of the storytelling, the mixed character of the gourmet audience, the social obligation not to monopolize the "conversation" nor to intrude with personal feelings bound to embarrass the company, have determined, far beyond the "frame" and the originally assumed conditions of novella-telling, lasting features of the genre: a fluent, cultivated manner of relating; avoidance of extremes in diction, whether melodramatic or vulgar, likely to make the mixed audience uncomfortable; stress on diversion of a sophisticated nature, not excluding the risqué but ennobling it by smooth presentation; relative brevity so as not to bore the listeners; stress on events rather than on subjective interpretation or preaching; perfection of vocabulary and style; tautness and limpidity of organization; and the discharge of audience tension through a *pointe*, the crowning last (or close to it) sentence of the novella, often with an ironic twist, derived from the usually witty *Pointe* of the anecdote, mother of the novella.

How has this entrenched novellistic tradition fared in the 20th century? The "frame" has survived in many variations, but is no longer central to the structure of the novella and, indeed, has not been so since Kleist. It still serves a purpose, if a perfunctory one, in Hauptmann's *Der Ketzer von Soana* (1918), where it is a moat protecting the author (alias editor) of a shocking story from possible recriminations of the public, or, more usefully, in Zweig's *Amokläufer*, where it helps in bridging the gap between an eerie story and the reader and becomes artistically significant in its own right, as it had done in the *Schimmelreiter* and as it will do, more emphatically still, in Zweig's *Schachnovelle* (1942). On a far higher level of existential, artistic, and novellesque import, Musil uses the realistic and politically tinged frame of the *Amsel* (1928) to bring out the mystic message of the three experiences related (see von Wiese [1962], pp. 299-318).

In *Der Ketzer von Soana, Amokläufer,* and *Schachnovelle* the frame has changed from the third person singular to the first; in Thomas Mann's *Mario und der Zauberer* (1930) to the half-objective, half-subjective first person plural. The change to the "I" occurs in a good many 20th century novellas with or without frames: Hofmannsthal's version of the *Erlebnis des Marschalls von Bassompierre* (1900), Hesse's novellesque tale *Die Marmorsäge* (1907), Kafka's *Ein Landarzt* (1919), Schnitzler's *Fräulein Else* (1924), and Musil's *Amsel.* The turn to the "I" in the age of impressionism and introspection is not surprising, but has not necessarily resulted in the loss of distance between teller and tale essential to the novella. The "I" form has also aided in preserving, while modifying, the oral tinge of the novella, its "registering aloud," its fresh immediacy, a kind of apparent disorderedness and incoherence (amazingly coherent, however, by hindsight) which maintains the rigorous obligation of the novella to tell what "happened" whether the teller understands it or not. *Mario und der Zauberer* offers a particularly sophisticated example of studied improvisation on the part of an author, or rather "reporter," who is still "confused" by a jarring occurrence. "If I knew the meaning, I would not need to tell you the story," says Musil in the next to the last sentence of *Die Amsel.* And he concludes: "But it is as if you heard a whisper or merely a rustling without being able to differentiate between the two." In an age of fragmentation and atomization, centripetal symbolism dissolves into centrifugality and allegorism. The symbol becomes a token, a signal (v. Wiese, 1962, pp. 21 ff., 299 ff.). Dream and reality are interchangeable (ibid., pp. 307-8). The novella seems to move back in the direction of the fairy tale (Kafka, Musil), with which it had long entertained largely unexplored links (Boccaccio, Wieland, Goethe, Tieck, Brentano, Chamisso, Keller).

Psychological depth-probing, the possibility, even probability, that everything points to everything (v. Wiese, 1962, p. 310), is dangerous if not fatal to the novella unless accompanied by the puritanic control of language of a Kafka, the exceptional literary finesse of Thomas Mann, or the somnambulant artistic tact of a Schnitzler and a Musil. Certain elements of 20th century existence – its cult of violence, the potential absurdity of life – have, to be sure, provided *novella* writers with new or intensified media of expression revitalizing the novella though artistically dangerous to a strict form. Among these are exacerbated irony, grotesque playfulness, dogged limitation to a small symptomatic segment of experience, the shrinking of symbols, open-endedness of experience and form, and layers of camouflage over the point of the story (see v. Wiese, 1963, p. 75). All these features, however, lend themselves as well, and probably better, to the short story. The "unheard of" constituent of the novella has become very usual in our cataclysmic age (Erné, p. 109); the short story derives some of its most telling effects from surviving shreds of the usual (e.g., a kitchen clock) emphasizing the chaos, the brokenness of postwar life (Borchert, "Die Küchenuhr", 1947). "Moreover, the degree of identification which a modern short story demands is incomparably greater than any demand of the sort among the stories of the *Decameron*" (Valency, p. 20).

What remains vital in the structure of the novella? The basic requirement of an "unheard-of actual happening" told with self-control, finesse, and objectivity persists, but the adventure tends to be more of an inward one. The unity formerly supplied by profiled action (silhouette, falcon) or, more externally, by a frame can now, in part, be expressed by a unity of mood, of style. The experience must be complete, not fragmentary as in the short story. The (particularly German) novella must continue to guard against moralizing (except in the frame), theorizing, melodramatic wallowing in sentiment, and lyric expansionism, against wordiness, excess of learnedness, and psychological implausibilities present in such highly heralded works as *Der Ketzer von Soana, Der Amokläufer,* Emil Strauss's *Der Schleier* (1920), Ernst Wiechert's *Hirtennovelle* (1935), and Stefan Andres's *Wir sind Utopia* (1943). Attempts to return to classic patterns of the novella (Paul Ernst's *Der Weg zur Form* [1906], Rudolf Binding, Ricarda Huch, Gertrud von LeFort, Wilhelm Schäfer, Wilhelm von Scholz) have been wholly (*Der Schleier*) or partly (Werner Bergengruen, *Die drei Falken,* 1937) unsuccessful.

Musil's definition of the Novella (1914) maintains continuity with the novellesque tradition while adapting it to 20th century existence: "A sudden, self-contained stimulation of the mind results in the *Novelle*" in which the writer should describe "something that befalls him, that shakes him up;

nothing that was in you from birth, but a dispensation of destiny. In this one experience the world is suddenly plumbed, or his eyes turn inward; in this one example he believes he can see how everything is really: that is the experience [*Erlebnis*] of the *Novelle* " (*Tagebücher* [1955], p. 684). The more hopeless the struggle of the individual against demonic forces (Kunz, Column 1834), the more admirable the artistic triumph of the author as the last and only remaining token of victory of order over chaos. The future of the novella, if there is to be one, lies in the direction of Kafka and Musil.

BIBLIOGRAPHY: Mitchell, Roger McB, *Heyse and his Predecessors in the Theory of the Novelle* (1915); Pongs, Hermann, *Das Bild in der Dichtung.* Vol. II (1939); Papst, Walter, "Die Theorie der Novelle in Deutschland (1920-1940)," *Romanistisches Jahrbuch,* II (1949), 81-124; Lange, Victor, Introduction to *Great German Short Stories and Novels* (1952); Papst, Walter, *Novellentheorie und Novellendichtung. Zur Geschichte ihrer Antinomie in den romanischen Literaturen* (1953); Arx, Bernhard v., *Novellistisches Dasein. Spielraum einer Gattung in der Goethezeit* (1953); Kunz, Josef, "Geschichte der deutschen Novelle vom 18. Jahrhundert bis auf die Gegenwart," *Deutsche Philologie im Aufriß,* Vol. II (1954; 2nd ed., 1960); Silz, Walter, *Realism and Reality: Studies in the German Novelle of Poetic Realism* (1954); Wiese, Benno v., *Die deutsche Novelle von Goethe bis Kafka,* Vol. I (1956; 7th ed., 1963); Lockemann, Fritz, *Gestalt und Wandlungen der deutschen Novelle. Geschichte einer literarischen Gattung im neunzehnten and zwanzigsten Jahrhundert* (1957); Steinhauer, Harry, Introduction to *Die deutsche Novelle* (1958); Koskimies, Rafael, "Die Theorie der Novelle," *Orbis Litterarum,* XIV (1959) 65-88; Valency, Maurice, Introduction to *The Palace of Pleasure* (1960); Klein, Johannes, *Geschichte der deutschen Novelle von Goethe bis zur Gegenwart* (4th ed., 1960); Martini, Fritz, "Die deutsche Novelle im bürgerlichen Realismus," *Wirkendes Wort,* X (1960), 257-78; Bennett, E.K., and Waidson, H.M., *A History of the German Novelle* (2nd ed., 1961); Doderer, K., "Novelle," in *Lexikon der Weltliteratur,* Vol. II (1961); Erné, Nino, *Kunst der Novelle* (2nd ed., 1961); Wiese, Benno v., *Die deutsche Novelle von Goethe bis Kafka,* Vol. II (1962);

Himmel, Hellmuth, *Die Novelle im Zeitalter der Massenschicksale* (1963);
Wiese, Benno v., *Novelle* (1963).

APPENDIX II
Trends of research on the German Novella: A Review

Books denouncing past theories of the novella as too rigid or too sweeping always seem to come up, in the end, with substitutes even less satisfactory or with the culprit in disguise.[1]   Through a circuitous route the severe critic returns to the original sin which he starts by rejecting and ends up by marrying if ever so coyly and therefore less effectively. Paine's well-written study is no exception.

Deconstructionist criticism of novella theory is no longer daring; on the contrary, it is now the thing to do. It can look back, by this time, on a long line of essays and books that, like Paine's, marshal their remarkable talents only to argue, sometimes at suspiciously great length, that no particular novella ever seems to fit all the criteria of novella theory and that every constituent of novella theory is also part of other genres, sub-genres, or types. Thus, in a nutshell and *cum grano salis,* Steinhauer (1936, 1958, 1969, 1970), Pabst (1953), von Arx (1953), Lämmert (1955), Schunicht (1960), Martini (1960, 1962), Polheim (1964, 1965, 1970), Malmede (1966), Kilchenmann (1967), LoCicero (1970), Johansen (1970, 1972), Leibowitz (1974), and Ellis (1974).

The 'minimalists', in effect, trivialize the novella as an art form by retreating to length as the sole or principal safe characteristic. Von Arx, reflecting Staiger, produces the spectacular conclusion, echoed by Ellis, that a novella is a 'tale of medium length', and to this day even otherwise more productive scholarship (Polheim, Leibowitz, Springer [1975], Good [1977]) seems to attach undue importance to this quantitative phenomenon.

---

[1]A review of J.H.E. Paine, *Theory and Criticism of the Novella*, Bonn, Bouvier & Grundmann, 1979, first published in *Comparative Literature Studies XX*, no. 3, Fall 1983, 346-350.

For fuller entries on some of the secondary literature mentioned in this review essay, see the Bibliography at the end of this book.

Indirectly, the 'deconstructionists' derive aid and comfort from the 'panoramists' who try to encompass the whole waterfront of tales presented as novellas, one by one; find, not surprisingly, that each of them is different, and thus arrive at the conclusion, implicit or explicit, that there is a great gap between general theory and each individual story (Bennett, 1934; Bennett-Waidson, 1961; Kunz, 1954; Klein, 1954, 1961; Himmel, 1963). In order to find *some* connection, 'panoramic' scholars like Kunz (1954, 1966, 1970), Lockemann (1957), or Thieberger (1968) latch on to a central idea or concept, an existential or metaphysical factor as a common thematic denominator (e.g. order vs chaos). By concentrating on cardinal themes of all literature rather than on generic structure, they, predictably, do not arrive at what might be specifically "novellistisch" and thus furnish grist on the mills of the 'deconstructionists'.

It is characteristic of the 'nominalists' that they set up most of previous *Novellenforschung* as a bogeyman and claim that it has been prescriptive if not dogmatic. If we are to believe them, prevailing scholarship on the German *Novelle,* principally by Germans, has amounted to the compilation of mechanical checklists of immutable novella characteristics that are contradictory or don't work out in practice. Malmede, whose pretentious book should have been entitled *Irrwege zur Novelle,* is an extreme example of this prosecution complex. Ellis, a first-rate mind, airily finds "the basic theory and its extensions. . . deficient in every particular" (*Narration,* p. 5), casts "doubt on the whole theory from beginning to end" (p. 12), and completes his indictment by concluding (assuming?) that "the traditional theory of the Novelle is logically faulty in all these respects" (p. 17). (As a judicious antidote to Ellis, read Werner Hoffmeister's superb review in the *Journal of English and Germanic Philology,* 74, 1975, 609-12). Even much more balanced scholars like LoCicero and Leibowitz deprecate past scholarship unnecessarily, and the sensible Swales (1977) feels impelled to declare: "Any attempt nowadays to produce a new definition of the novelle is non-sensical" (p. 17; see also p. 19).

There seems to be blissful ignorance or disregard of the fact that there has been much common-sense research on the novella (sometimes by the same scholars who have, in principle, adopted nominalist positions) occupying a middle-of-the-road position between analysis and synthesis, ideological/thematic and formal/aesthetic, historical and normative considerations (Silz, 1954, 1959; von Wiese, 1955, 1956, 1962, 1963 ff; Prang, 1959; Negus, 1965; Kunz, 1968; LoCicero, 1970; Ryder, 1971; Swales, 1977; Rolleston, 1980). The adherents to this position usually place main emphasis on sensitive, well-rounded interpretations of individual *Novellen* and cautiously posit the hypothesis of common but not necessarily pervasive characteristics: inductive, non-exclusive, relative norms.

The thrust that seems to have gained the most in the last two decades is the utilization but relativizing of the genre concept either by circumscribing it historically or by replacing it with different modes or types. As applied to the German novella, whose heyday occurred, unquestionably, in the XIXth century, the social, political, philosophical, and economic fabric of that epoch shapes and colors the novella in theory and practice (Silz, Lämmert, Polheim, Negus, Johansen/Baggesen, LoCicero, Hoffmeister, Swales). Paine, who joins (initially) the deconstructionist crowd by calling relevant German scholarship "an often contradictory melange of unsystematic pronouncements and reflections" (p. 13) and finally dismisses it summarily ("*Novellentheorie* has failed totally in its attempt to tell us what a *Novelle* is", p. 31), represents the second trend: the substitution of different and more 'open' norms for the old ones.

Unapologetically, Paine disavows any intention of proposing to "establish firm and finite criteria for the novella" (p. 11) and admits that he is leaving himself "vulnerable to the accusation of having said little . . . about the novella as a literary genre" (ibid.). But he does take, at least potentially, two steps forward. First, like the somewhat uneven but constructive Good (1977) just before him, he broadens his investigation of the novella to include non-German theory and works. This is, to be sure, more than overdue. After all, the novella is a genetically Romanic genre, flourishing in Italy, France, and Spain for more than three hundred years. But, with the French Revolution, there occurred a dramatic shift, in novella practice and theory, from *Romania* to *Germania,* with the result that since then structural awareness of the XIXth and XXth century novella in the Latin countries, in primary and secondary literature, seems much less pronounced than in German-speaking lands. Experts in newer Romanic literature have not abandoned the term but utilize it, in the wake of Pabst, with marked caution (Krömer, 1972; Eitel, 1977). In England, where features of the novella can be detected as early as *The Canterbury Tales,* the use of the term in creating and describing literature of the last two centuries has been casual and cursory; this also applies to North America.

This non-German reluctance to use "novella" seriously and actively in recent epochs corresponds somewhat to Paine's own predilection (for openness) and aversion (to norms). It is characteristic that he gives much scholarly credence to the impressionistic perceptions of the novella by Henry James who calls it "ideal," "beautiful," and "blest," attributes to it "possible neatness" as well as "control". Paine is willing to base, if in part, "a coherent and flexible theory of the novella" (p. 60) on these discerning but hardly comprehensive observations.

James leads Paine to his second step: testing selected recent comparative novella theory, in particular, and genre theory, in general, against a specific non-German literary text of distinction. The three theoretical studies chosen are Mary Doyle Springer's *Forms of the Modern Novella,* 1975; Judith Leibowitz's *Narrative Purpose in the Novella,* 1974; and Paul Hernadi's *Beyond Genre: New Directions in Literary Classification,* 1972; the text Joseph Conrad's *Heart of Darkness.* This elaborate exercise is to yield alternative theoretical criteria much more open and representative than the traditional norms of novella criticism.

Why does he choose these, and are his choices good? Springer sets up a typology of the novella derived from Sheldon Sacks' claim that "all relevant works of prose fiction are organized according to one of three mutually exclusive types: satire, apologue, or action" (Paine, p. 94). Springer's "device" orientation leads to engaging and bright interpretations of stories but, Paine discovers, seems to pay few dividends in terms of genre criticism. All the more so since Springer is disarmingly ignorant of German *Novellistik* before Thomas Mann and reveals no evidence of having sought first-hand access to German scholarship on a subject where the major contributions have precisely come from that direction. And Paine rightly finds her reliance on Anglo-American stories top-heavy.

This criticism cannot be leveled against Leibowitz who is directly familiar with German *Novellen* and scholarship about them, and who serves a balanced menu of German and non-German novella-type stories by Brentano, Stifter, Keller, Meyer, Hauptmann, Storm, Mann, Mérimée, Gide, Silone, Melville, James, West, and Spark. Paine finds the 'openness' and 'flexibility' of Leibowitz' theory more to his liking than Springer's 'exclusiveness ' and 'wholeness'. Leibowitz ascertains that the novella, unlike the short story, develops thematic richness but achieves the often noted compactness of the genre by a rhythm of contraction and expansion punctuated by repetitive structure. Paine's choice of Leibowitz is, all things told, a happy one.

Leibowitz, however, still does not have enough elasticity for Paine. So he stretches her "intensity" and "expansion" features along the lines of Hernadi's polycentric approach to genre. Hernadi works with modes of discourse, (thematic, dramatic, narrative, lyric), perspective (personal, dual, or private), scope (concentric, kinetic, ecumenic), and mood (tragic, comic, tragicomic). But, in my judgement, Hernadi's 'transcendence of genre' is too centrifugal to offer much structural promise for the novella. Besides, he is so preoccupied with the twentieth century that he suffers from a serious lack of historical perspective, and so much of his book consists of summaries of other scholars' theories that the specificity and impact of his proposed solution is impaired.

The last chapter of Paine's book, "*Heart of Darkness:* Penumbral Form," analyzes Conrad's magnificent story as a *novella,* probably for the first time. Joining criteria furnished by Leibowitz and Hernadi, Paine concludes:

> Repetitive structure and statement and reiteration of themes
> combine with the mode and perspectives of literary discourse
> employed in the microstructure of *Heart of Darkness* to
> produce the effect of intensity and expansion which marks

this work as a novella, and the amplitude of action and theme clearly set it apart from the one-dimensional structural and thematic kinesis of the short story. (p. 200, 210).

I agree with Paine that there are distinct novella-type features in the *Heart of Darkness,* though I must admit that I arrive at this conclusion by the systematic use of traditional novella criteria eschewed, at least apparently, by Paine. For, dare one suggest, may "intensity" and "expansion", to cite two of the main exhibits, not be related to more traditional novella criteria such as "Spannung" and "Entspannung," "Konzentration," "Wendepunkte," etc? Do Sacks-Springer's "action" and "apologue" add a great deal to the "objective" and "subjective" poles of the novella delineated by Friedrich Schlegel in 1801?

The book, alas, lacks a concluding chapter, one that would sum up the findings and transfer them, if tentatively, to a larger scale. Perhaps that is not just an unfortunate slip but has something to do with the meager results of so high-powered and meticulously researched an exercise. The author seems scared of suggesting that an exceptionally thorough analysis – sixty-nine pages, no less – in terms of genre of a major story like *Heart of Darkness* might possibly lead to something more than just elucidating one novella: "Novella theory tends to speak in generalities and to tell us a little about many works," he confides in his penultimate paragraph (p. 212), and for his last sentence he chooses, among a string of nuanced and penetrating observations on the *Novelle* by Robert Musil, the one which seems the most resigned, the most negative one. And so the mighty effort, two hundred and sixty pages on the theory of the novella, ends on a vacillating, indecisive note. Why expect so little of theory? Why should not theory be capable of telling us a lot about individual works? Especially if theory represents, as it can and sometimes does, the inductive quintessence of a number of significant texts, – not, as asserted far too often in a cavalier fashion, prefabricated dogma? What cultural reaction, what psychological resistance accounts for the anti-normative stance of present novella criticism? Is it the anti-canon complex?

When a mountain of sophisticated scholarly effort produces such a mouse, one may be excused for wondering whether the much maligned novella criteria worked out by generations of German *Novellenforschung* are, after all, not more productive, normatively as well as in their specific application to particular works, than "apologue," "intensity," "expansion," "kinetic scope," and all those "modes of discourse." Could it be that there *are* rather down-to-earth components characteristic of the novella art form that *tend* to give a story aimed in that direction a profile different from the fairy-tale or the *conte* or the short story, let alone the novel? Might not the diachronic continuity of the novella nucleus be inherent in its traditional *Gestalt* as a discursive drama, the genre with most structural persistence? (Current scholarship identifies the novella too lopsidedly with the centrifugal epic component). And are not the criteria elaborated by generations of scholars quite serviceable if one does not expect exclusiveness or omnipresence of them, if one allows varying combinations, clustering but not uniformity: the "sich ereignete unerhörte Begebenheit," the "Wendepunkt(e)," the "Krise > Katastrophe > Pointe," the "Falke > Dingsymbol > Leitmotiv," "Ironie" and "Paradox," the "Rahmen"? To which others could be added: "Bericht, nicht Rechtfertigung," "Handlung, nicht Interpretation," "Das Geschehnis spricht für sich selbst," "Sachlichkeit," "Sparsamkeit," "Straffheit," "Geschlossenheit," "Distanz," "Durchsichtigkeit der Sprache <–> Undurchsichtigkeit der Ereignisse," "Die Novelle als episch bewältigtes Drama". The next two steps being how these criteria work out, in detail, one by one, not in just one or two but two or three dozen German stories of artistic significance tending in that direction, and how they materialize in corresponding numbers of French, Spanish, Italian, Russian, Scandinavian, English and American equivalents. Is there such a premium on iconoclasm or semantic innovation in scholarship now that a reasonable application of generally understandable, relative norms has become an embarrassment? It is interesting to note that about the only straightforward, unselfconscious, normative (but not absolutist) approaches to the novella of recent times are to be found in surveys addressed to students and general readers, such as Gero von Wilpert, "Novelle", in *Sachwörterbuch der Literatur,* Stuttgart, Kröner, 1955, 386-389 ([5] 1969), or Albrecht Weber, *Deutsche Novellen des Realismus,* Munich, Ehrenwirth, 1975.

Is "continuity" a bad word even though there are six hundred years of evidence for a particular art form? Is it not about time to say that there is, to be sure, no such thing as THE novella, but that there *are* stories which show a preponderance of, a tilting toward (not a monopoly, not a perfect catalogue of) fairly specific but not pedantic structural components, parts that in their *combination* produce a "novellistische Wirkung"? Which does not mean such stories may not contain admixtures of lyric, epic, elegiac, sentimental etc. elements, but not dominant ones – and if they *are* dominant, then the term "novella," regardless of the labeling given to it, is a misnomer.

Paine's book, like Springer's and Leibowitz's, is a notable attempt to relocate some kind of equilibrium between the generic and the specific in literature. It makes many perceptive observations though it takes a roundabout way toward conclusions which it seems both to desire and to fear.

First publication of essays composing this book

1) "Goethe and the Novella", in *Goethe. One hundred and Fifty Years of Continuing Vitality*, ed. Ulrich Goebel and W.T. Zyla, pp. 133-155, Lubbock (Texas), Texas Tech Press, 1984. Reprinted by permission of the publisher. All rights reserved.

2) "Die novellistische Struktur des Gretchenabenteuers in *Dichtung und Wahrheit*", in *Stil-und Formprobleme der Literatur*, ed. Paul Böckmann, pp. 303-308, Heidelberg, Carl Winter, 1959. Reprinted by permission of the publisher. All rights reserved.

3) "Autobiography or Fiction? Johann Wolfgang and Johann Caspar Goethe's 'Schöne Mailänderinnen' and the 'Frankfurter Gretchen' as Novellas", in *Goethe and Italy, 1786-1986*, ed. Gerhart Hoffmeister, pp. 21-54, Amsterdam, Rodopi, 1988. Reprinted by permission of the publisher. All rights reserved.

4) "Die Novelle in der Klassik und Romantik", in *Europäische Romantik I*, Volume XIV of *Neues Handbuch der Literatururwissenschaft*, ed. Karl Robert Mandelkow, pp. 291-318. Wiesbaden, (c)Quelle & Meyer, 1982. Reprinted by permission of the publisher. All rights reserved.

5) "Theorie und Praxis der Novelle: Gottfried Keller" in *Stoffe, Formen, Strukturen*, Festschrift für Hans Heinrich Borcherdt, ed. Albert Fuchs & Helmut Motekat, pp. 424-440, Ismaning (Bavaria), Max Hueber, 1962. Reprinted by permission of the publisher. All rights reserved.

6) "Wendepunkt und Pointe in der deutschen Novelle von Keller bis Bergengruen", in *Wert und Wort*. Festschrift für Else Fleissner, ed. Marion Sonnenfeld, Robert Marshall, Helen Sears, & Barbara Kauber, pp. 45-56, Aurora (New York), Wells College Archives, Louis Jefferson Long Library, 1965. Reprinted by permission of the publisher. All rights reserved.

292

7) "Vinegar and Water. Allegory and Symbolism in the German *Novelle* between Keller and Bergengruen", in *Literary Symbolism*, ed. Helmut Rehder, pp. 33-62, Austin (Texas), The University of Texas Press, 1965. Reprinted by permission of the publisher. All rights reserved.

8) "Der Rahmen in der deutschen Novelle: Dauer im Wechsel", in *Traditions and Transitions.* Studies in Honor of Harold Jantz, ed. Lieselotte E. Kurth, William H. McClain, Holger Homann, pp. 246-262, Munich, Delp, 1972. Reprinted by permission of the publisher. All rights reserved.

9) "Thomas Mann als Novellist", in *Zeitgenossenschaft.* Festschrift für Egon Schwarz, ed. Paul M. Lützeler, pp. 103-122. Frankfurt a.M. Main, Athenäum, 1987. Reprinted by permission of the publisher. All rights reserved.

10) "Novella", in *Encyclopedia of World Literature in the XXth Century*, ed. Wolfgang Fleischmann, pp. 466-469, New York, Frederick Ungar, 1969. Reprinted by permission of the publisher. All rights reserved.

11) "Trends of research on the German Novella. A Review". Critical review of J.H.E. Paine, *Theory and Criticism of the Novelle*, Bonn, Bouvier & Grundmann, 1979, in *Comparative Literature Studies*, XX, No. 3, Fall 1983, pp. 346-350. Copyright 1983 by The Pennsylvania State University. Reproduced by permission of The Pennsylvania State University Press.

Bibliography (Works Cited)

Arx, Berhard von. *Novellistisches Dasein: Spielraum einer Gattung in der Goethezeit.* Zurich: Atlantis, 1953.

Auerbach, Erich. *Mimesis: The Representation of Reality in Western Literature.* Trans. Willard R. Trask. New York: Doubleday, 1957.

Aust, Hugo. *Novelle.* Stuttgart: Metzler, 1990.

Bastier, Paul. *La Nouvelle individualiste en Allemagne de Goethe à Gottfried Keller.* Essai de technique psychologique. Paris: Larose, 1910.

Behler, Ernst. "Die Zeit der Romantik." *Handbuch der deutschen Erzählung.* Ed. Karl Konrad Polheim. Düsseldorf: Bagel, 1981. 114-129, 571-573.

Bennett, E.K. *A History of the German Novelle.* 1st ed. London: Cambridge University Press. 1934.

---, and H.M. Waidson. *A History of the German Novelle.* 2nd ed. London: Cambridge University Press. 1961.

Block, Haskell M. "Allegory and Symbol: A Reappraisal." Synopsis. *Actes du IIIe Congrès de l'Association Internationale de Littérature Compareé.* 's-Gravenhage: Mouton, 1962. 346.

Borcherdt, Hans Heinrich. *Geschichte des Romans und der Novelle in Deutschland.* Leipzig: J.J. Weber, 1926.

Brinkmann, Richard. "Abstract Lyrics of Expressionism: End or
        Transformation of the Symbol?" *Literary Symbolism.* Ed. Helmut
        Rehder. Austin and London: University of Texas Press, 1965. 107-
        136.

Brown, Jane K. "The Renaissance of Goethe's poetic genius in Italy." *Goethe
        in Italy, 1786.* Ed. Gerhart Hoffmeister. Amsterdam: Rodopi, 1988.
        77-94.

*Champigny, Robert. "The *Swan* and the Question of Pure Poetry." *L'Esprit
        Créateur* I (1961), 145-155.

Child, C.G. "Achim von Arnim's 'Der tolle Invalide'." *Modern Language
        Notes* XII, 3 (1897): 188-189.

Doderer, Kurt. "Novelle." *Lexikon der Weltliteratur.* Vol. II. 1961. [Unable
        to relocate.]

Eitel, Wolfgang. *Die romanische Novelle.* Ars interpretandi 7. Darmstadt:
        Wissenschaftliche Buchgesellschaft, 1977.

Ellis, John M. *Narration in the German Novelle.* Cambridge: Cambridge
        University Press, 1974.

Erné, Nino. *Die Kunst der Novelle.* 2nd ed. Wiesbaden: Limes, 1961.

Feise, Ernst. "Kellers *Romeo und Julia* und Stifters *Brigitta:* Aufbau und
        Gehalt." *Xenion: Themes, Forms, and Ideas in German Literature.*
        Baltimore: Johns Hopkins Press, 1950. 153-179.

---. "Der tolle Invalide von Achim von Arnim." *Journal of English and
        Germanic Philology* LIII, 3 (1954): 403-409.

Friedenthal, Richard. *Goethe. Sein Leben und seine Zeit.* Munich: Deutscher Taschenbuch-Verlag, 1968.

Gardner, Helen. *The Limits of Literary Criticism.* London: Oxford University Press, 1956.

Gillespie, Gerald. "Novella, Nouvelle, Novelle, Short Novel?" *Neophilologus* 51 (1967): 117-127, 225-230.

Glaser, Rudolf. *Goethes Vater. Sein Leben nach Tagebüchern und Zeitberichten.* Leipzig: Quelle und Meyer, 1929.

Good, Graham. "Notes on the Novella." *Novel: A Forum on Fiction* 10 (1977): 197-211.

Grolman, Adolf von. "Die strenge Novellenform und die Problematik ihrer Zertrümmerung." *Novelle.* Ed. Josef Kunz. 2nd ed. Darmstadt: Wissenschaftliche Buchgesellschaft, 1973. 154-166.

---. "Goethes 'Novelle'." *Germanisch-Romanische Monatsschrift* IX (1921): 181-187.

---. "Novelle." *Reallexikon der deutschen Literaturgeschichte.* Ed. Paul Merker and Wolfgang Stammler. 3 vols. Berlin: de Gruyter, 1926-1928. 2: 510-515.

Henel, Heinrich. "Conrad Ferdinand Meyers Nach einem Niederländer'." *Wächter und Hüter: Festschrift für Hermann J. Weigand.* Ed. Curt von Faber du Faur, Konstantin Reichardt, and Heinz Bluhm. New Haven: Yale, 1957. 117-118.

Hennig, John. "Goethes Kenntnis der Schönen Literatur Italiens." *Literaturwissenschaftliches Jahrbuch der Görresgesellschaft* 21

N.F. (1980): 361-383.

Hernadi, Paul. *Beyond Genre: New Directions in Literary Classification.* Ithaca: Cornell UP, 1972.

Hernandez, José Luis Alonso, Martin Gosman, and Rinaldo Rinaldi. *Italia, France, España.* Amsterdam/Atlanta: Rodopi, 1993.

Heyse, Paul. "Einleitung": *Deutscher Novellenschatz. Theorie und Kritik der deutschen Novelle von Wieland bis Musil.* Ed. Karl Konrad Polheim. Tübingen: Niemeyer, 1970. 141-149. (Reprint).

---. *Jugenderinnerungen und Bekenntnisse.* 1900. *Gesammelte Werke.* 3 series. 5 vols. Zurich, New York: Olms 1985. III, 1: 3-312. (Reprint).

Himmel, Hellmuth. *Geschichte der deutschen Novelle.* Sammlung Delp 63. Bern and Munich: Francke, 1963.

Hirsch, Arnold. *Der Gattungsbegriff 'Novelle'.* Germanische Studien 64. Ed. Emil Ebering. Berlin: Emil Ebering, 1928. Nachdruck Nendeln/Liechtenstein, 1967.

Hoffmeister, Werner. "Die deutsche Novelle und die amerikanische 'Tale': Ansätze zu einem gattungspsychologischen Vergleich." *The German Quarterly* 63 (1990): 32-49.

Hofmannsthal, Hugo von. "Die Briefe des Zurückgekehrten." *Prosa II.* Frankfurt: S. Fischer, 1951.

Jaszi, Andrew O. "Symbolism and the Linguistic Paradox: Reflections on Goethe's World View." *Literary Symbolism* (1965). See under Brinkmann. 63-82.

Johansen, Jørgen Dines. *Novelleteori efter 1945.* Copenhagen: Munksgaard, 1970.

Kanzog, Klaus. "Rahmenerzählung." *Reallexikon der deutschen Literaturgeschichte.* Ed. Werner Kohlschmidt and Wolfgang Mohr. 2nd ed. 3 vols. Berlin: de Gruyter, 1968. 3: 321-343.

Kayser, Wolfgang. *Das sprachliche Kunstwerk.* 6th ed. Berne and Munich: Francke, 1960.

Kilchenmann, Ruth J. *Die Kurzgeschichte. Formen und Entwicklung.* Stuttgart: Kohlhammer, 1967.

Killy, Walther. *Deutscher Kitsch.* Göttingen: Vandenhoeck and Ruprecht, 1962.

Klein, Johannes. *Geschichte der deutschen Novelle von Goethe bis zur Gegenwart.* 4th ed. Wiesbaden: Steiner, 1960.

---. "Novelle." *Reallexikon der deutschen Literaturgeschiichte.* Ed. Werner Kohlschmidt and Wolfgang Mohr. 3 vols. Berlin: Walter de Gruyter, 1965. 2: 685-701.

---. "Wesen und Erscheinungsformen der deutschen Novelle." *Germanisch-Romanische Monatsschrift* XXIV (1936): 81-100.

Koskimies, Rafael. "Die Theorie der Novelle." *Novelle.* Ed. Josef Kunz. 2nd ed. Darmstadt: Wissenschaftliche Buchgesellschaft, 1973. 411-438.

Krämer, Herbert, ed. *Theorie der Novelle.* Stuttgart: Philipp Reclam Jr., 1976.

Krömer, Wolfram. *Die französische Novelle im 19. Jahrhundert.* Frankfurt:

Athenäum, 1972.

---. *Kurzerzählungen und Novellen in den romanischen Literaturen bis 1900.* Berlin: Erich Schmidt, 1973.

Kultermann, Udo. "Bildformen in Kellers Novelle *Romeo und Julia auf dem Dorfe.*" *Der Deutschunterricht* VIII, 3 (1956), 86-100.

Kunz, Josef. "Geschichte der deutschen Novelle vom 18. Jahrhundert bis auf die Gegenwart." *Deutsche Philologie im Aufriß.* Ed. Wolfgang Stammler. Berlin: Erich Schmidt, 1954. 2: 1739-1840.

---. *Die deutsche Novelle zwischen Klassik und Romantik.* Grundlagen der Germanistik. 2 vols. Ed. Hugo Moser. Berlin: Erich Schmidt, 1971.

---, ed. *Novelle.* Wege der Forschung 55. 2nd ed. Darmstadt: Wissenschaftliche Buchgesellschaft, 1973.

---. *Die deutsche Novelle im 19. Jahrhundert.* Grundlagen der Germanistik 10. Ed. Hugo Moser. Berlin: Erich Schmidt, 1970.

Lämmert, Eberhart. *Bauformen des Erzählens.* 5th ed. Stuttgart: Metzler, 1972.

Lange, Victor. "Introduction." *Great German Short Stories and Novels.* Ed. Victor Lange. New York: Modern Library, 1952. vii-xxi.

Langer, Susanne K. *Philosophy in a New Key.* New York: Pelican, 1948.

Leibowitz, Judith. *Narrative Purpose in the Novella.* The Hague: Mouton, 1974.

Lesowsky, J. "Der tolle Invalide auf dem Fort Ratonneau." *Archiv für das*

Studium der neueren Sprachen LXV (1911): 302-307.

LoCicero, Donald. *Novellentheorie: The Practicality of the Theoretical.* The Hague: Mouton, 1970.

Lockemann, Fritz. *Gestalt und Wandlungen der deutschen Novelle. Geschichte einer literarischen Gattung im neunzehnten und zwanzigsten Jahrhundert.* Munich: Max Hueber, 1957.

Lützeler, Paul M., and James F. McLeod, ed. *Goethes Erzählwerk.* Stuttgart: Reclam, 1985.

Malmede, Hans Hermann. *Wege zur Novelle: Theorie und Interpretation der Gattung Novelle in der deutschen Literaturwissenschaft.* Stuttgart, Berlin, Cologne, Mainz: Kohlhammer, 1966.

Martini, Fritz. "Die deutsche Novelle im bürgerlichen Realismus." *Wirkendes Wort* X (1960): 257-78.

Middleton, J. Christopher. "Two Mountain Scenes in Novalis and the Question of Symbolic Style." *Literary Symbolism. (1965).* See under Brinkmann. 83-106.

Mitchell, Robert McBurney. *Heyse and his Predecessors in the Theory of the Novelle.* Frankfurt/Main: Joseph Baer, 1915.

Mundt, Theodor. *Schriften in bunter Reihe, zur Anregung und Unterhaltung.* Ed. Theodor Mundt. Frankfurt am Main: Athenäum, 1971. (Reprint).

Negus, Kenneth. "Paul Heyse's Novellentheorie: A Revaluation." *Germanic Review* 40 (1965): 173-91.

Pabst, Walter. *Novellentheorie und Novellendichtung: Zur Geschichte ihrer Antinomie in den romanischen Literaturen.* 2nd ed. Heidelberg: Winter, 1967.

Paine, J.H.E. *Theory and Criticism of the Novella.* Bonn: Bouvier and Grundmann, 1979.

Paulin, Roger. *The Brief Compass: The Nineteenth Century German Novelle.* New York: Oxford University Press, 1985.

Petsch, Robert. *Wesen und Formen der Erzählkunst.* Halle: Niemeyer, 1934.

Peyre, Henri. "Seventy-Five Years of Comparative Literature." Yearbook of Comparative and General Literature. I (1952) 1-8.

Phelps, Reginald. "Keller's Technique of Composition in *Romeo und Julia auf dem Dorfe.*" *Germanic Review* XXIV, 1 (1949) 34-51.

Plotke, Georg, ed. *Der Briefwechsel zwischen Paul Heyse und Theodor Storm.* Munich: Lehmann, 1918.

Polheim, Karl Konrad. "Gattungsproblematik." *Handbuch der deutschen Erzählung.* Düsseldorf: Bagel, 1981. 9-16.

---. "Novellentheorie und Novellenforschung (1945-1963)." *Deutsche Vierteljahrsschrift für Literaturwissenschaft und Geistesgeschichte* Sonderheft XXXVIII (1964): 208-216.

---. *Theorie und Kritik der deutschen Novelle von Wieland bis Musil.* Tübingen: Niemeyer. 1970.

Pongs, Hermann. "Aufsätze zur Novelle." *Das Bild in der Dichtung.* Marburg: Elwert, 1939. 97-296.

---. "Die Novelle und das Dämonische." *Das Bild in der Dichtung.* 3rd ed. Marburg: Elwert, 1967. 251-296.

Prang, Helmut. "Formprobleme der Novelleninterpretation." *Hüter der Sprache: Perspektiven der deutschen Literatur.* Ed. Karl Rüdiger. Munich: Bayerischer Schulbuch Verlag, 1959. 19-38.

Rehder, Helmut. *"Romeo und Julia auf dem Dorfe:* An Analysis." *Monatshefte* 35 (1943) 401-434.

Remak, Henry H.H. *Novellistische Struktur. Der Marschall von Bassompierre und die schöne Krämerin (Bassompierre, Goethe, Hofmannsthal).* Germanic Studies in America 46. Ed. Katharina Mommsen. Bern and Frankfurt: Peter Lang, 1983.

Ritchie, James M. "Die strenge Novellenform im zwanzigsten Jahrhundert." *Dichtung Wissenschaft Unterricht.* Ed. Friedrich Kienecker and Peter Wolfersdorf. Paderborn: Schöningh, 1986. 252-264.

Rolleston, James. "Short Fiction in Exile: Exposure and Reclamation of a Tradition." *Exile. The Writer's Experience.* Ed. John M. Spalek and Robert F. Bell. Chapel Hill: University of North Carolina Press, 1982. 32-47.

Rowley, Brian A. [Essay entitled] *Kleider machen Leute.* London: Arnold, 1960.

---. "The Novelle." *The Romantic Period in Germany.* Ed. Siegbert Prawer. London and New York: Schocken, 1970. 121-146.

Ryder, Frank. *Die Novelle.* New York: Holt, 1971.

---. "Season, Day, and Hour: Time as Metaphor in Goethe's Werther."

302

Journal of English and Germanic Philology 53, 3 (1964) 389-407.

Salvan, J.L. *Dictionary of World Literature.* New York: Philosophical
Library, 1943.

Sembdner, Helmut. "Anmerkungen zu Kleist." *Sämtliche Werke und Briefe.*
Ed. Helmut Sembdner. 2 vols. Munich: Hanser, 1965. 2: 895-896.

Schefski, Harold K. "The Novelle in Russian Literature." M.A. Thesis.
(unpublished) Stanford University, 1970.

Silz, Walter. "Geschichte, Theorie und Kunst der deutschen Novelle." *Der
Deutschunterricht* 11 (1959): 82-100.

---. *Realism and Reality: Studies in the German Novelle of Poetic Realism.*
Chapel Hill: University of North Carolina Press. 1956.

Springer, Mary Doyle. *Forms of the Modern Novella.* Chicago: University
of Chicago Press, 1975.

Staiger, Emil. *Goethe.* Zurich and Freiburg im Breisgau: Atlantis, 1956.

Steinhauer, Harry. "Introduction." *Die deutsche Novelle: 1880-1950.* New
York: Norton, 1958. 3-22.

---. "Introduction." *Ten German Novellas.* New York: Doubleday, 1969.
IX-XXV.

---. "Towards a definition of the novella." *Seminar* VI, 2 (1970) 154-174.

Schunicht, Manfred. "Der 'Falke' am 'Wendepunkt'" Zu den Novelletheorien
Tiecks und Heyses." *Novelle.* Ed. Josef Kunz. 2nd ed. Darmstadt:
Wissenschaftliche Buchgesellschaft, 1973. 439-468.

Seidlin, Oskar. Review of *Thomas Mann: The Uses of Tradition*, by T.J.
Reed. *Journal of English and Germanic Philology* LXXV (1976),
268-271.

Smidt-Dörrenberg, Irmgard. *Angelika Kauffmann. Goethes Freundin in
Rom*. Vienna: Bergland, 1968.

Swailes, Martin. *The German Novelle*. Princeton: Princeton University Press,
1977.

Thieberger, Richard. *Le genre de la nouvelle dans la littérature allemande*.
Publications de la Faculté des Lettres et Sciences Humaines de Nice
2. Paris: Les Belles Lettres, 1968 (1969).

Trunz, Erich. "Anmerkungen zu Dichtung und Wahrheit." *Goethes Werke*
IX. 12th ed. Munich: Beck, 1981. 599-768, especially 670-681.

Vaget, Hans Rudolf. *Thomas-Mann-Kommentar zu sämtlichen Erzählungen*.
Munich: Winkler, 1984.

Valency, Maurice. "Introduction." *The Palace of Pleasure*. Ed. Maurice
Valency and Harry Levtow. New York: Capricorn, 1960. 2-28.

Weber, Albrecht. *Deutsche Novellen des Realismus*. Munich: Ehrenwirth,
1975.

Weing, Siegfried. *The German Novella: Two Centuries of Criticism*.
Columbia: Camden House, 1994.

Wiese, Benno von. "Bild-symbole in der deutschen Novelle." *Publications
of the English Goethe Society* New Series, XXIV (1955) 132-133.

---. *Die deutsche Novelle von Goethe bis Kafka*. 2 vols. Düsseldorf, Bagel,

304

---. *Novelle.* 8th ed. Stuttgart: Metzler, 1982.

Wilpert, Gero von. "Novelle." *Sachwörterbuch der Literatur.* 7th ed. Stuttgart: Kröner, 1989. 628-632.

Wortig, Ilse. "Der 'Wendepunkt' in der neuen deutschen Novelle und seine Gestaltung." Diss. Frankfurt am Main, 1931.

Zastrau, Alfred. *Goethe Handbuch.* Vols. 1 and 4. 2nd revised edition. Stuttgart: Metzler, 1962.

Name Index

Guidelines:

1. Authors of scholarly works are only listed here if they appear in an analytic/evaluative context; otherwise, see the end Bibliography. Judgment had to be used in borderline cases.
2. Anonymous works are listed as titles.

312

Topical Index

Guidelines:

1. Headings are listed under the language in which the term first appears. The translated term should appear either immediately after in ( ) or in (see under ....).

2. "See under" refers to the category under which the relevant pages are listed. "See also under" refers to a *related* category and as a rule will be used sparingly with [brackets].

NORTH AMERICAN
STUDIES IN 19TH
CENTURY GERMAN
LITERATURE

This is a series of monographs on post-Romantic literature of the nineteenth century in the German-speaking lands. The series endeavors to embrace studies in criticism, in literary history, in the interdependence with other national literatures, and in the social and political dimensions of literature. Our aim is to offer contributions by American scholars to the renovation of literary history, the reformation of the canon, the rediscovery of once significant authors, the reevaluation of texts and their contexts, and a renewed understanding and appreciation of a body of literature of acknowledged international importance in the nineteenth century.

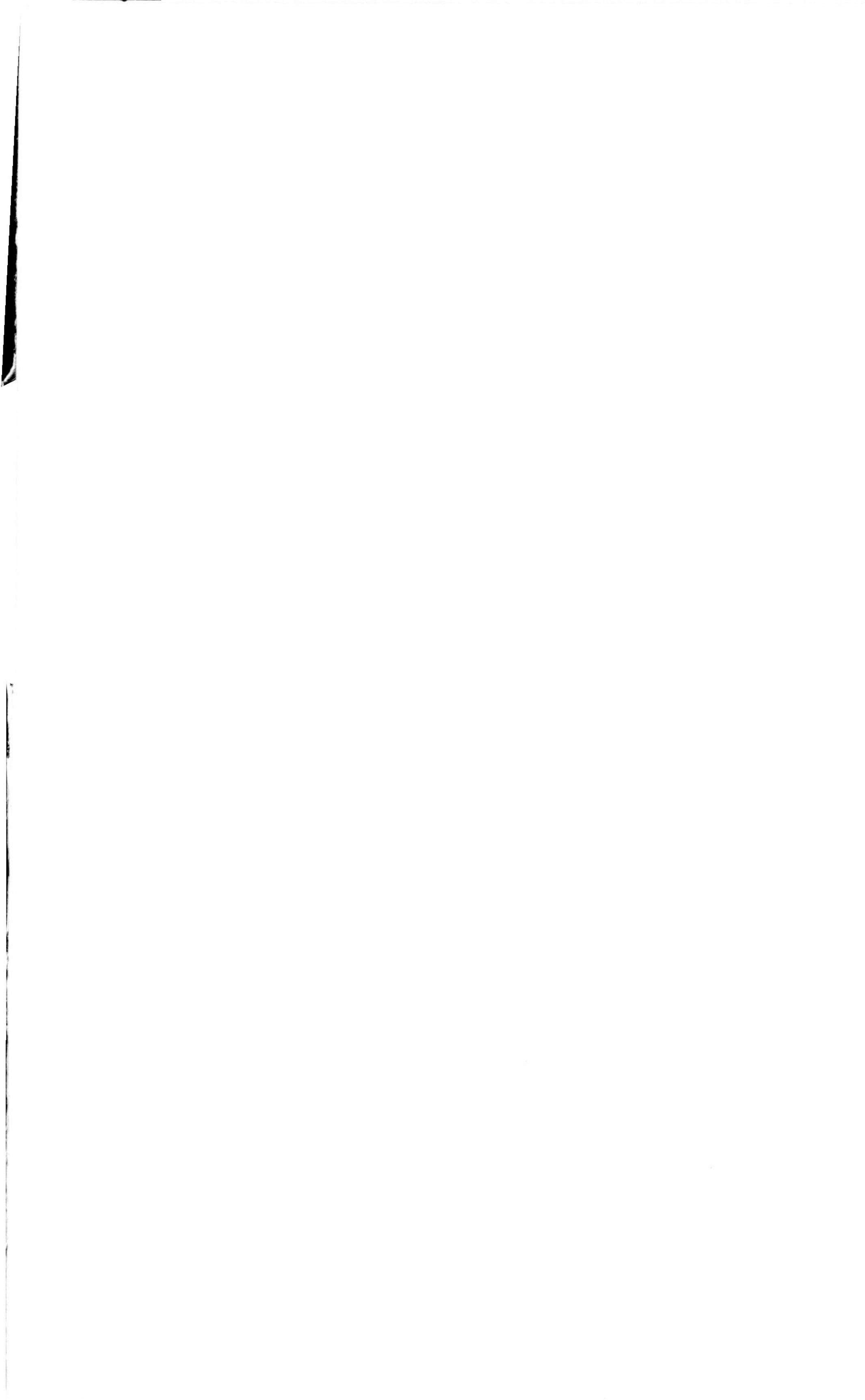